WITHDRAWN
UTSA Libraries

The Broken Olive Branch

Syracuse Studies on Peace and Conflict Resolution
Louis Kriesberg, *Series Editor*

OTHER TITLES IN SYRACUSE STUDIES
ON PEACE AND CONFLICT RESOLUTION

The Broken Olive Branch: Nationalism, Ethnic Conflict, and the Quest for Peace in Cyprus, Volume One, The Impasse of Ethnonationalism
HARRY ANASTASIOU

Cooperative Security: Reducing Third World Wars
I. WILLIAM ZARTMAN and VICTOR A. KREMENYUK, eds.

Cultures of Peace: The Hidden Side of History
ELISE BOULDING

*From Cold War to Democratic Peace:
Third Parties, Peaceful Change, and the OSCE*
JANIE LEATHERMAN

*Global Liberalism, Local Populism: Peace and Conflict
in Israel/Palestine and Northern Ireland*
GUY BEN-PORAT

Making Peace Prevail: Preventing Violent Conflict in Macedonia
ALICE ACKERMANN

Preparing for Peace: Conflict Transformation Across Cultures
JOHN PAUL LEDERACH

Scare Tactics: The Politics of International Rivalry
MICHAEL P. COLARESI

*Taming Ethnic Hatred: Ethnic Cooperation
and Transnational Networks in Eastern Europe*
PATRICE C. MCMAHON

*Thinking Peaceful Change: Baltic Security Policies
and Security Community Building*
FRANK MÖLLER

*Transnational Social Movements and
Global Politics: Solidarity Beyond the State*
JACKIE SMITH, CHARLES CHATFIELD, and RON PAGNUCCO, eds.

The Broken Olive Branch

Nationalism, Ethnic Conflict,
and the Quest for Peace in Cyprus

VOLUME TWO
Nationalism Versus Europeanization

Harry Anastasiou

SYRACUSE UNIVERSITY PRESS

Copyright © 2008 by Syracuse University Press,
Syracuse, New York 13244-5160

All Rights Reserved

First Edition 2008

08 09 10 11 12 13   6 5 4 3 2 1

The paper used in this publication meets the minimum requirements of American National Standard for Information Sciences—Permanence of Paper for Printed Library Materials, ANSI Z39.48–1984.∞™

For a listing of books published and distributed by Syracuse University Press, visit our Web site at SyracuseUniversityPress.syr.edu

Vol. 2 ISBN-13: 978-0-8156-3197-2
Vol. 2 ISBN-10: 0-8156-3197-9

Library of Congress Cataloging-in-Publication Data

Anastasiou, Harry.
The broken olive branch : nationalism, ethnic conflict and the quest for
peace in Cyprus / Harry Anastasiou. — 1st ed.
p. cm.
Includes bibliographical references and index.
ISBN 978-0-8156-3196-5 (hardcover : alk. paper)
1. Cyprus—History. 2. Cyprus—Ethnic relations. 3. Nationalism—Cyprus.
I. Title.
DS54.5.A82 2008
956.9304—dc22
2008032776

Manufactured in the United States of America

To the Greek and Turkish people,
with special recognition of Turkish Cypriots, Greek Cypriots,
Greeks, and Turks in both high and low places
who have toiled for peace in the eastern Mediterranean.

HARRY ANASTASIOU, a Greek Cypriot, was raised in Cyprus, experiencing firsthand most of the tumultuous years of civil and interethnic strife shaping that eastern Mediterranean island. In his quest to understand conflict and its transformation in the modern and postmodern world, he earned degrees in political science, philosophy, and peace and conflict studies from universities in the United States, Canada, and Holland.

Anastasiou holds a Ph.D. in international peace and conflict studies from the Union Institute and University in Cincinnati, Ohio, and a doctorandus degree in social science from the Free University of Amsterdam, Holland. He is a core faculty member of the Conflict Resolution Graduate Program and an affiliate of the International Studies Program at Portland State University, publishing numerous articles on peace and conflict issues, focusing on Cyprus, nationalism, peace building, and the European Union. An experienced practitioner of conflict resolution, he has, since the mid-nineties, played a leading role in the development and growth of a citizen-based peace movement in Cyprus and in Greek-Turkish relations. He has also been a participating member of the Harvard Study Group, a bicommunal think tank comprised of policy leaders and academics working on ideas and approaches for the peaceful resolution of the Cyprus problem.

Contents

Acknowledgments | ix

Introduction | xi

1. Globalizing Trends and the EU as a Catalyst for Peace: Political and Civil Changes in Greece and Turkey | 1

2. Rapprochement, Rising Civil Society, and Emerging Europeanization | 32

3. Seeking a Comprehensive Settlement on the Eve of European Integration: The Annan Plan | 52

4. Rising Ambiguities: The Competing Pulses of Peace and Conflict | 72

5. Cyprus at the Crossroads: Nationalism of the Past Versus Europeanization of the Future | 108

6. The Cyprus Referenda: Nationalism Versus Postnationalism | 139

7. Postreferenda Political Realities | 171

8. The Changing Parameters of the Cyprus Problem (I) | 205

9. The Changing Parameters of the Cyprus Problem (II) | 226

Conclusion | 260

Works Cited | *267*

Index | *277*

TABLE

5.1. TC Parliamentary Election Results, December 2003 | *118*

Acknowledgments

For their support of the Cyprus Peace Initiatives Project of Portland State University, under which the research endeavor for this book was undertaken, I wish to extend my gratitude to E. John Rumpakis, Cleo Rumpakis, Al Jubitz, the Jubitz Family Foundation, Douglas C. Strain, Gary Watson, Chris Garos, Effy Stephanopoulos, Isidoros Garifalakis, Maria Garifalakis, and numerous members of the Greek community of Portland, Oregon. By sharing a vision of peace and common humanity, they have morally and financially empowered our academic and practical efforts of contributing to democracy, peace, and reconciliation in the eastern Mediterranean region.

I wish to extend a special thanks to Dr. Marvin Kaiser, Dean of the College of Liberal Arts and Science of Portland State University; Dr. Birol Yesilada, my colleague from the Hatfield School of Government of Portland State University; and Dr. Robert Gould, Chair of the Conflict Resolution Graduate Program of Portland State University, for their encouragement and support.

For reviewing the manuscript, I wish to thank Dr. Louis Kriesberg, Professor Emeritus of social conflict studies at Syracuse University; Dr. Sean Byrne of the Arthur V. Mauro Centre for Peace and Justice of St. Paul's College, University of Manitoba, Canada; Dr. Benjamin Broome of the Hugh Downs School of Human Communication of Arizona State University; Dr. Maria Hadjipavlou of the Department of Social and Political Science of the University of Cyprus; and Dr. Erol Kaymak, chair of international relations at the Eastern Mediterranean University, Cyprus.

I wish to also express my appreciation to Roxane Christ, Susan Oretsky and Pieter Dykhorst for their valuable editing suggestions.

For challenging as well as empowering my spirit, while on the long journey that concluded with the completion of *The Broken Olive Branch*, I wish to extend a very special thanks to my wife, Theodora, and two sons, Anastis and Michaelangelo.

Lastly, I wish to thank my parents, Anastasios and Maria, for nurturing and orienting my early steps toward a world above and beyond the belligerent era in which I was raised.

Introduction

OVERVIEW OF *THE BROKEN OLIVE BRANCH*, VOLUME ONE:
THE IMPASSE OF ETHNONATIONALISM

From the perspective of peace and conflict studies, and more specifically of conflict analysis and resolution, the hope for peace in Cyprus had scarcely been within reach. Brief moments of hope around the 1977–79 top-level agreements, the 1983–84 negotiations, and the parallel efforts of the Ozal government in Turkey and the Vassiliou government in Greek Cypriot Cyprus in the early 1990s were quickly erased by the historical momentum of the problem. Of all the efforts, the UN-led initiative of 2003–4 marked the most substantive and tangible attempt for reaching a comprehensive resolution of the Cyprus problem. Unfortunately, this too failed. In its essence, the Cyprus problem remained intractable for more than half a century.

Among Cypriots, Greeks and Turks alike, the prospect for a settlement appeared so unlikely that over the years, people often consoled themselves with jokes about the intractability of the Cyprus problem. I recall one that asked who were the most useless among Cypriot lawyers. The answer was the leaders of the two communities, as they have been working on the same case for a lifetime without being able to bring it to closure. Another joke spoke of the Cypriots presenting the Cyprus problem to world's wisest persons, who were renowned for debunking the most complex of riddles. When faced with the challenge of resolving the issue, the wise men despaired and wept. Thereupon, the joke continued, the Cypriots decided to ask God for a solution. However, in confronting the Cyprus problem, God too despaired and wept.

While the Cyprus problem was often rendered artificially bearable through humor and habituation, its intractability weighed down on all Cypriots for decades. However, no aspect of the intractability of the Cyprus problem was accidental, as each had its specific historical and sociopolitical reason. According to the analysis in volume one of *The Broken Olive Branch, The Impasse of Ethnonationalism* (hereafter *IE*), one of the central historical factors that triggered and underpinned the evolution of the problem was the uncritical adoption of ethnocentric nationalism, first by Greece and Turkey and subsequently by Greek Cypriots (GCs) and Turkish Cypriots (TCs). Originating in nineteenth-century Europe and enshrined in the founding and development of the Republic of Greece and the Republic of Turkey respectively, ethnocentric nationalism consolidated an exclusivist, absolutist, and belligerent world view that essentially dominated the public political cultures of the people concerned (see *IE*, chapters 3 and 4).

As seen in *IE*, in its aggrandized and monoethnic concept of the nation-state, as well as in its adversarial orientation, the nationalist world view had an enormous historical influence on Cypriot politics. As explained, both prior to and decades following postcolonial independence, the identical nationalism of the respective Cypriot ethnic communities set the stage and largely determined the development and structuring of disparaging intercommunal relations (see *IE*, chapters 4 and 5). Ranging from the repeated cycles of interethnic violence between 1958 and 1974, to the polarizing manner in which Greece and Turkey became engaged in Cyprus, to the alienating modes of intercommunal communication, to the decades-long sterile approaches to negotiations, the impact of nationalism persisted as one of the most overwhelming determinants of the Cyprus problem. As reflected in *IE*, nationalism's historical potency was demonstrated in having severed the worlds of Greeks and Turks and in having mobilized and structured Greeks and Turks into exclusive ethnonational identity groups, which in the course of more than a century have related to each other primarily through conflict-conditioned modes of thought, action, and behavior.

A central question that is thereby forced to the forefront of the Cyprus problem in particular and of Greek-Turkish relations in general is whether democracy may be aligned with ethnocentric nationalism. Investigating an array of political, historical, and psychological phenomena in *IE*, the analysis revealed that nationalism skews and usurps democracy while decisively dissociating it from a culture and polity of peace. Democracy and nationalism proved to be fundamentally incompatible, especially in the context of the ethnically mixed morphology of Cypriot society.

From a historical perspective, the feature of nationalism that is most incongruous to democracy lies in nationalism's extraordinary capacity to legitimize and sustain belligerent interethnic relations, while viewing the recourse to the use of force or violence in the name and interest of *the nation* as an unproblematic, credible, and even moral option. Most devastating for the interest of interethnic peace has been the fact that the historical incorporation and usurpation of democracy by adversarial ethnonationalism has established the preconditions among leaders and public opinion to approach the potential or actual use of force or violence in the name of *the nation* as a legitimate, collective national right. As argued in *IE*, the dominant political cultures of Cyprus, Greece, and Turkey have been decisively conditioned by the belligerent predisposition and orientation of the nationalist world view (see *IE*, chapters 2, 3, and 5). It was not until late in 1999 and thereafter that the first deviations from the legacy of nationalism could be detected and observed in the political cultures of Cyprus, Greece, and Turkey.

Up until this time, the nationalist conditioning of Greek-Turkish relations and of GC and TC politics, particularly during the cold war era, precipitated into cycles of interethnic violence that not only scarred the history of Cyprus but also configured the collective memory of each of the Cypriot ethnic communities in alienating contradiction to that of the other.

Through its narcissistic psychology, the nationalism on each side of the ethnic divide appropriated the respective loss of life and human suffering and integrated them back into the conflict structure that nationalist rivalry itself generated. In so doing, nationalism perpetuated and maintained human pain and suffering while transforming it as supplementary fuel for sustaining, enhancing, justifying, and reinforcing adversarial interethnic relations and aggressive monoethnic agendas (see *IE*, chapter 5). For decades, the historical entrapment of each community in the narcissistic patterns of nationalist culture was perpetuated by the fact that the nationalism of each side, while highlighting one's own loss and suffering, consistently evaded and denied the loss and suffering of the other; and while accentuating one set of historical facts that disclosed one's own side as victim, suppressed another set of facts that disclosed one's own side as culprit. The master narratives of conflict-conditioned heroics that nationalism elaborated had locked GCs and TCs into a stagnating public mind-set where each side's heroes became the other side's villains, and where each side's losses became the other side's "rightful" retaliations.

As argued in *IE*, the antithetical ethnocentric worlds that nationalist rivalry generates and the divergent historical experiences it creates constituted a vital factor of intractability in the Cyprus conflict. It entailed, among other things, a structural breakdown of the interethnic communication process resulting from the respective, nationalist framing of history, perception, memory, and meaning. More fundamental than misinformation and misunderstanding, prolonged nationalist conflict precipitated a sociocultural institutionalization of *noncommunication* between GCs and TCs, and more generally between Greeks and Turks (see *IE,* chapter 6).

Underscored by the interethnic bloodshed of the 1960s and the Greek coup and Turkish invasion of Cyprus in 1974, the political impasse that stubbornly persisted for over half a century was largely a result of the antithetical, mutually alienating, and exclusive mental worlds that TCs and GCs, along with their respective motherlands, came to respectively inhabit as a result of their historical immersion into ethnonationalist rivalry. As nationalist assumptions and sociocultural dynamics continued to determine the context and content of the Cyprus problem, the marathon UN-led negotiations between the GC and TC leadership, in step with the Greek and Turkish governments, continued to bitterly fail, decade after decade. As both key antecedents and consequents of the Cyprus conflict, the ethnocentric concepts of history, identity, community, and, of course, statehood to which GCs and TCs had become habituated, repeatedly led with predictable precision to inconclusive and futile negotiations (see *IE,* chapter 7).

The Impasse of Ethnonationalism concluded with the Helsinki Summit of 1999 during which the European Union (EU) accepted Turkey's candidacy for future EU membership—a historic event that was made possible by Greece's abandonment of its traditional veto-backed policy of obstruction to Turkey's European aspirations. As the Helsinki Summit instated the European process in the eastern Mediterranean, the relationships between Greece and Turkey and between GCs and TCs assumed the potential of evolving in ways that could transform the agelong ethnonational rivalries between the Greek and Turkish people in the interest of peace, stability, and well-being for all concerned. Such a prospect hinged in a special way on whether the EU process would modify the nationalist monolith of the Turkish state and Turkish secessionist intransigence on the Cyprus issue.

THE BROKEN OLIVE BRANCH, VOLUME TWO:
THE HISTORICAL ENCOUNTER WITH
POSTNATIONALIST EUROPEANIZATION

Volume two of the *The Broken Olive Branch* explores the first historical shifts away from ethnocentric nationalism toward the gradual emergence of European-like postnationalist trends in the political cultures of Greece, Turkey, and Cyprus. In conjunction and in parallel with the challenging conciliatory processes of EU integration and enlargement, interethnic and international relations in the eastern Mediterranean started to embody in embryonic form the first-ever promise that peace and reconciliation between the Greek and Turkish people could become a tangible historical possibility. In the context of a rapidly globalizing world, the analysis that follows examines the dynamics of this possibility from the perspective of the historical competition between the peace-enhancing postnationalist politics that began to emerge since the late 1990s on the one hand and the traditional adversarial approaches of Greek/GC nationalism and Turkish/TC nationalism on the other. From this vantage point, volume two attempts a detailed assessment of the future viability of ethnocentric nationalism in contrast to a prospective polyethnic Cypriot polity within the broader framework of the multinational, peace-grounded democracy of the EU.

The analysis in volume two critically appraises the novel historical events and opportunities for a final settlement of the Cyprus problem, and for the normalization of Greek-Turkish relations, that precipitated during the years leading up to the Cyprus referendum of April 2004, and the subsequent integration of Cyprus into the EU. Furthermore, it examines the historic changes and new challenges that face Cyprus, Greece, Turkey, and the EU in the postreferendum era in light of future prospects. In its essence, the subsequent analysis is guided in its entirely by the fundamental question as to whether Greek/GC and Turkish/TC ethnocentric nationalism as the major historical determinant of the Cyprus conflict will prevail or be superseded in the interest of peace by the conflict-transforming capacity of European-based postnationalist politics.

The Broken Olive Branch

Globalizing Trends and the EU as a Catalyst for Peace

Political and Civil Changes in Greece and Turkey

THE PROGRESSION OF CONFLICT TRANSFORMATION

In his work *Building Peace: Sustainable Reconciliation in Divided Societies*, John Paul Lederach defined conflict as progression. In his words: "Conflict is never a static phenomenon. It is expressive, dynamic, and dialectical in nature. Relationally based, conflict is born in the world of human meaning and perception. It is constantly changed by ongoing human interaction, and it continuously changes by the very people who give it life and the social environment in which it is born and perhaps ends" (2002, 64).

The sociohistorical and human aspects of the Cyprus conflict analyzed in *The Impasse of Ethnonationalism (IE)*, volume one of *The Broken Olive Branch*, clearly reflect Lederach's thesis describing conflict as a progression. Based on this understanding, Lederach also defined peace building as a process engaging social and political actors in as many functions and roles and on as many levels of society as conflict does— if not more. Drawing from the work of Adam Curle, he identified four stages by which societies move from an entrenched conflict to a peace-building process with the propensity for dynamically orienting society toward sustainable peace.

The first stage is that of conflict entrenchment. During this phase, the people immersed in the conflict are quite unaware of its parameters regarding issues such as power symmetry and asymmetry, justice and injustice, and grievances and reparations. Becoming educated in diagnosing and understanding the roots and dynamic of conflict is a critical element in moving beyond this stage. This process of emerging from the state of immersion in the conflict, through diagnostic understanding, is the stage Lederach refers to as *the process of conscientization.*

The second stage is that of confrontation, where the pursuit of change brings the rival groups into a direct encounter. However, the confrontation involves a series of choices over means. These range from violent or nonviolent approaches to a combination of both. The quest for change in turn requires "the rebalancing of power in the relationship by which all those involved recognize one another in new ways" (Lederach 2002, 65).

This new recognition sets the foundation for moving toward the third stage, that of negotiation. In this phase, Lederach elaborated that "those involved increase the level of awareness of their interdependence through mutual recognition. In essence, negotiation means that the various people or groups involved recognize that they can neither simply impose their will on nor eliminate the other side, but rather must work with the other side to achieve their goals" (Lederach 2002, 65).

Moreover, this mutual acknowledgment that the other side exists and that it must be taken into account in opening up the future is "a form of power balancing and a prerequisite of negotiation" (Lederach 2002, 65). However, we need to clarify that while mutual acknowledgment does not automatically eradicate economic and military imbalances, it does induce a balance of power, in a political sense, at least as it is necessary to initiate and sustain meaningful negotiation.

The fourth stage in the peace-building process is negotiation and mediation that aims at establishing "a restructuring of the relationship that deals with the fundamental substantive and procedural concerns of those involved" in the interest of "more peaceful relations and increased justice" (Lederach 2002, 66).

One way or another, Cyprus started to move through these four stages during the late 1990s. During that decade, there were movements backward and forward with an increasing gravitation forward after 1999. Interestingly, progress through the four stages of conflict transformation occurred in the formal political realm as well as in the informal realm of civil society, through ever-evolving citizens' initiatives. Formally or informally, explicitly or implicitly, all four of Lederach's phases had increasingly engaged Cypriots. Numerous peace-enhancing processes gained momentum and manifested promise. These, identified broadly, were the catalytic framework of the EU, particularly through the accession process of Cyprus; the growth of the citizen peace movement as a vital aspect of the emerging Cypriot civil society; the general rapprochement between Greece and Turkey that commenced with the so-called "earthquake diplomacy"; and Turkey's candidacy to the EU.

To the degree that they became an integral aspect of the new reality of Cyprus, these initiatives and their impact enabled the erection of a multilevel historical and political configuration of potentially positive influences in the region. These influences and the patterns they enhanced were conducive to the possible emergence of conflict resolving and stabilizing processes intimately linking peace and security in a manner that could serve the interests of Cyprus and the Eastern Mediterranean region. Although slow-moving, wavering, and incomplete, a peace-building process started to come into view in the evolution of GC-TC and Greek-Turkish relations, even as the age-old conflict patterns persisted.

THE EU: CULTURE AND FRAMEWORK OF CONCILIATORY POLITICS

To appreciate more fully the contribution the European Union (EU) made as a catalyst for peace in Cyprus, some brief remarks on its historical background and its essence are in order. The EU was born out of the ashes of World War II. Originally comprised of a small number, the founding member-states, launching the idea of a united Europe, began the Herculean task of integration through a shared, far-reaching, and daring vision combined with very small but firm steps of implementation. The major objective of the European project was to remove the causes of war and to secure common processes and structures of democratic cooperation, multilateral decision making, and consensus building (Wood and Yesilada 2004). Nationalism as a world- and life view, the nationalist mode of institutional organization and behavior by nation-states, the fierce adversarial competition between the national economies of industrialized nation-states, and the relentless competition for colonies were the central factors of conflict that the EU founders sought to address and remove gradually (McCormick 2002).

The European historical experience revealed that the consolidation of populist nationalism around the modern nation-state precipitated into an arrogant, absolute, and aggressively uncompromising concept of national sovereignty that in practice proved not only defiant of both national and international laws, and indeed of democracy, but also catastrophic in its unparalleled legitimization of violence in the name of *the nation*.

For this reason, the visionaries and architects of European integration sought to systematically dissociate the nationalist mentality from both the political culture of the nation-state and the interrelationships of nation-states. This difficult and challenging European project gradually led to the establishment of the institutions and political culture of the EU, marking a novel historical attempt to enhance an intersocietal regime of equitable economic growth, human rights, and security within a framework by which democracy becomes intimately associated with peace. Having grown out of the European historical experience of war, the fundamental assumptions here are that warfare, violence, and the use of force are by nature erosive of democracy; that violence in all its forms is regressive to democracy, even when it is unavoidable; that the recourse to violence always marks political failure in that democratic thinking, acting, and relationships did not prevail; and that the means of democracy and the means of violence are incompatible.

These assumptions underpinning the rationale for the EU stand in sharp contrast to nationalism's affinity with, and legitimization of, violence in the name of democracy—of *the nation's* democracy.

The structure and logic of EU institutions are indicative of the unique manner in which the European experiment amplified, deepened, and expanded democracy above and beyond ethnocentric adversarial nationalism. Composed of the elected leaders of the member-states and the heads of the European Commission, the European Council, while representing the national interests of the members, makes broad consensual policy decisions that set the general guidelines for the development of the

EU. In effect, it forges the general parameters for joint participation in a shared enhancement of democracy and well-being.

As the highest executive body of the EU, the European Commission, composed of commissioners from the member-states, represents and brings forward in the decision-making process the interest of the EU as a whole, superseding the national interests of individual member-countries. It is precisely because of this focusing of attention on the transnational common good that EU commissioners are required to forego allegiance to their nation of origin in carrying out their tasks within the commission's areas of competence. At this level, the democratic process is thus institutionalized and conducted in the transnational dimension of politics.

Moreover, the Council of the EU (formerly known as the Council of Ministers) is responsible for bringing forward the specific and often diverse national interests of the individual states, which the members of this body explicitly represent. At this level, the democratic process assumes an intergovernmental structure and expression. Here, the overall decision-making process identifies, asserts, adjusts, and integrates the specific national interests of each member-state into the broader EU framework and objectives. National interests are thereby no longer pursued ethnocentrically and unilaterally, but rather jointly and multilaterally in an ongoing institutionalized fashion.

The multilingual European Parliament is yet another innovative expansion of democracy beyond ethnocentric nationalism. Each party bloc is composed of representatives from multiple ethnonational constituencies that cut across the national societies of the EU member-states. Each party brings together Germans, French, Dutch, Greeks, Italians, and other nationalities, elaborating citizen-based party politics across societies, ethnicities, cultures, languages, and nations.

Finally, the European Court of Justice ensures conformity of national and EU laws to the historical treaties that have furnished the foundations of the EU, thus raising the rule of law in its sphere of competency above the limitations of national law, while strengthening it within each of the member-states. Like the commissioners, the judges of the European Court act independently of the specific national interests of their home state.

In an era of increasing globalization, the combined structures and processes of the European Council, the European Commission, the Council of the EU, the European Parliament, and the European Court of Justice underscore the first conscious historical effort to open up and amplify democracy while freeing it from the constrictions and distortions of nationalism. The ethnocentric, narcissistic, and absolutist notion of national sovereignty that nationalism cultivated and operated within Europe until the end of World War II has been fundamentally modified by the EU political process and institutions. The EU transcended nationalism by systematically building and instating a regional edifice of democracy by which the sovereignty of nation-states is voluntarily pooled and jointly amplified with respect to the competencies and purposes of the EU. Despite the many difficulties, the launching of deliberations for an EU constitution (or its equivalent) marks a further step in EU integration and solidarity through the enhancement of democracy at the interstate and transnational levels of governance.

Insofar as the origins, principles, and framework of the EU are embedded in a historical effort to transcend ethnocentric nationalism within as well as between states, the EU system carries special significance and relevance for interethnic and interstate relations between the Greek and Turkish people in Greece, Cyprus, and Turkey, particularly in light of their respective nationalist legacies.

From the embryonic form that it assumed at its commencement in the Treaty of Paris of 1951, European integration has come a long way. The recent milestones of this process were the evolution of the European Community to the EU with the Maastricht Treaty of 1992; the introduction of the single currency, the euro, in 2002; and the decision at the Copenhagen Summit on December 12, 2002, for EU enlargement, which culminated in ten new countries, including Cyprus, joining the EU on May 1, 2004, bringing the number of members to a total of twenty-five countries.

EU enlargement is not merely a matter of expanding the borders of a united Europe. More importantly, it implies an institutionalized process whereby the candidate states are first required to meet specific criteria as a condition for initiating their accession process. Once that begins, the acceding countries start to harmonize their system of governance and socioeconomic institutions to the *acquis communautaire* (McCormick 2002). In this perspective, EU enlargement entails a process of fundamental social and political transformation that binds the candidate and acceding states wishing to join the EU. Preparing for EU membership implies a willingness to undergo radical changes. Among other things, candidates and acceding states and their respective societies are required to adopt a process of deepened democratization; establish open-market systems and attain levels of efficiency conducive to sustainable economic growth; develop a transparent and lean state with political accountability; become sensitive to environmental issues and standards; raise, establish, and implement human rights standards; and balance the traditional power of the state with the rights of individuals and subnational social and cultural groups.

Of utmost importance is the fact that the EU process requires each of the candidate and acceding states to adopt an approach and policy in their relationship to existing member-states that clearly forgoes the narcissistic, nationalist orientation of the old Europe. In contrast to the latter, they are to adopt conciliatory and consensual political processes and values as defined and established by EU treaties and institutions. This constitutes one of the fundamental features of the framework, in that it affects and transforms the traditional ethnocentric orientation of foreign policy by institutionalizing the democratic process on an intergovernmental, as well as transnational, transstate level. In this regard, the edifice of the EU reflects a structure of governance that is unprecedented in the world.

In light of the multiple benefits of EU membership, what is extraordinary about the enlargement process is the manner in which it induces and generates consent on the part of candidates and acceding states to adopt the values and institutions of the EU. In so doing, enlargement becomes a powerful catalyst for the social and political transformation of the joining states, as well as of member-states, such as one has never seen in modern history. The unique way in which the EU structures interstate, intersocietal, and trans-state cooperation and consensus building within its framework comes into sharp focus when one compares relationships between the member-states at present to those that prevailed under the shaping influence of nationalism from the nineteenth century to World War II. One may be critical of the EU with respect to innumerable issues and shortcomings. Yet, no one can dispute the fact that the EU edifice has marked the most creative and exemplary milestone in interstate and intersocietal peace, stability, and well-being. It is in the function of the EU as a peacebuilding and stabilizing system that one locates the novel impact of the enlargement process on Greek-Turkish relations and the Cyprus problem.

THE EU AS A FACTOR OF POLITICAL AND SOCIAL CHANGE

Greece

Greece has emerged from a troubled and complex past to become a respected, full member of the EU. The progress reflected in its historical trajectory is integral to socioeconomic and political changes, associated in great measure with the general process of Europeanization that has extended and deepened EU institutions, law, democracy, and culture within as well as between member-states and their respective societies (Keridis 2001).

Emerging from the devastating experience of World War II, Greece became embroiled in a terrible, ideologically driven civil war between the Communists and the Right (including the royalists). The defeat of the Communists through the first implementation of the Marshall Plan paved the way for Greece's membership in the NATO alliance. Facing severe economic problems, it continued with a quasi-democratic system reinforced and amplified by the strains and stresses of severe polarizations between right-wing and left-wing politics, under the heavy shadow of the cold war. This general trend culminated in seven years of military dictatorship by the Far Right nationalist colonels, spanning from 1967 to 1974.

The cumulative national crisis that resulted from the Greek junta's autocratic rule, its 1974 coup in Cyprus, and Turkey's military invasion that succeeded it had greatly discredited the traditional right-wing, militant nationalists in the eyes of Greek public opinion. This fact marked the beginning of the first serious attempt by Greek society to stir politics away from the past authoritarianism of the corporate state toward a more transparent and open democratic society. This new regime, what Greeks refer to as *metapoliteysi*, brought about numerous political changes that eventually earned Greece a place in the then–European Community. Its full membership in 1981 commenced an ongoing process of sociopolitical transformations in which Greece was compelled to gradually come to terms with its ideological and nationalist legacy on the one hand, and with its institutionalized, postnationalist, interstate partnerships within the European Community on the other.

The first break from traditional Greek politics came with the rise of Constantine Mitsotakis to the leadership of the right-wing New Democracy party in 1984. A nephew of former prime minister Elefherios Venizelos and critic of the abuses of the royalist nationalists, Mitsotakis was never a part of the Right's greater historical tradition (Keridis 2001). As Keridis explained, "Mitsotakis clarified New Democracy's ideological profile and freed the Greek conservatives from their authoritarian past, stepping up efforts initiated by Constantine Karamanlis in 1974 to turn New Democracy from the heir of royalists and national-minded anticommunists into a modern liberal European Party. New Democracy could no longer electorally afford the separation of Greeks into 'democrats' and 'right-wingers'" (6).

The juxtaposition of "democrats" to "right-wingers" had long been the tool by which the Communist Left sought to popularize its fierce critique of the abuses of the traditional Right. However, Mitsotakis's reform of Greek ideological politics came to its fullness when New Democracy made national reconciliation between the Right and the Left the rallying point of its political platform, while cultivating relations with the Communist Left.

The epitome of Mitsotakis's strategy for reforming the most septic aspects of polarized Greek political culture was the unprecedented formation in 1989 of the Tzanetakis government, a coalition between New Democracy and the Communist Party. In the context of the modern history of Greek politics and society, the significance of this event cannot be overestimated. "Since then, the rules of the political game have changed, and political life has been normalized, Europeanized, and liberated from artificial and obsolete divisions that had cast their shadows and constrained it for decades" (Keridis 2001, 7).

The European influence on Greek political life was evident as it began to yield certain substantive results. At least for key actors in the political leadership of Greece, Europe provided the model and the stimulus for the first phase in the effort at deconstructing the old militant nationalism of the Right and the radical ideological polarization between rightists and leftists within Greek politics. However, the full Europeanization of Greece was an enormous task, as it went against the grain of the country's nationalist history. This was evident in the relapse of nationalism in New Democracy under the leadership of Miltiades Evert between 1993 and 1996. The regressive trend reflected the party's internal crisis resulting from the struggle between the European-oriented, liberal reformists and the old-time nationalists, including royalists and junta sympathizers.

It was not until well into the 1990s, more than a decade after Greece joined the European Community, that the process of political and intellectual reform began to move decisively beyond the various brands of the old adversarial nationalism, including that of the Left. The reference here is to changes within the Pan-Hellenic Socialist Movement (PASOK). Founded by Andreas Papandreou as the first noncommunist Left party of Greece, PASOK exploded onto the political scene in the 1970s, mobilizing support from the traditional disenfranchised Left and from the old Venizelists. At the time, his success in raising PASOK to a powerful national party emerged mainly from the solidification of his political front through polarized rhetoric, and from a practice aimed at weakening the radical Left in favor of a centrist approach. "[PASOK's] strategy was based on ideological eclecticism, a catchall electoral appeal, the exploitation of strong, historically constructed, collective political identities of Greeks, [and] the use of the long traditional populism and nationalism in Greek politics" (Keridis 2001, 6).

This platform brought PASOK to power in 1981. Although Papandreou relativized political ideology at the party level, he reverted to nationalist rhetoric at the societal and national level. While it served as a politically expedient means of achieving broad support and internal unity, nationalism revitalized the dangers associated with ethnocentrism. This development resulted in heightened tension with traditional enemies and neighbors and raised deep concern within the European Community regarding the compatibility between Greek politics and European political culture. The crisis in the Balkans was also partly responsible for the reawakening of the familiar nationalism. The general frustration associated with PASOK's populist mismanagement of the economy turned into psychological fuel that fed the outburst of nationalism in Greece following the independence of the former Yugoslav Republic of Macedonia.

However, between 1990 and 1996,

> PASOK succeeded, at least on the level of leadership, in adapting to new trends, further promoting the modernization of the Greek political system. PASOK succeeded to the Socialist International, clarified its ideological profile, and made peace with economic rationality and Euro-Atlantic structures. It modernized its political message and went from being the embodiment of historic political polarizations to being the representative of European social democracy. (Keridis 2001, 7)

These significant changes coincided with the election of Costas Simitis to head PASOK as Papandreou's successor. Subsequently and to his credit, Simitis became the first Greek prime minister to forge a clearly postnationalist Greek government and foreign policy. Having overcome populist economics in the vein of traditional nationalism, the Simitis government was also the first to bring sound macro management to the Greek economy, enabling it to take full advantage of its place in the EU and to attain a growth rate of 3.5 percent per year by 2000.

The second half of the 1990s marked the Europeanization of Greek society and the two major parties of Greece. What Mitsotakis initiated in the New Democracy party, Simitis initiated and completed in PASOK and extended to the state and the governance of Greece. Henceforth, the major struggle within Greek politics and society was no longer along ideological party lines (what the left wing traditionally referred to as the struggle between the conservative Right and progressive Left), but across party lines between modernizing, European-minded Greeks and old-time nationalists from both the Right and the Left of the ideological spectrum. The key issues in this political environment centered more on the new role of the state in relation to the economy and to society in light of economic globalization, the rise of the information society, and the new opportunities opened up by EU enlargement. Inevitably, the nationalist concept of

Greek identity and its associated adversarial culture appeared questionable and even obsolete, at least in the eyes of those who were becoming attuned to the Europeanizing trends. As George Papandreou frequently asserted, the challenge centered on redefining Greek identity at a deeper level, extending and opening it up to the multicultural setting of Europe, the Balkans, and the Mediterranean (Papandreou 2000).

An indisputable fact in the postmodern era of globalization is the rapid narrowing of the gap that differentiates domestic from foreign policy. The case of Greece is no exception, as changes within its society and politics paralleled changes in foreign policy. Preoccupation with Turkey has always been at center stage of Greece's foreign policy, particularly as Turkey has been Greece's age-long, ethnonational rival, the occupier of Cyprus, and the giant, militarily powerful neighbor. Traditionally, Greece's approach to the Turkish threat and to its broader strategy in the region was grounded on a nationalistically conditioned foreign policy. It aimed at the isolation of Turkey and the obstruction of its European aspirations, resulting in Greece's refusal to engage Turkey in dialogue. The approach was based on the assumption that Turkey always was and always will be Greece's archenemy.

Since the late 1990s, this approach has been gradually but steadily changing. Fully consented to by Greece, the 1999 Helsinki decision by the EU to accept Turkey as a candidate-state marked the formal historical highlight of Greece's shifting foreign policy beyond the confines of nationalism. New political forces emerged in Greece that acknowledged the dangers of nationalism, challenged the populist approach to politics and the economy, questioned the corporate state and its ethnocentric, sociological hegemony, and gave credence to the new conditions of globalization. These new political forces were the same that prompted a new approach to foreign policy, particularly toward Turkey. Here again, the line differentiating those who favored openness and dialogue with Turkey from those who objected to it did not run between parties but across parties, at least in regard to the two larger ones, PASOK and New Democracy. The new political competition, now unfolding within each of the major parties, was between old-time nationalists and European, postnationalist reformers.

Along with acceptance of multicultural principles of governance and internationalization of the economy, Greece's Euro-reformers promoted the idea that the traditional policy of deterrence toward Turkey was no longer sufficient; it needed to be supplemented with a proactive policy of rapprochement founded on new, reality-based assumptions that were free from nationalist myths. Euro-reformers accepted the challenge to forge a new approach that was not only free from the outdated facts of the distant past and the stereotypical perceptions they gave rise to, but also was firmly grounded on the new facts of the present and the likely future promises they held. Keridis has given the most concise explication of these new assumptions. The new foreign policy, he explained, is founded on the claim that

> Turkey is not a monolith but a complicated and rapidly changing reality with a variety of constituencies. Some of these constituencies think of Greek-Turkish antagonism as a missed opportunity for the cooperation of the two most powerful Balkan states to the benefit of the whole region and are willing to engage in an honest dialogue with the Greek side to this end.
>
> Turkey is experiencing a phase of rapid social, political and economic pluralization, with such developments as the opening of its economy, the proliferation of private media outlets, and the further urbanization of a greater number of former peasants. During this process of seeking and achieving a post-Kemalist equilibrium, the risk exists for destabilization and increased tension, but great opportunities are created for cooperation with Greece through Turkey's emerging nonstate economic and social agents (the market and civil society), above and beyond official government channels.
>
> Greece has no interest in isolating its great neighbor or in excluding from the European political structures. On the contrary, Greece has only to gain from the Europeanization of Turkish society and the dissemination and further strengthening of European civil values inside Turkey. A stable, democratic, and peaceful Turkey with a market double the size of that of all the other Balkan countries combined and with strong cultural ties to Greece (such ties as folk culture, music, cuisine, language and mentality) would be the best partner for the joint construction of the new European, Balkan, and Near Eastern Order. (Keridis 2001, 14)

The changes in Greece's domestic developments and foreign policy, and the broader Europeanization of Greek society, were of tantamount importance as historical catalysts for contributing to both a prospective political settlement of the Cyprus problem and for peace and stability in the region in general. In essence, the challenges described above crystallized around a sociopolitical process by which Greece's Euro-reformers began to dissociate the ideas of democracy, economic well-being, and foreign policy from their entrapment in nationalism, and started to reconceptualize them politically, institutionally, and culturally in terms of a vision of peace and conciliatory politics.

Yet to attain a full appreciation of Europeanizing changes in Greek-Turkish relations and their bearing on Cyprus, particularly since the EU Helsinki Summit of 1999, it is imperative to address also parallel changes within Turkey.

Turkey

In the historical evolution of its society and politics, Greece had moved ahead of Turkey in its relationship with the EU. It became a member of the European Community during the time when European integration structures and institutions were still unconsolidated. The transformation of the European Community into the EU under the Maastricht Treaty of 1992 established a more cohesive inter- and transstate institutional framework, while the Copenhagen Summit of 1993 introduced a more rigorous accession process for candidate-states aspiring to join the EU. Along with these changes, the EU also put in place an upgraded, refined, and more efficient system of support and assistance to candidate-states. Turkey applied for EU candidacy following this shift in the European institutions and processes.

As Greece had done earlier, Turkey began to draw closer to Europe as it emerged from a troubled and ambiguous past (Kasaba and Bozdoğan 2000). Its history had been characterized by state-sponsored nationalism, with the military playing a central role in guaranteeing the overall structural integration of the Turkish state and its Western-oriented, Kemalist secular character. Highly centralized in its wielding of power, the Turkish state originally aimed at constructing, perpetuating, and securing a homogenized, state-defined Turkish identity. This nationalist project of creating a monoethnic nation-state was central to Turkey's evolution throughout the first half of the twentieth century. However, since Turkish society was originally multiethnic and highly stratified, it did not fit the nationalist model of an ethnically homogeneous nation-state. In the face of its polyethnic morphology, the adoption of monoethnic nationalism by the Turkish state was sustainable only though a powerful and leveling centralized state, backed by a strong military. Under these conditions, Turkey started as a one-party system. Later, Kemal Atatürk, the founding father of modern Turkey, sought to establish a multiparty system as another step in Turkey's Westernization; however, when the opposition party became the focal point of religious dissent to his reforms, Atatürk returned to a single-party system. It was not until the 1950s that Turkey introduced a multiparty system of governance. Even after this change, the crippled and quasi-democratic nature of Turkish state politics was manifested in the sustained overriding influence and intervention of the military in both the society and the political affairs of the state.

Civil Politics and the Turkish Army. The main thrust of Turkish state politics in the post–World War II era was the propagation of a secular, aggressively anticommunist nationalism and the maintenance of close ties with the West, particularly with the United States—ties initiated when Greece and Turkey joined NATO in the 1950s. Turkey's membership in NATO maintained and enhanced the political role of the military. The military had direct oversight of Turkish politics through the powerful National Security Council. The military coups of 1960, 1971, and 1980 marked the historical highlights of the military's prominent role in the country's internal affairs. Turkey's rigorous, pro-Western stance during the cold war era did not necessarily translate into democratization on the domestic front. Turkey was set on securing a Turko-national public order and a pro-Western foreign policy through the power of the military, while assuming that tolerating domestic political dialogue and dissent through the opening up of democracy and civil society would risk fracturing the Turkish state. The ideologically driven militancy of both the Right and the Left had been one of the phenomena imparting substance to this assumption, thus sustaining the state's authoritarian mode. Under these circumstances, the role of the state in maintaining public order was perceived not in relation to democratization but in relation to the preservation and enhancement of centralized state power. The military became an integral part of Turkey's system of governance, not only as the protector of the state but as the guarantor of its ideological identity: right-wing, secular nationalism and pro-Western anticommunism. Jenkins succinctly described this close historical association between Turkish state politics and the military:

> The Turkish republic evolved from the army formed to fight the War of Liberation against the victors of World War I. Six of the republic's nine presidents have been generals. The military has staged three coups in the last forty years. Each coup followed the collapse of civil authority. Each time, once it had restored order, the army returned power to a civilian government, only for the same process to be repeated again approximately ten years later. (2001, 32)

A further factor that helps explain the strong hand of the military in Turkish political history is the long-standing, intrinsic weakness of the civilian political elite. Although Turkey has allegedly been a multiparty democracy throughout the second half of the twentieth century, its political culture remained "dominated by traditional Anatolian values of personal allegiance, the precedence of collective over individual rights, and deference to authority" (Jenkins 2001, 21). The hierarchical and authoritarian structure of political parties thus constituted a more basic characteristic of Turkish politics that functioned over and above the right-versus-left ideological differentiations and polarizations. Civil politics and the civil bureaucracy thus became characterized by a trail of abuses and corruption. By contrast, the military, while remaining loyal to Kemalism, evolved into a highly efficient and generally corruption-free establishment, albeit with a narrow, self-serving focus. This phenomenon has been one of the major sociopolitical factors retarding the deepening of democracy in Turkey, as the instability and incompetence of the civil, political establishment reinforced dependence on the stability, robustness, and authoritarianism of the military.

The spectrum of Turkish politics has been spanned by clandestine groupings rather than institutionalized parties, with intense personal rivalries, even between leaders of parties that were ideologically identical. The weak and unstable coalition governments that emerged in the post–cold war era of the 1990s are cases in point. The June 1996 coalition between the Motherland Party under Mesut Yilmaz and the True Path Party under Tansu Ciller disintegrated in a few months. Even though both parties were ideologically centrist, the feud between the leaders led to a crisis in government. Similar ambiguities existed in the minority coalition that took power in May 1999. It brought together the centrist Motherland Party, the nationalist, left-wing Democratic Left Party, and the nationalist, right-wing National Movement Party. Paradoxically, the parties of the Center and the Left forged an alliance against the Right, to which both were strongly antagonistic, rendering effective governance impossible.

Jenkins further explained that

> [In Turkey,] political fragmentation is exacerbated by the autocratic manner in which party leaders run their parties. Advancement within the party is invariably the reward for loyalty to the leader rather than for ability. Dissidents face the choice between obscurity and resignation. The premium placed on loyalty has in turn encouraged a party leader's tolerance of corruption and nepotism, particularly in the awarding of state contracts, to the point where they are now virtually endemic. (2001, 22)

Under these conditions, the sociopolitical and economic landscape of Turkish society presented a characteristicly sharp contrast between the rich ruling politicians and the average Turkish citizens facing rising economic problems, the deteriorating effects of which bore most heavily on numerous marginalized groups, such as the migrants who moved from rural to urban centers, where they created squatters' towns. Income imbalances were accentuated among both social groups and regions, while tax collection was inefficient and inequitable. These trends gradually made clear to the public eye that while successfully serving their own economic interests, the civil political leaders were incapable of improving the economic well-being of the general population. Against this backdrop of political instability and continuing high inflation, the earthquakes of the 1990s brought decades of corruption and nepotism to explicit public consciousness. The result was a loss of confidence in the political establishment, which was coming under severe and unprecedented open criticism by the Turkish press.

The Kurdish Problem. The nationalism and power interests of the army, in conjunction with the weaknesses and unruliness of civil politics, created the conditions for a weak and wavering democracy that preserved and sustained the predominant role of the military in Turkish politics. Two other significant factors exacerbated the situation: the Kurdish problem and the rising influence of Islamic fundamentalism. Being in violent rivalry with Turkish state nationalism and the power of the army that backed it, the secessionist and militant Kurdish nationalism of the Kurdistan Workers Party (PKK) added to the perils and complexities of Turkish society. While largely ignored by the domestic mainstream media and political establishment, the level of violence brought by the conflict surrounding the Kurdish issue has marred Turkey's human rights record and further polarized Turkish society.

Under Abdullah Ocalan, the PKK counts the deaths of 4,151 members of the security forces and 4,472 civilians to its credit. For its part, the Turkish army is responsible for the death of 25,000 actual or suspected PKK members and the forceful evacuation and burning of more than 2,500 Kurdish villages in southeastern Turkey (Jenkins 2001, 28, 29). The conflict also polarized the Kurdish community, as 30,000 men from ethnically Kurdish clans became involved as village guards in fighting the PKK on the side of the government. Parallel to this was the PKK's policy of intimidation, resulting in the massacring of progovernment Kurdish families. The Kurdish issue also complicated Turkey's relations with northern Iraq, which became a Kurdish stronghold, as well as with Syria, which was known to harbor the PKK leader. These internal problems were a source of enormous stress and anxiety for the Turkish military, severely limiting innovations and creativity in policy development. The indecision of Turkey's handling the long-standing Turkish-Greek disputes and the Cyprus problem had much to do with the political paralysis induced by Turkey's internal problems—a fact rarely acknowledged by Greece and the GCs.

The Kurdish conflict subsided only after the capture of the PKK leader, Ocalan, in Kenya on February 15, 1999—an event that again strained Turkish-Greek relations because of disclosures that Greek officials, who were subsequently dismissed, had been unofficially harboring Ocalan without the knowledge of Prime Minister Simitis or his government. The capture of Ocalan, the internal rivalries among the Kurds, and the military weakening of the PKK forced to the forefront of the party's consciousness questions regarding the viability of violence as a means of securing Kurdish human rights. With a death sentence hanging over his head, Ocalan ordered the PKK to cease fighting. Having prevailed in the struggle for the PKK leadership, Ocalan's brother, Osman Ocalan, followed suit. In early 2000, following the organization's Seventh Congress, it was announced that the PKK was "halting its war with Turkey" (Jenkins 2001, 30). The Kurds renounced the use of violence while opting for the politicization and internationalization of the Kurdish problem, in which their human rights became increasingly associated with their autonomy within the Turkish state, rather than with full secession from the Turkish state.

A simultaneous political development that helped defuse the conflict was the EU's position on Turkey's aspirations to draw closer to Europe in its longing for future EU membership (Moustakis and Chaudhuri 2005). Although the EU had always been supportive of Kurdish human rights, it condemned both the terrorism of the PKK and the unsparing use of force by the Turkish army for their general impact on the Kurdish community. Gradually, the EU became a point of reference for reform within Turkey.

Simultaneously the EU became a vital stimulus in the search by Kurdish leaders for alternative, nonviolent ways to attaining their political and human rights goals. In light of the historical impasse that confronted the Kurds following Ocalan's arrest, the politicization of the Kurdish problem on a European basis appeared as a viable option. However, the high point of the EU's influence on the internal affairs of Turkey came into focus at Ocalan's trial. On June 29, 1999, Ocalan was convicted of treason and mass murder and sentenced to hang. However, the EU, having completely dissociated executions from the legitimate functions of the state, warned Turkey that carrying out the sentence would jeopardize its relations with the EU. On January 12, 2000, the Turkish government, against popular opinion, announced that it would postpone forwarding the sentence to parliament for the necessary ratification, pending the ruling of the European Court of Human Rights.

Under the direct prompting of the EU, the restraint exhibited by the Turkish government was partly responsible for the cessation of violence and creation of political and civil space for addressing the Kurdish problem in a new way. Although many setbacks followed, an alternative course of action opened up, leading eventually to decisive legislative reforms enhancing human rights and the legitimacy of ethnic pluralism within Turkish society. These developments marked a historical step in the direction of deconstructing the authoritarian, monoethnic nationalism traditionally espoused by the Turkish state and of simultaneously delegitimizing Kurdish secessionist violence as a means of attaining human rights.

As noted, a

> cessation of PKK violence would not only present a diversified, subtler challenge to the Turkish establishment's current concept of a culturally and ethnically homogenized unitary state. It would also increase Western pressure on Turkey to ease restrictions on the expression of Kurdish identity, while Ankara could not allow such a relaxation to be equated to a concession to terrorism. (Jenkins 2001, 31)

The EU's conciliatory political culture and process played a major part in the reframing of the Kurdish problem relative to both the Turkish state and the Kurdish community within Turkey. Interestingly, the increasing challenge for Turkey to forego monoethnic traditional nationalism and embrace ethnic pluralism and interethnic democracy was the same challenge confronting GCs and TCs, especially within the EU framework (Kasaba and Bozdoğan 2000).

Political Islam. Another central problem that accompanied both the impoverishment of civil politics and the Kurdish problem, keeping the military in the forefront of Turkish politics, was the rise of Islamic fundamentalism to a political force in the 1990s. Already in the 1980s, socioeconomic challenges and public disillusionment with mainstream politics provided fertile ground for the rise of the Islamist Welfare Party. Under the circumstances, the party leadership appealed to a very broad range of disappointed citizens to form its constituency.

> Although Islam was its binding force, the WP also supported elements of populist economics and nationalist nostalgia for the Ottoman Empire. Ideology was underpinned by a highly efficient party organization, including youth and women's groups, which combined political propaganda with services ranging from food handouts to hospital visits. The WP's electoral support covered a broad spectrum, from pious Anatolian conservatives to urban Muslim equivalents of European Christian Democrats to hardline advocates of sharia law with close links to Islamist terrorist organizations. (Jenkins 2001, 23)

In stark contrast to Kemalism's persistent extrication of religion from the public life, political Islam, particularly as it blossomed in the 1990s, initiated the first credible attempt at introducing religion into the edifice of Turkish nationalism by openly ushering it into public culture, politics, and potentially into the Turkish state. To the secular Kemalists this was an alarming development, especially since the incorporation of religion in Turkish nationalism could lend tacit legitimacy to the militant brand of Islamic fundamentalism, which had become a domestic as well as global phenomenon by the 1990s.

The Welfare Party was in essence the replacement of previous Islamist parties, such as the National Order Party, founded by Necmettin Erbakan, and its successor, the National Salvation Party—each abolished by the Turkish military in the 1971 and 1980 coups respectively. The new constitution of 1982 reaffirmed the secular nature of the Turkish state, forbidding both amendments as well as proposed amendments on the matter. However, the electoral support for the Welfare Party rose from 7.2 percent in 1987 to 21.4 percent in the 1995 elections, establishing it as the largest party in parliament. Forming a coalition government with Ciller's True Path Party, the Welfare Party assumed power, with Erbakan becoming the first professed Islamist prime minister of the Turkish republic.

This development ran against the historical grain of Kemalism and the secular nationalism it propagated, thereby provoking the intervention of the military, which was greatly alarmed at the prospect of an Islamic Turkish state. The Welfare Party itself was in an ambiguous situation as it was compelled to balance Islam with the secularism of its partner party. The fragility of Turkish civil politics was once again an obstacle to deepening civil society and democracy. Through intense but low-profile lobbying and direct efforts to influence public opinion, the military broke up the coalition government, forcing Erbakan to resign in the summer of 1997. In January 1998, the Turkish Constitutional Court outlawed the Welfare Party on the grounds that it had violated the constitutional provision of secularism. While this ban deepened divisions within the Islamist movement, this did not prevent political Islam from remaining a force to be reckoned with in Turkish society.

Although the leadership of the Welfare Party was banned from politics until 2003, the rest of its deputies joined the newly founded Virtue Party, which became the next political home of Islamists. As the Virtue Party prepared for elections, it faced a critical dilemma: either it could appeal to the Islamist constituency by presenting itself as the continuation of the Welfare Party, a strategy risking its closure by the Constitutional Court, or it could present itself as a completely new party at the risk of losing the Islamic constituency. Riven by internal tensions, the Virtue Party secured only 15.4 percent of the popular vote in the April 1999 elections, as many Islamists voted for the Nationalist Movement Party, whose explicit nationalist rhetoric provided a familiar ideological harbor.

General discontentment with the civil political process and the incapacity of the political leaders to bring about positive changes in Turkish society reinforced support for extremist violent groups at the edges of the Islamist movement. Terrorist organizations such as the anti-Atatürkist Islamic Raiders of Greater Eastern Front and the Turkish Hezbollah had carried out political assassinations, kidnappings, and robbery to promote their political cause and raise funds. Estimates indicate that Hezbollah alone was responsible for the deaths of between two and four thousand citizens, many from rival Islamist groups.

With the violence of Islamic fundamentalism in the background and the watchfulness of the constitutionally backed secular establishment in the foreground, one of the many ambiguities emerging within the broader Islamist movement was a growing division between traditionalists and reformists. Whereas the former opted for a religiously imbued nationalism, reverting to the Ottoman era as the appropriate source of Turkish national identity, the latter were increasingly open to deepening democracy and human rights, even as a way of securing the political rights of Islam itself.

Without a full appreciation of the impact of the EU's process and framework on Turkish politics in general and on Turkish Islam in particular, one cannot fully understand the developments then occurring within the Islamist movement. It is quite extraordinary that while the Kemalist forces that held power saw political Islam as one of the great threats to the secular identity and European orientation of the Turkish state and society, the reformists within Islam began to demand greater internal democratization by appealing to the EU. "During the late 1990s, as they came under greater pressure from the secular establishment, Turkish Islamists repeatedly stressed their commitment to greater democratization, freedom of speech, and even Turkey's eventual accession to the EU, which they believe will safeguard their political rights" (Jenkins 2001, 27).

The secular powers within Turkey had always been suspicious of reformist Islamists, believing that they were exploiting the EU values without really being committed to them. Clearly, the changes within Turkish political Islam left a residue of ambiguity. The echo of the traditional Islamists who claimed that democracy was a Trojan horse of Western cultural imperialism now stood in contrast to the voice of the new reformists. These reformists, having emerged from the Islamist movement, were demanding the institutional and cultural deepening of the European-like process of democratization. However, eventually history revealed that the political and formal linkage of Turkey to the EU, particularly following its candidacy in 1999, had the effect of increasingly delegitimatizing militant Islam as well as any form of military-backed, state-sponsored authoritarianism by the Turkish secular state. This dual process gradually curbed Islamic fundamentalism and its brand of nationalism, at least within formal politics, while posing a challenge to the state-centered absolutism of Kemalist secular nationalism. Directly and indirectly, the EU process challenged and impacted the nationalism of both the Islamists and the secular establishment, thus reinforcing the EU-oriented reformist forces in both camps.

The unprecedented ambiguities within the Islamist movement as well as the perplexing relationship between the secular Kemalist establishment and the pro-EU reformist wing of Islamists became even more prominent with the rise to power of the Justice and Development Party—a party arising from the general Islamist movement within Turkish society. The elections of November 3, 2002, introduced both a historical novelty and a great paradox within Turkish politics, when the Justice and Development Party won a sweeping victory, ousting from Turkish politics all traditional political parties except the Kemalist Peoples' Republican Party. The latter, while retaining the greatest ideological affinity with the military establishment, ended up being the only party of the opposition in parliament. The electorate, speaking through the ballot, voted in a manner that shocked and overwhelmed the traditional, long-established leaders in Turkish politics. However, the victory of the party signaled not so much a vote in favor of Islam as a vote of no-confidence in the traditional political parties. By voting for the Justice and Development Party, the citizens of Turkey in effect voted against the mismanagement of the economy, the corruption within the political establishment, the paralyzing feuds among political leaders, and all the negative phenomena they cumulatively identified with traditional Turkish politics. One may not regard the electorate's response, in this instance, as the direct expression of a fully established civil society but certainly as a sign of civil will posing the first open challenge concerning the accountability of the traditional political establishment.

However, there was also a paradox in the outcome of these elections. In coming to power, the leadership of the Justice and Development Party publicly renounced having an Islamist political agenda and strongly affirmed its commitment to the European orientation of Turkey and to resolving outstanding differences with Greece, including the most contentious issue, the Cyprus problem. It is extraordinary that at least in its political language, the party began to take a stance just as pro-European, prodemocratic, and secular, and just as oriented in favor of human rights as the reformists within the Kemalist political establishment. Interestingly, the first official overseas visit undertaken by the new Turkish government was to Greece, a move intended to indicate that Turkish-Greek rapprochement would remain an integral part of Turkish foreign policy.

One can easily identify two main reasons for the rising prominence of the reformist voices in the Justice and Development Party. First, party leaders clearly saw that their rise to power provided them with a historic opportunity to make their mark on Turkish politics and to deepen and accelerate the process of modernization at a critical moment in the evolution of Turkish society. Tacitly yet unmistakably, the new leaders of Turkey simultaneously acknowledged that in an increasingly globalized world, the most tangible and decisive option for Turkey's future was its orientation toward the EU.

This was certainly another demonstration of the continued impact that Europeanization had on Turkey through the EU process. This time, however, the transformational influence of the EU was bearing on the internal processes and deliberations of a Turkish government whose origins lay in the Islamist movement.

Whereas in the past, the restraints on the rise of Islamic fundamentalism and the dangers they posed to civil society were wrought through the intervention of the Turkish military into politics, now they were elaborated through the reforming political process of the EU. Directly as well as indirectly, the general EU political culture and the institutional processes linking Turkey to the EU subtly fostered political consent and self-deliberating reflection, reinforcing a reformist political agenda among key leaders of the Justice and Development Party. Moreover, the reformists within the party saw the EU process and Turkey's EU orientation as a powerful lever for addressing the residual democratic deficit inherited from the traditional political establishment, as well as for confronting and curbing the power that the Turkish military unduly exercised in civil affairs.

Similarly, the leaders of the party could not revert to Islamist fundamentalist policies and agendas. One may argue that their appeal to the EU, to reforms and deepened democratization was merely a self-serving tactical gesture. Indeed, for some within the Islamist movement it was just that. However, under the prevailing conditions, any serious adoption of Islamic fundamentalist politics was not only untenable but had the clear potential of proving detrimental to the political status and future of the Justice and Development Party, as well as to that of Turkey, both domestically and internationally.

This brings our analysis to the second reason—or better set of reasons—for the rising prominence of reformist voices within the Justice and Development Party. The fact that the latter came to power in the post–September 11 era is of crucial significance. The international condemnation of Islamic fundamentalism immediately following al Qaeda's terrorist attacks against the United States in September 2001, in conjunction with the track record of violence by the Islamic Raiders of Greater Eastern Front and the Turkish Hezbollah inside Turkey, essentially delegitimatized Islamic fundamentalist politics within broader Turkish society. Had the Justice and Development Party reverted to Islamic fundamentalism in any substantive way, it would have stood in violation of the constitutional provisions affirming the secular nature of the Turkish state at a time when the militancy of Islamic fundamentalism was emerging as a clear threat to Western democracies and open societies.

Under these conditions, the party would have not only confronted the political opposition of the Turkish military, and even of Turkish society, but also possibly tempted the military to intervene yet again in civil affairs at a time when Europeanizing trends and norms required the increasing disengagement of the military from politics. Thus any major reversion to Islamic fundamentalism would have been highly likely to trigger a major crisis in Turkey, which, in light of the EU process, culture, and political criteria bearing on Turkey as a candidate state, would have created a "lose-lose" situation for both the Justice and Development Party and the military, and subsequently for Turkish society. A confrontation between political Islam and the military would have ultimately resulted in a detrimental alienation of Turkey from the EU by provoking the EU's condemnation of Turkey, a fundamental setback in Turkey's EU aspirations, and a radical regression in domestic Turkish politics.

It gradually became clear to the leadership of the Justice and Development Party that since Turkey henceforth would be positioned within the EU system, the only way to secure the party's role as the new government of Turkey was to opt for European-style democracy. Equally significant was the realization that opting for democracy within the EU framework was also the only means to curb the power and interventionism of the Turkish military establishment, which traditionally had been the enemy of political Islam.

Reformists within the Islamist movement clearly understood that the only way the party could continue heading the Republic of Turkey in a manner that would grant it an open future was to start gravitating toward internal reform, democratization, and modernization, anticipating EU-related economic progress. Such an approach implied a willingness to pursue regional political solidarity, security, and peace.

This analysis does not intend to suggest that the dangers emanating from the extremities of Islamic fundamentalism had been eradicated, nor that Kemalist nationalism had disappeared, nor that the Turkish military had become politically neutral, but rather that Europeanizing trends had emerged as significant factors in the sociopolitical development of Turkish society. And to the degree to which they gained strength, they inevitably stood to play a critical role in modifying, among other things, the protracted Turkish-Greek conflicts and particularly the regional context of the Cyprus problem.

After its acceptance as a EU candidate-state at the 1999 Helsinki Summit, even against the backdrop of its complex internal problems, Turkey has embarked on a course of political and economic changes that would have been unthinkable without the EU process and requirements. From the beginning, Turkey was not fully aware of what EU participation demanded of it. Although Turkey's aspirations to become European provided the subjective motivation for change, the needed structural and institutional modifications have proven to be a considerable challenge. While initially the EU was not fully satisfied with the rate at which Turkey was reforming, by 2002 it viewed favorably a number of specific changes that Turkey had initiated in pursuit of its European aspirations.

The sweeping introduction by the Turkish parliament of new, EU-based legislation on August 3, 2002, signified the first notable effort for reform undertaken by the Turkish legislature. The new laws included the abolition of the death penalty from the civil code (except in time of war—a condition later removed altogether); the freedom to broadcast television programs in languages other than Turkish; the freedom of private schools to teach in languages other than Turkish; the abolition of punishable offenses for written, vocal, or pictorial criticism of the military, state institutions, parliament, the government, the justice system, and Turkish identity; the increase of prison terms for people or organizations aiding and abetting smugglers of people, particularly if immigrants are endangered; and the relaxing of regulations to allow religious and minority institutions to buy and sell property.

The new legislation further provided that Turkish foundations would be allowed to cooperate closely with similar institutions abroad, and foundations abroad would be permitted to set up branches in Turkey; that laws governing the operation of local and foreign nongovernmental organizations (NGOs) would be revised; that foreign NGOs would be permitted to operate in Turkey; that laws and regulations restricting public meetings and marches would be eased; that laws pertaining to the regulation of the press would be revised; and that some laws and regulations defining the duties of the police would be overhauled (Reuters 2002).

The most impressive of several democratization packages, these reforms were launched by the Turkish Parliament under the provision that activities flowing from the above freedoms must not compromise the secular constitutional principles of the Turkish state. However one assesses their immediate and long-term consequences, these changes introduced by the new legislation marked a significant step for Turkey toward the evolution of civil society and securing the rights of distinctive ethnic groups, including the Kurds, within Turkish society.

The EU applauded the action taken by the Turkish parliament. The European commissioner for enlargement, Günter Verheugen, called Turkey's decision "an important signal of the determination of the majority of Turkey's political leaders towards further alignments to the values and standards of the European Union" (ABC 2002). Simultaneously, the EU asserted that it anticipates the necessary institution building on the part of Turkey that will secure implementation of the new legislation. Concerning the reform package, Verheugen added that "much will depend on its practical implementation that will be closely monitored." What was equally interesting was the fact that the government of Greece, as well as the GC political leaders, publicly welcomed the reforms. In the web of traditional Greek-Turkish rivalry, this marked one of the first instances in recent history where the actions of one party were acknowledged as positive by the other.

Given Turkey's complex, historical, and sociopolitical domestic burdens and strains, it is doubtful whether it could have induced effective political, social, and economic changes in and of itself, based on its own internal will alone. Within the framework of the anticipated European integration requirements, however, the EU started to function as a lever for Turkey's domestic reforms. Through its steady process of enlargement, the EU manifested itself, among other things, as a function of domestic change within a candidate society (Keridis 2001; Keridis and Triantaphyllou 2001). This is a positive instance of what Keridis (2001) describes as the "domestication of foreign policy"—a process generally identified as one of the significant by-products of the phenomenon of globalization. Unlike its many chaotic and indeterminate episodes, the globalization process within the EU framework is institutionalized and regionally directed through a clear and specific agenda in accordance with a set of democratizing and peace-enhancing objectives.

This analysis does not intend to suggest that all of Turkey's internal contradictions and challenges were automatically resolved, particularly those at the critical juncture where civil politics and the power of the military establishment cross. Nor does the analysis insinuate that no more regressive events would occur that could jeopardize the positive steps that had taken place. But rather, it suggests that a significant process of constructive change had commenced within Turkish politics and society—change that carried the prospect of deepening democracy and, simultaneously, of rendering political developments conducive to regional stability.

Overall, the changes within both Greece and Turkey, particularly in association with the EU framework and process, began to gradually alter the relationship between the Greek and Turkish people, at both the interstate and intersocietal level. The modifications in Greece's foreign policy toward Turkey since 1999 and Turkey's candidacy for EU membership created a historical opportunity in terms of which new perspectives, strategies, and actions could be sought in dealing with domestic challenges as well as with the traditionally belligerent relationship between the two countries. Rooted in adversarial nationalism and subsequently reinforced by the accumulation of unresolved bilateral problems, ranging from the Cyprus conflict to the Aegean issues, the familiar approaches gradually started to yield to softer, more sober and constructive postnationalist ones.

Greece started to free itself from its sense of perpetual victimization—an integral part of its nationalist psychology of self-justification—while Turkey started to overcome its suspicion of foreigners, which constituted its nationalist psychology of introversion and hyperdefensiveness. In domestic and foreign policy, as well as in the general public political culture, Greece and Turkey alike began to exhibit small but decisive signs of change. Such change not only reflected the significant impact of the EU factor on the politics of the two countries and their relationship to each other, but in turn reinforced and amplified the function of the EU process as a positive catalyst in the internal and bilateral evolution of the two societies. As Keridis and Triantaphyllou aptly noted, contact with the EU

> demands the reconceptualization of the nation-state and the pooling and sharing of national sovereignty. It accelerates economic globalization by breaking down economic barriers and establishing a single market. It forces the modernization of backward polities and economies by promoting competition. Most importantly, by introducing the traditionally high democratic standards of northwestern Europe as the basis for a future political union, European integration has helped the democratization of the rest of the continent. It has focused the attention of policy makers and has provided useful roadmaps, linkages, and tradeoffs for painful institutional reform. Ultimately, it has initiated a learning process, spreading values, mentalities, and a behavior from Europe's northwestern core to its periphery. (2001, xix)

In both their domestic development and interstate engagement, Greece and Turkey had started to make significant strides forward as they became increasingly engaged in the general process of postnationalist Europeanization. The close association between democracy, economic well-being, and peace that the EU has been establishing in its evolving institutions and polity gradually extended to the Eastern Mediterranean. Inevitably, the Cyprus problem and the need for its definitive resolution was bound to assume new meaning and significance in light of the newly established regional trends.

Rapprochement, Rising Civil Society, and Emerging Europeanization

GREEK-TURKISH LOW-LEVEL POLITICS:
FIRST STEPS AT FORMAL RAPPROCHEMENT

As the history of the EU experiment demonstrates, deepening democracy within a particular state and society is inextricably intertwined with extending and institutionalizing democracy in one's relationship with neighboring states and societies. The commencement of low-level politics between Greece and Turkey in 1999, again within the broader EU framework, marked a small but vital step in positively modifying Greek-Turkish relations (Gundogdu 2001; Papandreou 2000). Low-level politics signaled the beginning of a modest peace-building process that disclosed the historical possibility of changing interstate and intersocietal relationships between two traditional enemy countries.

Under the joint leadership and vision of Andreas Papandreou and Ismail Çem, the foreign ministers of Greece and Turkey respectively, numerous committees under the two ministries began to work together on specific issues that were deemed cooperatively manageable. The process yielded both practical results as well as a tangible demonstration that Turks and Greeks could work together on specific social, cultural, and economic issues, even though outstanding differences on key political and national issues still prevailed.

Formal agreements for cooperation were signed in a number of areas of mutual interest and benefit. These included a series of provisions for cooperation in tourism and economic development; combating terrorism, organized crime, illicit drug trafficking, and illegal immigration; environmental protection; economic cooperation; and cultural cooperation.

By February 2000, nine bilateral agreements were signed between Turkey and Greece. Others soon followed, totaling seventeen bilateral agreements.

Without recourse to hyped publicity and lofty declarations, the effort ushered into the politics of both societies a new approach to building cooperation, albeit around matters and issues of secondary importance. It added another dimension to the rising, political culture of rapprochement, which became increasingly noticed by its sharp contrast to the adversarial, nationalist culture that had historically dominated Greek-Turkish relations (Gundogdu 2001; Papandreou 2000).

As a significant instrument in an ongoing process of conflict resolution and confidence building, low-level politics is often overlooked. Its meaning and practical transformational potential is not always appreciated or fully grasped. The basic assumption underpinning low-level politics is that while high-level issues, under conditions of protracted historical rivalry, cannot provide a basis for rapprochement and cooperation, low-level issues may furnish a starting point. The idea is that while two rivals may be incapable of forging agreements and cooperation on matters of high national priority, they may be able to see eye-to-eye on matters of lesser significance, or even on issues that may be altogether neutral with respect to the unapproachable, long-standing divisive issues. Engaging each other through a process of dialogue, exploration, and the development of mutually agreed upon strategies for cooperation on secondary issues constitutes a relatively low-risk task. However, in embryonic form it may include the conditions for taking greater steps and greater risks in the future. Achieving multiple agreements for cooperation through low-level politics has the potential of creating a sample culture of cooperation and promise that may in turn catalytically evolve, fertilizing public culture and politics. The words of the Turkish foreign minister following the first low-level bilateral agreements with his Greek counterpart are to the point. "Our countries," stated Çem, "have been engaged in a constructive process . . . to create a synergy in several fields such as tourism, environment, economic cooperation, culture, regional cooperation, and fight against terrorism and related issues. . . . This pattern of cooperation proved that with necessary willpower both countries can establish a close working relationship" (Greek-Turkish Forum 2002).

Success in low-level politics demonstrates in small but clear examples the viability of nonadversarial, postnationalist approaches to interstate and intersocietal relationships. In and of themselves, the cumulative effects of low-level politics leading to concrete outcomes may not amount to much. But in the broader context of sociopolitical change they may have potentially significant effects. In the process, low-level politics give policy leaders the otherwise barred opportunity to become directly acquainted and familiar with their counterparts from the enemy camp, to work systematically together, to deepen understanding of each other, to become jointly focused and creative, to share successes, and to learn the merits and prospects of consensus-based cooperation. Rendering this process publicly visible in the two societies introduces the public to actual and potential mutual benefits as the net outcome of developing and sustaining a culture and a practice of interstate cooperation.

In this context, high-level issues may be reframed in such a way as to warrant renewed consideration. What historically have been protracted and intractable differences may appear in a new light, giving rise to a new understanding of old problems. Generating positive change in the relationship between the two sides through the cumulative impact of low-level politics may in effect change the intractability of high-level issues by modifying the perspectives from which each side addresses them. As Fisher and Ury (1991) asserted, positions on difficult problems may be changed only as the relationship between the disputants begins to change, giving rise to new understanding and insight into each other's fears and concerns. This was precisely the approach pursued by the pioneering efforts of Çem and Papandreou. Papandreou clearly explicated this principle: "We have started a confidence-building measures procedure. I hope that in this way we will create the right psychology, the right atmosphere, and the right approach towards each other. Only in this way can we solve our more difficult problems" (Greek-Turkish Forum 2002). In the post-Helsinki interactions between Greece and Turkey, the strategy of addressing low-level politics as stepping-stones toward enabling the mutual management of high-level, divisive political and national issues became established as a specific instrument of conflict resolution akin to the one employed in erecting the first building blocks of the EU.

The work of Çem and Papandreou signaled the first significant effort by the political leadership of Turkey and Greece in almost half a century to move the two countries' relations beyond the adversarial modality of nationalist politics (Gundogdu 2001). A central underlying assumption was that insofar as the two countries continued to build on this foundation of rapprochement and mutual engagement, they might not only modify for the better their terrible record of bilateral relations but also provide a positive framework for addressing the Cyprus problem anew. In this regard, it was not at all surprising that an aspect of the Papandreou-Çem agenda was to institutionalize the rapprochement effort as much as possible, to dissociate it from the foreign ministers' own particular personal initiatives, while providing continuity through a structured process in which others may subsequently participate in promoting rapprochement between the Greek and Turkish people. Here again, the EU furnished the broadest and strongest institutional framework for engendering, empowering, and legitimizing this process.

CIVIL SOCIETY: THE EMERGING NEW VOICES FOR PEACE

Along with the Greek-Turkish rapprochement at the interstate level, a gradual awakening and mobilization of civil society in Cyprus, Greece, and Turkey also occurred around the unique role of citizens in the general process of Greek-Turkish rapprochement. Pioneering TC and GC citizen groups launched rapprochement efforts in the early 1990s, long before the EU process and its accompanying political culture began to exert its influence on Cypriot society, or the first signs of a possible paradigm shift in

Greek-Turkish relations crystallized. While keeping a low profile, these groups initially took small but determined steps in interethnic dialogue and peace-building reflections, projects and vision building (Broome 1998a, 1998b, 2005; Diamond 1997; Wolleh 2001).

Speaking about conflict transformation in divided societies, Lederach (2002) identified three conditional requirements for rendering the role of citizens effective in peace-building processes.

First, the "people who envision themselves as playing the role of peacemakers within the conflict setting must be identified" (94). Lederach reminds us that no matter how severe a conflict might be, one always finds people who have come to some vision of peace based on their experience of pain.

Second, the capacity of these people to find a voice that can be used as an agent for peace "depends on building bridges to likeminded individuals across the line of conflict" (94).

Third, "the recognition by the international community of these persons as valid and pivotal actors for peace is necessary to legitimize the space they need to develop their potential" (94–95).

In its modest but exemplary emergence, the citizen peace movement in Cyprus, steadily but unawares, met all of the conditions set forth by Lederach. The identification of relevant actors, the linkage with their counterparts in the rival community, and their endorsement by the international community, particularly the UN, the U.S., and the EU, occurred as the citizen peace movement grew in size and effectiveness in articulating a nonadversarial way of addressing the Cyprus conflict and the challenges for its resolution. It did so partly by design but also through the interest and momentum generated by the sheer spontaneity, energy, and commitment of the citizens involved.

In its embryonic stages, the citizen-based peace movement, otherwise known as the bicommunal movement, received the mediating assistance of numerous international scholars and practitioners of conflict resolution. However, during its subsequent development, the movement took on a life of its own. It evolved by assuming autonomous initiatives and responsibilities in generating strategies and implementing actions that eventually established the basis for a broad, locally grown, citizen peace movement. During the first half of the 1990s, the core leaders of the peace movement (of which I, too, was a part) received ample training in conflict resolution and peace building from some of the most notable international organizations, universities, and individual experts in the field (Wolleh 2001).

While any of the international third parties who contributed to this training may assert some legitimate claim to being the first to assist in the citizen peace process in Cyprus, one ought not overlook the central ingredient in this process. Indeed, one must duly acknowledge the long-term commitment and tireless determination of the local peace builders and their leaders in pursuing a peace-enhancing vision and peace-seeking options for Cyprus against much opposition. In fact, these qualities of the peace-building community transposed the academic and often abstract training offered by non-Cypriots into a practical, meaningful, and effective process of conflict transformation over the long term. It was the commitment, energy, and stamina of the local peace builders that furnished the vision-laden, human infrastructure that sustained the process and allowed it to widen and deepen in the face of stigmatization, ostracization, and, in some cases, life threats.

It is noteworthy that the most successful, hence most helpful, international peace scholars and practitioners working with Cypriots were those who approached their trainees not as recipients of conflict resolution skills and ideas, but rather as the local human resources for activating and sustaining the citizen-initiated peace-building process. The specific skills and theories of conflict resolution were indeed the contribution of the international experts who visited Cyprus from time to time. However, the unique manner in which this training was assimilated and integrated into the Cypriot culture had little to do with third-party mediation. It was the local, bicommunal peace builders, through their innovative and time-sensitive work, that rendered these learned skills and theories relevant to the unique setting of the Cyprus conflict, as they extended and transposed them from abstract techno-academic processes and principles to concrete, tangible, and place-specific peace-building initiatives. The totality of their work, both bicommunally and monocommunally, provided the seeds and the means for steadily defusing nationalist behaviors and values that were counterproductive to a culture of peace among the TC and GC communities. Working quietly but persistently across and within their respective ethnic communities, initiating a variety of activities and projects, the citizen peace builders became the local sociocultural resource for incubating, developing, and sustaining a citizen-based process of conflict transformation.

Nevertheless, having been directly involved at the forefront of the citizen peace-building initiatives, I can attest to the enormous difficulties and challenges that confronted the bicommunal effort from its inception in the early 1990s. Restrained by an unsympathetic and reluctant nationalist portion of the GC culture, and obstructed by a separatist and often directly intrusive nationalist TC administration, managing to organize and sustain bicommunal meetings was always a struggle. Innumerable meetings between TCs and GCs scheduled to take place in the buffer zone were cancelled by the TC authorities only moments before they were due to commence. The authorities often frustrated the efforts of the citizen peace-builders as though the objective was to break their spirit—the spirit of rapprochement. The media on both sides of the conflict regularly attacked and stigmatized the work of the peace builders as treasonous and denounced it as erosive of the national cause.

Yet even under such severe constraints, the citizens' work to promote interethnic dialogue and bicommunal peace-enhancing activities was formidably original. Over time, many bicommunal groups emerged and became active, providing a broad creative variety and diversity of rapprochement projects and demonstrating the perseverance and rising commitment of TCs and GCs to peace building and reconciliation. Among these groups were the:

All Cyprus Union Forum: A group formed to address trade and labor issues in relation to peace and the prospect of EU membership;

Brussels Business Group: A bicommunal group of prominent TC and GC business leaders that promoted various high-level peace initiatives;

Citizens' Movement for Reunification and Coexistence: A group promoting civil society and broad-based reconciliation between GCs and TCs;

EU Federation Study Group: A group engaged in dialogue on interethnic federation and the EU as the basis for peace in Cyprus;

Hade: A bicommunal publisher that published the first biethnic magazine in Greek, Turkish, and English;

Harvard Study Group: A high-level citizen think tank that generated creative ideas for the resolution of the Cyprus problem and conducted its work under the auspices of the Harvard-based World Peace Foundation;

Technology for Peace: A group focusing on the use of cyber-space and the Internet to foster bicommunal communication and peace-building projects;

Trainers Group: A group that received and provided ongoing training in conflict-resolution skills and strategies, and facilitated innumerable bicommunal peace-building workshops;

Women's Group: An all-women's forum for peace initiatives focusing on the empowerment of women as catalysts for peace; and

Youth Encounters for Peace: A group providing bicommunal peace-building workshops and projects for and by the young.

This list constitutes only a small sample of bicommunal peace-building groups intended to show the range, depth, and diversity of the ongoing activities and projects undertaken jointly by TCs and GCs. Besides bicommunal groups, numerous monocommunal groups were also formed to promote interethnic reconciliation within each community. Examples of monocommunal groups include the TC *This Country is Ours*, a consortium of forty-one organizations, and the GC *Cyprus Peace Center*. Despite innumerable difficulties, the animating vision and strategic tenacity of the peace builders enabled the growth and proliferation of the bicommunal citizen groups, rendering the small but new culture and the work they embodied seminally ahead of the politics and approaches of their respective political leaders.

Long before the EU integration process started to affect Cyprus as a catalytic factor in civil-society building, the bicommunal movement was articulating its vision of an emergent peace culture within a federal polity as the way forward. Years prior to acquiring full public visibility, at a time when bicommunal contacts were unnoticeable and marginal, the spirit of citizen-initiated peace building was represented and promoted in many small but suitably focused events and declarations. A case in point was a speech delivered in the Nicosia buffer zone in the mid-1990s before an audience of TCs, GCs, and third-party diplomats. Emphasizing that interethnic citizen rapprochement had to be pursued as an integral part of the political solution, I wrote the following:

> In the wasteland of our conflict-habituated history, the peace builders have formed numerous islands of hope around bicommunal concerts, social gatherings, poetry nights, conflict resolution workshops, identity seminars, women's groups, youth groups and many others. Seen by themselves, these events appear as a drop in the ocean, while the failure to achieve politically sanctioned federal structures across the traditional lines of conflict may be regarded as evidence that all efforts are but futile. But on the other hand, when seen in light of the vision of a future, these activities disclose in many significant ways the outlines of the anticipated society, the society of a federated Cyprus. Greek Cypriots and Turkish Cypriots gathering together, reflecting together, planning together, building together, even dreaming together, on equal terms, with their differences and similarities, under a single roof of federation.
>
> In this sense, the people involved in bicommunal activities are truly the first citizens of a federal Cyprus. Though as of yet they have no official political status, no federal passport, no federal voting rights, they are in effect the flesh and blood of the top-level agreements for a federal Cyprus. Imaginatively, these citizens have visited the future and have seen the wisdom and peace of a federal Cyprus. And they have returned back from the future, as it were, bringing with them its institutions, is values, its mentality, its cultures, to put into action today. (Anastasiou 1996b, 3)

The breadth and variety of issues and projects undertaken by the bicommunal peace-building groups provided a viable model of how citizen-initiated peace building constitutes a vital dimension of civil society and of how the process of deepening democratization is directly related to peace building as a factor of social transformation (Broome 2005). It is noteworthy that the popularization of the ideas of both civil society and nongovernmental organizations (NGOs) occurred concurrently and in direct relationship with the citizen peace movement, demonstrating the often-forgotten relationship between peace and democratization—a relationship brought to the historical forefront of Cypriot society and politics through the reinforcing influence of the political culture and institutions of the EU. In Cyprus, nationalism constrained, distorted, and suspended the development of civil society for generations (Mavratsas 1998). Ethnonational polarization, conditioned by the nationalist requirement of absolute loyalty to the alleged sacred status of *the nation*, sustained and perpetuated hierarchical, authoritarian, and closed political cultures and practices in both the institutions of state power and the mode of functioning of political parties.

Modernization brought about certain relative changes, more so on the GC side than on the TC side, as a result of the development and strengthening of the private sector within the GC community. But the advent and growth of the bicommunal peace movement, through its diverse, informal, often low-profile, yet decisive modes of operation, marked the first actions of political consequence by GC and TC citizens undertaken mainly independently and beyond the formal authority of the administration and the political party system in their respective communities.

GCs and TCs pioneered interethnic citizen peace building in that they took action long before there was any effort at interstate citizen rapprochement between the respective motherlands. In this sense, TCs and GCs led the way, providing the first citizen role model of a reconciled and reunited Cyprus. Two interrelated aspects characterized this model: First, the citizen peace movement effectively dissociated citizen responsibility from the traditional, nationalist notion of citizen identity. This identity defined the role of the citizen in terms of an esoteric, uncritical following of the leadership and an adversarial stance toward the other ethnic community. Second, the citizen peace movement redefined the identity and role of the citizen in terms of a shared vision of peace and mutual responsibility, in actions and attitudes that empowered the development of a public political culture conducive to the acceptance of difference and to multiethnic symbiosis. In other words, the new identity and role of the citizen, disclosed through the work and efforts of the citizen peace builders, emerged as one of active participation in the building and the forging of sustainable relationships of interethnic cooperation and power sharing.

Initially in principle and subsequently in publicly visible practices, the citizen initiatives provided the basis for elaborating in the public domain the first interethnic conceptualization of democracy. It was the first time in the political history of the Island that the idea of democracy expanded beyond the ethnocentric and monoethnic constraints of nationalism. It was the first time that democracy was entertained not merely as an intraethnic polity but also as an interethnic one worthy of its own value, actions, and vision. More significantly, through its persistent work, and in spite of its restricted executive powers, the citizen peace movement brought to the fore the central idea that the sustainability of democracy within, as well as between ethnic groups, is directly related to the emergence of a shared culture of peace, rooted in and guarded by the citizens. Through its practical engagements, the peace movement had affirmed Curle's articulation that there exists a structural linkage between the building of peaceful relationships and the opening up of justice and democracy (1971).

Speaking in the mid-1990s in the buffer zone, that peculiar space that hosted most of the bicommunal meetings, a friend and associate leader in the peace-building effort described the matter as follows:

> We are not politicians. It is not our job to solve the Cyprus problem. But we are the creators of a new culture, which will help resolve our conflict in a peaceful manner. Our dream is to help build a country where everybody's needs are everybody's concern. . . . We are unique since we are the only group in Cyprus that has a shared vision. We are unique because we have analyzed the conflict and created options and projects together. We are unique because we have gone deep into dialogue about some of the hottest topics. And our culture of peace is based on tolerance, understanding, and sharing. (Uludağ 1996)

From this perspective, the bicommunal peace movement, having proliferated its values and actions in the broader communities, helped create the first small but visible peace-supporting constituency, posing a challenge to the stifling nationalist cultures hitherto dominating the political public life of Cyprus. As Lederach (2002) stressed, one cannot underestimate the importance of a peace constituency as a vital sociocultural resource and catalyst of conflict transformation. Especially in divided societies, a peace constituency is an imperative dimension of the overall effort of resolving conflict, in both attaining and subsequently sustaining a final political settlement.

The core leaders and citizens who became involved in the rapprochement process, giving rise to the bicommunal peace movement, reflect what Lederach called the middle-range leaders in the process of conflict transformation and peace building. While the top-level leadership consists of public, official, and political figures and the grassroots leadership is made up of persons directly involved with the mass population, the middle-range leadership consists of, among others, "persons who are highly respected as individuals and/or occupy formal positions of leadership in sectors such as education, business, agriculture, or health" (Lederach 2002, 41).

Lederach explained that the unique position the middle-range actors occupy in society renders their work vital and irreplaceable in the process of conflict transformation and sustainable peace building in divided societies.

> First, middle-level leaders are positioned so that they are likely to know and be known by the top-level leadership, yet they have significant connections to the broader context and the constituency that the top leaders claim to represent. In other words, they are connected to both the top and grassroots levels. They have contact with top-level leaders, but are not bound by the political calculations that govern every move and decision made at that level. Similarly, they vicariously know the context and experience of people living at the grassroots level, yet they are not encumbered by the survival demands facing many at this level. (Lederach 2002, 41)

Lederach further noted that the status and influence of the middle-range leadership is not necessarily linked to political or military power or the desire to attain it. Rather, the effectiveness of their work derives from ongoing relationships and networking in society. Moreover, unlike the top-level leadership, they are not constrained by a constituency and the constant scrutiny of the public media. By virtue of these facts, the middle-range leadership has greater flexibility of thought and action in addressing and approaching the conflict. As described by Lederach, this flexibility and advantage in innovation and creativity enjoyed by the middle range actors is precisely the resource that the Cypriot bicommunal movement utilized in pursuing its strategies and end of interethnic peace building.

From its unique societal position and political vantage point, the citizen peace movement made many inroads to the grass roots of Cypriot society, triggering initiatives and group mobilizations. But it also established numerous relationships with top-level political leaders in the respective communities, as well as with representatives of the international diplomatic core working in Cyprus.

Some of the many subtle, often intentionally quiet ways in which the bicommunal peace builders went about their work in relation to the top-level echelons of Cyprus politics included: interacting with political leaders through informal discussions; sharing with political leaders conflict-resolving ideas and options that the peace builders developed in think tanks through the assistance of international organizations; meeting with UN personnel to explore ways to enhance bicommunal engagements; and compelling numerous embassies to add bicommunal citizen peace building to their Cyprus agendas.

Slowly but surely, the bicommunal movement also introduced the imperative of citizen peace building and interethnic rapprochement to the agenda of numerous political parties on both sides of the ethnic divide. The most notable example was the executive decision by the Central Committee of the GC Democratic Rally Party (DISY) to establish a specific rapprochement committee within its organizational structure to promote contact and dialogue between GCs and TCs. Although there was much disagreement within the party over the viability of interethnic citizen dialogue, this was an extraordinary intraparty development, given that the historical roots of this particular party lay in the tradition of far right-wing nationalism.

Furthermore, the bicommunal peace movement subtly added a reinforcing and transformative dimension to the TC opposition parties of the Left. For years the TC Left had vainly struggled to build bridges to the GC Left, but its absorption and energy-depleting preoccupation with deep Right-versus-Left ideological rivalries, combined with its inability to recognize and confront the malaise of ethnocentric nationalism, perpetually undermined its efforts. However, the gradual assimilation of bicommunal culture, approaches, and strategies by numerous leading citizens of the TC Left, introduced new political content and a new language of interethnic rapprochement that evolved beyond the stereotypical confines of classic left-wing ideology that traditionally characterized the TC opposition parties of the Left. The politics of the TC Left gradually underwent a process of transformation, in which the political and verbal militancy against the ruling TC and Turkish Right increasingly gave way to the politics of peace in relation to the GCs, and to the politics of democratization in relation to the EU. Interethnic reconciliation within a federal polity and the ensuing prospect of EU integration spilled over and cut across the old Left-versus-Right ideological boundaries, opening up broader, more diverse, and more integrative approaches to politics and democracy.

This transformation of the TC Left simultaneously eroded the grounds on which the TC Right had traditionally targeted it. The stereotypical concerns of the TC Right over the national threat became increasingly diluted and untenable, as the TC Left appeared increasingly propeace and pro-Europe. In this dynamic, the absolute adversarial posture that the TC Right had always assumed against the TC Left became unsustainable.

Interethnic rapprochement within the bicommunal movement engaged innumerable citizens from left-wing as well as the right-wing traditions in the respective communities. Also noteworthy is the fact that, having been seasoned by interethnic contact, many TCs and GCs from both the Right and the Left who became involved in citizen peace-building initiatives moved on to assume formal political positions, while others successfully ran for political office. For example, of the twelve GC and TC members of the Harvard Study Group bicommunal think tank, one GC became the government spokesperson, one TC became mayor, another GC became a government minister, while another was considered, albeit briefly, as a multiparty presidential candidate.

Over the years, the work of citizen peace builders gradually became not only visible in the eyes of both the Cypriot society and the international community but also an example of what needed to occur island-wide and of what political parties and leaders ought to support and even emulate. It had, in effect, set the basis for building legitimacy for peace through a small but emerging local, interethnic constituency.

In view of the complexities, constraints, and ambiguities of the conflict situation, the mode of operation of the bicommunal movement combined two contradictory elements. On one hand, it had to strategize constantly, adapt, and innovate to maintain a low profile whenever political conditions were such as to put the movement in jeopardy. On the other hand, it had to maintain its vigor, commitment, and vision of the future with numerous projects and agendas in place, ready for action in the public realm whenever the political circumstances warranted a well-calculated risk for public exposure and impact. One peace maker described the fight for peace as guerrilla warfare. He explained that you must know when to hide and when to come out to make your peace attack.

Citizen-initiated activities serving the interests of mutual understanding, peace, and reconciliation also emerged in Greece and Turkey. They were especially evident following the 1999 historical turning point marked by the confluence of Turkey's acceptance as an EU candidate state, the exchange of mutual humanitarian gestures between Greek and Turks during and subsequent to the terrible earthquakes, and formal Greek-Turkish rapprochement around low-level politics. In this context, numerous citizen initiatives took place to engender contact and engage in talks with the traditional rival society, moves quite independent of formal, "track-one" national politics.

Greek and Turkish academics and journalists began to interact directly, appearing jointly on nationally televised discussions, analyzing and exchanging ideas over the challenges and future of Greek-Turkish relations (Keridis 2001). Local artists launched a series of public appearances in each other's countries. Despite strong criticism by nationalists, popular singers grasped the vision for novel approaches and successfully staged several public performances in enemy territory, attracting thousands. In a conciliatory phenomenon like that occurring in postwar Europe, the twinning of a number of Greek and Turkish villages and towns was set up by mutual consent. With the endorsement of the Greek and Turkish foreign ministries, a citizen think tank known as the Greek-Turkish Forum was established, consisting of distinguished diplomats, journalists, and academics from Greece and Turkey committed to holding private meetings on an ongoing basis, to discuss the problems bedeviling relations between their two countries and to cooperatively seek peaceful paths and strategies for their resolution.

All these citizen-based efforts evolved under the critical scrutiny, protest, and objections of nationalists in both Greece and Turkey. Reservations and public criticisms of Greek-Turkish rapprochement came also from GC refugees, who could not fathom why their compatriots from mainland Greece were fraternizing with Turkey while Turkish troops were still occupying northern Cyprus. Simultaneously, however, the question that resonated around this issue was whether the refugee problem in Cyprus could have moved anywhere closer to a resolution had the citizens of Greece and Turkey continued on the familiar adversarial path.

SHIFTING ASSUMPTIONS BEYOND THE NATIONALIST MIND

Both as an antecedent and a consequent of the multilevel rapprochement process between GCs and TCs, and between Greece and Turkey, a gradual but distinctive shift occurred among engaged citizen groups and some political leaders away from the stereotypical nationalist assumptions and perceptions that had traditionally dominated the national political cultures of the Greek and Turkish peoples. Having emerged from various walks of life and social rank in Cyprus, Turkey, and Greece, these small but constantly rising groups of citizens and politicians began to orient themselves toward the quest for more constructive, sustainable, and effective ways of addressing the conflicts and differences between the traditional rivals. This new approach inevitably entailed a change in mental framework. And as epistemology asserts, whenever there is a change in mental framework, there is a change in mental purpose and interest, leading to new premises for knowledge, to new assumptions, and to new disclosures of reality. It is therefore not surprising that as the people engaged in rapprochement, they became increasingly focused on peace-enhancing options. Something quite fundamental in their mind-set began to change regarding the manner in which they viewed their own ethnonational group in relation to the other, as well as the manner in which they began to understand the nature of the protracted conflict.

Within the broader framework of the EU process, what subtly but surely transpired through peace-seeking engagements and struggles between the GC and TC communities, and between the Greeks and the Turks of the motherlands, echoed through an array of newly premised realizations. These realizations carried the potential for new alternative approaches, strategies, and actions above and beyond those that had been traditionally assumed, propagated, and propagandized by nationalism. While embedded in the complexities and contradiction of historical, social, and political events and processes, these newly emergent assumptions and realizations may be conceptually explicated and identified as follows:

• The perils of the past resulting from the protracted Cyprus conflict (as well as from the historical conflicts between the mainland Greeks and Turks) are not the absolute fault of one side. Rather, they are the outcome of the complex interplay of nationalisms, different political ideologies, events, and actions implicating all the relevant players—the GCs and the TCs, Greece and Turkey, and the international actors, including the cold war superpowers. Therefore, the causes of the conflicts and issues separating the GCs from TCs and Greeks from Turks are in fact blurred, ambiguous, overlapping, mutually reinforcing, and intertwined, rather than black and white.

• The pain and suffering of one's own ethnonational group emanating from the long history of conflicts and violence has a counterpart in the rival ethnonational group. Members of each community cannot and must not deny the pain and suffering experienced by members of their enemy community in the historical course of the conflict between TCs and GCs, Turks and Greeks. Therefore, open acknowledgment of each other's pain and the readiness of each side to accept a measure of responsibility for *our* common tragedy is a vital element in raising mutual understanding and addressing, comprehensively and inclusively, the concerns, fears, and hopes of all parties.

• Historical grievances concerning violations of human rights are not the exclusive prerogative of one side in the protracted Cyprus conflict. Each side has been both perpetrator and victim, albeit at different times and with respect to different historical events. Therefore, securing human rights is best served by comprehensive approaches that take cognizance of the historical landmarks of injuries, human rights violations, and need for security of all sides. Initiating and institutionalizing a process of reconciliation and peace building constitutes a sine qua non in rendering sustainable the cultural values and institutional guardianship of human rights.

• The traditional, adversarial, nationalist mind-set that TCs and GCs, Turks and Greeks have inherited and perpetuated cannot demarcate the way forward. Continuing to operate within the framework of ethnocentric nationalism would simply reproduce and amplify the conflict, leading to new deadlocks and more severe historical impasses. By contrast, developing and nurturing a new mind-set, guided by a dialogical, cooperative, and conciliatory mode of thinking and doing, is quite likely to yield positive results for all concerned as it stands to open up and amplify possibilities and options for the future, particularly in the context of the EU framework.

• National interests in the context of interethnic relations in Cyprus and interstate relations between Turkey, Greece, and Cyprus need not be cast in a win-lose framework, as is customary in the traditional nationalist mind. Rather, national interests need redefining in terms of cooperative approaches and mutual benefits, derived from the development and institutionalization of sustainable, peace-enhancing processes and alternative, nonbelligerent security systems.

• The matter of forging peace and security is not the exclusive task of politicians at the top level of formal politics. Nor is it merely a matter of military might. Such approaches reduce political accountability, leave society exposed and susceptible to perpetual fear and to adversarial politics and culture, and evade the need to engage the populace in the founding and building of an interethnic and an intersocietal regime of peace, security, and well-being. Peace and security are concerns that require the full engagement of not only the political leaders but also civil society on multiple levels and various socioeconomic and cultural fronts. Peace can be achieved not only through diplomacy and political agreement, but also through a process of social transformation, whereby citizens play a central and active role in moving society and its politics from a condition of conflict to one of resolution and normalcy.

- In the context of globalizing trends, opportunities for economic growth and well-being for GCs and TCs and for Greeks and Turks cannot be effectively seized under conditions of perpetual ethnonational rivalry, and by extension, of absolute, ethnonational economic competition. On the contrary, economic gains and well-being may be optimized for all concerned in an environment of regional peace and stability, and in pursuance of cooperation and common ventures at various levels, including intergovernmental, private sector, and intersocietal initiatives.
- Globalizing trends render nationalist politics of unilateralism, isolationism, intransigence, and introversion untenable and detrimental to the national interests of states and societies. The shrinking of the world through increasing economic and technological interdependence poses new political challenges and adaptation requirements, which are best managed through peace-enhancing, collaborative, and consensual approaches in international, interethnic, and intersocietal relations.

The gradual emergence of these new assumptions marked a historical novelty in the perceptions toward each other of GCs and TCs, and of Greeks and Turks. One may question how prevalent these assumptions were in Cypriot, Turkish, and Greek society to make a difference. One may also question the degree to which these assumptions affected policy decisions in the everyday running of political affairs. However, what is certain is that these assumptions have been growing in strength and clarity among increasing numbers of citizens, political leaders, business leaders, intellectuals, and journalists. These groups may have been a minority in the entire population of each society concerned, but they included significant opinion formers with effective access to the worlds of public media and politics. Thus they began to function as vital catalysts of sociopolitical change, increasingly attuned to the domestic and international challenges of the times.

Prompted to some degree by the EU enlargement and integration process, the relative but clearly observable changes in Greek-Turkish and GC-TC relations reinforced, empowered, and bespoke the possible birth of an alternative new system in the Eastern Mediterranean societies and region. As the diverse and multilevel efforts in rapprochement evolved, they stood to create a mutually reinforcing dynamic that added increasing legitimacy to interethnic democratization and conciliatory politics and culture in the contesting societies. To the degree that such a trend was sustained, it carried the propensity for undermining the nationalist agendas and outlook still held by various groups and centers of power in Cyprus, Greece, and Turkey.

Seeking a Comprehensive Settlement on the Eve of European Integration

The Annan Plan

The long-standing, interethnic, citizen peace-building initiatives in Cyprus, the rising citizen and top-level rapprochement between Greece and Turkey, the EU accession process of Cyprus, and Turkey's EU orientation gradually gave rise to an unprecedented convergence of the interests of TCs, GCs, Turks, and Greeks, and the association of these interests with peace. It was precisely in relation to this new context of Cypriot, Greek, and Turkish politics that the UN launched its historic proposal entitled *Basis for the Comprehensive Settlement of the Cyprus Problem*. On November 11, 2002, the UN secretary-general, Kofi Annan, announced his plan for the reunification of Cyprus, presenting it as a historic opportunity for peace. As the culmination of top-level negotiations that began in late 1999, the Annan Plan, as it came to be known, was the most elaborate and sophisticated proposal ever presented to the rival ethnic communities of Cyprus. In light of the complex history of the Island's conflict, the array of grievances and suffering of each side, and the divergent fears, concerns, and interests of each community, the general structure of the Annan Plan may be characterized as a masterpiece in conflict-resolution diplomacy.

More than 150 pages of the UN proposal presented a comprehensive plan covering the basic aspects of the Cyprus problem, namely, governance, territory, refugees, property, and security, with certain details left open for further negotiation and later closure. Building on the original Treaty of Establishment, Treaty of Guarantee, and Treaty of Alliance by which Cyprus first became an independent state, the Annan Plan delineated the creation of a loose, bizonal, Swiss-modeled federation, accompanied by additional treaties with Cyprus's traditional guarantor powers in light of the anticipated entry of a united Cyprus into the EU. The following summary of the Annan Plan gives the basic principles that underpinned the elaborate UN proposal.

- The Treaty of Establishment, the Treaty of Guarantee, and the Treaty of Alliance shall remain in force, but new treaties will also be signed with Greece, Turkey, and Britain on matters related to the new state of affairs in Cyprus.
- Cyprus shall sign and ratify the Treaty of Accession to the EU.
- Cyprus shall maintain special ties of friendship with Greece and Turkey and shall support Turkey's accession to the EU.
- Any unilateral change in the state of affairs, in particular, the union of Cyprus or part of Cyprus with any other country or any form of partition or secession, is prohibited.
- The status and relationship of the State of Cyprus, its "common state" government, and its "component states" is modeled on the status and relationship of Switzerland, its federal government, and its cantons.
- The new Cyprus will be composed of one common state and two component states with political equality.
- The common state will be the voice of one Cyprus internationally and fulfill the island's obligations to the EU.
- The component states, of equal status, within the limits of the constitution, sovereignly exercise all powers not vested by the constitution in the "common state" government, organizing themselves freely under their own constitutions.
- The component states shall cooperate with each other through cooperation agreements and constitutional laws, and they will not infringe upon the powers and functions of each other.
- There will be a single Cyprus citizenship and special majority, "common state" law that shall regulate eligibility for Cypriot citizenship.

- All Cypriots will enjoy internal "component state" citizenship status, which will complement and not replace Cypriot citizenship.
- Greek Cypriots and Turkish Cypriots residing in specified villages in the other "component state" shall enjoy cultural and educational rights and shall be represented in the "component state" legislature.
- The "common state" parliament will be composed of two chambers, the Senate and the Chamber of Deputies.
- Each chamber shall have forty-eight members. In the Senate each "constituent state" shall be represented on a 50-50 basis, while in the Chamber of Deputies each "constituent state" shall be represented in proportion to its population, provided that each "component state" receives no less than 25 percent of the seats.
- Decisions of parliament will require the approval of both chambers by simple majority.
- The Presidential Council shall consist of six members elected on a single list by special majority in the Senate, and approved by majority in the Chamber of Deputies.
- The offices of president and vice president shall rotate every ten months among members of the Council. No more than two consecutive presidents may come from the same "component state."
- The Treaty of Alliance shall permit Greek and Turkish contingents not exceeding an unspecified four-digit figure, and a UN peacekeeping operation shall monitor the agreement along with a monitoring committee from the guarantor powers.
- The supply of arms to Cyprus shall be prohibited. All Greek Cypriot and Turkish Cypriot forces, including reserve units, will be dissolved and their arms removed from the island in phases along with the redeployment of Greek and Turkish forces.
- Cyprus shall not put its territory at the disposal of international military operations other than with the consent of Greece and Turkey.
- The Supreme Court, comprising nine judges—three Greek Cypriots, three Turkish Cypriots, and three non-Cypriots—will resolve disputes between the component states.
- On entry into force of the agreement, the leaders of the two sides shall become copresidents of Cyprus for three years.

- Areas subject to territorial adjustment which are legally part of the Greek Cypriot component state upon entry into force of this agreement shall be administered during an interim period no longer than three years by the Turkish Cypriot component state. Administration shall be transferred under the supervision of the UN to the Greek Cypriots in agreed phases ninety days after entry into force of this agreement.
- In areas subject to territorial adjustment, properties shall be reinstated to dispossessed owners, but in areas not subject to territorial adjustments the arrangements will be on the basis of compensation.
- Dispossessed owners who opt for compensation or whose properties are not reinstated shall receive full and effective compensation on the basis of the value at the time of dispossession plus inflation.

The executive summary did not go into the details of specific territorial adjustments, but made reference to a map that formed part of the proposal. In its overall structure as well as in its detail, the Annan Plan embodied certain unique features that reflected its conflict-resolution perspective and scope. In delineating the new system of governance, it moved beyond the nationalist extremities of both the ethnomajoritarian concept of a unitary state, and the ethnocentric, exclusivist concept of a secessionist state. In proposing a tristate system of two equal component states and a common federal state, the plan gave credence to the distinctive identity and relative political autonomy of each of the Cypriot communities, while simultaneously providing a joint structure of governance based on shared powers, privileges, and responsibilities. The provision for a unifying single citizenship in regard to the international status of Cypriots, combined with a complementing but differentiating internal citizenship, bespoke the same conflict-resolving integration of concerns and relevant factors.

Moreover, the Annan Plan introduced the EU factor as a novel element that would henceforth be intrinsic to the new system of governance, guarantees, and security of Cyprus. The relationship between the new Cyprus, Greece, Turkey, and Britain was reframed in terms of the anticipated entry of a united Cyprus into the EU, and in terms of the broader EU institutional framework. As far as the sustainability of the proposed settlement was concerned, this dimension was crucial precisely because, in carrying out its business, the common federal state in which GCs and

TCs would be working jointly in their legislative, executive, and judicial capacities would be operating mainly within the broader framework of the EU institutions, addressing mainly EU-related issues. The GC and TC representatives of the new Cyprus would in effect be working in continuous and close association with the representatives of all the other EU member-states—a provision that fundamentally dilutes the conditions for the reemergence of GC and TC nationalist antagonism in the common governance of Cyprus.

Another central aspect of the Annan Plan was that, compared with the original structure of the Republic of Cyprus, it considerably decentralized political power by diffusing it and diversifying it at the highest level of government. In instituting a new system of power sharing, the plan shifted the center of power from its former hierarchical concentration in the presidential office to a bicommunal presidential council. This aspect of the UN proposal entailed the devolution of political power, not merely in terms of the proposed tristate structure of governance, but also in terms of the specific executive powers of the federal state government. The general devolution of power from the center to the periphery was essentially modeled after the most advanced concepts of European democracy, as multiethnic and multinational systems of governance based on multicentered power structures superseded earlier, centralist concepts of state power based on ethnomajoritarian and/or ethnosecessionist nationalism.

The above aspect of the plan was also reinforced by the fact that the offices of president and vice president rotate between the members of the bicommunal presidential council on the basis of very brief terms. This arrangement constituted a key safeguard against the institutional centralization and the monopolization of power by either ethnic community—an arrangement imperative for transcending the legacy of ethnocentric nationalism in ethnically mixed societies.

The two-chamber structure of the parliament of the common state as proposed by the Annan Plan was yet another central feature reflective of the deconstruction of nationalist politics. The equal representation of TCs and GCs in the Senate and the population-based, proportional representation in the Chamber of Deputies presented the constitutional resolution to the traditional conflict between the GCs and TCs over what should be the basis of Cypriot democracy. On the one hand, GC nationalists traditionally asserted that democracy ought to be based on the ethnic majority of Cyprus, a position that amounted to the political paralysis and disempowerment of the TC minority. On the other hand, TC nationalists argued that democracy ought to be based on equality between the two communities irrespective of numbers, a stance giving each citizen of the smaller TC community disproportionately greater political power than each citizen of the larger GC community. Each version of nationalism represented by these positions skewed the application of democracy.

Superseding this nationalist-conditioned impasse, the Annan Plan's proposal for a parliament composed of both a Senate and a Chamber of Deputies effectively integrated and balanced the concern for equality between the ethnic communities with the concern for equality between individual citizens at the level of their ethnic representation in the legislature of the common state.

The intention of the UN plan to move beyond the old nationalist approach to governance was strengthened by the provision that TCs and GCs residing in the other community's zone would be represented in the legislature of the other community's component state legislature. (This provision was later replaced, in response to objections by the TCs, with more flexible regulating the residency of GCs in the northern TC constituent state.)

The arrangements proposed for the legislatures of the component states and the common state, as well as for the structure of the Presidential Council, spoke of the plan's intention of raising the principles and institutional processes of democracy above and beyond the traditional, ethnocentric nationalism of the two Cypriot communities. From its very inception, nationalism had conceived of democracy as an exclusively intraethnic principle of governance, confined and restricted to political relations within homogeneous ethnic groups. Inviting the GCs and TCs to break free from nationalism, the Annan proposal elevated and extended democracy to both an intraethnic and interethnic institution and process of governance. Monoethnic democracy was not only secured but also complemented, balanced, extended, and amplified by polyethnic democracy.

In view of the fact that, relative to population, the UN characterized Cyprus as one of the most militarized areas in the world, the Annan proposal for the radical demilitarization of the Island marked one of the most decisive directives in changing the historical course of Cyprus from the path of nationalist militancy to one of peace and cogovernance. It ought to be stressed, however, that this aspect of the plan could not have emerged within the realm of viable possibilities outside the broader evolving and consolidating EU process, transforming and integrating both GC-TC and Greek-Turkish relations.

Perhaps the best indication that the Annan Plan offered a sound basis for negotiating a final settlement was the fact that as soon as it was made public, it was fiercely rejected with identical characterizations by the hardcore nationalists on both sides of the ethnonational divide. Both TC nationalists, who uncompromisingly continued to support ethnically clean secession, and GC nationalists, who still strove for a single island-wide Hellenic state, strongly opposed the federal interethnic nature of the proposed solution. Strikingly, but not surprisingly, both viewed the plan as national treason. The shockingly similar positions of both groups of the traditional hardliners on the UN plan could only mean one of two things: Either the plan was completely irrelevant to reality in Cyprus, or it was so relevant that it exposed and challenged the intolerant ethnocentrism of persons and groups still entrapped in the nationalism that had created the Cyprus conflict in the first place.

The nationalists were confronted with an unprecedented ambiguity in that their absolute rejectionist position ran against the grain of the UN, the EU, and the unparalleled diplomatic mobilization of the international community. Outright rejection of the Annan Plan by the nationalist leadership was thus not a simple or straightforward matter. The more strategically minded core nationalists soon realized that the political cost associated with outright rejection of the plan would be undeniably high. The plan's historical significance could not be evaded or ignored without consequences. To defeat it, therefore, the nationalists on both sides would have to resort to more subtle tactics. In light of the converging trends in favor of a Cyprus settlement, ranging from the evolving Greek-Turkish rapprochement to the EU process, the core nationalists concurred that the only way to defeat the Annan Plan was to delegitimize it in the eyes of the public and the various ethnonational opinion-forming centers.

In contrast to the rejectionism of the nationalists, many GCs, TCs, Greeks, and Turks saw the Annan Plan as an unrepeatable historical opportunity that ought to be seized, particularly in view of the growing interethnic and interstate rapprochement between the Greek and Turkish peoples and the upcoming entry of Cyprus into the EU. In an opinion column entitled *The Annan Plan: A Historic Challenge for the Cypriots*, a colleague and I jointly asserted that the Cyprus problem had reached a critical and unprecedented juncture and should be handled with utmost care and responsibility (Anastasiou and Yesilada 2003). We noted that while the time frame for a final settlement was narrowing, never before in the protracted history of the Cyprus problem had political leaders, civil society, and the international diplomatic community invested so much effort and energy to forge a settlement. Equally important, never before had there been such a confluence of favorable conditions for arriving at a comprehensive settlement.

If both the GCs and TCs rejected the UN plan, we argued, the consequences of failure would seriously damage not only GC-TC interests, but also Greek-Turkish relations, the region in general, and the security interests of the Western alliance at a critical historical moment. Failure to reach a settlement would set off a series of events including the indefinite suspension of UN peace-making efforts, the consolidation of the division of Cyprus, and further polarization of GCs and TCs as the former continued to seek EU membership and the latter moved toward integration with Turkey. Moreover, we reasoned, rejection of the plan would throw Cyprus's EU membership in doubt, seriously damage Greek-Turkish relations, eclipsing the progress made since 1999, deeply undercut Turkey's aspirations for future EU membership, and strain relations between NATO and the European Security and Defense Identity (ESDI). Finally, in this worst-case scenario, those GCs and TCs who had spent their lives hoping for peace and reconciliation on their Island would become the prime losers (Anastasiou and Yesilada 2003).

All of these scenarios were based on a projected elaboration of the consequences if both GCs and TCs rejected the Annan Plan. If both sides agreed to negotiate and proceed with finalizing the UN peace plan, however, we predicted that the positive consequences would be historically staggering, with enormous benefits outweighing all the relative losses that each side would incur in reaching the compromises required by the plan. These benefits would include:

- the entry of a united Cyprus into the EU, thus engrafting the GC and TC societies and their future development into a broader system of stability and security, a dimension absent from all previous efforts to settle the Cyprus problem;
- the instatement in all of Cyprus of the EU's conflict-preventive and peace-building institutions and political culture as a determining factor in both TC-GC and Greek-Turkish relations;
- economic benefits from EU membership for all the people of Cyprus;
- the freeing of new generations from the shackles and burdens of a problem they had no part in creating, but which had been laid on their shoulders by previous generations; and
- the consequent reorientation outward of the energy of these new generations toward creating a new society within the EU framework. Furthermore, not only would Turkey's advancement toward the EU be greatly enhanced, but
- relations between Turkey and Greece would improve significantly, allowing progress on other outstanding issues, such as those related to the Aegean;
- Cyprus, and consequently Turkey and Greece, would provide the first much-needed example of Muslim and Christian societies and states operating securely, freely, and cooperatively within Western, secular, and democratic institutions at local, national, and regional levels;
- the EU framework would be extended and deepened in the Eastern Mediterranean region, bringing its conciliatory and stabilizing institutions and political culture to the doorstep of the troubled Middle East as envisioned in the Barcelona Declaration; and
- TCs, GCs, Turkey, and Greece would offer the world a success story in peace and reconciliation, at a time when the world is in dire need of hope (Anastasiou and Yesilada 2003).

Given such possibilities, it was clear by the most elementary criteria of intelligence and reason that the benefits of a settlement to TCs, GCs, Turkey, Greece, and the Eastern Mediterranean region would overwhelmingly overshadow all of the traditional objections put forward by each of the parties. The benefits lying within reach at this historical juncture went far beyond any of the gains that the two sides had striven for through their traditional nationalist positions and struggles.

The Annan Plan, the EU, and the Turkish Cypriot Peace Rallies

With the elaborate Annan Plan on the negotiating table and the accession of Cyprus to the EU clearly in view, the TC citizens in particular started envisioning a new world of peace, security, and prosperity that was both realistic and beneficial for the entire TC community. Increasingly, in the eyes of the TCs, a likely settlement of the Cyprus problem under the umbrella of the EU appeared truly far-reaching. Joining the EU through a settlement of the Cyprus problem would mean an immediate end to the TCs' international isolation; unprecedented economic opportunities; a new dimension of security in addition to that provided by Turkey; international legitimacy for the TC administration through a reunited Cyprus; and the acquisition of European citizenship, with benefits and privileges far beyond those that the Turkish Republic of Northern Cyprus (TRNC) alone could ever provide.

Most TCs experienced heightened anxiety and anticipation as the UN time frame for achieving a settlement on the basis of the Annan Plan ran parallel to the formal EU integration process of the GC-controlled Republic of Cyprus. It was common knowledge that the UN was pushing for acceptance of the plan and for ratification of an outline agreement before the EU's upcoming summit on December 12, 2002, during which the decision was to be made to include the Island (along with nine other countries) in its next enlargement wave in 2004. Simultaneously, to stimulate and orient Turkish and TC opinion toward a UN-based settlement with the GCs, Brussels reiterated its position that it would admit Cyprus into the EU with or without a settlement. EU leaders and officials engaged with

Cyprus were hoping the prospect of EU membership for the entire island would spur a solution to the conflict, with a subsequent normalization of relations between Greece and Turkey and between Turkey and the EU. In close coordination with the UN, the EU's conflict-resolution strategy for Cyprus and for Greek-Turkish relations leaned more toward mitigating the long-standing intransigence that the traditional TC and Turkish nationalist leadership had historically entrenched.

For the majority of the TC community, it was clear that the Annan Plan was the bridge that could decisively and immediately link their future to the EU. Increasing awareness of how wide the political and economic horizon would open with the prospect of a united Cyprus joining the EU intensified the TC community's sense of their political isolation and international marginalization under the status quo of their breakaway state, the TRNC, an awareness that amplified their desire for a comprehensive settlement of the Cyprus problem. Thus a rapidly growing number of TCs saw the Annan Plan as having pivotal historical significance.

Against the backdrop of a decade of growing TC-GC citizen peacebuilding initiatives, reinforced by Greek-Turkish rapprochement since 1999, the launching of the plan led to an unprecedented series of peace rallies in the Turkish part of the capital, Nicosia. Through these, a constantly growing number of TCs began to express openly their ardent desire and support for a peaceful settlement. The first peace rally, on November 28, 2002, involved between fifteen and twenty thousand participants of all ages and walks of life: ordinary citizens, political leaders of the opposition, and ninety-two NGOs, many of whose leaders had been longtime participants in the bicommunal citizen peace movement. All the participating organized groups signed a declaration entitled *Vision of the Turkish Cypriots for a Solution and Joining of the EU.*

Interestingly, the TC media refrained from covering the event in spite of its historical novelty and political significance. Meanwhile, the nationalist newspaper *Volkan* (named after the militant, nationalist movement of the 1950s) had called on the TC authorities to ban the rally, arguing that the prosolution TCs were undermining the national cause and the national interests of the TC community. But given the prevailing conditions, nothing could stop the mobilization of the TCs. Shops were closed, students were let off school, and even civil servants defiantly took the day off to attend (*Cyprus Mail* 2002b; *Phileleftheros* 2002). A month later, on December 26, 2002, a second mass peace rally was launched. This time the numbers rose to thirty thousand (*Cyprus Mail* 2002a). This was followed by an even bigger mobilization of TCs on January 14, 2003. CNN estimated fifty-five thousand participants, while Reuters put the number to eight-five thousand (CNN 2003). Regardless of the accuracy of the numbers, the rallies directly involved anywhere from a third to half of the estimated TC population of Cyprus.

The successive rallies marked an unprecedented effort by the TCs to send an explicit and powerful message to their leader, Rauf Denktash, urging him to proceed with a final settlement on the basis of the Annan Plan. Speakers at the rallies stressed that "if we do not return to the negotiating table we cannot defend our rights" (*Cyprus Mail* 2002b). The crowds waived banners with the word *peace* written in Turkish, Greek, and English, while many carried or wore olive branches on their heads. EU flags and banners bearing pro-EU slogans also abounded, with the demonstrators chanting, "Yes to the plan! Yes to the EU!" These images were most distasteful to the nationalists who had dominated Cypriot political life since the advent of the Cyprus problem. Neither olive branches nor interethnic democracy had ever been part of the nationalists' political outlook.

The TC mobilizations were primarily peace rallies in support of reunification, but they also served as clear protests against Denktash, whose intransigent, secessionist nationalism was gradually but surely being seen by an increasing number of TCs as the main obstacle to a Cyprus settlement. The rallies were saturated with banners that read, "Denktash quit," "You will be accountable," "You have no right to play with our future," and "Denktash move aside and let peace come through." While initially attempting to dismiss the significance of the rallies, Denktash could not evade the challenge to his leadership—a leadership unquestioned for decades. In the midst of criticizing the event as one of mere excitement and yelling, lacking in prudence and reason, Denktash admitted that the calls for him to resign had reduced him to tears.

During the peace rallies, the red and white flag of the TRNC was hardly noticeable, while the blue flag of the EU and thousands of blue balloons carried by the TCs in the streets of northern Nicosia were seen everywhere—public, nonverbal semiotics expressing the views of the majority of the TC community. This signalled an unprecedented historic questioning of the TRNC as a viable state necessary to protect and guarantee the well-being and future of the TCs. TC opinion was clearly shifting from demands for recognition of the TRNC to demands for a federal settlement of the Cyprus problem under the Annan Plan and EU membership, severely undercutting the traditional, unilateral secessionist agenda of the TC and Turkish nationalist leadership. The economic hardships that the TC community had borne as a result of the perpetuation of the Cyprus conflict and the collapse of the banking system in northern Cyprus in the late 1990s further stimulated support for the vision of united European Cyprus.

The TC peace rallies received wide coverage by the GC media and induced favorable public responses from forward-looking GC personalities. One such response came from the former GC mayor of Nicosia, Lellos Demetriades. His written address to his own community also sent a clear message to the TCs: "We [the GCs] are with them [the TCs] for peace." A second notable response came from Michalis Papapetrou, then the GC government spokesman. He described the rallies as astonishing and assured the TCs that their messages were loud and clear, stressing that the GC side had received them in a positive spirit. He asserted, "We unite our voices with them for Cyprus." In unison with the TCs he declared full support for "reunification, accession of a united Cyprus to the EU, and a solution to the Cyprus problem based on the Annan Plan by February 28," the date that the secretary-general of the UN had set for a decisive outcome. It is noteworthy that both Demetriades and Papapetrou had been longtime participants in the bicommunal rapprochement process—the process in which I and others had been inextricably engaged from its pioneering days. Both men had been inexorably drawn into the bicommunal process as it began to take shape over the years, gradually involving persons of influence from the higher echelons of politics.

A significant aspect of the TC peace rallies hinged on the fact that never before in the postcolonial history of Cyprus did the TC community express its will in such a public manner and through such huge numbers. More importantly, it was the first time that the TC community had taken autonomous political action outside the direct regulation and authorization of the TRNC authorities. The rallies embodied the TC community's first potent and direct expression of civil will and the first clear sign of an emerging broad-based voice for civil society and culture on the TC side.

The significance of the confluence of these factors was that it gradually cultivated and engendered the association of human rights, civil society, and democracy with interethnic peace and reconciliation. Explicitly or implicitly, consciously or unconsciously, this dynamic brought the cause of peace to the forefront of the political process and public culture of Cyprus. This novel development had greatly empowered the TC citizens in a dual way: It created potent legitimacy for civil society and citizen-initiated action, while simultaneously delegitimizing the centralized, statist power structure and nationalist authoritarianism residual in traditional TC and Turkish politics. Popular support for a comprehensive settlement that entailed power sharing with the GCs and entry into the EU amounted to a fundamental erosion of nationalist ethnocentric politics and associated monoethnic notions of society (Lacher and Kaymak 2005). Even more importantly, TC public opinion demonstrated a historic tacit questioning of the viability of secessionist and monoethnic statist concepts of democracy, the very nationalist approach to governance that had driven Cypriot politics to interethnic violence and the subsequent decades-long impasse.

Comparing the TC rallies in favor of the Annan Plan to the results of the GC presidential elections of February 16, 2003, one is compelled to conclude that the TCs more strongly favored the Annan Plan than the GCs. This difference was illuminated by an opinion poll commissioned by GC newspaper *Politis* and the TC *Ortam* and conducted by researchers Amer/Nielsen and KADEM. The surveys carried out in the north and south showed that 59 percent of GCs rejected the UN proposal for a settlement and 28 percent supported it. On the Turkish side, 52 percent supported the draft and 40 percent opposed it. The polls also showed that public understanding of the Annan Plan was a problem, with only one-third of respondents on each side saying they felt sufficiently informed about it. Both sides, however, said they would consider the draft as a basis for negotiations.

One set of issues both sides disapproved of, albeit for different reasons, were the proposed territorial adjustments. Sixty-two percent of TCs said they did not approve of the plans, which would shrink their territory to 28.5 percent of Cyprus from the 36 percent they had controlled since 1974. Of the GCs, 63 percent opposed the plan out of concern about access to their properties in the area to remain under Turkish Cypriot control and fear of restrictions on their ownership rights.

According to the poll, the sharpest difference in views between the two sides centered on the proposal for joint governance by veteran leaders Glafkos Clerides and Rauf Denktash for an initial three years from the date of agreement. Seventy-two percent of Greek Cypriots opposed this provision, compared with only 31 percent of Turkish Cypriots—results reflective of the perennial polarization between the GC tendency for a strongly integrated unitary state and the TC tendency for increased separatist powers and autonomy.

The survey was based on a relatively small sample, 390 people in the south and 400 people in the north, and may therefore be approached with skepticism. However, the general pattern that it reflected is reinforced by direct observation of the political phenomena under consideration. On the Turkish side, the indicators of the survey were reflected in the huge and escalating numbers of TCs participating in each successive peace demonstration. On the Greek side, the election of Tasos Papadopoulos to the presidency of the Republic of Cyprus was clearly reflective of that portion of the GC population most reluctant to accept the Annan Plan as the framework for negotiating a final settlement.

THE HAGUE TALKS

As noted already, when Kofi Annan announced his Cyprus plan, he did so not only in light of the preceding developments in Greek-Turkish rapprochement, GC-TC citizen peace building, and the overarching EU process—all factors conducive to a final settlement of the Cyprus problem. He also did so in view of upcoming, date-specific events carrying enormous historical significance for the Island. The earliest one was the signing of the Treaty of Accession to formally establish the anticipated entry of Cyprus into the EU, set for April 16, 2003. The next crucial historical landmark, the full and complete integration of Cyprus into the EU, was planned for May 1, 2004.

With the TC peace rallies in the background and the April 16 milestone immediately ahead, the secretary-general of the UN took direct action to advance the diplomatic process for the resolution of the Cyprus problem. In spite of remaining disagreements between the two sides, Annan requested that Denktash and Papadopoulos plan for a referendum to allow the TCs and the GCs to vote on the Annan Plan as the basis for negotiating and finalizing a comprehensive political settlement. Annan asked the two leaders to meet him in the Hague on March 10, to give him their decision about a referendum on March 30, 2003. The hope was that if the Cypriot leaders said yes and the GCs and TCs voted in favor of a reunified Cyprus, then Denktash and Papadopoulos, as temporary copresidents of the United Cyprus Republic, would sign the Treaty of Accession to the EU in Athens on April 16, 2003, with the remaining details of the agreement to be worked out after that date.

The two Cypriot leaders did meet Annan at the Hague, along with senior officials sent by Greece and Turkey in support of their respective Cypriot communities. Special envoys from Britain and the United States also joined in support of the talks. However, to the great disappointment of all that looked to the top-level meeting in hope, particularly the TCs, the Hague talks ended in failure. While the secretary-general convened the meeting simply to formalize a commitment for a referendum, the two Cypriot leaders embarked on the discussions with strong reservations about the UN plan itself. Denktash believed that the plan would dislocate TCs, creating new refugees, whereas Papadopoulos argued that the plan committed the GCs to sharing disproportionate power with a minority and restricted the number of GCs able to return to their former homes. Prodded by Greece, Papadopoulos reluctantly consented to accept the plan as the basis for further negotiations, thus implying openness to the possibility of proceeding with the requested referendum.

However, because of Papadopoulos's well-known nationalist past and hard-line, ethnocentric rigidity, the TCs assumed that he, like Denktash, rejected the idea of a referendum (Birand 2003). Annan urged the two leaders to keep negotiating until March 28 and move the referendum to April 6 and declared that Papadopoulos was ready to keep trying but Denktash ruled out further immediate talks. "The two leaders," he explained, "have expressed their willingness to continue talks, but without a firm commitment to proceed energetically to a conclusion. . . . " Hence, on March 11, the UN secretary-general announced that the talks between the GCs and the TCs had collapsed and that the effort to reunite the Island before Cyprus's accession to the EU had been terminated (Reuters 2003).

It was evident that the main reason for the failure of the talks was the lack of sufficient political will by the two sides to formally commit to a referendum on the Annan Plan. Denktash's outright intransigence and Papadopoulos's uneasiness combined to bring the talks to a deadlock. This, however, was not the only reason for the failure of the Cyprus talks. Critical events rapidly unfolding on the international scene at the time were also a deterrent. Upon announcing the collapse of the talks, Annan stated that the search for a Cyprus settlement had been "overshadowed by the atmosphere of crisis and great anxiety that is affecting the whole world, the question of Iraq and its disarmament" (Reuters 2003). The intensity of the events surrounding the crisis over Iraq, in which the international community had become stressfully embroiled, had deflected the attention of the international players most influential on the Cyprus issue, particularly Britain and the United States. The abortive talks underlined the fact that political realities, however place-specific, were becoming inextricably bound to the conditions of globalization. If the energy of the international community within the UN had not been so completely focused on the Iraq crisis, conditions surrounding the Cyprus negotiations would have been more favorable, possibly allowing resolution.

The international fixation on Iraq facilitated Denktash's resistance to the Annan Plan by creating the conditions that enabled him to definitively reject it at the Hague. Known as the most intransigent of the parties concerned, Denktash staked his decision to reject the Annan Plan outright on the intensely strained internal politics of Turkey, resulting mainly from the Iraqi crisis. At the time, the United States was strongly pressing the Turkish government to allow the deployment of American troops on

Turkish soil for the pending military operations against Iraq. This created a chaotic political climate within Turkey. The tension between the government of Abdullah Gül and the conservative nationalist circles within the Turkish political and military establishment dissipated and drained the government's energy.

The attempts of the United States to communicate directly with the Turkish military aroused the indignation of the Turkish government. For the first time, the government publicly yet cautiously accused the United States, Turkey's strongest traditional ally, of curbing the progress of Turkish democracy by attempting to bypass the legitimate, civilian government and deal directly with the military. The Turkish press stated that "though the Gül government did want a solution in Cyprus, the fact that it lost control in general during the quarrel over the US troop deployment motion was the biggest factor" in enabling Denktash to evade the pressure that the government was exerting on him for a final Cyprus settlement. In this environment, Denktash "managed to stir into action the conservative circles that rule Turkey, creating, in the end, the climate he wanted." Prime Minister Gül and his government were up against the "'No to a solution' front that has been 'orchestrated' in an excellent manner by Denktash" (*Turkish Daily News* 2003). The notable Turkish journalist Mehment Ali Birand asserted that "the Turkish Armed Forces played the most effective role in bringing about the rejection of the Annan Plan" (Birand 2003). Ahmet Necdet Sezer, the Turkish president, also aligned his position with the armed forces in rejecting the Annan Plan. The stance and continuing influence of the Turkish military had in fact provided the empowerment for Denktash's negotiating strategy and final objective at the Hague meeting.

Furthermore, the Republican People's Party, the sole opposition party in the Turkish Parliament since the sweeping victory of the Justice and Development Party in the elections of November 2002, launched an antisolution-based attack on the Gül government under the slogan, "Not a pebble of it [Cyprus] be given away!" Again according to Birand, the Republican People's Party, "considering its social democratic nature, . . . has staged an incredible show of conservatism and nationalism on Cyprus" (2003). On the one hand, the Iraq issue heightened the tension between the conservatives among the military establishment and the government; on the other, the intensive nationalist critique by the opposition party created an internal political paralysis around the Cyprus issue. As noted by the *Turkish Daily News,* Prime Minister Gül became wary, "thinking that on top of the loss of prestige he suffered over the Iraq issue he might now be accused of high treason. In the end Gül was left all alone and Denktash won" (2003). The assertion expounded by Alter (1994) that crisis always creates favorable conditions for hardened nationalism was fully reflected in the course of these events.

The overall pattern emerging from this highly profiled episode brought into focus, yet again, the fact that between, as well as within, the societies with a stake in the Cyprus question, the central axis of struggle was between the traditional nationalists and the postnationalists struggling for reform and sociopolitical change. Clearly, the agenda for peace did not lie in the nationalist camp. Within Turkey, the struggle was emerging through a complex web of competing and contradicting approaches and understandings. The nationalist establishment of the Turkish military was caught between its guardianship of the unity of the secular Turkish state and democratic reforms initiated by the civilian government of the Justice and Development Party—a party that had denounced the agenda associated with its Islamist origins, gradually adopting the European path. Traditionally, and as late as the 1990s, the Turkish military had suppressed Islamic fundamentalism in defense of the constitutionally based secular character of the Turkish state. Simultaneously, however, the conservative core of the Turkish military was beginning to emerge as an obstacle not only to Europeanizing and democratizing domestic reforms but also to the unfolding efforts to resolve the Cyprus problem.

Unlike in the past, when the public was compelled to a strong reliance on and trust in the military establishment, it was now starting to view the military as a force potentially stalling and impeding Europeanization, an objective that had been clearly associated with Turkey's national interest. As part of the EU's formal requirements and expectations, democratizing reforms and constructive support for a solution of the Cyprus problem were bound to become the most potent historical challenge to the nationalist conservatives within Turkey's traditional military and political establishment (*The Economist* 2003).

The failure of the Hague talks left the TC community deflated and disappointed. The Papadopoulos government recoiled in ambiguous relief, retaining its antifederalist legacy but also holding the upcoming EU accession of Cyprus as a victory card. The EU warned Turkey that the failure of the talks would have a direct bearing on EU-Turkish relations, hindering progress toward Turkey's goal of becoming a member of the EU (*Phileleftheros* 2003). This was a reiteration of the earlier assertion of EU enlargement commissioner Verheugen that "it would be difficult to see how it would be possible [for Turkey] to start accession negotiations under such circumstances" as the failure in the peace talks (Reuters 2003). The outcome temporarily satisfied the ideological and psychological compulsions of the nationalists. Objectively, however, it marked a setback to Turkey's European aspirations and to the speed by which it needed to reform in attaining the European standards of peace and democracy.

Rising Ambiguities

The Competing Pulses of Peace and Conflict

FREE MOVEMENT: THE UNEXPECTED
AND UNPRECEDENTED EVENT

On April 23, 2003, shortly after the collapse of the Hague talks, an extraordinary event took place in Cyprus. With Turkey's consent, the Denktash administration decided to partially lift restrictions on citizen movement across the green line—the 1974 cease-fire demarcation that over twenty-nine years had become a hardened ethnic boundary. Under this decree, TCs could travel to the GC south and GCs could visit the north, initially for only one day from 9 A.M. until noon, but, soon after April 23, for three days, including overnight stays. The announcement came as a great surprise to all concerned, and as a pleasant shock to GCs, whose longing to revisit northern Cyprus had long been impeded. The unexpected change was especially emotional for the thousands of GC refugees who had been forced to flee from the north, where their lives and history were rooted. Relaxing the restrictions to free movement also came as a great relief to TCs, who could now visit the south after decades of isolation and confinement. The international community was also caught by surprise, particularly the mediators who had formally abandoned the Cyprus problem following the collapse of the Hague talks.

The historical and political question that naturally arises is why the Turkish side decided on this unexpected shift in policy on an issue that for years marked the cornerstone of its secessionist agenda. To anyone outside the narrow circle of policy leaders at the upper echelons of power, the precise reasons and motives are not readily accessible, as objective observation is not possible nor reliable information available. However, in view of the historical significance of the decision, one is compelled to hypothesize as to the reason. A cluster of time-specific, interrelated phenomena may provide the answers.

In the eyes of both the UN and the EU, the blame for the failure of the Hague talks—and consequently for not putting the Annan Plan to an islandwide referendum—weighed heavily on the Turkish side. Since the GC leader had agreed to put the plan to a referendum, albeit reluctantly, the Turkish side was left politically exposed. One can argue that this was not the first time that one side or the other suffered international political exposure because of its particular national policy decisions. However, conditions in April 2003 were radically different from all those previously encountered by the TC and Turkish authorities.

The collapse of the top-level talks came as an overwhelming anticlimax for all who had invested hope in the UN-mediated negotiations. This was particularly true for the TCs. The experience again highlighted the marginalized political status of their community. Yet, this time it did so in a manner that was provocative, psychologically violating their longstanding sense of economic and political deprivation. In view of their anticipation for the long-awaited restoration of their international political status through a Cyprus solution and entry into the EU, the TCs felt that their leaders had failed them, even humiliated them. From a certain diachronic sensibility, it seemed as though the disappointing outcome of the top-level talks reawakened in many TCs the memory of siege, isolation, and entrapment they had experienced during the 1960s, when they lived in enclaves cut off from the rest of the world. Only this time, the major factor in their enclavement was not the GC-run Republic of Cyprus and the GC nationalist militias but the political entity and leaders that had been their protectors and guardians—namely, the TRNC, Denktash, and his political associates. As long as the key issue was whether to unite with the GC south, the TRNC, with all its shortcomings, still offered TCs a minimum foundation for security, identity, and political independence. Within the EU framework, however, particularly in an era of rapid globalization, the TRNC and its personification in the leadership of Denktash began to be perceived as a restraint and even as an obstacle to TC interests.

The domestic difficulties encountered by Turkey, combined with the negative economic impact that its economy had on the TC community over the years, were additional factors discrediting the TRNC. Moreover, in a society as small as that of the TC north, the disparity in wealth and well-being between those closely associated with the ruling regime and the rest of the community had emerged as another distasteful reality. In recent years, TC opposition parties and civil groups had frequently identified this disparity as partly a result of unwarranted privileges and even of corrupt practices by those in power. The opposition argued that a small elite of the politically and economically privileged had a vested interest in maintaining the status quo, and had therefore functioned as the main obstacle to achieving a solution to the Cyprus problem.

In the context of the overwhelming forces of globalization within which the EU offered a secure and promising harbor, an increasing number of TCs viewed the resistance of the TRNC leadership to a final settlement of the Cyprus problem as a blow to the specific interests and future of their community. In their eyes, it now appeared that what the constraining Turkish enclaves were in the 1960s in relation to the rest of Cyprus, the TRNC and Denktash had now become in relation to the rest of the world, especially the world of the EU. The severe economic problems suffered by the TC community, in combination with the lost prospect of EU membership, rendered the experience of life in the TRNC reminiscent of that in the enclaves during the 1960s. This parallelism of experience was by no means absolute, especially regarding security. Yet in terms of economic deprivation and political disenfranchisement, the experience was comparable.

Two significant developments created an unprecedented situation that the TC and Turkish leadership had to reckon with: first event being the ardent mass support in favor of the Annan Plan exhibited through the TC peace rallies, and second, the fact that following the failure of the Hague talks, the GC-led Republic of Cyprus had moved forward with the signing of the EU Accession Treaty on April 16. Conjoined, these two developments posed a great challenge to the policy leaders on the Turkish side, placing the Denktash administration of the TRNC and the Turkish government in a very precarious position. That the failure of the talks had not halted progress toward the EU integration of the GC-led Republic of Cyprus had the potential of driving the Turkish authorities on a collision course with the newly found civil will of the TC community. Had such a confrontation materialized, the Denktash administration, along with the Turkish government and military establishment, would have been compelled to face an overwhelming and unprecedented loss of legitimacy within the community. Furthermore, such a confrontation would have forced the TRNC and Turkish authorities to make an unpleasant decision as to whether to take drastic measures to maintain order. Repressive action by the authorities in a confrontation with the civil will of the TCs would have immediately invited the condemnation of the EU, as such a move would have signaled a reversion to autarchic forms for governance. Such a scenario would have damaged Turkey's EU ambitions, particularly at a time when the country was clearly struggling to implement EU-aligned reforms in the midst of its traditional domestic and international challenges.

In this context, the enormous psychological energy that had built up among the TC community in anticipation of an Annan-based settlement, in conjunction with the feelings of despair and even anger that followed the failure of the talks, was precipitously dangerous to the government of northern Cyprus. In lifting the restrictions and allowing citizens to move freely to and from the two sides, a key objective of the TC administration was to defuse this energy, which arisen from the TCs' first-ever collective posture of civil assertiveness in relation to their formal political authorities.

The partial lifting of restrictions to free movement also served as a tacit attempt on the part of the TRNC to eliminate unilaterally the impact of the economic isolation of the north by opening avenues of contact with the wealthier south. The implicit hope here was that such a move would at least partially relieve the economic pressure weighing on the TCs by opening up economic opportunities for the TC community, while simultaneously leaving the structure of the TRNC intact. In taking this risky but desperate decision, the Denktash administration and Turkey were still acting within the framework of their traditional strategy. The idea was that through a partial open-borders approach to the south, the TRNC would somehow be legitimized by default. This strategy was artificial, however, precisely because in unilaterally allowing contact with the GC south, the Turkish side simultaneously refrained from becoming decisively engaged—through the Annan Plan—in solving the Cyprus problem.

In addition to the internal factors pressuring the TRNC and Turkey, one indirect external factor played a significant role in the decision to relax restrictions on movement. It derived from an emerging confrontation between European law and Turkey. Two legal cases were of exceptional importance. The first concerned GC refugee Titina Loizidou, who filed a suit with the European Court of Human Rights accusing Turkey of obstructing access to her property in northern Cyprus. In December 1996, the court found Turkey liable, since its military presence in northern Cyprus supported and underpinned the regime that was denying the plaintiff access to her property (*Loizidou v. Turkey* 1998). The court concluded that Turkey was guilty of human rights violations and ordered Ankara to pay Loizidou damages and to allow her access to her property.

Initially Turkey attempted to evade its legal obligation, but in 1998 the European Court of Human Rights ruled that Turkey must pay damages of nine hundred thousand dollars. Since then, hundreds of GC refugees have appealed to the European court, with many more queuing up to follow in the footsteps of Titina Loizidou. Though Turkey attempted a defense arguing that the property issue ought to be settled in the context of the future political arrangements bearing on the Cyprus problem, its position did not stand in the European court. Under these conditions, against the historical backdrop of its unqualified support of the TRNC, Turkey was at great risk, facing embarrassing international political exposure and hefty fines.

Even though the jurisdiction of the European Court of Human Rights extends to signatory states beyond members of the EU, compliance to the rule of law on human rights issues is viewed by the EU as a cornerstone of its regime. From this perspective, Turkey's readiness to comply with the ruling of the court was a litmus test of the authenticity of its European aspirations. As a country that had officially accepted the authority of the European Court of Human Rights, Turkey found itself caught between its obligations toward European law and its traditional secessionist policy on Cyprus. By December 2003, Turkey had agreed to pay damages to Loizidou in the order of € 1.2 million, setting a precedent for other GC plaintiffs. The case brought the property aspect of the unresolved Cyprus problem to the forefront through the due process of law. Unavoidably, it also highlighted the human rights dimension associated with obstructing the free movement of citizens.

The most critical confrontation between European law and Turkey, however, came from another appeal to the European Court of Human Rights. Although the case did not receive the wide publicity given the Loizidou case, especially on the GC side, it marked an extraordinary challenge for the Turkish and TRNC authorities, as the plaintiff was not a GC but rather a TC. The embarrassing entanglement of Turkey, and by implication of the TRNC, with European law centered on the case of *Djavit An v. Turkey*. A critic of the regime of northern Cyprus, Djavit An had been a leading member of the Movement for an Independent and Federal Cyprus, an unregistered association of TCs and GCs founded in 1989. Djavit An appealed to the European Court of Human Rights, accusing Turkey of obstructing him from freely assembling with GCs by refusing him permission to cross the green line. As a signatory of the European Convention of Human Rights, Turkey disputed its liability for the allegations, claiming that it was imputable "exclusively to the TRNC, an independent and sovereign State established by the Turkish Cypriot community in the exercise of its right to self-determination" (*Djavit An v. Turkey* 2003). But

> the Court recalled that States which had ratified the European Convention on Human Rights could be held responsible for acts and omissions of their authorities which produced effects outside their own territory. Such responsibility could also arise when, as a consequence of military action, the State concerned exercised effective control of an area outside its national territory. The obligation to secure, in such an area, the rights and freedoms set out in the Convention, derived from the fact of such control, whether it be exercised directly, through its armed forces, or through a subordinate local administration. It was not necessary to determine whether Turkey actually exercised detailed control over the policies and actions of the TRNC authorities; it was obvious from the

large number of troops engaged in active duties in northern Cyprus that the Turkish army exercised effective control over that part of the island. Such control entailed her responsibility for the policies and actions of the TRNC. Those affected by such policies or actions therefore came within the "jurisdiction" of Turkey. (*Djavit An v. Turkey* 2003)

Addressing the substance of the matter, the court's judgment was that in fact Turkey was in violation of European law. According to the press release issued by the court registrar,

> During that period [March 1992 until April 1998] the Turkish Government refused to grant a substantial number of permits to the applicant; in particular, only 6 out of 46 requests were granted. In some cases, permits were granted to other people who had submitted requests, but not to the applicant. Between February 2, 1996 and April 14, 1998 the applicant was refused all permits requested to attend bicommunal meetings in southern Cyprus (10 in total).
>
> The Court considered that all the meetings the applicant wished to attend were designed to promote dialogue and an exchange of ideas and opinions between Turkish Cypriots living in the north and Greek Cypriots living in the south, with the hope of securing peace on the island. The refusals to grant these permits to the applicant in effect barred his participation in bicommunal meetings, preventing him from peacefully assembling with people from both communities. Accordingly, the Court concluded that there had been an interference with the applicant's rights to freedom of peaceful assembly.
>
> As there seemed to be no law regulating the issuing of permits to Turkish Cypriots living in northern Cyprus to cross the "green line" into southern Cyprus to assemble peacefully with Greek Cypriots, the manner in which restrictions were imposed on the applicant's exercise of his freedom of assembly was not "prescribed by law." There had, therefore, been a violation of Article 11. (*Djavit An v. Turkey* 2003)

The significance of the judgment lay in the fact that it asserted and effectively defended the rights of a citizen against a powerful, highly centralized, statist regime accustomed to exercising executive power from the top down with little if any interference. But more significant than the vindication of Djavit An was the fact that the verdict of the court sent a clear and strong message to both the TRNC and Turkey regarding human rights and state accountability under European law. It administered a potent dose of what European law and political culture require and expect, particularly of those states aspiring to EU membership. The fact that freedom of assembly, and by implication freedom of speech, was the issue at the heart of the court's judgment directly exposed the TRNC's and Turkey's perennial policy of restraining the movement of citizens across Cyprus's north-south divide.

The historical confluence of all these events confronted the TC authorities and Turkey with pressures emanating from the rising tension between their past policy of secessionist nationalism and the challenges for a conciliatory, postnationalist, European future. The fact that Denktash and his supporting nationalist, political elite were not quite capable or willing to break decisively from the conflictual past offers a point of reference for intuitively deciphering the intention and scope of the historical decision to resort to the free movement policy.

For Denktash and his nationalist supporters embedded in the TC and Turkish power structure, instating free movement did not in essence amount to opening the cease-fire line but rather to opening the state border between the TRNC and its neighboring GC state in the south. The implicit agenda was that if spontaneous contact proved successful and risk-free, the argument could then be advanced that open interstate relations through citizen contact appeared to be working. As such, it would be an affirmation that the two-state scenario was in fact a viable option. Hence, it was hoped, legitimacy would be conferred to the TRNC by default. In contrast, if free contact proved unworkable and potentially destabilizing, then the argument could be advanced that since the two ethnic communities could not coexist even through limited contact, then TRNC recognition would appear the sole practical and consequently legitimate option. Founded on these hypotheses, Denktash's free movement policy amounted to an effort to forge retroactively an exit path from the UN framework after the failure of the Hague talks without losing face or political credibility.

In spite of the Turkish and TC authorities' willingness to proceed with political reforms, their stubborn resistance to external and internal pressure and their persistent efforts to obtain a priori recognition of the TRNC demonstrated that the traditional nationalist mentality maintained by the military and political hardliners was keeping Turkish politics within its old conservative statist framework. This held true even in light of the TRNC's unexpected change in policy regarding free movement. If we recognize that the Turkish side was sandwiched between the pressures to move forward with conflict-transcending positive changes and its inability to decisively move out of the box of nationalism, its allowance of free movement may be interpreted as a desperate, long-shot attempt to bring the TRNC into the EU framework through the back door, as it were, through tacit acceptance of its state status. Given the fact that the GC-controlled Republic of Cyprus had signed the EU Accession Treaty, and that the EU viewed the GC government as legitimate, the Denktash administration assumed that by normalizing relations with the GC south, the TRNC would somehow also become normalized and hence legitimized as a state entity under the umbrella of the EU. This approach was a novel extrapolation of the perennial, nationalist, secessionist demand by the TRNC administration, namely, that the EU deal with it directly and independently of the GCs. Of all the hopes that the Denktash administration associated with its free movement policy, this was the most unrealistic, given the institutional EU process and law.

FREE MOVEMENT: THE UNINTENDED CONSEQUENCES

Overall, the decision to lift partially the restrictions to free movement did not yield the outcome intended by the Denktash administration. Though the international community, including the United States and the EU, welcomed the move as a gesture of good will, it also noted that free movement, while an important positive step, left the political problem essentially unchanged. In his report, the secretary-general of the UN stated that the new freedoms that came into effect did not constitute a substitute for a comprehensive settlement of the Cyprus problem. He added further that without a genuine political commitment to his proposal it would be "highly unlikely that such a settlement can be achieved" (United Nations 2003b).

The most stunning outcome resulting from the easing of restrictions on freedom of movement was the manner in which the TC and GC communities began to interact as they came in direct contact with each other after four decades of separation. From the very first day the barricades were removed, GCs and TCs flooded into each other's areas. TCs crossed to the south mainly to reconnect with old friends and to see how the other side was living. GCs crossed to the north primarily to revisit their homes, villages, and towns. The difference in motivation was reflective of how the conflict had impacted each side. In the 1960s and in 1974 the TCs fled from their homes in order to find safety, first into larger TC enclaves and then to the north. Hence, their interest in the south was motivated not so much by a desire to return to their former homes but to find old friends from the GC side who were remembered as faithful fellow residents of their villages and cities who had taken no part in the violent exchanges, but from whom they had been severed as a result of the hostilities. These old friendships, which TCs sought to rekindle, were yet another reality that the respective nationalism of each side had denied, suppressed, forbidden, and kept at bay for decades. Meanwhile, the overwhelming flow of GCs to the north was essentially motivated by the pain of having been forced out of their homes by the Turkish army where they had enjoyed a life of relative security and well-being. It was motivated by the psychological desire of return, even under the increasing acknowledgment that much of what had happened in the past and much of the current situation was historically irreversible.

What was extraordinary about this historic, direct interaction between TCs and GCs was that it occurred in a spirit fundamentally defiant of their respective nationalist inheritance, and of the mistrust, animosity, and suspicion typical of longtime adversaries. The nationalist stereotypes of the moral *us* and demonic *them* had somehow undergone a process of dilution, as though in some inner space of conscience people, over the course of time, had silently engaged in conflict-transcending reflections and visions.

The new freedom of movement inevitably released intense emotions among the TC and GC communities alike (Hadjipavlou-Trigeorgis 2007). In the psychological realm, it entailed a peculiar admixture of revisiting past loss and anticipating future hope. But these emotions were by and large contained in, and directed by, an overarching vision and desire for peace and the mutual benefits that would ensue from it. The easing of restrictions on movement, even under the shadow of the tragic past, allowed many defining moments of personal reconnection with *the other*. People from each side had friends from the distant past knock at their door; GCs visited the long-missed Kyrenia Harbor in the north for a cup of coffee; TCs visited the longed-for Paphos Beach in the southwest. Others came to the doorsteps of their former homes to be greeted by the current inhabitants with *Kopiaste* or *Hoşgeldin*, the words for *welcome* in Greek and Turkish respectively. To the surprise of many, both in Cyprus and the world, these Greek and Turkish words apparently opened renewed channels of communication to the hearts and minds of the GC and TC peoples—peoples fatefully separated by nationalist ethnic conflict and forced to live in different worlds while continuing to inhabit their common Mediterranean island.

The gestures of good will that permeated Cyprus after the two communities came in direct contact were innumerable (Hadjipavlou-Trigeorgis 2007). No formal inventory contains all the stories. However, the unreserved expressions of good will, and the positive experiences they helped create islandwide, became a living narrative in the recent memory of all Cypriots. For instance, upon visiting her home in the north, a GC woman was presented with the wedding dress that she had left behind twenty-nine years earlier as she fled from the fighting. The TC family that moved into her home had kept it since 1974 and returned it to her in April 2003. This story is representative of hundreds of others in which people had kept valuable family items belonging to the original occupants from the other community, such as photos, jewelry, and other mementoes, only to return them three decades later.

With intense emotion, a close friend told me of his visit to his former home in the northern part of Nicosia. As it was late at night when he arrived, his wife was concerned about disturbing the TC family that was living there. Instead of knocking at the door, they decided just to leave a note and a gift at the doorstep and come back another day. But as this friend went to place the gift at the doorstep, the door opened. He found himself face-to-face with the TC occupants of his house. When the GC couple introduced themselves as the legal owners of the house, the TC family immediately invited them for a treat, as it is customary in Cypriot culture. The TCs wanted to cook for their visitors, but the GCs convinced them not to, as it was too late. After spending time talking, reminiscing, and sharing their hopes for the future, my friend asked the TCs if he could take a look at his old room, where he had spent his teenage years. Being somewhat of a technical wizard as a youngster, he had set up a little engineering laboratory there. Upon visiting his old accommodation, he found it intact. The TC family had kept all the items—his tools and laboratory instruments. He was shocked and amazed. Both he and his wife shed a tear or two as they gazed at this preserved moment from their past. The TC family assured them that they had wanted to keep things as they were in case the original owners one day wanted to have those articles back.

Stories of this nature surfaced in an overwhelming and unprecedented manner since the instating of free movement. A prominent peace builder who had worked for years promoting rapprochement between the two Cypriot communities noted in April 2003, "The phenomenon is amazing! All the journalists and historians might be working around the clock and still they can only capture and record only the tiniest part of the enormity of what is going on. So many stories to tell" (N. Anastasiou 2003a).

However small the good will gestures may seem from the perspective of power politics, these stories bear a unique kind of witness to the magnanimity of the human spirit. They are an extraordinary testimony to the fact that even under conditions of ethnic violence and alienation, ordinary people, concealed from the public eye of nationalist politics, had the courage to preserve a sense of dignity and humanity through tokens of respect and honor toward the mostly anonymous owners of those homes they were fatefully driven to occupy.

Under the new conditions of unimpeded interethnic contact, a central aspect of Cypriot culture that came to the forefront with the innumerable gestures of good will was that of hospitality. It was the first time since the establishment of Cyprus's independence in 1960 that hospitality played a role in shaping the spontaneous interactions between the two communities in a way that was publicly transparent and politically relevant for civil society. The historical shaping of public political culture by ethnocentric nationalism had precluded both the open acknowledgment of shared cultural values and the expression of conviviality between the two communities, as nationalism placed a premium on ethnic differences and polarization. The grip of nationalism on the politics of the Island had essentially displaced from the public domain shared traditional culture, particularly that of hospitality. In effect, it submerged the shared elements of public culture to the realm of private culture, thereby marginalizing them to irrelevance.

In his analysis, Lederach (2002) reminds us that in divided societies, regardless of the alienation that ensues from protracted conflict, people from rival sides do in fact share cultural values that may function as civil resources in the pursuit of peace and reconciliation. Cypriot hospitality, and the particular manner in which it came to color the interactions between TCs and GCs, was revealed as being one of these vital local cultural resources. Though the culture of hospitality had never been tapped in the interest of building and sustaining peace, free movement reawakened and activated it in the public domain of civil society, to the great surprise of many, especially the hard-line nationalists. It constituted one of the cultural elements crucial to the emergent, widespread meltdown of the old stereotypes generated by the conflict in the respective communities.

What was even more astonishing was that TCs and GCs extended these gestures of good will and hospitality while the Cyprus problem remained unresolved, while the cease-fire line was still manned, and while Turkish troops in northern Cyprus and the Greek-supported GC National Guards in southern Cyprus were still poised as enemy forces. Simultaneously, however, the general stance exhibited by GCs and TCs in their personal gestures of mutual respect and good will gave rise to a general sentiment and a public culture potentially capable of rendering the traditional presence and role of the respective military systems obsolete. What one encountered at this juncture was a genuine case of conflict transformation directly involving the society at large. These events constituted a stark affirmation of what Lederach (2002) meant when he stressed, to the bewilderment of the conflict-habituated mind, that connections across conflict lines always exist on the level of citizens, and that these connections are a vital resource in peace building. In the case of Cyprus, these interethnic connections, though buried beneath the rubble of historical layers of bloody conflict, surfaced spontaneously with the partial lifting of the restrictions on free movement.

There were also some minor negative incidents on both sides that fortunately were swiftly contained before causing any damage. The authorities of the TRNC had arrested a number GCs for entering the north from an unauthorized crossing. The GCs were taken to court but were soon released. Upon crossing to the south to visit their former home, a TC couple and their GC taxi driver were attacked and beaten by the two GC refugee brothers residing there. The GC police swiftly moved in and placed the brothers in custody. What made the containment of these and other small incidents possible was not only the decision of the authorities to defuse them quickly, but also the general public climate of hope and anticipation generated by the thousands of positive contacts between TCs and GCs. The culture of rapprochement embodied in the mutual gestures of good will was a subtle behavioral expression of direct democracy that even the most hard-line nationalist leaders could not ignore without political cost.

Direct contact between the two Cypriot communities also brought to disclosure certain tragic aspects of the past. A GC who was known to have killed TCs decided to visit his former ethnically mixed village in the north. His name was on the TC authorities' monitoring list of GCs barred from entering the Turkish side of the island. This GC, however, managed to slip through one of the crossings without being detected and proceeded to his former village. Upon his arrival, he sat at the coffee shop in the village square. Soon after, a TC woman showed up. She was the wife of a TC he had killed more than thirty years earlier. Recognizing the GC as her husband's murderer, she demanded that he tell her where he had buried the body, since it had never been recovered. Commotion and tension ensued, but the TC police arrived just in time to avert a potentially ugly turn of events. The perpetrator quickly returned to the south. But other GC villagers, who had known about this tragic old story, communicated to the TC widow where they believed her husband's body had been buried.

Among the tales of revisitations to the tragic past were stories of healing, as victims and culprits alike were compelled to face the ghosts and shadows of those violent motives and actions that the spirit of ethnic nationalism had demanded of them—ghosts and shadows that have haunted and chastened them through time. A case in point was a story that appeared, along with many others, in a bicommunal electronic circular. It stated: "A TC went to Paphos looking for his covillager who tried to kill him in 1964. He wanted to say that he had forgiven him and when he found out that the GC had died two months earlier, he cried. . . . He told the other GCs that he also had done terrible things and asked for forgiveness" (N. Anastasiou 2003b).

Inevitably, this incident raises the existential question of why this TC shed tears over the death of his attempted assassin. Perhaps it was because he was a covillager, a person he knew quite well, possibly since childhood. But it may be also because his relationship to this man embodied the pain and anguish of a personal and communal history gone terribly astray. Although at the political level the GC covillager had been his enemy, at the deeper human level the man had been an identical image of the TC. Both had been imbued by the hatred and the violence of ethnic nationalism. Both had resorted to unspeakable actions. And both were in dire need of being freed from their haunting past.

It is very likely that in shedding tears for his dead GC covillager, the TC was also shedding tears for himself—for the wrongdoings he himself had committed long ago. What is extraordinary about this TC is that while he visited his former village with the intention of forgiving the man who tried to kill him four decades before, he ended up requesting forgiveness from his GC compatriots, who had gathered around him as he told his story. It was as though in doing so he was also redeeming his dead GC counterpart (Fitzgibbons 1986).

Other stories that arose from the direct contact between TC and GC communities revealed some of the most concealed aspects of the tragic past. These concerned supreme expressions of humanity that occurred during the actual times of interethnic violence, at the darkest moments of the Island's history. Here is one story as an eyewitness told it:

> In 1974 as the GCs of the mixed village of Afania were fleeing from the Turkish army, the soldiers were firing at them. A 15-year-old GC boy was shot dead. His mother and the other members of the family were also in grave danger. They were saved by an 18-year-old TC from their own village. A few days ago, 29 years later, the mother who lost her son went back to her village looking for the young TC who saved the lives of the rest of her family so she could thank him. She went to the house of this TC and saw his mother. She told her that the TC young man was also killed during the war in 1974, just a few days later. . . . The two mothers embraced and wept and with them the GCs and TCs of the village of Afania who witnessed this tragedy. (N. Anastasiou 2003a)

This incident thrusts to the forefront of consciousness both the tragedy that lies at the heart of interethnic nationalist conflict and the long concealment and erasure of acts of interethnic humanity from the pages of adversarial nationalist historiography. But the event also stands as a monumental witness against those fundamental lies of nationalism. It challenges the latter's doctrines: that humanity and identity are fundamentally defined and contained by ethnicity; that ethnicity is the sole and exclusive criterion of community; that identity, humanity, and group interest stop at the boundaries of ethnonational identity; and that the interests of different groups are absolutely ethnocentric, forever competing, and ultimately irreconcilable. The story of the TC and GC boys is perhaps the greatest condemnation of the nationalist view of life, as it destroys and exposes the destructiveness of its spirit, of its basic assumptions and related actions. In the context of the long history of ethnonational strife in Cyprus, this event marks not just the tragedy of the GC and TC boys' deaths but the tragedy of interethnic conflict in general, conflict that occurs whenever the precepts and agendas of nationalism are believed and acted on.

But on another more profound level, the TC boy's supreme expression of humanity toward his ethnic enemies, followed by his untimely death from Greek fire a few days later, stands as a spiritual landmark of the victory of human dignity and care in the face of danger and indifference. It signifies the victory of neighborliness in the face of rivalry; of interethnic friendship in the face of interethnic animosity; and of love in the face of hate. This is the victory that nationalism has never been capable of offering to the people of Cyprus, or for that matter to those of any other ethnically mixed society. The victory of humanity over the spirit of nationalist rivalry in the action of the TC boy was revealed twenty-nine years after its occurrence in that tear-filled embrace between his mother and the mother of the GC boy who also perished in 1974. The meeting of the two mothers resulting from the instating of free movement in April 2003 is perhaps the most profound metaphor of hope for Cyprus—a hope that was planted with the death of the GC and TC boys and that outlived the decades of nationalist conflict and interethnic animosity through that defining moment of their mothers' embrace.

During the decades of separation initiated by the violence of the 1960s and 1970s, eventually culminating in full geographical ethnic segregation, each side related to the other through its own nationalist stereotypes of the all-good "us" versus the all-bad "them" that were generalized and fixated in the public culture of each community. This marked the general process and content of interethnic communication within the public realm, in spite of the existence of particular positive contacts between GCs and TCs in the private spheres of society. Public, intergroup communication between the two sides occurred, by and large, through the mediation of absolutely adversarial nationalist stereotypes. Verbal as well as nonverbal communication directed at one's community and/or at the other community was filtered and conditioned by these stereotypes, as they had taken over the realm of public culture and conditioned the political criteria of legitimacy. The very violence that militant, ethnocentric nationalism had helped induce had in turn facilitated the crystallization of these self-justifying stereotypes of "us" versus "them."

In general, under conditions where the communicative process occurs through the mediation of nationalist stereotypes while the rival sides are physically separated, interethnic communication deteriorates to a process that enhances alienation between the ethnicities and supports the thriving of propaganda (Ellul 1973). Or, as we suggested earlier, it instates a process of institutionalized noncommunication. Since the establishment of the Republic of Cyprus in 1960, two self-alienated processes of intraethnic monologues had prevailed, under which each side, while assuming that it was communicating with the other, was in fact communicating with its own projected stereotype of the other side. In turn, as each side spoke to the projected stereotype that it created, that stereotype reflected back to the community its own assumptions, perceptions, and assumed legitimacy. Each side was thus captive to an alienating, circular process of esoteric communication, which amounted to reducing the fundamental meaning and content of public political culture to a grand tautology.

Under these conditions, neither assumptions, perceptions, nor the meaning of facts could be subjected to a reality check, as each side, having no direct experience and knowledge of the other, was completely severed from the reality of the other side. The phenomenon reflected very accurately David Bohm's analysis of the breakdown of genuine dialogue. As he explained, dialogue is barred whenever in the human mind the presentation of the other and of reality is replaced and eclipsed by the mental *re-presentation* of the other and of reality (Bohm 2000).

By contrast, as attested in advance by participants in the original, bicommunal, citizen peace movement, direct interpersonal contact and communication between members of the two communities created conditions allowing old nationalist stereotypes to be implicitly questioned and new relationships, transcending the prejudicial confines of the adversarial stereotypes, to be built. Under conditions of relative calm, a by-product of the direct contacts between the two Cypriot communities that commenced in April 2003 was a first meltdown of the old nationalist stereotypes that had dominated public culture. A general process of intercommunal refamiliarization commenced as GCs and TCs found themselves interacting in the same physical and social spaces, ranging from private homes, restaurants, shops, mountains, and beaches to cooperating in NGOs and at an increasing number of bicommunal public events. Encounters with concrete persons from the other side gradually revealed that members of the other ethnic community were considerably different from the traditional nationalist enemy image through which they were collectively perceived. The image of the all-bad "them" that had saturated the respective public culture of each ethnic community for so long contrasted increasingly with the face-to-face experience of the other as ordinary human beings—human beings with basic concerns and hopes for the future much like those of one's own community.

Direct experience and knowledge revealed to the GCs that not all Turks were ruthless barbarians, and to the TCs that not all Greeks were murderers—the dominant images inherited from the past. Even with the tragedies of the not-too-distant past still in memory, GCs and TCs alike, having moved beyond the specific facts and events that originally underpinned the nationalist stereotypes, discovered that people from the other side could also be pleasant, kind, hospitable, respectful, and genuinely concerned. Employing Bohm's terminology again, direct contact started to restore in the perceptions of each community the *presentation* of "the other" over and above the old and skewed mental *re-presentation* of "the other," thus rendering genuine, interethnic citizen dialogue a historical possibility (2000).

Though limited within a specific time frame, the direct interactions across the ethnic divide gave rise to innumerable experiences akin to those reflected in the work of Papadakis (2005), in which he vividly documents his long journey from the esotericsm of nationalist socialization to the stark, experiential realization that the "other side," while having its own story, also has a human face. Even against the backdrop of painful memories, in encountering each other under conditions of calm and hope, the two communities, at least in the intensity of this unique historical moment, came face-to-face with an undeniable fact: Despite the many ills separating Greeks from Turks, and beyond the stereotypical characterization of "the other" as merely the barbarian and the villain, the enemy also has a basic humanity that awaits discovery.

Overall, the spirit of peace that permeated the unhindered mixing and daily interactions between GCs and TCs after April 23, 2003, constituted a fundamental first violation, in the public realm, of the belligerent spirit of ethnocentric nationalism. By word, by deed, and by sentiment, it marked the first islandwide, grassroots, verbal, and nonverbal declaration by GC and TC citizens alike that they were historically ready to break from the conflict-prone, monoethnic nationalism of the past. It signified the expressed preparedness of GCs and TCs to trade their war-torn history for a new arrangement of shared and balanced governance, for an open, multiethnic civil society, and for a secure and prosperous future within the framework of the EU.

It seemed that the decades spent apart had given the GCs and the TCs a small measure of mental space to reconsider, reflect, and make fundamental decisions about their relationship to the other community and the future. The tangible promise embodied in the vision of a united and prosperous European Cyprus retroactively activated this inner mental space while expanding it enormously. It was clear that each community had covered some distance on the road from interethnic nationalist rivalry to interethnic coexistence and, even further, to interethnic cooperative symbiosis. In part, the EU process, the exemplary actions of the citizen peace movement, and the general rapprochement between Greece and Turkey induced and stimulated this development. But much of the new intercommunal spirit was also reinforced by an intrapersonal and intracommunal dialogue on what had occurred in the past and the type of spirit and posture that should prevail for an alternative and hopeful future. Given these facts, the historical challenge that emerged from the positive behavior and attitude exhibited by the two communities through the new opportunities for free contact was whether their political leaders would follow suit. The question was whether they would build on the good will expressed by their respective communities and start working decisively toward a comprehensive negotiated settlement.

In any event, the political phenomena and events that preceded and converged with the direct contact and free mixing of the TC and GC communities marked a historical highlight in the evolution of the Cyprus problem. The changes reflected in this highlight may be understood from the two-pronged perspective of, first, assessing how far each community had managed to disengage from the original nationalist agenda in which the Cyprus problem was rooted and, second, ascertaining to what extent each side had moved toward a symbiotic and conciliatory political culture conducive to a formal resolution. By the time free movement came into play, more TCs than GCs had adopted conciliatory politics in support of a loose federation. However, while all GCs disengaged from their original nationalist agenda of *enosis* (union with Greece), not all TCs abandoned *taksim* (ethnic partition). This fact differentiated the parameters of the intracommunal political debate within the TC community from the one that was taking place within the GC community.

Having relinquished the demand for *enosis* to the relics of history, the GCs were now struggling with the question of whether the solution to the Cyprus problem should be founded on a stronger or a weaker form of federal integration in reuniting the Island. Within the TC community, public opinion generally favored a loose federation, while the core of the political establishment wielding power preserved and maintained the original TC nationalist demand for *taksim*. Within the overall pattern of the Cyprus problem, this fact rendered the intracommunal tension within the TC community far more severe and intense than the one emanating from its counterpart debate within the GC community.

Hence, following the collapse of the Annan-based Hague talks and the widespread spirit of rapprochement permeating the direct contact of the two communities, tension and antagonism between prosolution advocates and the antisolution secessionists within the TC community mounted to unprecedented heights. This tension placated a number of TCs whose jobs depended directly on the TRNC administration, while it frustrated many others, particularly those identifying with the opposition parties. Simultaneously, those in power, namely those with a vested interest in ethnic separation and secession, resorted to power posturing and tacit intimidation tactics.

For both Denktash and the TRNC administration, this phenomenon was a historical novelty. In view of the historical prioritization of TC physical security, the regime in northern Cyprus had been accustomed to governing over a relatively passive and submissive TC community. This was no longer the case. Under the new precipitating sociopolitical conditions, it was anticipated that the intracommunal antagonism between the antisolution and the prosolution TCs would be played out at the political level, reaching its climax at the December 2003 TC elections—the first elections after the failure of the Annan-based negotiations and following the broad grassroots, interethnic, citizen rapprochement. The emerging struggle within the TC community was one between the traditional, nationalist old-guard with its top-down, statist model of governance, and the newly founded forces of TC civil society, with their increasingly European vision of democracy and governance.

Under these conditions, the domestic nexus of the Cyprus conflict underwent a subtle shift. The emergent constituencies among GCs and TCs favoring the UN-based settlement and interethnic reconciliation were gradually posing a challenge to those in their respective communities who persisted in the old mode of adversarial, ethnocentric nationalism. This fact slowly started to blur the familiar, clear-cut interethnic polarization as this polarization was starting to be traversed by a rising propeace community comprising both GCs and TCs. Such a shift was indicative of historical movement away from the hitherto entrenched structure of the interethnic conflict, to commencing a substantive process of conflict transformation.

POSITIVE AMBIGUITIES AND UNILATERAL GESTURES BY THE GREEK CYPRIOT AND TURKISH CYPRIOT ADMINISTRATIONS

With the failure of UN-led talks in the background and the pending EU integration of the Island under the flag of the GC-controlled Republic of Cyprus, the partial removal of restrictions to free movement created certain unprecedented, sociopolitical conditions that drove a wedge into the hitherto structure of the Cyprus problem. The fact that the mass remixing of TCs and GCs has not only been free from major regressive incidents but also created a general climate conducive to peace provided the strongest tangible demonstration that the two communities had encountered each other in a spirit of readiness for a settlement and peaceful coexistence under a new polity. The phenomenon revealed that, despite numerous reservations, the communities were prepared to move forward. Combined with the reality that the TRNC administration was highly anxious to present itself to the international community in a positive light following its rejection of the Annan Plan, the positive outcome of mass contact between the two Cypriot communities rendered the instated freedom of movement irreversible.

The array of TC demonstrations in favor of the Annan Plan and the exemplary behavior of respect and humanity expressed in the direct contacts between TCs and GCs essentially brought to the forefront of political developments the significant role of civil society as a vital catalyst of conflict transformation. From a historical point of view, of crucial importance was that the mobilization of civil society had occurred not only through monocommunal NGOs and citizen and professional associations but also, and for the first time, bicommunally on the basis of a spontaneous, increasingly popular vision of interethnic reconciliation and peace. Both directly and indirectly, this fact highlighted the historical justification and rising legitimacy of the bicommunal, citizen peace movement initiated in the early 1990s in the midst of severe criticism and even harassment by the respective centers of the traditional nationalist establishments.

Under the new conditions created by free movement, bicommunal meetings and activities were no longer restricted to the narrow confines of the buffer zone and the threatening scrutiny of the hard-line nationalists. The available social space for interethnic contact had expanded from one that was scarce, politically controversial, and ridden with the risk of stigmatization, to one that was ample, generally acknowledged as legitimate, and immediately accessible to all TCs and GCs islandwide. Those of us who had toiled for more than a decade to build bridges across the ethnic divide were overwhelmed by the fact that the possibilities and social space for continuing citizen peace building had widened beyond anyone's wildest dreams. As a prominent citizen peace builder noted,

> In Cyprus we are going through a process of condensing of history: so many events of tremendous importance packed in every day. The wall [of ethnic separation] is full of cracks. It is not down yet, the political solution is still not here, there is a lot of work to be done, stretching the peace building–community to the limits of human endurance, there are dangers ahead of us, but still we are drunk with the wine of victory, celebrating in unheard of circumstances. There are so many new bridges being built every hour, every day, that it is impossible to break them down; in my opinion the people have taken over and the process is now irreversible. . . . All the bridges we built all these years are being made wider and more people are walking on them. (N. Anastasiou 2003a)

Indeed, under the cloud of perpetual political controversy, the silent but persistent work of the small, bicommunal, peace-building community had provided the leaven for what had transpired through the now open and unimpeded direct contacts between the GCs and TCs. The citizen peace builders had provided the example, the language, the culture, the approach, the vision, and the challenge for peace. To a large measure, the broader community on each side had followed suit. Spontaneous crossing to the other side and the freedom to meet with members of the other community anywhere on the Island had both strengthened and added legitimacy to the work of the citizen peace-building movement. In turn, it optimized possibilities for expanded, bicommunal interactions, political as well as social. Strongly endorsed by the EU as being aligned with its own political values and expectations, the political culture initiated by the small, persevering, citizen peace movement was now compounded by an explosion of rapprochement phenomena.

Although for years many had fought and condemned the efforts of the original peace-building movement, while others dismissed it as marginal and irrelevant, the general rapprochement following the lifting of restrictions on movement on April 23, 2003, came as a surprising affirmation of the significance of the work done during the previous years. One of the greatest vindications of the long and arduous work of the citizen peace-builders came from Denis Chubais, first secretary of the EU Delegation in Cyprus, as recorded by the *Financial Mirror*:

> Referring to the positive attitudes of Cypriots towards each other since being allowed to mix together, Chubais paid tribute to those who have been active in the bicommunal arena over the years. "It is not by chance. You cannot put the soiled laundry of history into the washing machine of time and 30 years later everything is perfectly bright," he said. "I think that all the bicommunal actions, all the people who were trying to build bridges, have led to this result and I would like to congratulate whoever took part." (*Financial Mirror* 2003)

Ironically, the Denktash and Papadopoulos administrations that were currently in power were traditionally known to have led those nationalist factions and to have represented that part of public opinion in the respective communities that had been most resistant to bicommunal contacts and rapprochement. The exception in the Papadopoulos administration was the Communist Progressive Workers Party (AKEL), in that while it accepted rapprochement, it nevertheless restricted its efforts to contacts merely with the TC Left. Political thinking in the Denktash tradition rejected interethnic citizen contacts because they allegedly enhanced conditions that undermined the TC demand for state recognition, which was always set forth as a prerequisite for interethnic relations. According to the Denktash line, citizens should be forbidden free contact until the GCs officially recognize the TRNC and accept the latter on the basis of equal sovereignty. Political thinking in the Papadopoulos tradition likewise rejected interethnic citizen contacts because they allegedly reinforced the conditions for the recognition of the breakaway TC state of the TRNC. According to the Papadopoulos line, citizens from the two sides should not be allowed to come in contact freely until the TRNC forgoes its demand for recognized secession, Turkey withdraws its military from Cyprus, and the territorial integrity and sovereignty of the Republic of Cyprus are restored. In their unique manner, these ethnocentric, nationalist approaches to statehood, which in turn propagated the subjugation of civil society to state power, for years have kept citizen rapprochement and any kind of citizen-initiated peace building blocked and captive to the intractable political structure of the conflict.

However, under the circumstances that led to the 2003 decision to allow free movement across ethnic lines, and in light of the events that transpired from the decision, it became quite clear that opposing rapprochement between the two communities would no longer carry political expediency or legitimacy, especially in light of EU democracy.

With direct contact and access to each other's zone, TCs and GCs became party to a proliferation of rapprochement activities and events such as the Island had not seen for decades. The bicommunal movement that pioneered interethnic dialogue, contact, and peace-enhancing initiatives no longer needed to work in obscurity under the accusing and threatening eye of nationalists. Nor did participation in bicommunal activities need to be restricted to the most committed and risk-taking TC and GC citizens. Peace-building rapprochement was now open to all citizens, under conditions that had considerably reduced the danger of ostracization, marginalization, threats, and accusations of treason.

Innumerable organized and spontaneous rapprochement events and actions flourished during the period following the instating of free movement. Commenting on just the bicommunal activities assisted by the UN Force in Cyprus (UNFICYP), the UN secretary-general reported that soon after direct, intercommunal contacts, UNFICYP facilitated forty-nine bicommunal events at the former Ledra Palace Hotel. By November 2003, the secretary-general reported that UNFICYP had facilitated 128 bicommunal events, bringing together eleven thousand TCs and GCs (United Nations 2003c). In May 2004, he reported the facilitation of 138 bicommunal events, while noting 3.7 million crossings by GCs to the north and TCs to the south (United Nations 2004d).

To these events, one ought to add a huge array of more permanent bicommunal activities, ranging from GCs and TCs appearing on each other's mass media and joint TC-GC TV-panel discussions and public lectures, to ongoing contacts between TC and GC political parties, municipal authorities, journalists, academics, labor unions, teachers' associations, chambers of commerce, and others. Through all these events, TCs and GCs became spontaneously engaged in an unprecedented and ongoing public dialogue on vital issues, such as the shape of the political settlement-to-be, the obstacles ahead needing attention, the relevance of the EU to the future of a new Cyprus, and hundreds of other topics of mutual interest and concern. Numerous party leaders from the two sides even resorted to spontaneous rapprochement, as many of them began to invite each other to their homes for informal dialogue and social interaction. Bicommunal choirs and dance groups already in place from previous years started to perform all over Cyprus, while new groups of artists launched their own rapprochement initiatives. Regular narratives of human suffering from the past, especially of innocent civilians, as well as of stories of interethnic humanity and kindness, began appearing in the press. Only this time, each account cited and presented GC and TC cases side by side, in the very same articles. Citizens of all ages, but especially the youth, started to visit places of interest and events of the neighboring community (Montville 1993).

One of the most extraordinary events that followed the opening of the checkpoints was an UNFICYP-sponsored, bicommunal blood donation event. "A blood sample collection drive to identify a compatible bone marrow donor for a five-year-old Turkish Cypriot girl with leukemia was the largest bicommunal event, with 13,400 donors turning up from both sides" (United Nations 2003b). It is profoundly interesting that in this mutual gesture of humanity, the nationalist concept of blood was shattered. Nationalism has always propagated that identity ought not to be watered down by the mixing of blood across ethnic lines.

As a sequel to a previous drive, this blood sample collection drive blossomed into a huge humanitarian rapprochement event, rallying not only the GC and TC communities but also Greece and Turkey. The giving of blood under the UNFICYP project marked yet another public affirmation by GCs and TCs that humanitarian actions need not be confined to one's own ethnic group, but may extend in magnanimity and conciliation to the other ethnic community. The event disclosed a symbolic as well as a substantive shift away from the nationalist association of blood with ethnic purity and identity and toward a free, humanistic view of blood as a means of sustenance that conjoins ethnic groups as it transcends ethnic boundaries.

The magnanimity and humanity expressed by the respective communities in their strong joint response to the call for blood samples stood in sharp contrast to the past. A number of years earlier, in a rare humanitarian gesture, a very sick TC boy was set to receive a blood transfusion from a GC hospital. Thereupon, the boy asked if the blood he was to receive was bad blood, since the hospital was Greek and not Turkish. Told by the boy's cousin, who had become involved in the bicommunal peace movement, the story reflected the degree to which a conflict-ridden environment impacts children's view of the world. Clearly, the boy's perception that Greek blood is bad cannot be explained as merely the result of naïveté because of his youth. Rather, it drew on the subtle internalization of ethnocentric meanings that an adversarial nationalist culture had inculcated into his mind through the natural process of socialization. The free giving of blood by GCs and TCs at the 2003 UNFICYP event had certainly annulled the nationalist perspective that the boy had learned from his adult community.

The spirit exhibited by TCs and GCs in the bicommunal blood donation demonstrated that when blood is given as a peace offering, freedom is immensely enhanced; blood need not become the price of freedom and the sacrifice of human life need not be the payment for liberty. In this joint act of giving, interethnic humanity was restored and liberated, demonstrating as a lie the nationalist maxim that "there is no freedom without blood." In effect, it brought into sharp relief the existential truth that, far from freedom requiring human life, as nationalism would have it, it is human life that requires freedom.

These and many other acts demonstrated that refamiliarization between the GC and TC communities was becoming an integral part of the overall sociopolitical process and a vital aspect of conflict transformation. It added a new dimension to the continuing Cyprus problem, signaling the new reality of Cyprus.

The positive results emanating from the free movement of GCs and TCs, in conjunction with the widely recognized prospect of a common future within the EU, placed the two administrations in a very precarious situation. Each found itself directly confronted with the reality that it had traditionally criticized and vehemently resisted—namely, a growing and widening interethnic rapprochement between GCs and TCs. Moreover, the two administrations were inadvertently confronted with positive citizen rapprochement taking place quite independently from, and even in defiance of, the political preconditions the current leaders of the respective communities had traditionally demanded. In effect, they were compelled to come to terms with the fact that a vast majority of the population of the Island was spontaneously following the footsteps of the original bicommunal citizen peace-movement, which the nationalist-oriented parties currently in power had always fought. On both sides, the nationalists seated at the core of political power were forced to observe that citizens in general had joined the rapprochement process, and that they had done so irrespective of their individual stances on what final shape the formal solution should take. Before the eyes of the two administrations, the culture and work of the formerly dissident citizen peace movement was gradually vindicated through both the positive contacts by the broader population and the commendations of the EU.

The ushering in of the Annan Plan, with its popular support by the TCs, its formal, albeit reluctant, acceptance by the GC government, the watchful eye of the EU, and the initial conciliatory attitudes exhibited by the two communities, created a framework from which the respective administrations could not escape without enormous political cost. Consequently, contrary to their traditional political posture, they too felt compelled to resort to positive gestures of good will, for such a policy decision constituted the minimum requirement for remaining aligned with the rising, popular trend of peaceful rapprochement and with the expressed expectations of the EU and the UN.

In the midst of innumerable political ambiguities and inconsistencies resulting from the emergent clash between the past and the prospective future, what transpired was extraordinary and unprecedented in the history of the Cyprus problem. The two administrations quite independently from each other embarked on an array of good will policy decisions that added yet another dimension to the progression of events toward rapprochement.

With the lifting of restrictions to free movement by the Turkish-backed TC administration, the GC side took measures to facilitate the transportation of the TCs visiting the south by providing free buses and administrative services. The TC authorities took further steps by opening more crossings along the buffer zone, as the existing checkpoint crossings could not cope with the flood of people, particularly GCs, wanting to visit the other side. GCs were permitted to drive their own cars to the north provided they purchased temporary insurance from the TC authorities. The GC administration soon decided to allow TCs to drive their cars to the south by finding ways of formally bypassing the perennial GC official position, which viewed TCs as driving illegally imported cars without a legitimate driver's license. The TC administration took measures to reduce the red tape at the various crossings that initially created bottlenecks, congestion, and long delays for the GCs visiting the north. The GC side likewise improved its methods of service for the TCs visiting the south. Soon after the opening of the checkpoints, the TC authorities announced that the GCs could visit and stay in the north for three consecutive days instead of the single day originally allowed.

As members of the two communities started to move back and forth across the great divide, the respective authorities became increasingly conscious of the impressions of those visiting their former places of residence. In the context of EU expectations and challenges, the GC side, even before the lifting of restrictions on movement came into effect, had taken measures to restore certain sights of cultural and religious significance to the TCs. With thousands of GCs crossing to the north, the TC side likewise felt compelled to restore and improve certain places of importance to GCs. As a sign of respect to the returning GC visitors, local TC authorities cleaned up certain GC cemeteries that had been long abandoned to the elements of nature and time, while the GC government also announced that with the start of the next academic year, Turkish language courses would be offered as an option for GC students attending the public school system. And very significantly, the GC side made public its hitherto concealed list of missing TCs.

It is extraordinary that all of the above events took place while those in government on both sides were the parties most committed to a nationalist outlook and most intransigent with regard to negotiating a political settlement. The combined factors of EU political culture and institutions of peace and security, and a citizen-based, peace constituency gave rise to conditions of hope strong enough to compel even those who had staked their patriotic identity on hard-line, nationalist approaches to compromise their ethnocentric, partisan politics.

Nevertheless, it ought to be stressed that up to this point the political problem of Cyprus remained unresolved. While the authorities on each side each took numerous significant steps that enhanced the general progress of interethnic rapprochement, such unilateral initiatives were quite inadequate for achieving the formal resolution of the political problem. For the latter, nothing less than full bilateral engagement in direct negotiations would suffice. Even as the respective administrations were compelled to adopt policies of citizen rapprochement, they were simultaneously criticized by members of their respective communities for indecisiveness in negotiating a final settlement. TC parties of the opposition and an emerging broad spectrum of citizen organizations launched ongoing and mounting criticisms of Denktash's refusal to negotiate on the Annan Plan. On the GC side, political leaders and citizens criticized Papadopoulos for numbness and reservation in clearly and decisively appealing to the UN for the reopening of the Annan-based negotiation.

However, what was particularly stunning regarding the free interaction among TCs and GCs was the extension of many of the consequences of peaceful rapprochement beyond the traditional, official political boundaries. While in theory the official positions of each side did not change, in reality the formerly clearly drawn lines of political conflict gradually blurred.

As the TCs began to cross over to the GC side, and knowing that the entry of the Republic of Cyprus into the EU was imminent, they started applying by the hundreds to the GC authorities for official Republic of Cyprus identity cards and subsequently for passports. Acknowledging the ambivalence and bleakness surrounding the future of the TRNC after Denktash's blatant rejection of the Annan Plan, the TCs resorted to this action to secure EU citizenship. This TC move constituted a fundamental violation of the traditional position of the TRNC and the Denktash administration, which maintained that the Republic of Cyprus did not represent in any way the TC community, and that the TRNC would not recognize the Republic of Cyprus as long as the GC government did not recognize the TRNC. As TCs sought to obtain Republic of Cyprus identity cards and passports, the TRNC administration was faced with realities it had no way of determining or containing within the framework of its traditional policy on the Cyprus problem.

Given these facts, the critical question facing the TRNC was what status to accord TCs obtaining passports from the GC-led Republic. Were they to be viewed as citizens of the Republic of Cyprus and also of the TRNC? As holders of passports issued by a state that the TRNC did not recognize, were these TCs to be considered illegitimate citizens? Were they to be considered traitors? Ought the TRNC take legal action against them? All these issues, and many others contingent on them, remained fundamentally unanswered, as they blurred the familiar political lines.

The situation for the GC authorities was no different. Free movement and spontaneous interaction between the two communities created new issues challenging the traditional formal politics of the GC side as well. As GCs flooded to northern Cyprus, they were required by the TC authorities to show their passports at the crossing points. As they crossed over in their cars, GCs were also required to buy insurance that would be valid on the TC side in accordance with the laws of the TRNC regime. How, then, should the GC government regard its citizens' compliance with the conditions set forth by the TRNC for entering the north? Did this compliance imply recognition of the TC breakaway state? Were the GCs visiting the north in violation of the official policy of the GC government? Should the GC government prohibit GCs from visiting the north under these conditions, after it had spent decades accusing Turkey and the Denktash administration of obstructing GC access to the north? The problem became even more complicated for the GC government when the TC administration allowed GCs to visit the north for three consecutive days, with overnight stays. Should the GC government allow its citizens visiting the north to briefly reside in GC hotels and property that had been forcefully taken by the Turkish army. Some hard-liners actually argued that the GC government should prosecute GCs staying overnight in the north on the grounds that they were party to the use of stolen property.

Furthermore, the GC government was faced with the peculiar and unprecedented situation of seeing thousands of GCs spend money in the north, when the official position had always been to forbid any trade with the TC side on the grounds that such action would reinforce and endorse the illegal occupying regime of Denktash and Turkey. Within the first two weeks after the restrictions to free movement were relaxed, the GC visitors to the north had spent about 2.5 million Cyprus pounds (approximately $5 million) there—a considerable amount given the size of the population. Did this spending contravene the GC trade embargo on the TRNC, the official policy that the GC side pursued so vehemently since 1974? Had the economic embargo, in effect, been lifted on domestic trade in tourism between the two communities, while remaining in place for foreign trade in general? Do all these developments and actions inadvertently facilitate the official TC demand for recognition of the TRNC as a separate state entity? These and many affiliate questions remained suspended in the air. Just like the TC leadership, the GC leadership had to tolerate a subtle but critical fading of the all-too-familiar conflict lines and positions.

While stunning, the free mixing of the Cypriot communities wedged new political realities into the heart of the Cyprus conflict. Operating as indirect catalysts, they injected into the fossilized, conflict system political elements that were gravitating toward the deconstruction of the traditional conflict pattern of the Cyprus problem. They introduced positive ambiguities that started to expose as unsustainable the formal status quo and each government's respective, decades-long approach, conditioned and institutionalized by the nature of the Cyprus conflict. The new ambiguities decisively pointed to the fact that the TC and GC political leaders alike were gradually pulled into a state of limbo, suspended between the blurring of their traditional political positions and the absence of a final political settlement. While never recognizing the Republic of Cyprus in principle, the TRNC could not completely evade it in practice as an entity carrying international legitimacy. And, while never recognizing the TRNC as an independent state in principle, the Republic of Cyprus could not stall in practice the indirect acknowledgment of the existence of a northern administration.

Free contact between the TC and the GC communities thus had the unintended consequence of undermining fundamental aspects of the traditional positions of the two sides. This in turn made clear that while there was no way of reverting to the old sharp demarcation of the conflict lines, there was no way forward other than negotiating a final political settlement. Moreover, external factors were also undermining the status quo. The obligations emanating directly from the EU integration process had their own complementary impact on the course of events.

THE GREEK CYPRIOT GOVERNMENT WITHIN THE EU FRAMEWORK: PRIVILEGES AND OBLIGATIONS

In the recent history of the Cyprus problem, the side that had moved closest to the EU—the GC side—inevitably appeared privileged politically, socially, and economically. However, having established a structural relationship with the EU through the process of harmonization and formal accession, the GC side was also burdened with the greater obligation of exhibiting conciliatory and peace-enhancing policies and attitudes toward its TC counterpart.

Despite its hard-line, nationalist legacy, the Papadopoulos government had no choice in this. From the moment it assumed power under the claim of representing the legitimate Republic of Cyprus, the entity acceding to the EU, the Papadopoulos government was obliged by EU law and political culture to treat TCs on equal terms with GCs. Even though the political problem remained unresolved, and even though all concerned recognized that the original formal structure of the Republic of Cyprus did not represent the structure of the settlement-to-be, the GC-controlled government of the republic was obliged to behave and legislate in accordance with the letter and spirit of EU polity.

Through its elaborate process of enlargement, the development of the EU has been marked by the broadening and deepening of its institutionalized system of interethnic, transnational, and interstate symbiosis and cooperation in the interest of peace and security. This same process was manifested in the EU's relationship with Cyprus as the EU announced specific measures designed to promote economic development in northern Cyprus for the betterment of the TC community. In early June 2003, the European Commission announced the release of a financial aid package of € 12 million for the promotion of trade between northern Cyprus and the EU and for actions to bring the TCs and the GCs not only closer to each other but also closer to the EU. The program of economic assistance would be implemented in cooperation with the UN, with the major part of the package going to the building of infrastructure as well as to studies on preparing the TC part of the Island for EU membership after the reunification of north and south. In the event of a settlement, an additional € 206 million for the period of 2004–6 was promised to the TC side. This combination of pre- and postsettlement aid constituted an integral element of the EU's peace-enhancing incentives and strategy on Cyprus. Worthy of note here is the fact that the EU's presettlement aid package to the TCs directly contravened the economic embargo that the GC side had successfully propagated since 1974. Banking on the internationally recognized status of the Republic of Cyprus, the official policy of the GC government had been to maintain a persistent economic blockade of the north until Turkey withdrew its troops from Cyprus.

The EU impact on the GC-led Republic of Cyprus did not end there. Prior to the full accession of Cyprus to the EU and pending a settlement of the Cyprus problem, the European Commission proposed that, with the consent of the GC government, the TC Chamber of Commerce (not the TRNC) be given the authority to issue certificates for the movement of products. The significance of this proposal must be considered, however, against the backdrop of the 1994 ruling of the European Court of Justice that, as an unrecognized state entity, the TRNC could not issue certificates of origin for its exported products and thus could not benefit from the Association Agreement between the EU and the Republic of Cyprus. The EU's 2003 proposal went beyond strictly legal considerations by adding a complementary rapprochement element to its approach to TC trade. By proposing to authorize the TC Chamber of Commerce to issue certificates for products under the umbrella of the Republic of Cyprus, the EU now sought to uphold its legal standards regarding trade while simultaneously pursuing a strategy of conciliatory politics in relation to the TCs. The EU–Cyprus Association Council thus complemented the 1994 protocol concerning the certification of products by adding a dimension of interethnic administrative cooperation that would grant the TC part of the Island preferential access to the EU market.

Hence, contrary to the traditional GC policy, the Papadopoulos government was compelled to follow the EU lead and act upon recommendations in line with EU political values. The GC government spokesman thus announced that "the government has authorized the Turkish Cypriot Chamber of Commerce to issue certificates of origin. Exports of goods will be made with the further certification by the government to ensure the EU specifications are met and then products will be exported through the legal ports of the Republic" (*Financial Mirror* 2003).

In its impact on Cyprus, the EU began to dissociate TC and GC economic interests from their old, politically competing, monoethnic nationalisms and to reconstitute them in relation to peace and interethnic symbiosis. Contrary to the traditional nationalist linkage between economic interest and ethnocentric politics, the EU elevated and transposed economic well-being to a function of interethnic peace and security. Within its framework, the respective economic interest of each Cypriot ethnic communities was to be transformed from one based on ethnic rivalry to one based on peace-engendering cooperation. In all these ways, both the Denktash and the Papadopoulos administrations found themselves in a political straitjacket—a straitjacket of European making, specifically designed to curb nationalist politics and their related adversarial political cultures and economies.

These developments marked a decisive deviation from the TC secessionist nationalism as well as from the GC assimilative, majoritarian nationalism. The EU-influenced outcomes contradicted the long-standing Denktash prerequisite—demand for recognition of the TRNC—as well as the perennial GC position that any conciliatory contact with the north, particularly through formal institutions, entailed an implied recognition of the TRNC. The EU process of accession had definitively communicated to the hard-line Denktash administration and the nationalists within the Turkish establishment that state recognition through forced secession was not tenable in the world of the EU, and that legitimacy for the TC administration could result only as a consequence of a negotiated political settlement within the framework of the UN proposal.

The EU process likewise compelled the GC government to recognize that while heading the legitimate Republic of Cyprus, it could no longer act as though the state was an instrument of exclusive GC ethnic interest. By acknowledging the Republic of Cyprus as the Island's legitimate state in accordance with international law, the EU had certainly reinforced the status of the GC-controlled state—but EU policy and strategy toward the GC government also delegitimized the nationalist politics that had long driven the governance of the republic, particularly the politics typical of Papadopoulos's Democratic Party (DIKO). The impact of the EU on GC politics had thus initiated a process of both deconstructing and dissociating nationalism from the functions of the state. It marked the commencement of a historical process that increasingly challenged the GC-run state to transcend its traditional, ethnocentric mode of governance, as this was a fundamental prerequisite for rendering possible the establishment of an alternative system of cooperative, interethnic, and multiethnic governance.

5

Cyprus at the Crossroads

Nationalism of the Past Versus

Europeanization of the Future

RENEWED NATIONALIST TEMPTATIONS:
NEW WINE INTO OLD WINESKIN

Even as numerous steps toward rapprochement were being taken at this critical historical moment, with the EU acting as catalyst in creating and sustaining momentum, the hardcore nationalist traditions represented by the ruling administrations of the TC and GC communities remained a potent factor. Under the circumstances, to expect these governments to abandon nationalism in favor of reconciliation and a political settlement by either side would have been unrealistic. Though tempered by the EU process and modernizing social change in general, the nationalist mindset and behavior—albeit desperate and bewildered—persisted in the Denktash and Papadopoulos administrations.

In many respects the significant peace-enhancing changes taking place appeared provocative and even disturbing to the nationalists in the two administrations because they disrupted the familiar conflict lines and rules of the belligerent, ethnocentric game they had become so accustomed to. The broad and unimpeded citizen rapprochement evident in the spontaneous mixing of the two communities, the 50 percent–plus popular vote among the TCs favoring reunification and the entry of a united Cyprus into the EU, and the continuing rapprochement between Greece and Turkey—all these trends appeared highly problematic to those still confined to the nationalist mentality. Under the circumstance, to the measure that the two Cypriot administrations continued to operate from a nationalist mindset, each faced the temptation of attempting to integrate the new historical developments into the old adversarial patterns.

On the GC side, the Papadopoulos administration started to interpret phenomena such as the TC rush to the GC south for the purpose of securing passports not so much as a desperate and ardent desire by the TCs to attain EU citizenship, but as an entrenchment and even an endorsement of the legitimacy of the Republic of Cyprus. The same rationale was evident as the administration succumbed to EU recommendations to accept the formal processing of TC products through the TC Chamber of Commerce and subsequently through the republic's government for export to EU markets. Again, the Papadopoulos administration perceived this development not, as the EU intended it, primarily as a gesture of good will meant to facilitate efforts to reach a political settlement but as a political and legal validation of the status of the Republic of Cyprus.

The Papadopoulos administration presented the positive outcome of intercommunal contacts as proof that the two communities could coexist and that separation was merely the result of Denktash's and Ankara's secessionist policy. But because it refrained from voicing its position on the solution in light of the UN plan, the administration appeared to imply that the positive intercommunal contacts amounted to a first step toward reintegrating the TCs into the Republic of Cyprus—a move, it was thought, that would reinforce the republic's legitimacy and continuity. The fundamental, yet unexpressed, assumption underlying Papadopoulos's nationalism was that the TCs would be gradually absorbed into the GC-controlled republic, thus, pending certain peripheral adjustments, a de facto resolving of the Cyprus problem. The GC administration assumed that this process would in principle restore the republic while effectively dissolving the self-declared TRNC.

Rather than seizing the rapprochement process as the civil foundation for the diplomatic pursuit of a final political settlement, the Papadopoulos administration was regressing to a nationalist usurpation of the process, particularly the part initiated by its government. The repeated impression projected by the administration was not surprising, given the hard-line nationalist approach historically associated with Papadopoulos's DIKO party. The impression was that propagating the political and legal status of the Republic of Cyprus in partisan nationalist fashion was more central to its policy than resolving the Cyprus problem in accordance with the UN federal model. If negotiations were to be pursued, Papadopoulos's objective would be the restoration of the republic as close to its original unitary form as possible, and not the establishment of a new bicommunal, bizonal federation, as anticipated by all UN resolutions.

From Papadopoulos's perspective, the flourishing positive contact between GCs and TCs was not a basis of a new political order but grounds for absorbing the TCs back into the republic, which he nationalistically conceived as an exclusively Hellenic state. Reintroducing the old GC political notions of the 1960s and early 1970s, he presumed that the solution entailed the assimilation and diffusion of the TC community into a Hellenic GC society and state as a way of substantially liquidating the communal representation and hence political power of the ethnic minority. Here, political equality before the law would exist only between individual citizens and not between ethnic communities represented by their own internal constituent administrations.

In Papadopoulos's thinking, real negotiations should simply focus on minor modifications to the Republic of Cyprus—some internal security guarantees for the TCs and the creation of a certain number of TC positions with marginal power in government—in exchange for the withdrawal of all Turkish troops from the Island and the return of all GC refugees to the north. Such an approach would avoid completely establishing a new political system as a basis for biethnic governance, cooperation, and unification. Clearly, this plan was not only illusory from a historical and practical point of view but also antithetical to all of the UN resolutions on Cyprus and particularly to their embodiment in the Annan Plan.

The Denktash administration responded in a similarly ethnocentric manner by attempting to frame the rising and broadening civil rapprochement as a phenomenon supporting and reinforcing the secessionist agenda of traditional TC nationalism. Prior to lifting the restrictions to free movement, Denktash and his supporting nationalists had denounced and regularly obstructed contact between TC and GC citizens. In the positive climate that developed during the remixing of the two communities, they endorsed intercommunal contact. However, they presented interethnic rapprochement not as a secure foundation for the finalization of the UN-based negotiations, but as a phenomenon supporting the logic of secession.

According to Denktash and his nationalist constituency, the calm and incident-free citizen contacts were indeed a positive phenomenon, but one proving that Cyprus's residents were ready for the full normalization of "interstate" relations between the TRNC and the de facto GC state administering the south. The citizens of the two states, TC and Turkish nationalists noted, were now getting along fine. For all practical purposes, the Cyprus problem appeared solved. The only requirement left for final settlement was for the GC side to recognize the TRNC and formalize its relationship with it. From this vantage point, the solution to the Cyprus problem was more a matter of settling peripheral political and legal details than of engaging in serious negotiations for a comprehensive new polity for Cyprus.

The entrapment of the nationalist mind in the vicious cycles of its own tautologies is evident here. The perspective informing and shaping the above-mentioned strategy reflects the artificiality by which the ethnocentric narcissism of the nationalist mentality distorts peace-enhancing, interethnic relations. The approach of the Denktash administration amounted to not only an attempt to impose a nationalist framework on interethnic rapprochement (and thus denature the political intentions and goals of the citizens engaged in it), but also to again place the Cyprus problem outside the parameters of the UN and specifically of the Annan Plan. Soon after the failure of the Hague talks and the mixing of the two communities, the TC administration announced the establishment by the TRNC of a Claims Settlement Council to which GC refugees were invited to appeal for the purpose of formally settling their property claims. By unilaterally addressing the claims of individual GC plaintiffs, Denktash's goverment sought to draw GCs into a formal legal relationship to the TRNC, thus asserting and establishing recognition of TC state sovereignty.

The Denktash administration assumed that attempting to settle the property issue by dealing with individual GCs would resolve a major issue at the heart of the Cyprus problem without resorting to negotiations to establishing a new interethnic federal order of reunification. By default, the Denktash administration reasoned, this process would confer independence, legality, and recognition on the TRNC. Denktash's breakaway state vainly anticipated that success in such a strategy would also curb the European Court of Human Rights and render irrelevant the precedent set by its ruling in the Loizidou case. Persistent secessionist nationalism motivated the Denktash administration to evade the historical requirement for negotiating a comprehensive settlement of the Island's long-standing problem.

During this phase of the evolution of the Cyprus problem, the TC and GC administrations appeared to be competing in the political exploitation of the peace-enhancing, conciliatory interactions between the two communities, as each administration propagated unilaterally its same old nationalist agenda—that is to say, secession on the part of the Denktash administration and a return to a unitary state by the Papadopoulos administration. Both sides attempted the peculiar feat of incorporating the new conciliatory and fundamentally postnationalist rapprochement phenomena into the old adversarial nationalist frameworks—an effort to put, as the saying goes, new wine into the old wine skins.

The political inauthenticity of the monoethnic unilateralism of both administrations was revealed in their treatment of the powerfully emerging rapprochement process. One of Papadopoulos's ministers explained in a personal conversation to a close associate of mine that Papadopoulos—in noting that Denktash was trying to exploit the positive outcome of intercommunal contacts—had privately emphasized to his administration that the GC side ought to downplay the significance of the rapprochement process and even discourage it from occurring through direct citizen initiatives. If there was to be any rapprochement, Papadopoulos stressed, it should be exclusively a function of the GC-controlled Republic of Cyprus.

This position reflects the perennial alarm felt by nationalist leaders in the face of independent, civil society initiatives. They saw citizen rapprochement as an instrument of the state serving ethnocentric state ends—never as a conciliatory civil society process occurring independently from the state—a viewpoint demonstrating the antidemocratic nature of nationalist politics. As always, the presence of an autonomous, interethnic, peace-supporting, and peace-seeking civil society—a fundamental ingredient to any genuine democracy—was strongly distasteful and threatening to the nationalist mind.

Remarkably, the positions of both Denktash and Papadopoulos on the issue of rapprochement converged to an identical pattern. Each attempted to usurp the citizen rapprochement process by transposing it into an extension and legitimization of his particular state, while simultaneously skewing the independent initiatives of civil society. At the formal government level, each leader sought to appear publicly to support citizen rapprochement, but only as long as it was politically exploitable in the interest of ethnocentric state politics. At the same time, each denounced such exploitation when accused of it by the other. In either case, when challenged and threatened by authentic expressions of rapprochement by civil society, nationalist politics continued to undermine peace-enhancing phenomena that had burst out of the monoethnic nationalist frameworks and agendas.

The prospect of resuming negotiations based on the UN peace plan at the formal, diplomatic level produced the same pattern of reluctance and unilateralism evident in the responses of the two administrations to the broadening civilian rapprochement. One could argue that Papadopoulos's strategy of emphasizing and relying on the international legitimacy of the Republic of Cyprus did not differ from the one pursued by all the previous GC administrations. Yet, with regard to the final political objective, there was a distinctive difference between the Papadopoulos presidency and the previous ones of Glafcos Clerides and George Vassiliou. Papadopoulos's predecessors, while affirming the international recognition of the Republic of Cyprus as their starting point for negotiating a settlement, understood that the republic, as originally established, did not constitute the settlement's final structure. Papadopoulos, however, viewed the recognized republic not merely as the starting point for negotiations but also as the essential state structure that defined the final settlement—a position that fell outside the designated parameters of all the UN resolutions. It took President Clerides a term and a half of his double presidency to acknowledge that while the Republic of Cyprus constitutes the only recognized Cypriot state entity, it could never be construed as the structure of the solution of the Cyprus problem. Papadopoulos's approach was essentially a regression to the point at which Clerides began his presidency in 1993—a return to the old nationalist approach.

Papadopoulos's dealings with the Cyprus problem increasingly gave the impression that his exclusive and incessant emphasis on the legitimacy of the Republic of Cyprus was not merely tactical but substantive. It was therefore no surprise that, with the Annan Plan still on the negotiating table, he exhibited no attempt for months after the failure of the Hague talks to move the situation beyond the status quo. Despite some general and ephemeral verbal statements in favor of a settlement, his administration remained passive in the sphere of diplomacy, exhibiting few if any signs of an intention to reactivate negotiations within the framework of the Annan Plan. As a result, the Papadopoulos government tacitly communicated that it was resigned to waiting passively for Cyprus's full admission to the EU in May 2004.

Nationalists in Papadopoulos's circles, and those on the Greek side in general, were operating on the fundamentally misplaced judgment that if negotiations were delayed until after Cyprus joined the union, then the GC side would secure the formal status and perpetuity of the republic, thereby increasing its negotiating power. This judgment was based on the same unfounded assumption by which GC and Greek nationalists originally supported the accession of Cyprus to the EU—namely, that they could use the power of the EU as a partisan, ethnonational political instrument against the TC side and Turkey, now an EU candidate. This position reflected a gross misunderstanding of EU principles. It also revealed a nationalist approach to European law resulting in an ethnocentric, sterile legalism foreign to European political culture and values. The old adversarial nationalism preserved in the Papadopoulos political tradition continued to subvert and postpone a genuine understanding and appreciation of the EU as a conciliatory, democratizing, and peace-enhancing interethnic and transethnic polity.

The same delaying tactics reflected in Denktash's approach were in fact no different from his long-standing ones. His outright rejection of the Annan Plan, followed by his brief and superficial proposal of talking points for direct negotiations with Papadopoulos, were but a failed attempt to bypass the mediation of the UN and approach Cyprus as an interstate problem between the TRNC and GC administrations. However, the resulting diplomatic stalemate, to which Papadopoulos was also resigned, was not necessarily outside Denktash's aims and expectations. Papadopoulos's preference for delaying negotiations until after the full entry of Cyprus in the EU also worked for Denktash; if diplomatic inaction could drag on until Cyprus's full entry into the union in May 2004, he reasoned, the attempt to negotiate a comprehensive settlement for reunifying Cyprus would be more likely to fail, leaving partition and thereby secession, as the default result. Certainly, such an outcome would have created a heavy political toll for Turkey, as it would have jeopardized its EU aspirations. Denktash's strategy appealed solely to the anti-European forces in Turkey, not to its reformists, and this constituted his greatest political gamble and challenge.

To summarize, Denktash and Papadopoulos employed identical tactics in delaying any resumption of negotiations in order to sustain the political impasse beyond May 1, 2004, the date Cyprus was due to join the EU. The difference was that Denktash sought to delay the negotiations in the hope that the entry of a divided Cyprus into the union would reinforce partition and hence secession, while Papadopoulos did so in the hope it would reinforce and perpetuate the status of the Republic of Cyprus. Denktash's approach was one of misconceived political "cleverness," while Papadopoulos's was one of unfounded legalism. Both approaches proved historically regressive and politically barren, having deviated from the UN directives and expectations as well as from the essence of EU political culture.

While the international community considered Denktash's intransigence more severe than that of Papadopoulos, both sides persisted in their unilateral approaches to the Cyprus problem. At a time of converging, positive civil trends—with the UN plan still on the table, with full EU membership just around the corner, and with Greece and Turkey working toward positive rapprochement—Denktash and Papadopoulos were still on divergent paths.

CHANGING TRENDS IN THE TURKISH CYPRIOT COMMUNITY AND TURKEY: CHALLENGES TO DENKTASH'S AND PAPADOPOULOS'S NATIONALISMS

Shortly before the December 14, 2003, parliamentary elections in northern Cyprus, GC president Papadopoulos publicly stated that he would have rejected the Annan Plan had Denktash accepted it at the Hague. Strategically, the statement was not only unnecessary but also diplomatically damaging to the GC side, particularly after Denktash had received most of the blame for the failure of the Hague talks and after the Accession Treaty with the EU had been signed by the GCs. The statement, however, disclosed Papadopoulos's reluctance to accept a biethnic, federal solution, which he would have to negotiate if talks were to resume. In the midst of the party campaigns for the parliamentary elections, Denktash swiftly utilized Papadopoulos's statement to combat his TC prosolution critics, who saw Denktash and his supporting nationalists as the main obstacle to a settlement. Papadopoulos's statement did not empower the prosolution, pro-EU parties in TC northern Cyprus, but rather allowed the antisolution forces in the TC community to deflect the criticisms against them for rejecting the Annan Plan onto the GC side. Only Papadopoulos knew whether this outcome was intentional. What is certain, however, is that given his nationalist inclinations and opposition to the Annan Plan, Papadopoulos would have had far greater difficulty negotiating with the propeace TC moderates than with Denktash.

In a manner typical of nationalist rivals conditioned by protracted conflicts, Papadopoulos and Denktash, while being enemies, assisted each other in rationalizing their respective rejectionist approaches and in evading genuine pursuit of a settlement. Papadopoulos's statement, as well as Denktash's response to it, signified a reversion to the monoethnic and unitary concept of statehood. It brought to the foreground, yet again, the perennial incompatibility between the monoethnic polity of nationalist governance and the polyethnic polity of pluralistic, civil governance—an incompatibility that Papadopoulos and Denktash mutually sustained and perpetuated as a way of resisting any prospect for an interethnic, federal settlement.

The universally accepted common ground among all who have invested time and energy pursuing a historically viable peace for Cyprus—be they citizens, states, or international institutions—entailed three fundamental interrelated assumptions: that state legitimacy for the TCs could not be achieved outside a negotiated settlement with the GC side; that the constitutional structure of the GC-controlled republic did not represent the general structure of governance for the resolution of the conflict; and that a political settlement should be sought within the framework of a bizonal, bicommunal federation, as recommended by the UN resolutions and supported by the EU, the United States, and the international community in general.

The way the Papadopoulos administration handled the Cyprus issue following the failure of the Hague talks, including its approach to the intercommunal rapprochement process, suggested a full acceptance of the first of these assumptions but an implied rejection of the second and third. This rejection was evident from the administration's avoidance of a public commitment to federation as the basis for the solution of the Cyprus problem, as proposed by the UN. The Denktash administration's handling of the matter implied an acceptance of the second assumption but a rejection of the first and the third. Denktash continued to consider federation as an ethnonational anathema for TCs. The above positions constituted the net outcome of persisting nationalist approaches by the governments of the two Cypriot communities in spite of the growing positive civil and regional developments within the general EU framework and process. Papadopoulos soon faced psychological isolation in EU circles, even though his formal institutional participation in the EU process remained intact. Denktash, in contrast, operating outside the EU and UN framework, was coming under increasing criticism at home, from Turkey, and internationally for being the major obstacle to a Cyprus settlement.

The TC parliamentary elections of December 14, 2003, marked yet another unprecedented development in northern Cyprus. Against the backdrop of the massive TC peace rallies of a year earlier, the elections were perceived as an indirect referendum on the Annan Plan and thus on TC opinion regarding joining the EU within a reunited Cyprus. The

TABLE 5.1

TC PARLIAMENTARY ELECTION RESULTS, DECEMBER 2003

Party	Percentage of Vote	Seats
Republican Turkish Party (CTP), left wing	35.18	19
National Unity Party (UBP), right wing	32.93	18
Peace and Democracy Movement (BDH), left wing	13.14	6
Democrat Party (DP), right wing	12.93	7
Nationalist Peace Party (MBP)	3.23	0
Solution and EU Party (CAP), left wing	1.97	0
Cyprus Justice Party (KAP)	0.60	0

contest during the preelection campaigns was intense, clearly differentiating the political forces favoring a solution from the secessionist nationalist forces favoring perpetuation of the status quo. The outcome of these historic elections is set out in table 5.1 above.

The political forces favoring an immediate settlement and entry into the EU won a marginal victory over those opposed to the Annan Plan and the reunification of the Island. However, in the distribution of parliamentary seats, the blocs of both prosolution and antisolution parties secured twenty-five seats each, preventing any of the blocs from forming a government. Under the circumstances, the prosolution, pro-EU parties could not establish their own government nor relieve Denktash of his duties as negotiator. Even so, this was the first time the propeace, anti-Denktash votes exceeded the 50 percent mark, a result signaling a fundamental paradigm shift in the TC community.

Against the backdrop of the unique election results in northern Cyprus and continuing EU-propelled reforms in Turkey, the Europeans were signaling willingness to give Turkey a date for starting accession talks. The deliberations, based on the Copenhagen criteria by which the EU commences accession negotiations with candidate states, entailed a strict, formal, and objective process. In applying these criteria, the EU repeatedly emphasized to Turkey that unless Turkey helped resolve the Cyprus problem within the framework of the UN directives, its European aspirations would be in peril. Nevertheless, and prior to the Cyprus referendum, the EU maintained the possibility of granting Turkey a date to start accession talks even without a settlement of the Cyprus problem.

The EU's willingness to entertain this possibility may be interpreted as a fallback position in the eventuality that Turkey superseded Denktash's intransigence and the Papadopoulos administration continued to balk at negotiating a UN-based settlement. In such a case, Turkey would not bear exclusive, or perhaps even primary responsibility, and the EU would reserve the right to accord to each party its measure of responsibility for failing to settle the Cyprus problem. Further, if in the final analysis Turkey proved forthcoming in constructively supporting the UN process for a Cyprus settlement, the EU would then cease to insist on politically linking Turkey's accession to a solution of the Cyprus problem. Though never explicated at the time, this prospective approach by the EU appeared tacit in its varied responses to the unfolding political dynamics in anticipation of the integration of Cyprus into the EU.

The possible dissociation of Turkey's accession process from the solution of the Cyprus problem was in principle the same as the hitherto upheld dissociation of the Republic of Cyprus's accession process from the solution. In the latter case, the EU's message was that Turkey, as a non-member of the EU and an occupying force, had no right to hold Cyprus hostage and prevent it from proceeding toward European integration. In the former case, the EU implied that by the same logic, neither could the GC side hold Turkey hostage and politically obstruct its European aspirations, particularly if Turkey met the Copenhagen criteria and was judged not responsible for failing to solve the Cyprus problem. Under such circumstances, the Europeans were implying, the assessment of Turkey's qualification for accession would be conducted independently of Cyprus. Interestingly, following the TC parliamentary elections of December 2003, Turkey announced that it accepted the Annan Plan as the basic framework for the Cyprus negotiations and proposed some modifications.

By this time, the EU-induced reforms in Turkey were beginning to bear fruit. As a society whose identity was traditionally conceived and grounded in the power of its highly centralized state, Turkey was starting to take some significant steps toward opening up institutionally and politically. It was beginning to overcome its perennial fear that any relaxation of state power over Turkish society and its citizens would break up the country. The evolution of the Kurdish issue was a case in point. The enactment of laws granting further rights to the culturally and linguistically diverse ethnic communities within Turkish society, together with the Kurdish PKK's cessation of violence in early 2000, opened up new prospects. It demonstrated that it was possible to commence restructuring Turkey's system of governance by grounding it in democratic pluralism and evolving civil freedoms, rather than in the weighty monolith of the military-backed "deep state."

Although in the summer of 2004 a splinter faction of the PKK revoked the earlier declaration of a cease-fire, its power had become weakened and diffused enough for Prime Minister Recep Tayyip Erdogan to reinforce the reforming trends by publicly stating that a Turkish citizen could call himself a Kurd if he so wished. The implication was that it was fully legitimate for a citizen to be both a Turk *and* a Kurd. In June 2004, a Turkish appeals court ordered the release of four Kurdish former members of parliament who had been convicted ten years previously of belonging to an outlawed separatist group. Among those freed was Leyla Zana, whose campaign for Kurdish rights had made her internationally renowned. Though incomplete, such moves toward the formal acceptance of ethnic pluralism contrasted with the earlier nationalist stance of the Turkish state, in which Turkism was officially the sole identity of citizens at the expense of, and often in fierce rivalry to, other ethnic identity assertions in Turkish society. All of these changes were later confirmed by the European Commission's recommendation report on Turkey.

In this ongoing process of relaxing state power in relation to civil society, the National Security Council, the most powerful executive organ of the Turkish state dominated by the Turkish military, was demoted to a consultative body with a reduced representation of the military. As a response to one of the central demands of the EU, this gradual depoliticization of the Turkish military marked the formal beginning of one of the most radical transformations of the Turkish state since Atatürk.

This first-ever subjugation of the Turkish military to civilian control constituted one of the most significant reforms toward deepening democracy and strengthening civil society since the founding of the Republic of Turkey. By reason of traditional habit and historical momentum, the military's informal influence continued, but its power lost its legal and formal foundation. The subsequent removal of all military representatives from the boards of universities throughout Turkey is indicative of the new powers that civil political authorities have acquired as a result of these reforms. As the European Commission's report noted, "Civil-military relations are evolving towards European Standards" (Europa 2004).

For Cyprus, these changes meant that Denktash, who had perennially enjoyed the backing of the Turkish military establishment, could face eventual weakening and possibly even opposition from the civilian Turkish government. The latter could now question his approach without incurring the enormous political cost the governing parties of Turkey traditionally faced every time they attempted the slightest move forward on the Cyprus issue. In fact, for the first time in the history of the Cyprus problem, Denktash and his nationalist supporters appeared dissociated from Turkish national interest, as Turkey was slowly redefining its goals in terms of EU-related opportunities that had more to do with regional stability, integration, and peace than with adversarial, ethnocentric nationalism.

The gradual liberalization of the Turkish media, a key aspect of Europeanizing reforms, initiated a continuous stream of public dialogue on the Cyprus issue, in which the merits of a negotiated settlement for Cyprus were openly entertained in a historically unprecedented manner. Increasingly, the media told the Turkish public that Turkey's national interest and European aspirations could be better served in supporting a negotiated political settlement for Cyprus than in continuing to pursue the old policy of "no solution is the solution"—the policy that had traditionally bolstered Denktash's secessionist nationalism and intransigence. In this opening up of the media process, Denktash's public image gradually underwent fundamental deconstruction in Turkish public opinion. From a preeminent national figure symbolizing Turkish pride, heroic resistance, and unyielding national determination, he was demythologized into a fallible, self-serving political leader with historical responsibilities warranting public accountability.

In their work *Peace and Conflict Studies,* Barash and Webel (2002) noted that in general there is a correlation between the degree to which a country is internally democratic and that to which it is open and constructive in its foreign-policy decisions. The changes gradually taking place in Turkey reflected to a certain measure this principle. Though never consciously articulated, the deliberate process of deepening democracy and empowering civil society within Turkey contributed to a gradual shift in Turkey's perception of the Cyprus problem and consequently to a gradual modification of what its policy leaders deemed an acceptable solution. The further Turkey gravitated toward democratic and pluralistic governance regarding its own society, the more open and flexible it became to entertaining a pluralistic and multiethnic state solution of the Cyprus problem.

These reforming changes within Turkey, combined with the electoral victory of the prosolution moderates among the TCs, furnished enough political leverage for Erdogan to circumvent the objecting nationalists among the Turkish military and political establishment, as well as the "archduke" of nationalist intransigence, Denktash himself. The slow but steady evolution of Turkey toward European democratization was beginning to overtake Denktash's politics of nationalist stagnation.

It was under these conditions that the Turkish government declared its acceptance of the Annan Plan as a framework for a final settlement of the Cyprus problem. The announcement by Erdogan's government came soon after another public confrontation with Denktash, following a statement he had made that the Annan Plan was nothing but a trap for the TCs. In response, the Turkish government openly reprimanded him for his derogatory remarks concerning the secretary-general's intentions and hastened to add that the UN is not in the business of setting traps. This confrontation was yet another severe blow to Denktash's political credibility and legitimacy. He, like all nationalists, had never viewed the UN as a credible international organization whose peace and security mission ought to be respected and strengthened but merely as an instrument to be usurped whenever possible for unilateral ethnocentric ends.

Publicly, the Turkish military appeared aligned with the position and course of action adopted by the Turkish government regarding Cyprus and the Annan Plan. Privately, however, deepening divisions between reformists and nationalist conservatives were brewing within the military establishment. In light of the hegemonic role traditionally played by the Turkish military, the fact that the reformist postnationalist trends associated with the EU political culture and process were gradually empowering the authority of civil politics and slowly eroding the familiar monolith of the Turkish military was of historical and political importance.

Along with domestic developments within Turkey, the rapprochement process of low-level politics between Greece and Turkey continued even in the midst of the obstacles impeding resolution of the Cyprus problem. In the face of continuing, though reduced, tensions and disagreements over military flight paths and Flight Information Region (FIR) regulations pertaining to the Aegean Sea, the two countries maintained active, bilateral diplomatic contacts and cross visits by political leaders. Civil society initiatives through direct citizen contacts were also continuing, while the international press was talking about Greeks and Turks rediscovering each other as neighbors. Articles started to appear suggesting that Greeks and Turks were beginning to overcome what their respective nationalism had suppressed and denied for decades—namely, that the two peoples share a great deal in the areas of culture, music, and sentiment. Emphasizing this ongoing rediscovery of Greek-Turkish historical and cultural overlaps, fusion, and similarities, the *International Herald Tribune* remarked:

> While the business of presidents and generals is to draw lines and enforce them, art can deal with ambivalence, worlds that overlap and boundaries that blur. And in that most ambivalent of all post-Ottoman relationships, between Greeks and Turks, the role of culture has never been so important.
>
> To understand this, recall some recent dates in Istanbul's cultural diary. A book of children's stories by a Greek diplomat has been published in Turkish. A Turkish folk singer, Muammer Ketencoglou, has made haunting music with his Greek friends, one of whom is an accomplished church chanter.

> Among Muammer's audiences was the Lausanne Treaty Foundation, a voluntary group that brought together Turkish and Greek historians, conservationists and literary critics for a meeting in Istanbul. They included Turks who deplored the dilapidation of Anatolia's churches and Greeks who acknowledged their country's neglect of mosques. Anyone following these events would conclude that the process of segregating this region's component parts had finished, and a new dynamic of cultural and political reintegration had begun. (2003)

Greek-Turkish rapprochement did not stop with the cultural sphere but also extended to that of politics, even at the highest level. By February 2004, Turkey and Greece had officially ratified a pact, signed in Salonika the previous year, proposing construction of a two-way natural gas pipeline between the two countries. Under the agreement, they would separately construct and operate their respective segments.

Regarding Cyprus, Greece and Turkey agreed for the second consecutive year to cancel the annual military exercises in and around Cyprus that each had traditionally conducted jointly with the military forces of its Cypriot ethnic counterpart. This decision was complemented by Turkey's becoming an official signatory to the "Olympic Truce," an initiative of the Greek government ahead of the Athens 2004 Olympics, revitalizing the three-thousand-year tradition of ceasing hostilities during the Olympic games. Furthermore, an agreement was signed for the removal of mines along the Greek-Turkish land border, to be implemented under Canadian supervision.

The launch of the first cross-border economic pact between Greece and Turkey, backed by the EU, was another milestone for Greek-Turkish rapprochement. The agreement entailed a program worth € 66 million, 35 million of which would be disbursed by the EU. Announcing endorsement of the pact by Brussels, the Greek Ministry of Foreign Affairs explained that the project, which geographically spanned more than 17 percent of Greece and 8 percent of Turkey, was aimed at "creating conditions for economic growth and employment through business cooperation between Greece and Turkey." The goals of the project also included "improvement of the quality of life, protection of the environment and the preservation of cultural heritage." Greek finance minister Nikos Christodoulakis declared that "for the first time, Greece and Turkey are embarking on a joint endeavor to implement infrastructure in sectors including tourism, communications, and transport." He explained that "this will give impetus to joint economic cooperation, which is to the benefit of both countries" (Demiris 2004).

Emulating the peace-enhancing instruments developed and implemented in the EU, this cross-border infrastructure conjoining the national economic interests of the two countries was conceptualized, among other things, as a means of reducing border friction and of politically decompressing border issues that in the past have proven to be a potential source of conflict escalation. A case in point was the border dispute over Imnia/Kardak, an uninhabited rock islet in the eastern Aegean that almost led the neighboring countries to war. By contrast, the mutual interests associated with the newly launched cross-border pact had set a precedent that caused the repetition of such conflicts to appear irrational, if not altogether meaningless.

All of these developments signified a strengthened willingness by Greece and Turkey to continue moving forward with conciliatory and confidence-building projects irrespective of the residue of unresolved problems in the two countries' relations. Again, the EU provided the historical example, institutional process, and political culture that enabled forward-looking Greek and Turkish political leaders and citizens to continue redefining national interest and security in nonadversarial terms and restructuring them in ways that increase the potential for mutual economic growth, cooperative politics, peace, and regional stability. Strengthening Greek-Turkish relations gradually reinforced the regional framework that could prove conducive to resolving the Cyprus problem. The transformational trends, emanating from the motherlands' steady bilateral shifts toward postnationalist, foreign-policy approaches, progressed to encircle both Denktash and Papadopoulos.

At the international level, the indirect yet determined involvement of the United States facilitated the effort to restart the Cyprus talks. However, the reactivation of American interest in the resolution of the Cyprus problem after a year-long lull occurred under peculiar circumstances.

According to statements made by the UN secretary-general, the failure of the Hague talks the previous year was partly a result of the failure of the international community—particularly the U.S.—to weigh in sufficiently on the negotiation process, as attention was diverted to the unfolding crisis over Iraq. Now, a year later, the United States reactivated its interest in Cyprus not because it was past the Iraq crisis, but because it was terribly entrenched in it.

The instability, violence, and general social, political, and economic mess plaguing Iraq following the American military's overthrow of Saddam Hussein left the U.S. politically and morally exposed in the eyes of the UN and the world. Diplomatic relations between the U.S. and the EU, as well as between the U.S. and most of its transatlantic allies, have never been more strained. International disenchantment with the unilateralist foreign policies of the Bush administration, of which the invasion of Iraq was considered the most serious, placed the U.S. in dire need of an internationally visible diplomatic success. Cyprus appeared as a great opportunity. In an article entitled "Why the White House Is Pushing Cyprus Solution," *The Christian Science Monitor*, referring to expert opinion, noted that "sudden US interest in Cyprus exemplifies the administration's desire to show its 'we're-all-in-this-together' side in the post-Iraq-war period. It also suggests the weight the White House places on ties with Turkey as a key to stability and reform in the Middle East." The article further noted that according to John Hulsman, a United States–Europe relations expert at the Heritage Foundation, "The US is also exercising its leverage with Turkey, pressing for a Cyprus accord as a way to show the Europeans its diplomatic side and its desire to move beyond last year's falling out over Iraq" (LaFranchi 2004).

With the November 2004 U.S. presidential elections drawing near, the Bush administration desperately needed a nonmilitary international success story to counter the controversy over its decision to attack Iraq. The UN effort to restart the Cyprus negotiations thus coincided with a time when political choices and global realities for the U.S. government had come full circle. Before the Iraq war period, the Bush administration had cut short the unfinished national and international dialogue over Iraq only to strenuously resume it—not freely but of necessity—after the invasion. Similarly, it indifferently dropped the Cyprus problem before the Iraq war period only to pick it up again zealously in the invasion's aftermath, this time in a climate of rising political anxiety over the future of Iraq and the marred international credibility of the U.S. The insistent U.S. prodding and pressuring of Turkey, as well as of the GC and TC policy leaders to restart the Cyprus negotiations must be viewed in light of this ambiguous and paradoxical background. Be that as it may, the U.S. emerged as yet another factor in the ever-changing, international political context of the Cyprus problem, favoring a conclusive Cyprus settlement along with Greece, Turkey, the EU, and the UN.

As these historical trends converged, Papadopoulos was again feeling rising pressure. The old rejectionist nationalism he and his associates embodied was being countered by Greece's postnationalist, rapprochement policies and directives; Greece's strong support for the resumption of negotiations on the basis of the Annan Plan; Turkey's declared acceptance of the Annan Plan; the marginal but historic victory of the TC moderates; and strong pressure by the EU and the United States to resume negotiations that would bring the Cyprus problem to closure by May 2004.

Not surprising, by the first week of January 2004, Papadopoulos explicitly yet reluctantly stated that the GC side was ready to respond to an invitation by the UN secretary-general to resume negotiations on the basis of the Annan Plan without terms or conditions (*Cyprus Weekly* 2004).

RESUMPTION OF TALKS

Under these conditions, UN secretary-general Kofi Annan invited the GC and TC leaders to meet with him yet again in New York on February 10, 2004, to recommence negotiations based on his plan. Unlike previous diplomatic efforts, Annan enlisted the help of both Greece and Turkey, who agreed to send representatives to the New York talks. The objective of the negotiations was to put a complete text for a comprehensive settlement to separate referenda in April 2004 in the hope that, given a positive outcome, a reunited Cyprus would accede to the EU on May 1, 2004. Both Turkey and Greece welcomed the resumption of talks and made independent statements anticipating that the negotiations would yield a fruitful and conclusive end. Turkey emphasized that the solution ought to take cognizance of "the realities" on the ground, reiterating the concerns of the Turkish side that the settlement secure the political equality between the TCs and GCs as distinct ethnic identity groups. Greece, in contrast, anticipated a positive outcome on the assertion that the solution be "workable," stressing its concern that the settlement secure the unity of Cyprus in the political and administrative functionality of the new arrangement.

With Greece and Turkey backing the resumption of talks on the basis of the Annan Plan, Denktash was grudgingly dragged back to the negotiating table and Papadopoulos inevitably had to follow suit. However, UN officials who knew Denktash were deeply concerned that he was still leading the TC delegation. One UN official stated that Denktash's "resignation as a negotiator, to reject discussing a plan he refused to accept, would have been more consistent and would have been understandable. His current attitude is very suspicious. There are some who suspect that he will resign in the near future to prevent the plan from being implemented before May 1" (*Turkish Daily News* 2004c).

The constant attention given Denktash's intransigence gave indirect cover to Papadopoulos's own hard-line nationalism. But some UN officials expressed apprehension about Papadopoulos as well. Although hopeful about the reactivation of the negotiations, numerous European-oriented GC politicians, such as former president George Vassiliou, were concerned as to whether Papadopoulos's nationalism and related maximalist diplomacy could yield positive results.

The three-day negotiations were tough and intensive. International powers with a stake in the Cyprus problem strongly supported the UN-led process. U.S. Secretary of State Colin Powell and his British counterpart, Jack Straw, intervened during the talks, prodding and encouraging the Cypriot leaders to follow the secretary-general's lead for a successful outcome. In contrast to former negotiations, certain novel elements came to frame the New York talks. For the first time since the 1970s, Denktash did not have free reign in the negotiations. As the *Turkish Daily News* reported, the accompanying presence of the newly elected "prime minister" of the TRNC, Mehmet Ali Talat, as a member of the negotiating delegation was a sign that "Denktash would not be doing as he pleases." Simultaneously, Turkey exerted enormous pressure on Denktash, "who was widely blamed for the collapse of an earlier round of talks last March" (*Turkish Daily News* 2004c). Denktash, who always took pride in his absolute, nationalist loyalty to Turkey, faced the greatest challenge of his political career when Prime Minister Erdogan stated: "We have given a road map to Denktash. We will see how loyal he will be" (*Cyprus Mail* 2004f). And when the prime minister was asked what would be the consequences of Denktash's objection to the road map, he replied: "The TRNC would pay the bill" (*Turkish Daily News* 2004c).

As a result, the negotiations at the UN headquarters in New York yielded an interesting outcome that could be characterized as historically unprecedented. The GC and TC leaders agreed to Kofi Annan's proposals for rapid negotiations on the basis of the UN plan that would lead to a finalized version, to be put to simultaneous separate referenda in the GC and TC communities on April 21, 2004, just ten days before Cyprus was due to join the EU. What was novel about the approach of the secretary-general was that he secured the commitment of all sides to a negotiation process that had closure and a referendum at a specified time. The talks, it was agreed, would continue between the Cypriot leaders, and if they could not reach a deal by March 22, the governments of Greece and Turkey would be brought into the process. If no final text for an agreement was produced by March 29, Annan would fill in the blanks and the referendum would proceed.

Given the history of the Cyprus problem, this was an extraordinary outcome. It set the stage for concluding the half-century-long negotiations and providing the Cypriot people a historic decision in the interest of peace and a new future. The European Commission welcomed the commitment made by the Cypriot leaders and stated that "the accession of a united Cyprus on 1 May remains the clear preference of the EU." Commission president Romano Prodi highlighted the historic meaning of the EU in relation to Cyprus. "The Commission considers that the chances for a comprehensive settlement have never been better," he stated. "It would bring to an end a division that has been there already too long. There is no place for barbed wire, minefields, and peace-keeping forces in the EU" (EU Business 2004b).

Under Alvaro de Soto, UN special representative, the negotiations between the GC and the TC leaders based on the Annan Plan commenced in Cyprus on February 19 following the New York agreements. The time between the start of the talks and March 22, the date agreed upon for the involvement of Turkey and Greece if needed, saw an array of tactical twists and turns, objections and counterobjections from the GC and TC leaders, and public-opinion debates and exchanges. The talks focused on outstanding issues in the areas of territory, security, properties, and the return of refugees. During the process, Papadopoulos accused Denktash of becoming more intransigent, while Denktash complained that Papadopoulos was rejecting all of his demands. The reality was that at the forefront of events were two adversarial nationalists with maximalist approaches to negotiations; the TC leader was still attempting to "negotiate" a secessionist solution and the GC leader was still pursuing a "settlement" that resembled the unitary state of the pre-1974 era.

In the midst of these developments, the Erdogan government demonstrated its willingness and persistence to move Turkey beyond its fruitless traditional position on Cyprus. In a heated three-hour debate in the Turkish parliament, the opposition Republican People's Party fiercely accused the government of unacceptably deviating from Turkey's decades' old national policy on Cyprus (*Turkish Daily News* 2004a). The Turkish government did not relent but rather remained determined to approach the Cyprus problem from within the parameters of the UN-led initiatives. The framework of the EU process, the continuing rapprochement between Greece and Turkey, and the emergent prosolution voice of the TCs created facilitative conditions for the Turkish government to redefine Turkey's national interest in terms of a negotiated settlement of the Cyprus problem based on the Annan Plan. The process marked yet another step in the erosion of traditional Turkish nationalism and the restructuring of national policy on Cyprus in a way that embraced nonbelligerent problem-solving approaches as expected of EU candidate states.

Meanwhile, in Greece, political developments took a new turn. On March 10, the long-standing socialist government of the Panhellenic Socialist Movement (PASOK) lost the elections to the center-right New Democracy Party. Overall, the removal of PASOK from power was not necessarily a setback for Greece, as New Democracy had evolved beyond its far-right nationalist origins, transforming into a European-styled party.

However, New Democracy had not been in power for more than a decade. The realities and challenges had also changed.

According to *The Economist,* Greece was now "enjoying an economic growth rate well ahead of the European average." Its international image had become "substantially better," and "its chronically weak public finances [had] improved thanks to the discipline of the euro area (which Greece joined in 2001)." As noted by international observers, neither the former prime minister, Costas Simitis, nor Foreign Minister George Papandreou was perceived as dishonest. But "they were faulted for failing to crack down on networks of cronyism and maladministration that continued to flourish all around while they concentrated on foreign affairs and on the broad lines of macroeconomics" (*The Economist* 2004b).

Hence, in its electoral victory, New Democracy inherited not only PASOK's shortcomings but also what was internationally deemed outstanding achievements in the economic and foreign policy domains. The stakes of governance were now much higher, less nationalistic, and more European. Having come to power in this context, New Democracy was also facing two major issues that warranted immediate attention: the organization of the summer Olympics, which had fallen victim to the long-standing Greek malaise of maladministration, and the final phase of the Cyprus negotiations with the prospect of a conclusion. The critical question was whether New Democracy could rise to the challenge quickly enough to sustain the Cyprus effort.

Against the backdrop of the political momentum PASOK had generated in recent years regarding its conciliatory and constructive rapprochement policy toward Turkey and its positive and determined contributions toward the resolution of the Cyprus problem, New Democracy appeared to be in a state of political numbness. Moreover, across the Aegean, it was facing a rapidly transforming Turkey, which rendered the old, adversarial, nationalist approach to foreign policy increasingly obsolete. New Democracy was compelled immediately to engage with Turkey at the very time Turkey made the decision to change its policy on Cyprus in pursuit of a negotiated settlement within the framework of the UN.

As expected by the most sensitive observers, the talks between Denktash and Papadopoulos reached an impasse. This was not surprising given the nationalist orientation of the interlocutors. A similar mono-ethnic concept of statehood motivated the overall approaches of the two Cypriot leaders. Their immediate strategies were also alike in that both had attempted to impede the success of the negotiations for keeping the Cyprus problem open beyond the May 1 deadline, when Cyprus was due to join the EU. The only essential difference between Denktash and Papadopoulos were their tactical reasons for preferring to delay a possible settlement. Denktash was hoping to entrench the partition of the Island by having the TRNC de facto diverge and break away from the GC-controlled Republic of Cyprus, as it was assumed that only the GC part of Cyprus would be formally integrated into the EU. Papadopoulos was hoping that by having the Republic of Cyprus join the EU without a settlement, he could impose the republic's recognized status on the TCs through its strengthened European membership status. The politics of both leaders were diametrically opposed to both the fundamental political culture of the EU and the negotiation framework and intent of the UN peace plan—a plan that reflected the distillation of more than four years of negotiations between GCs and TCs.

When the Denktash-Papadopoulos talks ended in failure by March 22, the UN secretary-general directed the process to its second phase as agreed during the New York meetings. The negotiations were thereby moved from Cyprus to the Swiss resort of Bürgenstock with the extended participation of Greece and Turkey. Interestingly, but not surprisingly, Denktash refused to attend the negotiations in Switzerland. With the now inevitable April referendum looming, he preferred to spend his energies promoting a "no" vote for the Annan Plan among the TC community. Equally interesting, but again not surprising, was that Papadopoulos, who grudgingly attended the talks, refused to engage in direct negotiations with his counterpart, opting instead for indirect proximity talks. Papadopoulos's refusal to negotiate directly came at a time when the interlocutor on the TC side was not Denktash but Mehmet Ali Talat, one of the most outspoken moderates and peace supporters among the TC leaders. In diplomatic circles, this fact exposed Papadopoulos, disclosing yet again his perennial tactics of relying on Denktash's rejectionism to conceal his own hard-line nationalist approach to the Cyprus problem.

But Denktash was no longer around, and as a result Papadopoulos fell into a tactical vacuum.

On the Turkish side, Serdar Denktash, the son of the long-standing TC leader, and Abdullah Gul, the Turkish foreign minister, joined Talat. On the Greek side, the GC party leadership, former president Glafcos Clerides, and special advisors accompanied Papadopoulos. The historical significance of this four-party effort was highlighted by the fact that both Greece's and Turkey's prime ministers Costas Karamalis and Tayyip Erdogan joined Kofi Annan during the last phase of the negotiations. Even with the involvement of Greece and Turkey, once again, the two sides could not conclude a finalized document of the UN proposed plan. Subsequently, as was agreed in New York, the secretary-general assumed the responsibility of filling in the blanks, thus bringing the negotiations to a close. The fifth and final version of the Annan Plan was complete and ready to be put to a referendum.

OUTCOME OF NEGOTIATIONS AND IMPROVEMENTS OF THE FIFTH AND FINAL VERSION OF THE ANNAN PLAN

Contrary to the perception and position of nationalist hard-liners on both the TC and GC side, the fifth and final version of the Annan Plan featured considerable improvements. Nearly all the concerns that both sides had put forward during the Bürgenstock talks, were incorporated in a number of creative ways.

According to the UN secretary-general, "the plan was significantly improved" to address numerous issues that the GCs had requested, including changes regarding the functionality of the federal government. The Presidential Council was enlarged from six to nine members (with the additional three being nonvoting); the offices of president and vice president "would not rotate among all members through the five-year term of the Council, but instead alternate on a twenty-month basis between one member from the Greek Cypriot State and one member from the Turkish Cypriot State, starting with the former." (This meant that over the five-year term, GCs would hold the presidency for forty months and the TCs for twenty months.) Also, the period of the transitional government was shortened from thirty months to two months. The structure of the Central Bank was overhauled and the Court of Primary Federal Jurisdiction was created. All these changes were "inspired by the Greek Cypriot proposals." Further, "131 federal laws (almost all based on Greek Cypriot drafts)" were completed "to ensure that in all these vital areas the United Cyprus Republic would be fully functional from day one" (United Nations 2004c).

GCs were further concerned about assurances that the TCs and Turkey would fully implement the plan. "To this end the mode of entry into force [of the plan] was changed to ensure that the guarantor powers would be fully and irrevocably legally committed to the settlement upon signature, with all necessary internal parliamentary approval or ratification procedures already completed." Further, the Monitoring Committee was strengthened and the UN monitoring of political developments was enhanced. Moreover, the UN would "assume territorial responsibility over areas subject to territorial adjustment in the last phase before the transfer." This was a response to the GC demand that the timely hand over of territory "was not dependent on the good will of the other side" (United Nations 2004c).

On the security issue, the GC proposal to "add a reference to the commitment of Cyprus and the guarantor powers to international law and the Principles of the Charter of the UN" was incorporated in the Annan Plan. "As for troop levels [Greek and Turkish] permitted by the Treaty of Alliance, which stood to 6,000 under the plan . . . the Greek Cypriot concern that these be significantly reduced was met in exchange for meeting a Turkish Cypriot concern that a symbolic presence be permitted in accordance with the levels provided by the Treaty of Alliance [i.e., 950 Greek troops and 650 Turkish troops], even after the EU accession of Turkey" (United Nations 2004c).

In satisfying GC concerns at the Bürgenstock negotiations, the question of property rights underwent the most fundamental changes. According to the UN report,

> The property scheme was radically overhauled by removing all overall ceilings on property reinstatement, and instead providing that most Greek Cypriots would have some property reinstated in the Turkish Cypriot State (usually their former home and one third of the land,

though more [often all] for small landowners, and all for returnees to four Karpas villages and the Maronite village of Kormakiti). The effect of this change was that the overall amount of property in the Turkish Cypriot State eligible to be reinstated to Greek Cypriots would be roughly doubled as compared with the previous version of the plan, and more evenly distributed among the dispossessed. The Property Board was restructured and the scheme was backed by guaranteed bonds and certificates linked to real property assets to enhance economic viability. While residency ceilings were slightly lowered as part of the package discussed with all parties at Bürgenstock, they were also made to rise earlier, thus bringing forward the day when Greek Cypriots could begin returning to their homes. Restrictions on the establishment of secondary residences by Cypriot citizens anywhere in Cyprus were removed. (United Nations 2004c)

These changes on GC property rights were in addition to the previous plan, which provided for the majority of GC refugees (60 percent) to return to their homes under GC administration and to have all their property reinstated.

During the Bürgenstock negotiations, the TC side voiced its own concerns regarding improvements of the UN peace plan. Because of their fear of being politically and economically overwhelmed by the GCs, the TCs expressed a firm desire to strengthen the bizonal character of the settlement. In response, the secretary-general slightly reduced the residency ceilings relevant to TC concerns about property affected by the events of 1963 and provided greater simplicity and certainty while reducing the economic impact of the property scheme on the constituent Turkish Cypriot state. The strengthening of the bizonal aspect of the plan was compensated for by the fact that it "doubled the amount of property that could be reinstated to Greek Cypriots." A safeguard relating to residency was also introduced "to ensure that no less than two thirds of its Cypriot permanent residents spoke its official language as their mother tongue (this would effectively allow over time some 100,000 Greek Cypriots to take up permanent residence in the Turkish Cypriot State, in addition to the unlimited provision for secondary residence)" (United Nations 2004c).

The TCs were also concerned about securing political equality—not just among individual citizens, but also between the constituent states of the new federal Cyprus. The secretary-general introduced changes requiring that the voting of federal senators representing the TC constituent state would be based on mother tongue rather than internal, constituent citizen status. However, political rights at the constituent state and local levels were to be exercised based on residency status regardless of mother tongue.

A further worry of the TCs was the legal security of the settlement. The TCs feared that the GCs might challenge the settlement in the EU courts. To alleviate this fear, "The European Commissioner for Enlargement, consistent with the EU's policy of accommodation of a settlement in line with the principles on which the EU is founded," assured the secretary-general that "the Commission was committed to submitting the draft Act of Adaptation contained in the [Annan] plan for consideration by the Council of the EU prior to 24 April 2004, and adoption after a successful outcome of the separate, simultaneous referenda before 1 May 2004." The settlement would then become part of EU primary law, thus ensuring legal certainty and security within the framework of the European legal system. Moreover, the plan already provided for the United Cyprus Republic to request of the European Court of Human Rights that the new federal republic be "the sole responsible State party" to settle matters regarding property. However, "individual right of recourse to the European Court of Human Rights should the domestic remedy prove inadequate was in no way limited" (United Nations 2004c).

Security, which always ranked high on the TC agenda, was reinforced in the final version of the plan by "allowing Turkey and Greece to sustain symbolic force levels as already provided by the 1960 Treaty of Alliance (namely, 650 Turkish troops and 950 Greek troops) even after EU accession." This provision was made in exchange for considerably reducing the number of troops in the interim, a response to a GC concern. According to the final version of the Annan Plan, upon agreement, Turkish troops would be reduced from their current 40,000 to a mere 6,000, with the provision of the introduction of an equal number of Greek troops. By the year 2011, the Greek and Turkish troops would be further reduced to 3,000 until 2018, or earlier if Turkey joined the EU.

Thereafter, the Greek troops would number 950 and the Turkish troops 650. The plan also anticipated the possibility for the complete withdrawal of Greek and Turkish troops from the Island through mutual consent.

In accordance with the UN peace plan, about a quarter of the TC population would be required to relocate as a result of the territorial adjustments necessary for the formation of the TC and GC constituent states. This fact was troubling to the TCs. To ease the process of TC relocation, "the Relocation Board's range of activities was strengthened, the time period for adjustment of territory was extended by six months, and the Turkish Cypriot State would be entitled, for a transitional period, to maintain a slightly larger number of police than under the previous versions of the plan" (United Nations 2004c).

According to the final version of the Annan Plan, the federal government would be "fully functioning" from the very outset, immediately following agreement based on a positive outcome of the referendum. While agreeing to this aspect of the plan, the TCs were concerned that they "would need more time in practical terms to make the necessary economic and structural adjustments" particularly as regards harmonization with the EU *acquis communautaire*. Addressing this concern, the secretary-general introduced a federal law "suspending the application in the Turkish Cypriot State of certain federal laws which transposed provisions of the *acquis communautaire*." In conjunction with this, "the Central Bank law included provision for a branch in the Turkish Cypriot State (but within the central [federal] structure) with clearly defined functions. Its purpose and functions would be reviewed after six months by experts from the International Monetary Fund and the EU, and it could only be extended beyond one year by agreement" (United Nations 2004c).

In brief, these were the improvements made to the peace plan by Kofi Annan to accommodate the concerns of the GCs and TCs respectively during the Bürgenstock negotiations. As evident from the above, improvements along the concerns of one side did not necessarily entail losses on the part of the other. In the greatest number of changes, both sides received the maximum of what they requested.

The outcome of the negotiations appears as an unacceptable loss only when measured using the traditional objectives of the respective ethnocentric nationalisms that created the Cyprus problem in the first place. When the plan is assessed either from the perspective of the TC nationalist notion of ethnic secession or the perspective of the GC nationalist idea of Cyprus as a unitary Hellenic state, then the peace plan indeed appears unacceptable. However, the aim of the secretary-general was the creation of a new state of affairs that would reconcile the legitimate concerns of the stakeholders as well as free the Island from its captivity to the long-overdue political stalemate of competing nationalisms. This objective was embodied in the establishment of the United Cyprus Republic, as articulated in the fifth and final version of the Annan Plan. In this regard, no matter how balanced and comprehensive the plan may have been, peace could not be attained and sustained as long as either side remained locked into the traditional nationalist framework. The Annan Plan has been described as the most elaborate and creative plan ever devised by the UN in solving interethnic conflict. (In fact, it wouldn't be surprising if the Annan Plan becomes a key resource and model for addressing and resolving other interethnic conflicts around the world.) But the plan's unprecedented merits, particularly in relation to the historic moment of Cyprus's entry into the EU, becomes evident only as one begins to break free from the skewing vision of ethnocentric nationalism and its monoethnic concepts of statehood.

The secretary-general was hoping to formalize and thus diplomatically legitimize the outcome of the agreed-upon process by having the interlocutors sign onto the final draft of the plan. While the Turkish side was ready to do so, Papadopoulos refused. In spite of the gravity of the situation, Greece's role in the process had been lukewarm and lacking in leadership. Consequently, Greece simply followed in Papadopoulos's footsteps.

6

The Cyprus Referenda

Nationalism Versus Postnationalism

THE HISTORIC REFERENDA OF APRIL 24, 2004

The Greek government requested changing the date of the Cyprus referenda, as the original date of April 21 suggested by the UN coincided with the dark anniversary of the 1967 rise to power of the Greek military junta. The date was therefore moved to April 24. The separate, simultaneous referenda held in the GC and TC communities were unprecedented, as it was the first time in the history of Cyprus that GCs and TCs had been asked to participate directly in shaping the polity and future of their common homeland.

Unfortunately, the outcome of the referenda, on the eve of the Island's entry into the EU, was a great disappointment to all who had worked and hoped for a final political settlement of the Cyprus problem. On the TC side, 64.9 percent of the electorate voted in favor of the Annan Plan, while 35.1 percent voted against it. On the GC side, 75.8 percent of the electorate voted against the Annan Plan, while 24.2 percent voted in favor. It was historically telling that the two Cypriot leaders who felt utterly satisfied with this outcome were Papadopoulos and Denktash. Papadopoulos's rejection of the plan had been fully secured and justified by the GC vote. Denktash thanked God for the GC "no" vote, as it fulfilled his aim of destroying the Annan Plan while simultaneously relieving the TC side of political blame (*The Economist* 2004c).

In view of the enormous work that had been done—from the comprehensive UN peace plan to a new anthem and flag—the failure to conclude the Cyprus problem at this critical and most opportune historical moment was perhaps the greatest political setback in the history of the Island since independence. The rejection of the plan by the GCs by a margin of three to one and its acceptance of the plan by the TCs by a margin of two to one appeared irrational and even shocking to outside observers. Yet, to those with insight into the subjective, political dynamics internal to Cyprus, the referenda could not have yielded anything different given the leadership of Papadopoulos on the GC side and Denktash's eclipsing political influence on the TC side. How, then, can the results of the referenda be tangibly explained in view of the unprecedented convergence of historical and political factors bearing on the Cyprus process leading up to April 24?

A long-term, time-sensitive study conducted by a group of scholars, combining expertise on the Cyprus problem and Expected Utility Analysis methodology, yielded interesting results that are relevant to the above question. The study was significant in employing state-of-the-art methodology to predict and analyze outcomes of the Cyprus negotiations and the anticipated referenda on a solution. The study used an agent-based model to analyze the political debate on the core issues of the Cyprus problem among all involved stakeholders (GC, TC, Greek and Turkish governments, parties, media, labor unions, various civil society organizations, and international agents such as the EU, UN, and United States). Moreover, the methodology combined game theory, decision theory (bounded rationality), risk, and spatial bargaining, providing predictions based on an explanation of how the policy positions of competing interests evolve over time.

A series of studies over the years (Fall 1998; May 2003; December 2003; February 2004; March 2004) employing an Expected Utility Analysis methodology indicated that overall, the positions of the Cyprus stakeholders had started to gravitate toward agreement. Particularly in the study of March 2004, undertaken immediately prior to the referenda, the outcome showed an unprecedented level of convergence between GCs and TCs on all the issues with the exception of territory. On that issue, the study recommended direct contact between the Papadopoulos administration and the Turkish government, as the analysis pointed to the probability of arriving at consensus. Unfortunately, neither the Papadopoulos government nor Turkey heeded this recommendation. But even with the issue of territory left open and ambiguous, there was considerable convergence on all other issues. More significantly, this convergence coincided with the parameters of the Annan Plan (Yesilada et al. 2004). Interestingly, the methodology employed in the study had a well-documented track record of success. It had been used for an internal assessment of more than two thousand issues around the world by policy development agencies, which had found the approach to be accurate more than 90 percent of the time.

By all indications, in its March 2004 application to Cyprus, the time-sensitive Expected Utility Analysis was predicting a high probability for agreement on the UN peace plan, with Turkey and the GCs in considerable accord on the issue of property. However, the outcome of the April 24 referenda reflected an enlarged gap between GC and TC opinion. And in a subsequent study conducted in May 2004, the Expected Utility Analysis yielded high divergence on the issues of territory, settlement, and property rights, all of which emerged as highly contested since the referenda.

More stunning was the fact that a survey conducted between September 2004 and January 2005 by local experts, five months after the referenda, concluded that 67 percent of each community converged in favor of a federal settlement based on the Annan Plan. Even though the survey indicated that the first preference of the GCs was not federation, it also concluded that the majority of GCs viewed an Annan-type federation as an acceptable compromise. Interestingly, the survey also pointed out that while the majority of the TC youth were in favor of reunification, that of the GC youth were not (Lordos 2005).

The overall trajectory of GC and TC opinion thus indicates that while there was convergence in March 2004, by April and May there was considerable divergence because of changes of opinion on the GC side, and by September 2004 and January 2005 there was again a shift showing greater GC tolerance for an Annan-based federal settlement. These findings raise the natural question: What changed between March and April 2004, the period of time immediately prior to the referenda, that can explain the final divergent outcome in the GC and TC votes, particularly in view of the fact that a few months later, majority opinion among GCs and TCs again reflected possibilities for convergence? Furthermore, what can explain the paradoxical fact that at the time of the referenda and thereafter, it was GC youth, rather than their TC counterparts, who were found to prefer ethnic separation to a reunified Cyprus? Given their historical and political significance, these questions warrant careful scrutiny.

Papadopoulos's intention not to pursue a settlement was already evident during the talks prior to the finalization of the Annan Plan. The deluge of documents presented by the GC side to the UN mediator appeared to be designed to arouse the indignation of the other side in the hope that the negotiations would be stalled rather than to pursue constructively a final settlement (United Nations 2004c). Exhibiting a spirit reminiscent of Denktash, Papadopoulos did not attend the talks for the purpose of concluding an agreement, nor did he embody the necessary political will required to move the process forward to a successful outcome. Rather, he was drawn into the negotiations as a result of the historical momentum generated before his presidency by the increasing convergence of the efforts of the UN, the EU, the previous governments of Greece, the Republic of Cyprus, Turkey, and the TC community, and—though belatedly—the United States.

With the talks in Switzerland coming to a close, Papadopoulos found himself in the same predicament that had earlier confronted Denktash. Papadopoulos had no options left in pursuing and sustaining his quasi-camouflaged, antifederalist and hence antisolution position than to propagate a "no" vote among the GCs. A possible rejection of the Annan Plan by the GC electorate became the last place of refuge for Papadopoulos and his nationalist agenda. Swaying the electorate to reject the plan emerged as Papadopoulos's last political standoff and the last instrument by which to oppose a solution based on a multiethnic, bicommunal federation as finalized in the plan. It is for this very reason that, on his return to Cyprus, Papadopoulos spent all of his energy and used all of the private and public means at his disposal as president to campaign against the peace plan.

The formal launch of Papadopoulos's "no" campaign was marked by his national address of April 7, 2004, delivered in the middle of the Greek Orthodox Easter week. Similar to Denktash's earlier appeal against the UN plan, Papadopoulos's televised address was tearful and impassioned.

In a delivery reminiscent of political speeches of the 1960s, the GC president called on his electorate to vote a "resounding no" to the Annan Plan—the very plan on the basis of which he had formally agreed to negotiate in good faith and, if need be, to accept the UN secretary-general's final version.

The anachronism of his speech was reflected in the emotive nationalist fervor of its delivery, the repeated use of the old nationalist-laden phrase "Hellenic Cypriot people," and his attempt to simulate the outdated role of ethnarch reserved for archbishops who functioned as national leaders in times gone by. In content, tone, and gesture, Papadopoulos attempted to emulate the late Archbishop Makarios, whose image and legacy could be psychologically transposed into a source of political legitimacy for Papadopoulos's nationalist agenda. The decision to address the GCs during Easter week insinuated an attempted subliminal association between Papadopoulos and the archbishop. It certainly denoted the familiar trend within certain brands of nationalism, in which the religious sentiment of the masses is psychologically associated with, and eventually integrated into, the hyperpolitics of nationalism and their maximalist agendas.

Overall, Papadopoulos's speech included little that went beyond the age-old ideological rhetoric that the GCs were accustomed to hearing throughout the decades of unbending TC and Turkish nationalist, secessionist politics. While contrary to regional sociopolitical trends and EU politics, the call by Papadopoulos for a "resounding no" had a psychological affinity to the traditional habituation of GCs to past TC and Turkish intransigence. For years, GC public opinion merely reacted morally and ideologically to the unacceptable position of the Turkish side, without ever considering genuine political options with attainable goals, ones carrying real consequences and requiring real responsibilities. Never before did the GCs encounter the possibility of a Cyprus solution in concrete and practical terms; nor did the GC leadership ever sufficiently prepare them for one. If anything, with brief exceptions, GC politics had over the years atrophied into a regurgitated political culture of ideal and untenable objectives, grounded on simply saying "no" to the other side's nationalist position. Though practically fruitless, this GC approach was sustainable because of the ease by which GC leaders could simply object to Denktash's secessionist extremism without incurring any political cost. The ingrained pattern of this residual psychology of inconsequential reaction and rejection was the mass psychological resource that Papadopoulos managed to tap in mobilizing support against the UN peace plan. Thus his speech opposing the Annan Plan gave no consideration whatsoever to the political consequences of a "no" vote by the GC side, assuming that, as always in the past, a GC "no" not only would change nothing on the ground but also would reinforce the political position of the GC side.

Papadopoulos's speech shocked and amazed outside observers, including the UN, since it retroactively posed serious questions as to why the GC president had bothered to attend the UN-led negotiations at all. Papadopoulos's real motives for going to the talks were revealed in the speech itself. He explained that the main reason for attending was to avert any accusation that the GC side was unwilling to negotiate. This admission earned Papadopoulos great international discredit by placing in question his motives, sincerity, and responsibility as a head of state. In the cloud of nationalist passions stirred up during the referenda campaigns, GC public opinion failed to grasp the enormous political and diplomatic damage incurred by Papadopoulos's initiative to defeat the UN effort.

In his attempts to influence the outcome of the referenda, Papadopoulos employed two interrelated schemes: First, he tapped into the dormant nationalist memory and sentiments of the GC community, stirring, reactivating, and amplifying nationalism to the point of saturating the public debate and drowning out the prosolution voices. Second, he reawakened the GCs' sense of victimization and reintegrated it into the nationalist framework, thus reassociating the GCs' sense of injustice with the typical reactionary culture of adversarial nationalism. Triggering this mental connection enabled him to capitalize on the historical fears of GCs rather than building on their current strengths and hopes for a new future. This two-pronged approach prompted a public resurgence of nationalism just at the point when it could have been relegated to the past. Papadopoulos not only reactivated GC nationalism but explicitly identified it with his administration's formal position and approach.

Through his negative approach to the Annan Plan, Papadopoulos succeeded in reviving the GCs' old nationalist worldview. In his Easter week speech, he emphasized that the Annan Plan did not satisfy "our minimum requirements." He painted the plan in dark colors, neglecting to acknowledge that as the authorized negotiator for the GC side, he had originally consented to the UN process that led to the final version of the plan.

One of the most populist arguments against the Annan Plan, hinging on the fears and nationalism reawakened by the "no" campaigners, was that the UN plan was nothing but a conspiracy of "the foreigners" to serve the interests of Turkey—the embodiment of an underhanded act of betrayal "against Cypriot Hellenism" by "outsiders." This grossly simplistic interpretation came not only from GC nationalist factions fighting zealously against the peace plan but also from Papadopoulos, who propagated it both within the domestic GC community and among GC and Greek communities living abroad.

The idea that the "foreign powers"—primarily the United States and Britain—had fabricated the Annan Plan for the sole purpose of getting Turkey into the EU was an attempt to capitalize on an old but familiar GC grievance. After independence, GC nationalists argued that the 1960 constitution that had established the Republic of Cyprus had been imposed on the GCs by outsiders. Papadopoulos anti-Annan campaign was now insinuating that the proposed UN plan was no different: that it, too, was being imposed on GCs from without. The argument against "foreign powers" articulated in 2004 was intended to sway public opinion back to the nationalist, anticolonial mentality and to reactivate a half-century-old perception among GCs and Greeks, thus rendering the rejection of the UN peace plan as the logical and patriotic choice.

The widespread argument that the Annan Plan was a foreign, anti-Greek ploy penetrated the most sensitive and most vulnerable aspects of the GC psyche and historical memory. Through several tacit and explicit arguments and associations, the leaders of the "no" campaign communicated to the public that there was nothing new on the historical scene and that now, just as in colonial times, the foreign powers were selfishly working against the interests of the GCs. Reawakening fears from the distant colonial past, the approach was not only blind to changing historical realities but also evasive concerning the new opportunities for peace, stability, and well-being for Cyprus and the Eastern Mediterranean that were within reach. Anything linked to future opportunities for a settlement was suppressed, while a "yes" vote for the Annan Plan was presented as dangerous, risky, and ethnically suicidal, thereby amounting to national betrayal. In contrast, a reversion to nationalist anticolonialism, the grievances of the past, and the preservation of the status quo until further notice were presented as the ethnically responsible, moral, and sacred choice—the choice that would be enacted by voting "no." Papadopoulos's presentation of the UN peace plan to the GCs was not only out of step with history, but also alien to the politics of the EU, which the Republic of Cyprus, as a state joining the union, was supposed to share.

The artificiality of the nationalist position that the Annan Plan was a "foreign conspiracy" was evident when one considered that both the Greek government and PASOK, the main opposition party, had supported it. Yet Papadopoulos and opponents of the plan among both the GC community and the Hellenic diaspora never took issue with Greece; instead, they preferred to engage in collective denial. Presumably, they should have accused Greece of being a coconspirator, working in collusion with the "foreign powers" against the national interest of Cyprus. Moreover, the argument that the sole objective of the Annan Plan was to get Turkey into the EU bypassed the historical fact that the last two governments of Greece openly supported Turkey's European aspirations. The Greek government had supported Turkey's desire to draw closer to Europe since 1999, with the proviso that Turkey contribute to the solution of the Cyprus problem within the UN framework. This fact was never addressed by those favoring a "no" vote. Had they done so, they would have had to either acknowledge disagreement with the foreign policy of the motherland—a cardinal sin according to ethnocentric GC nationalism—or, worse, accuse Greece of betrayal. All the ambiguities were glossed over by the nationalists' overarching emotional appeals for "the survival of Cypriot Hellenism" in their determination to defeat the Annan Plan. Once again, the internal inconsistencies of the nationalist mind were revealed at the juncture where objective reality clashed with nationalism's unique ability to create an unreal, mental world and reside in it as though it were real.

But Papadopoulos's incessant and exaggerated negativity reached its peak of effectiveness when he directly linked the allegedly harmful aspects of the plan to the security concerns of the GCs. Having fed and fueled the fears of the GCs, Papadopoulos propagated his nationalist agenda and rejectionist strategy by generating among the GC community intense emotions of uncertainty and anxiety over the viability of the settlement. Yet again, nationalist populism won. But what were the specific security provisions of the UN plan, and how did they profile against the backdrop of the EU?

Contrary to the claims of the rejectionist camp, the final version of the Annan Plan provided for a steady reduction of Turkish troops to commence with the plan's implementation. As already noted, Turkish troops were to be initially reduced from the current forty thousand to six thousand, and eventually phased out to a merely symbolic number. As stated in the plan, the chronological milestones marking implementation of these provisions were as follows:

i) each contingent [Greek and Turkish] not to exceed 6,000 all ranks, until 2011;
ii) each contingent not to exceed 3,000 all ranks thereafter until 2018 or the EU accession of Turkey, whichever is sooner; and
iii) the Greek contingent not to exceed 950 all ranks and the Turkish contingent not to exceed 650 all ranks thereafter, subject to three-yearly review with the objective of total withdrawal (United Nations 2004a).

Moreover, the Annan Plan added that "Cyprus shall be demilitarized, and all Greek Cypriot and Turkish Cypriot forces, including reserve units, shall be dissolved, and their arms removed from the Island, in phases synchronized with the redeployment of and adjustment of Greek and Turkish forces." And further, "the supply of arms to Cyprus shall be prohibited in a manner that is legally binding on both importers and exporters," a process to be jointly monitored by a committee chaired by the UN and comprised of Greece and Turkey as guarantor powers, the federal government, and the constituent states of Cyprus (United Nations 2004a).

In spite of these fundamental security provisions in the plan, the rejectionist camp led by Papadopoulos chose to emphasize that it allowed for the continuing presence of Turkish troops, thereby suggesting that the plan was essentially legitimizing the partition and military occupation of Cyprus. The nationalists could sustain this argument only by neglecting to acknowledge publicly its provision for the progressive withdrawal of more than thirty thousand Turkish troops, to commence with the signing of the agreement. Equally important was their silence about the added security that European integration would introduce for all Cypriots—presumably the major reason that the GCs chose to join Europe. Contrary to the actual provisions of the plan, the impression projected by the "no" campaigners to the GC public was that Turkish troops would continue to occupy Cyprus and that joining Europe had no security implications for the Island. The nationalists projected this impression among the GC community not through direct references to the actual text of the Annan Plan, but rather through the heightened emotionalism by which they linked support for the plan with national treason.

More striking, however, was the fact that the concept of security elaborated by the GC "no" camp was identical to that propagated and used for decades by Denktash and his longtime supporter, the Turkish military. Typical of nationalists, it entailed the view that security is exclusively a military issue. This view is valid only under belligerent or battlefield conditions, being derived from, and conditioned by, violent conflict situations. To the degree that this concept of security drives perception and policy, it inevitably reproduces the original belligerent conditions that gave rise to it, keeping its proponents entrapped in conflict, suspicion, and mistrust. Associating a public sense of safety exclusively with firepower tends to stall politics indefinitely from ever transcending military means and conflict-habituated policies. As a rule, the nationalist mind equates the search for improved security and peace with the search for more potent firepower. But in so doing, it holds politics hostage to conflict and the adversarial mentality. Politics thus becomes a mere subsystem of a militarist concept of security.

Within the nationalist framework, only two basic policy options exist: either make the enemy militarily weaker, or make oneself militarily stronger—an approach that precludes any prospect for resolving conflict in the direction of sustainable, positive peace. Military matters do constitute a critical dimension of the security framework of any political settlement between rivals. But when military considerations are deemed the sole basis of security, conflicts can never be solved, as one side's security always translates into the other side's insecurity. Within the international setting, the two world wars marked the abysmal failure of this nationalist concept of security as it led to devastating mutual destruction.

By contrast, the strong sense of security that EU member-states have built and enjoy owes its success to the abandonment of the nationalist concept of security and to its restructuring as a multidimensional political, social, and economic system beyond mere military considerations. The EU concept of security has been founded on economic interdependency and well-being; on shared interethnic, interstate, and trans-state political institutions for joint democractic decision making; on strengthening civil society and citizen initiatives across ethnic, societal, and national lines; and most importantly, through all the above, on building relationships between former enemies and between old and new members of the union. The military, though important, is the last factor in the EU system of security and is itself integrated as a subsystem of all the factors laid out above. For the EU it is "soft power" that constitutes the foundation of security, not "hard power" (Rifkin 2004). Many different historical elements have played a role in shaping the European security system. The fact that integrating the militaries of the member-states into the union is one of the last remaining steps in completing the European edifice strongly suggests that the European concept of security was not designed primarily in terms of military power but instead in terms of building economic ties, political cooperation, social integration, peace-enhancing relations among the members, and an ever-growing system of shared law and political values.

This would have been the appropriate and up-to-date security framework from which to address the historic decisions leading to the Cyprus referenda—a framework that could have been reinforced and built on had Cyprus entered the EU a united country. And this framework was precisely the basis of the Annan Plan's security provisions, regarding both the internal arrangements of a new Cyprus and the external relations of Cyprus vis-à-vis its integration into Europe and subsequent normalization of the Island's regional ties to Greece and Turkey.

However, given the nationalist premise of their politics, neither Denktash nor Papadopoulos was able or willing to operate within the European post–world war concept of security, despite the fact that the peaceful mixing of their respective communities offered them a firm basis for doing so. By refusing to think outside the nationalist box, Denktash and Papadopoulos were compelled to operate outside the European and UN concept of security. Papadopoulos, even more than Denktash, desperately attempted to convey the impression that he was adhering to both the EU and the UN framework. But the marginalization of Denktash by the Turkish side revealed Papadopoulos's adherence as merely legalistic and never political. Neither the sharing of power nor the building of interethnic relations was ever profiled in the political record of these leaders. They were politically and ideologically unqualified to understand that interethnic, political cooperation, common economic interests, and relationship building constitute a vital aspect of any sustainable security-system conducive to democracy.

In mobilizing mass support against the Annan Plan, the Papadopoulos-led rejectionists among the GCs took full advantage of the revived nationalism. Old slogans were pulled out of the historical closet and employed in the battle against the plan. Most notable was the saturation of the public environment with images of the Greek word *OXI*, meaning "no." The slogan originated in 1940 when the mainland Greeks said "no" to the advancing Italian army, an event commemorated since through an annual national holiday observed on October 28. In 2004 the GC nationalists exhumed the slogan and transposed it into a populist psychological motivator for engendering a "no" vote to the Annan Plan. It was precisely on this anachronistic *OXI* idea that Papadopoulos grounded his appeal to GCs to voice a "resounding 'no'" on the day of the referenda.

Those GCs reinfected with the old nationalist fever missed a historical irony, however. Whereas in 1945, the mainland Greeks said *OXI* to foreign troops entering their country, in 2004 the GCs were saying *OXI* to foreign troops leaving their country. By choosing to vote "no" to the Annan Plan, the GCs were in effect voting for the indefinite presence of Turkish troops in Cyprus. As always, nationalism was forfeiting reality for an abstract universe of populist slogans, symbols, and references to past glories and heroics having less to do with the discernment of concrete, historical realities and possibilities than with mythical, self-deluding, untenable, and often destructive outcomes. The intoxicating satisfaction ensuing from reagitated nationalist emotions was paid for by political blindness to an unprecedented historical opportunity that could have brought the problematic past to a decisive conclusion and create a new future for Cyprus.

NATIONALIST FEVER AND HUMAN RIGHTS VIOLATIONS

But the Papadopoulos-induced relapse into obsessive nationalism and reactionary politics did not stop there. Just as the Denktash regime had practiced for years in northern Cyprus, Papadopoulos usurped the state apparatus to propagate his "no" agenda in the south. A report by the Cyprus Action Network (CAN) reflected the lingering influence of Denktash in the north and the resurgence of populist nationalism in the south. This action group included overseas Cypriots and non-Cypriots concerned about the various violations of human rights that often occur on both sides in Cyprus, particularly under the guise of patriotic objectives. Drawing from the current local and international media, CAN summarized the respective intracommunal abuses leading up to the referenda. On April 23, 2004, a day before the referenda, CAN published the following:

> The Cyprus Action Network would like to bring to the international community's attention the flood of human rights violations that have taken place in the days preceding the referenda on the 24th of April. These violations fall into the following categories:
>
> South Cyprus:
>
> • Government misinformation: Local media and politicians reported that state ministers and officials terrorized government employees, claiming that if the Annan Plan were to be accepted there would be salary cuts, benefit and job losses. In particular, the employees targeted were in the police force, in the military, and in the tourism industry (one of the largest, more profitable industries in the South).
>
> • Education: Teachers in public schools have been pressuring students to support a "NO" vote, encouraging nationalistic behavior and

refusing room for discussion in the classroom. A discussion on the plan to be held at the English school was cancelled, and the student organizing it was threatened. Threats for the son of a high ranking civil servant who resigned because of his disagreement with the government were written on the walls.

• Media misinformation: Both UN and EU mediators have been prevented from exposing their views in private and public media in the South. Moreover, there are claims from politicians that the government had interfered with the operation of the state television channel, CyBC, and organized the president's interview right before the end of the campaign period to avoid the response of the "yes" side.

• Miscellaneous: A Greek Orthodox bishop threatened voters with damnation if they supported the UN plan. The Church's influence in the South should not be underestimated, where there is still a large number of practicing Greek Orthodox citizens.

North Cyprus:

• State supported terrorizing of citizens: The well-known ultranationalist group, Grey Wolves, have been threatening citizens in the North, and are among those suspected of beating up motorcyclists carrying "vote yes" banners. The Grey Wolves are openly supported by the leader of the North, Rauf Denktash.

• Government voting manipulation: The government refuses to allow Turkish Cypriots living in the South the right to vote in the referenda, so that roughly one thousand Turkish Cypriots are ineligible to vote. . . .

The Cyprus Action Network is concerned that the instances recorded are undemocratic and in violation of the Cypriot citizens' rights. Moreover, many of the articles [referred to by CAN] suggest that these violations are to be directly blamed on the respective governments in both sides. We ask for immediate international attention on these issues. (Cyprus Action Network 2004)

In the north, the rise to power of Talat's propeace Republican Party acted as a countervailing force to Denktash's nationalism. In the south, however, the rise to power of Papadopoulos's DIKO party reintroduced and reestablished the nationalist agenda at the core of the GC government's political vision, policy, strategy, and tactics. This approach was so evident that at his own political risk, Anastasiades, the leader of DISY, the main opposition party, fiercely attacked Papadopoulos for abuse of power, underhanded tactics, and meddling in the civil service to bring about a "no" vote. Stating his intention to report Papadopoulos to the EU, the leader of DISY asserted:

> I would like to make clear that the letters I was going to send to the President of the [European] Commission, to the EU Presidency, to the President of the EU Council, to the EU Broadcasting Authority and the President of the EU Parliament will be sent tomorrow. . . . And I have facts, like letters to public servants, letters to the police, the circular by the Education minister, Mr. Papadopoulos's interview on Thursday, and the abuse of air time by some channels through influence or otherwise, in order to express only what the Presidential circle wants to express. . . . So let the government start acting like Europeans, let them stop using their usual methods of talking of traitors and of people being sold out. . . . For the first time after decades we hear the words "traitor," "an instrument of foreign interests," from all those who think they are selling patriotism. . . . Let them know that from May 1, the EU will know about their methods, and what happens in Cyprus will be known. The vampire of the past will stay in the past, and those who live in the past will have to answer to the EU. (*Cyprus Mail* 2004d)

Already, EU and UN officials were expressing dismay and concern that both private and public broadcasting stations had prevented European and UN representatives from giving interviews for the GC public. The officials had accused private GC channels of refusing to interview Günter Verheugen, the enlargement commissioner, "who had steered Cyprus over the past five years through difficult accession negotiations to be ready to join the Union on May 1." Moreover, officials stated that GC media had also prevented Alvaro de Soto, the UN's special envoy to Cyprus, from giving interviews, cancelling his planned appearance on CyBC, the state broadcasting channel. In what was described as a moralistically toned posture, typical of the nationalist presumption of absolute rightness and of justified defiance toward "outsider foreigners," the GC government categorically denied any form of intervention. European Commission officials, however, insisted that their claim of the GC government's undue interference was a fact, while diplomats asserted that Papadopoulos was behind the media plan. Having reserved all the nationwide television stations in the GC community, and having identified himself as the head of the "no" campaign, Papadopoulos granted an interview broadcast by all channels during the last hour of the campaign.

The actions of Papadopoulos and his government provoked severe criticism both locally and internationally. Vassiliou, former president of the republic and former chief negotiator for Cyprus with the EU, publicly protested the interview as an unprecedented, antidemocratic action, since Papadopoulos spoke both as president and as leader of the "no" campaign.

The outcome of the GC referendum was clearly dependent on the GC political leadership and mass media. The reactionary, nationalist tidal wave launched by Papadopoulos with his Easter week address created in public culture a clear association between the official GC position and the absolute rejection of the Annan Plan. At this juncture, the nationalist elements still embedded in the institutions of the mass media—newspapers, television, and radio—were reawakened to what seemed to be a renewed legitimacy. If the president of the GC-led Republic of Cyprus could utter a "resounding no" from the highest position of public office, why couldn't any other citizen, including journalists and media centers, join the rejectionist camp with just as much zealotry and nationalist fervor?

In alignment with the Papadopoulos government, the GC media played their own role in shaping GC public opinion. Under the impact of the anti-Annan initiative of the Papadopoulos government, a power struggle broke out witin the news media as nationalist journalists sought to monopolize control. As gatekeepers of the power of the public media, the most ardent nationalists among the journalists violated basic codes of conduct by not only leading fierce, opinion-forming efforts against the Annan Plan, but also by directly and indirectly muzzling the voices of its advocates. Nonnationalist journalists favoring a more European approach were displaced, intimidated, and professionally delegitimized.

A week following the referenda, the *Cyprus Mail* published a study conducted by the media research firm AGB on how air time was allocated in the public debates on the Annan Plan occurring between February 16 and April 21, 2004. According to the AGB study,

> 59 per cent of the time (183.4 hours) allocated by the four TV channels—CyBC, Sigma, Mega, and ANT1—was dedicated to "no" supporters compared to 35 per cent (109.3 hours) reserved for those in favor of the [Annan] plan. Only six per cent of airtime was given to other analysts.... Mega showed the greatest imbalance and gave 'no' campaigners almost double the airtime than to the 'yes' advocates. CyBC came a close second and ANT1 third. Sigma gave 37 percent more time to those wishing to express negative opinions on the plan. (*Cyprus Mail* 2004g)

Not surprisingly, the report noted that of all GC politicians, President Papadopoulos "had the most air time of 11 hours and 25 minutes, as his speeches were broadcasted simultaneously on all four channels"—the channels carrying the highest national ratings.

Within the EU, questions were raised as to whether the Republic of Cyprus under Papadopoulos was in breach of the union's Copenhagen criteria, which make freedom of the press a main precondition for accession. Not wanting to add to the dire political situation at the most critical juncture of the Cyprus problem, the European Commission refrained from openly stating whether the GC government was violating European accession rules. At issue, according to the Europeans, was the skewed manner in which the Papadopoulos-led "no" campaign was presenting the Annan Plan to the GC public, and its power to derail the historic opportunity for reunifying the Island.

Another protagonist that played a key role in the "no" campaign was the Greek Orthodox Church of Cyprus. Historically influenced by the rise of Hellenic nationalism during the nineteenth century, the church's uncritical assimilation of impassioned ethnocentrism had rendered inert and meaningless the transcendent spiritual directives of mercy, reconciliation, and peace that its faith allegedly espouses. Also, sadly, nationalism had driven the church into confusing its spiritual task with the extremities of adversarial politics under the banner of patriotism. Of all the institutions in GC society, the Greek Orthodox Church has been the least capable of shedding the idolatry of nationalism and the least interested in constructive and peace-enhancing spiritual renewal.

Just before the populist "patriotic" fever overcame the GCs with the launch of the referenda campaigns, the church had exhibited isolated and timid attempts to follow the interethnic, conciliatory process that had grown since the late 1990s. The bishop of Morphou, for example, began speaking publicly against the evils of nationalism and in favor of peace with the Turks, not merely as a matter of practical political wisdom but as a moral imperative of the faith. Moreover, not long before the referenda, the church had joined the movement toward interethnic contacts that flourished with the opening of the checkpoints by inviting TC clerics to an interfaith conference focusing on the perils of the past and the need for reconciliation and a peaceful future.

However, the church's vulnerability to ethnocentric nationalism was revealed by how quickly and zealously the mainstream of its establishment and leadership were mobilized behind the "no" campaign following Papadopoulos's populist appeal to GCs to reject the Annan Plan. The church became a vital agent of the campaign, reinforcing and disseminating Papadopoulos's nationalism to the grass roots of GC society—a nationalism all too familiar to the modus operandi of the Greek Orthodox Church. Adding to the populist rhetoric of the rejectionist camp, Bishop Chrysostomos of Paphos—the acting church leader because of the ill health of the archbishop—warned against the plan's advocates. Insinuating that he had information about "foreigners" arriving on the Island, allegedly to distribute pamphlets and literature in favor of the Annan Plan, he discredited the supporters of peace by associating them with "foreign interests." He strongly warned the GC devout against listening to them. "We must close our eyes and our ears to these people," he said, "so that without any distractions we can vote 'no' if we are to continue living in our forefathers' land which has been Greek for three thousand years" (*Cyprus Mail* 2004b).

By lumping together all non-Greeks as conspiring foreigners, Bishop Chrysostomos fully aligned himself with Papadopoulos and the hardcore nationalists in his party. The bishop's dark suspicion of all foreigners, his references to the nationalist, anticolonial fighters of 1955–59, and his politically unfounded assertion equating Cyprus's accession to the EU with the old idea of *enosis* attest to the regressive nationalism that overtook the GC leadership. Ironically, the idea that Cyprus's accession to the EU is another way of achieving *enosis*—of uniting Cyprus with Greece—was the very argument propagated by Denktash as grounds for objecting to European integration—a position that politically discredited Denktash in European eyes, as a notion without merit or connection to reality.

The quintessential expression of nationalism by the GC Orthodox Church was manifested in the "hellfire sermon" against the Annan Plan delivered by Bishop Pavlos of Kyrenia (Silver 2004). Understandably, under the federal settlement proposed by the Annan Plan, the northern city of Kyrenia would have remained under the administration of the TC constituent state. But the question never asked by those opposing the plan was whether their all-or-nothing rejectionism could ever realistically lead to a sustainable outcome or generate a polity more effective for a settlement than the opportunity for peace offered by the historic UN plan. The nationalism articulated by Bishop Pavlos was not at all concerned with the specific content of the peace plan. In an unrestrained, wholesale identification of the Annan Plan with an ultimate form of injustice, punishable with eternal damnation, the bishop declared, "Those who say 'yes' will be party to this injustice, will lose their homeland and the kingdom of heaven!" (*Cyprus Mail* 2004b).

Ultimately, the synergy between Papadopoulos's speech, the mobilization of his party's political leaders and constituency, the utilization of the infrastructure of the civil service, and the roles of the media and the church created an emotionally charged nationalist tidal wave inducing extreme anxiety and dissonance among the public. Sadly, it did so just when the GC community was called upon to make a historic decision of tantamount importance for the future of Cyprus—a decision that presumably ought to have been made with utmost seriousness and clarity of mind.

In stifling the voices favoring the plan through intimidation, potent nationalist rhetoric, and the revival of the fears and anxieties of the past, the rejectionists generated not just the emotional hype of obsessive reaction but also great confusion among many ordinary GC citizens—possibly among the greatest number of GCs. Given the historical gravity of the choice confronting the GCs, the factor of confusion clearly favored a "no" vote to the Annan Plan. In an explosive government-led political climate of psychologically aggressive rejectionism, many GCs, confused as to the right choice, eventually became inclined to vote "no." Mass confusion always creates favorable conditions for blinding emotionalism; when people must choose between the painful but familiar past and a confusing, unknown future, they naturally opt for the familiar. This is precisely the psychological mechanism that the induced relapse into nationalism activated among a large portion of the GC electorate.

Central to the GC rejection of the Annan Plan, in which fanatical conviction as well as widespread confusion played a role, was the revival and reinstatement of the nationalist mindset in public culture by the Papadopoulos administration and its supporting coalition associates, namely the socialist party EDEK, the communist party AKEL, and smaller parties such as the Green Party. Since ethnocentric nationalism implies a fundamental aversion to any sort of interethnic cooperation, political or cultural overlap, or interethnic power sharing, it harbors the confining perception that democracy is essentially an intraethnic polity, never an interethnic one. It was solely through the reactivation of the nationalist mind in the public realm that the leaders of the "no" campaign managed to draw GC opinion into the anti-Annan camp, as the emotive energy of the newly launched ethnocentrism eclipsed the UN plan. At this juncture, the fundamental incompatibility between nationalist politics and multiethnic federation became clear, an incompatibility not merely between nationalist politics and certain forms of multiethnic federation, but between nationalist politics and *any* form of multiethnic federation.

Thus the complex array of psychological and ideational conditions that led the majority of GCs to reject the UN peace plan pose a serious question: whether the 76 percent "no" vote had anything to do with the actual content of the Annan Plan. The GC rejection of the UN peace proposal seems to have had less to do with the specifics of the plan than with the potent emotional reaction generated by the anachronistic references, symbolism, and rhetoric of a repopularized, monoethnic nationalism. The greater this emotionalism became, the more abominable the Annan Plan appeared, regardless of its content and the historical opportunities it presented. In reality, the GC "no" vote was directed less against the plan's objective content than against a nationalistically fabricated mental image of it—an image that abstractly and artificially associated it with a perceived anti-Hellenic "foreign conspiracy" that absolutely and exclusively served Turkish interests, that vastly endangered GC security, that undermined democracy, and that violated "the will of God."

THE ROLE OF NATIONALIST EXTREMISTS:
DISEMPOWERMENT AND EMPOWERMENT

Historically, all the GC parties that had come to power since the late 1980s were eventually compelled to undergo internal reform and a change in attitude as a result of their interactions with the EU. At least at the leadership level, this was particularly the case with DISY, the party traditionally rooted in and identified with the far-right brand of militant GC nationalism. Like Papadopoulos's DIKO, when DISY first came to power in 1993, it unleashed and reactivated an obsessive nationalism that drove the Cyprus problem into a highly dangerous cul-de-sac. But during its second term in office, under the second presidency of its founder, Glafkos Clerides, and the reforming, Europeanizing influence of Greece's Simitis government, DISY became increasingly outspoken about interethnic rapprochement, the EU vision, and a UN-based settlement. By 2004, Anastasiades, following the lead of Clerides and having undergone his own political transformation, became the first GC leader openly to lead DISY in support of the Annan Plan.

By contrast, DIKO, a party representing a mere 14 percent of the GC electorate and still locked into ethnocentric nationalism, came to power through the support of communist AKEL, a party of anachronistic mentality, and socialist EDEK, a party that, like DIKO, still embraced the old nationalist mentality. Papadopoulos's DIKO party had not been in power since 1988. Upon winning the presidential election in 2003, it appeared to pick up where it had left off in the 1980s, taking office in the same nationalist spirit and pursuing the same arbitrary, partisan usurpation of the state apparatus as it had in the past. Like other GC parties that had been in office, the Papadopoulos-led DIKO and its unreformed coalition partners were in time bound to crash against the postnationalist politics and institutions of the EU.

Over the years, it was common for the EU to question Denktash's intransigent nationalism and his Turkish-backed, quasi-military style of governance. But with the phenomena that transpired in the GC south during April 2004, many EU officials also questioned whether the politics and tactics of the Papadopoulos government befitted the presidency of a country that was about to join the EU. As with Denktash, the objections to the Annan Plan articulated by Papadopoulos and the "no" advocates in general appeared valid only in terms of a perspective that located the solution of the Cyprus problem outside a federal, interethnic model. The objections made sense only on the assumption that the solution sought ought to have been based on a monoethnic concept of statehood. From this perspective, interethnic power sharing was at best viewed as a distorted form of polity and as an enemy of national self-determination—a nationalist concept antithetical to EU culture and polity, as well as to all the UN resolutions on Cyprus.

One of the dire effects of the nationalist climate created by the Papadopoulos administration was the public political cover and empowerment it bestowed on the most extreme nationalists among the GC community. It created political space and legitimacy for the most fanatical and chauvinistic elements to play a role, yet again, at the forefront of events in both the public and private domains of society. Under these conditions, the momentum of the nationalist wave in the GC community did not stop with impassioned nationalist rhetoric and underhanded media tactics. It created an atmosphere allowing certain extremists to dare to cross the line from stirring nationalist sentiments among citizens and intimidating those supporting the Annan Plan to violent actions and threats against the plan's leading proponents.

The head of the DISY party, the first to declare formally its support of the UN proposal, had a hand grenade thrown into his house. Alecos Constantinides, the chief editor of the center-right newspaper *Aletheia*, received anonymous calls "threatening his life and expressing anger at the line the newspaper was following during the referenda." On numerous occasions, Constantinides restrained his family from getting into his car until the vehicle was checked for bombs. Known for his outspoken support of peace with the TCs and his backing of the Annan Plan, Michalis Papapetrou, a former government spokesman and close associate of former president George Vassiliou in the United Democrats Party, was placed under police protection. The action of the police resulted from credible information that his life was in danger from extreme GC elements supporting the "no" campaign (*Aletheia* 2004).

These events in the GC community paralleled phenomena in the TC community during the run-up to the referenda. The most notable were the heavy beatings of propeace youths by the Grey Wolves, an extremist nationalist group rooted in Turkey's far-right nationalist past. Furthermore, TC militants bombed the house of Mehmet Ali Talat, Republican Party leader and propeace "prime minister" supporting the Annan Plan. Reactionary forces also bombed the offices of *Kibris,* a newspaper known for promoting peace with the GCs, supporting a negotiated settlement to reunify the Island, and criticizing the intransigent nationalism of the Denktash regime.

Fortunately, no injuries occurred in these incidents in either community, but the events revealed, yet again, that reawakened nationalist passions enabled sinister forces to be incubated and unleashed into society in a manner that could easily become unmanageable. As always, the affinity between nationalism and aggressive primitive instincts had the psychological and even moral propensity to legitimize extreme actions. Yet the sporadic cases of militant interventionism by nationalists in the two Cypriot communities during the referenda campaigns disclosed an interesting difference between those occurring in the north and those occurring in the south. The militant attacks on the TC side betrayed the panic of nationalists who had been put on the defensive, since the new TC administration, backed by the Turkish government, favored a settlement and supported the Annan Plan. In contrast, the militant attacks on the GC side reflected the determination of nationalists committed to taking the offensive in support of a political position directly aligned with the official position of the Papadopoulos administration. The GC government might have formally denounced the incidents of violence as unacceptable, but it could not circumvent the essential fact that the militants' political ends were identical to its own, and, further, that its own nationalist approach had actually empowered the militants.

To understand the particular historical phase to which Cyprus had evolved by April 2004, it is essential to stress that, astonishingly, none of the incidents of tension noted over the year beginning with the free mixing of the two Cypriot communities and lasting until the referenda were interethnic, but rather were intraethnic. This was a stunning sign that interethnic relations at the citizens' level had withstood the test of intercommunal contact better than had intra-Greek or intra-Turkish relations within the respective Cypriot communities. In the effort to arrive at a final settlement, the critical issue was thereby one of leadership. From this perspective, the incident-free, interethnic relations stood as a great historical condemnation of the rejectionist portion of the TC leadership as well of the Papadopoulos coalition government.

Evidently, GC opinion offered an opportune range of possibilities for finalizing a supportable settlement. The GC leadership, however, chose to steer GC opinion in the direction of reaction, confusion, and rejection. The rejectionist camps of both Denktash and Papadopoulos failed to build their political agendas on the positive political capital that was available in the readiness of the TCs, the flexibility of GC opinion, and the positive outcomes of intercommunal relations. Rather, they opted for ethnocentric agendas and approaches that perpetuated the captivity of their people to the divisive and belligerent remnant of their nationalist past. Perhaps the saddest impact of the reawakened nationalism on the GC side was the lasting effect it had on the more suggestible portion of the community—namely the GC youth, most of whom maintained a stance opposing the interethnic reunification of Cyprus, contrary to the very goal that perennially constituted the primary aim of the GCs (Lordos 2005).

These were the perils and challenges of a society in transition, which could have easily seen the process of change set in the direction of creative renewal and peace-enhancing reunification, had the governing GC leadership seized the unprecedented, historical moment presented by the April referenda. A positive outcome would have meant not only a comprehensive political settlement but, just as importantly for the sustainability of peace in Cyprus, the decisive defeat of nationalism on both sides of the Island—the nationalism that bred the ethnocentrism that had fueled the Cyprus conflict in the first place. Having failed to transcend its own nationalism, however, the Papadopoulos government remained blind to the political and historical prospects at hand.

THE ROLE OF PARTY POLITICS: AKEL

The communist, left-wing party AKEL, credited with helping Papadopoulos and his hard-line DIKO party come to power, bears a great deal of responsibility for the events leading to the failure of the Annan Plan. Given AKEL's long-standing, interethnic rapprochement policy and ongoing contact and dialogue with the TCs, most people, especially among TCs, expected it to support the Annan Plan. In fact, following the release of the final version of the plan, AKEL declared that it was viable since it contained many more positive elements—in the interest of GCs—than negative ones. However, it soon became evident that hard-line nationalists within the communist party, upon sensing that their party was inclined to vote "yes," reacted vehemently and publicly, threatening to leave. Given the monolithic and esoteric culture of AKEL, the party leadership clearly viewed potential or actual party attrition not as merely undesirable, but as the ultimate threat, to be combated at any cost. Always a central feature of AKELIst political culture, this attitude derived from the historical residue of the communist ideology, which perceived the party as the "sacred cow" of politics. Within such an ideological framework, no political values, agendas, or objectives existed beyond the unconditional self-preservation, self-worship, and aggrandizement of the party. This culture was activated among the leadership in the face of the reaction of AKELIst nationalists, who opted for total rejection of the Annan Plan.

At work here was the familiar but grossly overlooked traditional blind spot of communists regarding the nationalism harbored within their own ranks. Historically, ethnocentric nationalism has not been the exclusive monopoly of traditional right-wing politics, flourishing just as well within left-wing traditions (Pfaff 1989). The huge mistake the Left had made from its initial appearance was to perceive nationalism not as a conflict-habituated, sociocultural phenomenon but merely as an ideological one restricted to right-wing parties and movements. Communists remained blind to their own belligerent nationalism and its adverse effects on interethnic and international relations.

This historical blind spot left AKEL unprepared for the political blackmail applied by its own ethnocentrically fixated party members toward the party leadership in the approach to the referenda. The combination of the challenges from nationalists within the party and the sacred status communists attribute to it became AKEL's historical entrapment. AKEL had either to denounce nationalism and face party attrition as its nationalist members joined more explicitly nationalist parties (especially Papadopoulos's DIKO party and socialist EDEK party) or follow the nationalist agenda and maintain party cohesion. This dilemma had plagued AKEL since the 1950s, starting with the *enosis* movement.

Moreover, in making a final decision on the Annan Plan, AKEL also had to confront issues of political power and privilege vis-à-vis its participation in the coalition government that had reverted to nationalist politics. If AKEL were to support the UN plan, it would have had to break ranks with the Papadopoulos government just when the party had won more ministerial positions than ever before. Voting "yes" for the plan would have required AKEL to give up unprecedented party power in government. Inevitably, AKEL began to waver, rescinding its original, publicly expressed intention to vote "yes"—a position that would have surely ended with an overall endorsement of the plan by the GC community. AKEL's mixed messages and political wavering added to the high anxiety, confusion, and negativity among the GC community already generated by Papadopoulos's anti-Annan campaign. The party's traditional policy of rapprochement toward the TCs and its long-standing, professed support for reconciliation and the reunification of Cyprus began to appear dull, unconvincing, and lacking in political credibility.

As expected, AKEL was politically and morally challenged by the TC Left, which had always considered it a trustworthy partner in the struggle for reconciliation and a final political settlement. Moreover, AKEL came under political pressure from the Americans who had placed great stakes on a positive diplomatic outcome in Cyprus for reasons, as mentioned previously, that had much to do with their efforts to restore their badly damaged international credibility resulting from their invasion of Iraq. The strong sense of desperation in the American approach perhaps did more to alienate AKEL than to assist it in constructively assuming its historical responsibilities.

However, the great shame of AKEL was disclosed when DISY, the traditionally far-right party and ideological archenemy of AKEL, decided to support the Annan Plan in the referenda. DISY, founded by former president Clerides in the 1970s, was the party that absorbed the 1974 GC coupists and carried the historical stigma of the excesses of the far-right brand of GC nationalism. DISY was the party that AKEL had always identified as the bearer of the historical legacy of fascism and the one that shared little with what AKEL called the "progressive democratic forces" of the Island. Unlike in Greece, where the traditional Right and the mainstream Left underwent a conscious process of national reconciliation, leaving behind the mar of the Greek civil war and the paralysis of belligerent, ideological politics, the historical alienation between AKEL and DISY persisted, even up to the critical moment of the Cyprus referenda. But to its credit, DISY had evolved beyond its problematic historical legacy of belligerent, far-right nationalism. The change in DISY had occurred as its founder, Clerides, abandoned nationalist approaches during his second term as president, in a shift coinciding with the formal accession process of Cyprus to the EU; as the leadership of DISY subsequently began increasing contact with Europeans, thus becoming exposed to postnationalist politics; and as prominent DISY members and officials started to become engaged in rapprochement initiatives with TCs, thus encountering interethnic perspectives on the Cyprus issue.

The historical irony was that Papadopoulos's DIKO party, with which AKEL colluded at the most crucial moment in the history of the Cyprus problem, had always been fundamentally nationalistic in its approach. In fact, DIKO, which had been presenting itself as the traditional "moderate Center Right," had preserved and sustained a far more hard-line, ethnocentric, nationalist outlook than the allegedly far-right DISY had done in recent years. The effective leadership and major portion of the Socialist Party EDEK, which also coalesced with Papadopoulos during the presidential elections, had similarly been a preserver and propagator of ethnocentric nationalism. AKEL's historical and ideological fallacy lay in the fact that, while paying lip service to an antinationalist agenda and refusing to cooperate with DISY when the latter was moving away from its nationalist past, it aligned with the most nationalistic parties, both in the presidential elections and eventually in the referenda of April 24. All AKEL managed to achieve was the empowerment of DIKO, which represented a mere 14 percent of the GC electorate, by enabling it to set the political agenda of the GC community through the formal seat of governmental power.

The traditional bitter rivalry between the GC communists and the GC rightists throughout the 1950s, 1960s, and 1970s exacerbated the interethnic conflict between GCs and TCs, culminating in the Greek-led coup d'état and the Turkish invasion of 1974. The militancy, hatred, and nationalism exhibited in the Right-Left conflict skewed and undermined interethnic relations, while fueling and amplifying TC nationalism. Among other things, the Cyprus referenda of 2004 should have been viewed as a historic opportunity for the traditional GC Right and the GC communists to transcend their bloodstained past. The referenda presented a great historical moment for AKEL and DISY to reconcile in the interest not only of restoring intra-Greek relations but also of achieving broader interethnic peace in Cyprus by joining hands in support of the plan. DISY's readiness to do so was revealed when it ventured out as the first party to announce officially its support of the Annan Plan at a time when the tidal wave of Papadopoulos's "no" campaign was in full sweep—and in view of the fact that it stood to lose some diehard nationalist members. In light of the pending accession of Cyprus to the EU, the historic stance of DISY revealed a subtle response to its own psychological need for redemption—one that would finally relieve it from its weighty nationalist baggage.

By contrast, AKEL proved incapable of attaining the political transcendence called for by the dramatic run-up to the referenda. It failed to reform itself sufficiently to overcome the residue of its monolithic, communist psyche and its self-denying, unattended nationalism. Not surprisingly, AKEL, despite its unease, chose to align itself with the nationalist rejectionism of Papadopoulos and the socialists. Once again, this brought to the surface the fact that AKEL's gestures of rapprochement toward the TCs had not been primarily and fundamentally interethnic (between the two ethnic communities), but rather intra-ideological (between its members and TC communists and leftists).

In the past, by assuming that the primary ideological agenda was to collaborate with left-wing parties in an all-out political war against the Far Right, AKEL practically turned a blind eye to the nationalism within its own ranks and thus its own vulnerability to nationalism. As always, when confronted with the historical options between political ideology and ethnocentric nationalist loyalties, the Left subjugated the former to the latter. This occurred even as it fought its right-wing compatriots, identifying them as traitors to the national cause in the same manner that right-wing nationalists had traditionally perceived and treated the Left.

The contradictions in its thinking about the referenda, particularly given its traditional rapprochement rhetoric of "the Turks are our brothers," made it hard for AKEL to choose a clear position. Shortly before the April referenda, therefore, in a desperate attempt to attain "moral cover" for gravitating toward the Papadopoulos camp, AKEL conjured up an extraordinary approach, arguing that while it had intended to support the Annan Plan, there was not enough time to convince its supporters of its merits.

In a communication to the UN secretary-general, AKEL requested a six-month postponement of the referenda. Needless to say, this position served Papadopoulos's strategy of pursuing the May 1 entry of Cyprus into the EU without a settlement—a strategy that intended to use the subsequent European status of the republic as a negotiating weapon against the Turks. Clearly, the UN rejected AKEL's request. After all, the entire logic behind the four-and-a-half years of negotiations culminating in the extraordinary diplomatic effort undertaken by the UN, the EU, and the United States was to achieve a comprehensive settlement before the Island's entry into the EU. A postponement would have meant a contradiction in principle of what had been agreed and a total dislocation of the diplomatic process that had led to the engagement of all the stakeholders: the TCs, the GCs, Greece, Turkey, and the EU.

However, still awkwardly caught between its professed support for the Annan Plan and its rapprochement with the TC Left on the one hand, and its power interests and tacit nationalism on the other, AKEL continued its desperate quest for a credible way out of its political and moral dilemma. Its new tactic was to argue that while the Annan Plan was viable and supportable, it needed institutional assurances by the international community guaranteeing its implementation, such that Turkey would not evade or disrupt the execution of the plan. If such guarantees were secured, AKEL asserted, the party would then offer its support. Otherwise, it would call on its constituency to reject it at the referenda.

Even as objective observers questioned whether Turkey would gain anything from disrupting implementation in the event of a settlement, a UN draft resolution aimed at granting to the GCs the institutional guarantees that AKEL had requested was launched jointly by the United States and the UK. While the draft circulated for finalization among the members of the Security Council, Papadopoulos unexpectedly dispatched foreign minister George Iacovou to Moscow. When the final version of the resolution was put to the vote at the UN, fourteen of the fifteen Security Council members voted in favor. Surprisingly, Russia vetoed it. The uneasiness and awkwardness so evident in the public posture and statements of the AKEList leadership revealed that AKEL was party to Papadopoulos's efforts to secure Russia's veto of the UN resolution on Cyprus—the very resolution that AKEL had requested. As for dispatching the foreign minister to Moscow, the explanation given when questions were raised was that the trip had been planned prior to the drafting of the proposed resolution.

Parenthetically, it ought to be mentioned that a survey conducted by Drs. Christophorou and Webster, released in spring 2004 following the referenda, revealed that while 51 percent of GCs preferred a unitary-state solution, only 11 percent preferred a federal one. Simultaneously, however, the survey indicated that 62 percent of GCs were willing to support a solution based on the Annan Plan if guarantees were given for its safe implementation (Christophorou and Webster 2004). In other words, GCs were willing to opt for the UN federal solution pending implementation guarantees—the very guarantees that, to the expressed contentment of Papadopoulos, had been blocked by the Russian veto.

This dire diplomatic episode brought to light the tactical machinations of Papadopoulos's nationalism, in which AKEL had participated. As usual, nationalism's absolutist approaches to politics, its maximalist "all-or-nothing" principles, and its confusion of democracy with monoethnic, absolute majoritarianism led to one type of diplomacy—subversive, not constructive. Within the same framework, international law and the institutional processes that support it are always perceived and employed by nationalists as mere legal weapons for conducting maximalist politics in the arena of diplomatic warfare. Even when the law is set up in the service of pluralistic democracy, nationalists perceive it not as a nonpartisan, common framework within which to conduct politics, but rather as a tactical instrument for waging ethnocentric political battles.

Nationalists rarely use the law in the spirit of the law. They simply usurp it as a dead letter into which they import an alien spirit, namely the belligerent nationalist spirit. In essence, nationalists scarcely view themselves as being under the law. To the degree that they operate within the its framework, they do so solely for tactical reasons, never for substantive or principled reasons. They see themselves as fundamentally positioned outside of it precisely because, in nationalism, the value of "the nation" is above the law—a position that extends to the nationalist concept of national sovereignty. Although nationalists find it prudent in times of calm not to violate the law overtly, they nevertheless readily usurp it and its institutions in the interest of their ethnocentric objectives, which lie outside its spirit and intent.

Papadopoulos's tactics vis-à-vis the UN reflect the manner in which nationalism is played out in the formal processes of international law and related institutions. Papadopoulos's behavior and tactics were clearly reminiscent of how Denktash conducted politics for decades. Ironically, Papadopoulos had caught up with Denktash-like nationalist politics at the historical moment when Denktash's own nationalism was being curbed.

AKEL's approach at this crossroads of the Cyprus problem can only be described as a grand travesty of political thought and action, reflecting an unprecedented case of collective denial and evasion. The absence of political astuteness and sense of responsibility on its part emerged when its leader, Christofias, explained his party's decision to vote "no" during the referenda. He asserted that AKEL's "no" was not like those of the others, since his party's "no" was intended to postpone the referenda in order to prevent the failure of the plan during its implementation (Cyprus News Agency 2004).

Sadly, ideological blind spots and political power concerns made AKEL an amateur player in its handling of the diplomatic and political affairs of Cyprus. All that AKEL managed was to become an extension of Papadopoulos's "no" campaign, partaking of his nationalist rejectionism, which marked the referenda with the psychological realienation of the two ethnic communities. Knowing Papadopoulos's long-standing, ethnocentric nationalism, one could not expect anything beyond his traditional, reactionary intransigence. But AKEL, as a party proud of its rapprochement efforts and alleged support for federation and reunification, appeared in the worst of lights, particularly in the eyes of the TC Left. Unlike the Labor Day celebrations of 2003, which saw a massive festive gathering of GC AKELists with TC parties and labor unions, the celebrations of May 2004 saw a shamed AKEL celebrating alone.

The overall political bankruptcy in the approach of the ruling GC parties was fully disclosed in the stark contrast between their delirious activism before the referenda and their disoriented numbness afterward. Their feverish and relentless anti-Annan rhetoric and mobilization was followed by an anticlimax of silence and agenda-free passivity. It was as though their victory in defeating the Annan Plan had ended in a political void, with nothing left to do. This silence and political inaction paralleled the political passivity and diplomatic immobility characterizing the Papadopoulos government after the referenda. By contrast, Turkey's prime minister, Erdogan, declared that the Cyprus referenda marked "the most successful event in the last 50 years of Turkish diplomacy," to which *The Economist* added, and "also the Greek-Cypriots' biggest diplomatic disaster in 30 years" (*The Economist* 2004a).

7
Postreferenda Political Realities

UN OUTRAGE AT PAPADOPOULOS

Given the UN's and the EU's enormous effort to bend Turkish and TC nationalist intransigence paralleling four-and-a-half years of formal negotiations, the international political fallout following the referendum was considerable. Though the Papadopoulos administration downplayed its significance, the open condemnation by the international community of the government's role in the GC rejection of the UN plan was clear, explicit, and firm. Both the EU and the UN were shocked and outraged at the politics and tactics of Papadopoulos and his administration. Initially, the GC rejectionist camp either evaded the international community's response or recycled it back into the treadmill of the nationalist mind, interpreting the overwhelming disenchantment of the international community with the GC vote as a sign of Hellenic victory against the foreign conspirators.

However, a more grounded approach to the events in Cyprus leads to a very different understanding of what shaped the opinion and stance of the international community. While officially accepting the outcome of the referendum, the EU and the UN held the GC side primarily responsible for derailing the effort to resolve the Cyprus problem, mainly in view of certain vital political and diplomatic facts centering on Papadopoulos's leadership and his supporting coalition government.

First, during the New York talks in early April, Papadopoulos had agreed with the UN secretary-general that the Cypriot leaders would commence negotiations on the basis of the Annan Plan; Greece and Turkey would join the negotiations if the Cypriot leaders were not able to conclude; and the secretary-general would fill in the blanks of the UN plan, which would then be put to a referendum prior to Cyprus's entry into the EU.

On the basis of diplomatic protocol, the understanding of the UN and the EU was that Papadopoulos's formal commitment to this process meant that he had accepted, at least at a minimal level, the framework of the Annan Plan; he had endorsed the possible contributions of Greece and Turkey; and he had welcomed, if necessary, the final drafting of the plan by the UN secretary-general.

The Europeans, in particular, felt strongly offended that after giving his formal consent to the process, the GC leader had resorted to nationalist appeals to his community to vote "a resounding 'no'" to the Annan Plan. These facts were echoed in the UN secretary-general's postreferendum report of May 28, 2004 (United Nations 2004c).

Second, those citizens and diplomats who had invested their energy and hope in a negotiated settlement were shocked at Papadopoulos's explanation as to why he had participated in the negotiations that were so explicitly based on accepting the framework of the Annan Plan. In his Easter week speech, Papadopoulos explained to the GC people that he had agreed to participate in the UN talks because, had he not done so, he would have acted contrary to the perennial policy of the GC National Council—that the GC side seeks a solution to the Cyprus problem through negotiations under the auspices of the UN. Such a statement revealed that Papadopoulos's participation was formalistic and tactical rather than substantive. His original objective was to have the negotiation process end in failure, with the TC side blamed for the impasse. However, having underestimated the change in Turkish policy over Cyprus, Papadopoulos was left politically exposed. His diplomatically impoverished explanations as to why he participated in the talks were a retroactive rationalization of an approach that went sour. However, it raised disturbing questions regarding his political credibility and true motives. The central issue was that Papadopoulos had concealed his position on the peace plan until the referendum (Loizides 2004).

Third, the European and the UN officials were stunned at Papadopoulos's articulation of his rationale for rejecting the Annan Plan. In his Easter week broadcast, the GC leader explained that his negative position on the Annan Plan was justified because accepting the plan would have meant "doing away with our internationally recognized state [the GC-controlled Republic of Cyprus] at the very moment it strengthens its political weight, with its accession to the European Union" (Papadopoulos 2004). The statement revealed that Papadopoulos's priority was not the solution to the Cyprus problem and the accession of a united Cyprus to the EU, which had grounded the entire logic of the UN talks. Instead, it was the preservation of the Republic of Cyprus, even at the price of perpetuating the Cyprus problem and, further, of ushering the conflict into the union. Moreover, his adamant fixation on preserving the Republic of Cyprus rather than supporting the finalization of a new united Cyprus republic, reveals that his assessment of the Annan Plan was not based on the plan's own merits but on his overshadowing preference for perpetuating the old nationalist ideal of attaining a unitary, ethnocentric state. This ideal has proven disastrous whenever pursued by any faction in any society of multiethnic composition.

Referring to Papadopoulos's explanation, the UN secretary-general asserted, "I was surprised at this statement, in light of what Mr. Papadopoulos had said to me in Brussels in January. I was also surprised at his interpretation of the plan, since the plan was designed to allow each side to maintain its position on how the new state of affairs would come into being" (United Nations 2004c; see also United Nations 2003a, pars. 66–67). Not surprisingly, in a briefing to the Security Council immediately following the Cyprus referendum, undersecretary-general for political affairs Kieran Prendergast stated that while the results of the referendum were respected, the UN characterized them as "disappointing." Regretfully, it was noted, "the United Nations had come closer than ever before to solving one of the most delicate and complex conflicts on its agenda" (United Nations 2004b).

In light of both the historic displacement of Denktash by the moderate Talat—with the backing of the Turkish government—and Greece's original support of the Annan Plan, Papadopoulos emerged as the new leading figure of intransigence in the Cyprus problem. From the EU and UN perspectives, Papadopoulos had undertaken the role and status previously attributed to Denktash. In the changing and novel political context, this was so striking that the UN explicitly profiled Papadopoulos's nationalist rejectionism in its official reports. Addressing the Security Council, Prendergast asserted that

> The reasons given by Mr. Papadopoulos [for rejecting the Annan Plan] were wide-ranging and far-reaching. His rejection of the plan meant that he had joined company with Rauf Denktash—the leader of Turkish Cypriots—who had also given wide-ranging and far-reaching reasons to reject the plan. Paradoxically, each leader had claimed that the plan, as finalized, threatened the security and safety of his people and gave in to all the key demands of the other side. (United Nations 2004b)

For his traditional nationalist politics, Denktash had earned the title "Mr. No." This characterization circulated in the diplomatic corridors of the international community, denoting his absolutist and anticonciliatory approach to the Cyprus problem. But with Denktash overtaken by the new leadership in both the TC community and Turkey, the leader of the GC side now assumed the stigma of rejectionism and nationalist intransigence formerly carried by the leader of the TC side. It was thus no surprise that less than a week after the referendum, *The Economist* was profiling Papadopoulos as "a new Mr. No" (*The Economist* 2004c).

The new political realities were succinctly formalized in the UN secretary-general's report on Cyprus of May 28, 2004, which in essence set the stage for the politics of postreferendum Cyprus. In his report, Annan elaborated in chronological and thematic detail the up-to-date process and outcomes of the Cyprus negotiations, including their implications for the postreferendum era.

Traditionally, the reports of the UN secretary-general tended to lay the burden of responsibility more on the TC and Turkish side for the failure to resolve the problem. But the May 2004 report placed the responsibility for the impasse on the GC side. And it did so in a manner that marked a decisive change in the UN's perspective and language on Cyprus. The international diplomatic mobilization leading up to the referendum and the entry of Cyprus into the EU marked the most extraordinary, elaborate, and comprehensive diplomatic and political effort for resolving the Cyprus problem ever undertaken. It entailed a long and arduous process during which Turkey had clearly changed its position in favor of a settlement, the TCs had shifted their stance in favor of reunification, Denktash's secessionist nationalism had been marginalized, and Greece had expressly backed the Annan Plan in parallel with its conditional support of Turkey's European orientation. With this unprecedented historical convergence, the swaying of GCs by their leadership to vote "no" to the UN peace plan was truly tragic. The sad and depressing outcome was reflected throughout the secretary-general's report (United Nations 2004c). That the report included a scathing critique of GC president Papadopoulos was not surprising. The report made explicit references to Papadopoulos's undermining of the agreement of the February 2004 negotiations (2); to his tactics of delay and excessive objections (6, 12); to his making new demands on what had been earlier agreed (15); to his ambivalent, postnegotiation statements about preferring to preserve the republic rather than opting for a final settlement (16); to his inaccurate presentation of the Annan Plan to the GC people (17); to objecting having the UN provide further institutional security guarantees for the GCs; and to his indifference to and absence from the international pledging conference for Cyprus organized by the European Commission in Brussels (17).

By comparison, the secretary-general's criticisms of the TC side were few. Moreover, he explicitly acknowledged both the positive change in the TC position (p. 4) and the steadfast commitment of Turkey to solving the problem in accordance with the UN plan (p. 2). The only serious criticism was that their delay in changing their position in favor of a settlement had weakened the incentives for the GC side. The reference was to Denktash, whose rejectionism drove the beleaguered negotiation process past April 16, 2003, thus permitting Papadopoulos to sign the Accession Treaty with the EU with no binding commitment for a UN-based settlement of the Cyprus problem. But in the final analysis, given the extraordinary convergence of historical factors in favor of a settlement, the secretary-general attributed the failure to bring the Cyprus problem to closure mainly to the GC leadership.

PAPADOPOULOS'S MONOETHNIC NATIONALISM AND OUTRAGE AT THE UN

While Greece remained passive, the Papadopoulos administration responded vehemently to Annan's report to the UN Security Council. The rebuttal by GC foreign minister George Iacovou stated publicly that the secretary-general suffered from a "writer's syndrome." Uttered by the representative of the side that for decades had staked its position on its alignment with the UN, such a statement was deemed by third parties as crude and highly inappropriate. President Papadopoulos responded with a strong letter of complaint to the UN accusing the secretary-general of partiality and prejudice against the GC side. Within UN circles, however, Papadopoulos's response was not taken seriously. Based on the role he had played in the negotiations and the referendum, his letter was perceived as nothing more than a discredited moralistic defense of his untenable nationalist position. Besides, it contained nothing concrete or constructive on how to proceed toward a solution of the Cyprus problem. Overall, Papadopoulos's attack of Annan's report fell on deaf ears. The result was merely a deepening alienation between the GC leadership and the UN. Stunningly, the fruitless diplomatic situation in which Papadopoulos found himself as a result of his nationalist politics was identical to the one Denktash had been in for decades because of his barren nationalism. Indeed, a role reversal had occurred.

To the secretary-general's questioning of Papadopoulos's commitment to a federal solution, the GC president responded that no evidence substantiating such doubts exists. In light of the traditional position of his party, DIKO, and his political record, Papadopoulos's claim that he was never opposed to federation is extraordinary and unconvincing. DIKO and its leadership's opposition to a bicommunal, federal solution had been common knowledge in Cyprus for decades. What, then, did Papadopoulos mean by stating in his letter to the UN that he did not oppose federation? The answer can be pursued through two possible avenues. One is to conclude that Papadopoulos is a liar. This, however, is too simplistic, as it renders incomprehensible the passion and moral tone of Papadopoulos's self-defense against the UN. A more appropriate approach for understanding Papadopoulos's response is to explore the meaning he attributes to the term *federation*. To do this, one must consider the particular manner in which the meaning of federation may be refracted once processed through the prism of nationalism.

Reflective of his party's traditional approach to the Cyprus problem, Papadopoulos's overall handling of the negotiations and the referendum revealed a particular dimension of the democratic deficit typical of nationalist politics. It concerns the ethnocentric, majoritarian understanding of democracy, which conceives it as an exclusively intraethnic polity and never an interethnic one. The political ramifications of the nationalist concept of democracy were precisely what impeded Papadopoulos from moving toward a settlement. While he accepted the principle of political equality between individual citizens, he fundamentally rejected the principle of the political equality between ethnic groups, as do all nationalists. Papadopoulos revealed this in an interview with the Dubai-based *Khaleej Times* in September 2004, in which he bemoaned the federal arrangement proposed by the Annan Plan. The GC president explicitly rejected political equality between GCs and TCs, arguing that it would be unworkable. "Democracy in principle," he asserted, "is based on the majority opinion"—meaning the opinion of the *ethnic* majority. He made it clear that he would not concede to the minority TC community the same rights as the GC majority (*Khaleej Times* 2004). The antifederalist implication here is that since at the community level the TCs never can have rights equal to those of the GCs, the TCs never ought to be constituted as a federated state. Hence, the idea of creating a bicommunal, bizonal federation that would include GC and TC constituent states is meaningless and unacceptable.

In the nationalist mind, ethnic majorities alone constitute the basis of democracy, popular sovereignty, and state power. On the basis of this presumption, ethnic minorities are at best obliged to accept undifferentiated absorption into the society of the dominant ethnic majority, with their rights secured before the law solely as individuals, but never as a sociopolitical identity group sharing decision-making power. It is precisely this perspective that caused Papadopoulos and the anti-Annan intelligentsia to reject the UN peace plan, since it attempted to balance not only the rights of GCs and TCs as individuals before the law but also their rights as ethnic communities before the law. As a rule, nationalists do not accept that ethnic majorities and minorities should have equal rights as communal entities in a country, particularly in wielding state power; they instead view the power of the state as a monopolistic right of the ethnic majority. Strikingly, exactly the same perspective had shaped Denktash's secessionist politics as far back as the 1950s. His objective was to carve out of Cyprus a state in which the TCs would be the majority, which in turn would establish a TC majoritarian "democracy," with the TC community monopolizing political power at the collective state level. For three decades the administration of the TRNC deprived the small GC minority remaining in the north of any political power or substantive representation. The foundation of Denktash's and Papadopoulos's politics was in fact identical, reflecting the political extremities and blind spots of nationalist majoritarian politics.

If this analysis is credible, though, how can one explain that while still in the nationalist mode, Papadopoulos argued in his letter to the UN that he never rejected federation? His forceful tone and sense of conviction strongly suggest that in his mind he had in fact been unquestionably benevolent to the other side. His response was in fact articulated as a moral argument asserting that while he had been decisively generous toward the TC side, the UN secretary-general accused him of rejecting federation and derailing the anticipated settlement. How can this be so?

Papadopoulos's sense of benevolence toward the other ethnic community was essentially derived from his nationalist assumption that although Cyprus is a "Hellenic state" that should rightfully be governed by the GC ethnic majority through a monopoly on state power, he nevertheless openhandedly consented to consider a measure of secured TC representation in the organs of the central state.

As already mentioned, nationalist majoritarian politics only accepts the political participation of the other ethnic community as individual citizens, never as an ethnic group. Even less acceptable to nationalists is to have the ethnic minority represented as a constituent, federated state on equal standing with that of the ethnic majority. In this sense, the maximum limit of Papadopoulos's "benevolence" was for the TCs to participate as a sum of individuals in proportion to the sum of GC individuals—not as an ethnic community or federated state with the same rights as the GC community and GC federated state. Of course, this amounted to the TCs' having no more than 18 percent of the decision-making power in the overall system of governance, particularly at the federal level. Prevalent in the Papadopoulos camp, this perception revealed an attempt to subsume the meaning of *federation* to a monoethnic concept of democracy. By definition, then, it precluded the possibility of any form of interethnic, federated/federal polity. It is in view of this perception that Papadopoulos's strong reaction and even "moral outrage" at Annan's report can be understood. When he asserted that he *accepted* federation, what he really meant was that, having compromised beyond the boundaries of what a "proper democracy" ought to be (which in his nationalist mind is the unquestionable monopoly rule of the ethnic majority), he was willing to accept some form of guaranteed TC representation and power. This was in essence what Papadopoulos understood whenever he referred to an "acceptable form of federation."

Whether GC or TC, nationalists failed to confront the fact that historically their majoritarian concept of democracy always resulted in the ethnic majority overwhelming the ethnic minority. This was the key political orientation of both GC nationalism, as it attempted to prevail during the interethnic conflicts of the 1960s, and TC nationalism, as it attempted to instate by force a Turkish state in northern Cyprus. The impasse of both GC and TC ethnocentric, majoritarian politics was the central problem that the Annan Plan aimed at overcoming. But Papadopoulos and his nationalist supporters did not understand federation in the sense and for the purpose that the plan intended. Rather, they saw it as the most extreme point of a compromise, in that while the ethnic majority ought to hold full control over state power, it was nevertheless willing to cede some power to the other (minority) ethnic group.

Needless to say, this ethnomajoritarian concept of governance was the same underpinning Denktash's politics of secession. Because of their monoethnic concept of statehood, nationalists feel that anything beyond the full rule of the ethnic majority constitutes a compromise of democracy. For this reason, while interethnic democracy is fundamentally excluded from their concept of federation, when nationalists accept even a skewed notion of federation, they feel they have been outrageously tolerant and giving. On both sides of the Cypriot ethnic divide, the familiar anger, frustration, and moralizing arguments of nationalists over national injustice and unfairness is a direct derivative of their monoethnic contrivance of democracy.

A prevalent argument put forward by numerous GC nationalists was that interethnic federation is in essence racist because it divides power along ethnoracial lines. It is stunning how the same people who have grounded their politics on this argument can believe simultaneously that ethnocentric majoritarianism, which shrinks democracy to merely an intraethnic polity, is not racist but the pinnacle of democracy. Then again, the nationalist mind had always attempted the alchemy of turning the raw iron of ethnocentric intolerance into the gold of democracy.

Nationalists maintain that if ethnocentric majoritarian democracy is rejected, then the alternative is for the minority to rule the majority. This belief is the inevitable outcome of a mind entrapped in a nationalist concept of democracy. The dilemma disappears only when one accepts that democracy is *also* an interethnic category. For both the UN and the EU, the comprehensive settlement for Cyprus proposed by the Annan Plan was founded on an interethnic concept of democracy, especially since the historical problem it addressed was a protracted interethnic conflict.

Moreover, the interethnic democracy recommended by the UN plan also provided for the numerical representation of the GC and TC communities to reflect the differences in their respective size. The UN concept of federation was thus built on the principle of equality applied to both the relationship between individual citizens and the relationship between the major ethnic identity groups of Cyprus. For example, the Annan Plan's proposal for a federal parliament composed of two chambers, the Senate and the Chamber of Deputies, underscored the principle of interethnic democracy. The proposed Chamber of Deputies was composed in proportion to the number of citizens in each ethnic community of the constituent states, while the Senate was composed of an equal number of GCs and TCs. What did this arrangement achieve? It balanced the numeric representation of each side, establishing equality between individual citizens, to the communal representation of each side, establishing equality between the communities. The GCs were granted higher representation in the Chamber of Deputies, reflecting their proportional numeric representation. In the Senate, GCs were granted equal representation with the TCs, reflecting the equality of the communities and their respective constituent states.

In other words, the Chamber of Deputies upheld the principle of equality between individual citizens, while the Senate upheld the principle of equality between the ethnic communities. This logic of balancing equality between individual citizens before the law and equality between communities before the law runs throughout the many details of the Annan Plan. In essence, acceptance of the Annan Plan by the TCs meant a transcending of the nationalism embodied in the political legacy of Denktash. Rejection of the plan by the GCs meant a relapse into the nationalism embodied in the political legacy of Papadopoulos.

Interestingly, when considering the type of democracy and power sharing enjoyed by Cyprus within the EU, GC nationalists tended to ignore the very arguments and principles they employed for rejecting the Annan Plan. If the principle of ethnocentric majoritarianism was to apply to the EU bodies, based on merely the numeric representation of the member-states, then GC Cyprus, with a population of 700,000 in a Europe of 450 million, should have been allocated only 1.1 seats of the total 732 in the European Parliament, rather than the 6 seats given. And in the Council of the EU, Cyprus should have been granted only 0.5 votes of the total 321, instead of the 4 votes given.

What often evades the nationalists is that in accordance with the EU's concept of democracy, countries that have relatively small populations are overrepresented, while those that have large populations are underrepresented. Such balances reflect the European reframing of governance that dissociated democracy from nationalism's past distortions, where democracy was confused with the uncompromising rule of ethnic majorities over ethnic minorities. Equally noteworthy is that nationalists, who espouse ethnocentric majoritarianism, arguing that interethnic federation is unworkable, persistently evade any reference to successful states that have been structurally established as peace-founded interethnic democracies, such as Belgium, Switzerland, and Canada.

EU OUTRAGE AT PAPADOPOULOS

Judging that the entry of the Republic of Cyprus into the EU would strengthen its "political weight," Papadopoulos grossly overlooked the fact that, although the institutional status of the republic would be affirmed as the recognized state entity until a final settlement was reached, the nationalist politics and adversarial diplomacy accompanying it would inevitably erode the GC government's political credibility.

Addressing the European Parliament during the aftermath of the Cyprus referenda, EU commissioner for enlargement Günter Verheugen explicitly accused Papadopoulos of having misled him in the handling of the Cyprus problem. "I feel cheated by the Greek Cypriot government," Verheugen announced. "For months on end I have done everything I could in good faith to make it possible for the Greek Cypriot side to accept this plan on the understanding that this is what they intended to do. Now things look very different" (Quetteville 2004). As the commissioner was rarely heard using such strong language in his political conduct, his official reprimand of the GC leader at the highest level of an EU institution reflected the gravity of the matter in the eyes of the Europeans. Verheugen went on to say that "if the Greek Cypriot government had publicly supported it [the Annan Plan], the Yes vote would have won" (Europarl 2004).

The political gravity of the situation was further attested by the discussion that followed in the European Parliament. It was noted that "the No vote by the Greek side is due to a feeling of insecurity. But accession to the European Union by a reunified island would have brought better guarantees of security" (Europarl 2004). Other members of Parliament strongly disapproved of the statements made by the GC cochairman of the EU–Cyprus Joint Parliamentary Committee, who reiterated Papadopoulos's approach by arguing that the central issue at hand was that Turkey, a candidate-state for European membership, was allowed to occupy Cyprus. In light of the GC rejection of the UN plan, which provided for the progressive demilitarization of Cyprus, such arguments sounded to Europeans empty of substance and lacking in seriousness and political credibility. In fact, another parliamentarian described the arguments of the GC representative as "reactionary and nationalist." Verheugen also stressed that "the UN plan called for a withdrawal of the troops" and that "without this plan there will probably be more troops" (Europarl 2004). The Europeans were so stunned by the un-European attitude exhibited in the official GC position that some questioned whether the

GC-controlled Republic of Cyprus had in fact met the Copenhagen political criteria for membership.

Further indignation was expressed when a Greek member of the European Parliament, aligning himself with the official GC position, questioned in what capacity TC "prime minister" Mehmet Ali Talat was invited to be present at the European Parliament's discussion. The question was perceived as very provocative, particularly as Talat, who supported the UN plan, had been a long-standing critic of Denktash and an ardent advocate for peace and reunification. The explanation given to the Greek representative was that the "European Parliament . . . [is] not bound by diplomatic constraints" and that it wished "to hear the views of all parties in order to understand the situation better" (Europarl 2004). The GC and Greek representatives suggested to the European Parliament that in all its dealings with the TCs, it ought to go exclusively through the GC-controlled Republic of Cyprus. Under the circumstances, this struck the Europeans as nationalistically partisan, regressive, and contrary to the political culture of the EU as well as to the explicit goals of the UN-led Cyprus negotiations. The situation was summarized by Verheugen in an interview on Germany's ART Television. "The political damage is large," he stated. "There is now a shadow over Cyprus's membership."

The accession of Cyprus to the EU had confronted the Europeans with a critical question regarding the political culture(s) that new member-states usher into the union. The set of chapters by which the union defines the criteria and process of harmonization for acceding countries lack a key element: the explicit and demonstrable adoption by the countries concerned of an expanded concept of democracy that includes interethnic and transethnic conciliatory values. Though exceedingly significant, the current EU chapters defining norms of harmonization are primarily legal and administrative and essentially technical in nature. But as Cyprus has demonstrated, it does not suffice to assume that technoadministrative harmonization alone automatically leads acceding countries to adopt the political culture of the EU.

With the establishment of the EU as a political entity in 1992, advancing European integration further than the former European Community, the conditions were created for moving beyond mere functionalist and neofunctionalist approaches to harmonization. What could have been added to the harmonization requirements was for acceding states to adopt explicitly the interethnic and transethnic political values and culture of the EU. Such a requirement would expect the acceding countries to forego, in principle, the ethnocentric, adversarial nationalism that has marked the historical legacy of European countries. The bodies that would be expected to adhere to this postnationalist, politicocultural harmonization may range from the government to the major political parties of acceding countries, but could extend to their major educational institutions and the mass media.

European values could be elaborated as a set of specific norms to be adopted by acceding countries as the professed orientation of their national sociopolitical organizations. Such an approach would certainly complement but also go beyond technoadministrative harmonization to the declared and institutionalized acceptance of postnationalist political norms. Otherwise, the process of enlargement leaves the union vulnerable to the importation of covert nationalism through the new member-states. Following the Cyprus referendum, the discussion in the European Parliament and the confrontational exchanges between the GC representatives of the Papadopoulos government and European parliamentarians underscore the EU's failure to effectively manage, and decisively transcend, the contradiction in principle between the union's political culture and the lingering, traditional nationalism of new member-states.

POSTREFERENDUM CYPRUS: A REVERSAL OF ROLES?

Under the shadow of the failed referendum, the entry of Cyprus into the EU marked a defining moment in both the evolving structure of the Cyprus conflict and the ensuing challenges for a final settlement. Considering the shift to conciliatory politics under the TC "prime minister," Talat, and the relapse into nationalist politics under GC president Papadopoulos, a remarkable phenomenon occurred during the period following the referenda and the republic's integration into the EU: a role reversal by the two sides on a considerable array of positions in their respective approaches to the Cyprus problem.

TC politics and diplomacy attained an unprecedented level of international credibility, particularly in the eyes of the UN and the EU. As far as the international community was concerned, the political vision and actions that led to the TC vote in favor of the Annan plan during the referendum constituted a final and decisive affirmation that the TC choice for reunifying Cyprus had surpassed the barren traditional demand for monoethnic secession and recognition for the TRNC. By contrast, GC politics and diplomacy encountered international contempt and disappointment. While the "no" vote of the GC majority was formally respected, the international community viewed the nationalist politics and tactics by which the GCs were led to their decision as anachronistic, fundamentally regressive, and clearly antithetical to both the UN and the EU directives and expectations. This marked the new state of affairs in postreferendum Cyprus, even though the TCs continued not being fully integrated into the European legal framework of the *acquis communautaire*, while the GCs were. Until the end of the autocratic and nationalist leadership of Denktash and prior to the presidency of Papadopoulos, the political realities in Cyprus were quite the opposite: While the TCs were politically and diplomatically alienated from the UN and the EU, the GCs were seen as more aligned with and politically empowered by the UN and the EU.

Even with full and formal participation in the EU, the Papadopoulos government was bound to further lose political credibility to the degree that it did not abandon its nationalist politics. Moreover, as the EU normally sees no credibility in such politics, Papadopoulos stood to barricade himself behind a merely legal approach to the Cyprus problem—a position that would compel him to resort to the law belligerently and excessively, yet without the prospect of a final political resolution. Bankrupted nationalist politics coupled with an increasingly desperate reliance on EU law would inevitably end in a formalistic legalism that would further expose Papadopoulos's antifederalist politics. This contradiction between nationalist politics and legality was disclosed as the Papadopoulos government seriously entertained taking the EU to the European Court of Justice over the commission's proposal to open direct trade with the TC north. Stunningly, the threat to take such legal action came only a few months after the GC-controlled Republic of Cyprus joined the EU, following the latter's gigantic efforts and long-standing influence that helped align the TCs and Turkey with a prosettlement policy on Cyprus.

Beneath Papadopoulos's nationalism lay the same political position (though not the same legal position) propagated for years by Denktash and his nationalist supporters in the Turkish military and political establishment—namely, "no solution is the solution." In his persistence to preserve the Republic of Cyprus at the expense of a final settlement for a united Cyprus republic, Papadopoulos had in fact adopted this approach at the very same historical moment when the Turkish side abandoned it. He and his supporters believed that following the accession of the Republic of Cyprus to the EU, the administration of the unrecognized TRNC would naturally weaken and disintegrate, leading to the inevitable absorption of the TC community into the Republic of Cyprus. EU law, they reasoned, would in and of itself solve the Cyprus problem by imposing the republic's recognized status onto the TC community, rendering the requirement to negotiate a comprehensive settlement superfluous. This approach demonstrates that Papadopoulos's refusal to pursue a settlement prior to accession was an attempt to treat the Cyprus problem as merely legal in nature, rather than deeply political as well.

Another shift in positions occurred when both the perennial GC economic embargo on the TC north and the traditional intransigent TC demand for recognition of the TRNC underwent fundamental erosion. Before the referendum and entry of the Republic of Cyprus into the EU, GCs had viewed the economic embargo imposed on the TC community as the most effective bulwark against the TRNC's secession and formal recognition. After the referendum, however, the GC government began to view increasing economic assistance to the TC north as the greatest weapon against TRNC recognition. The "yes" vote by the TCs and the "no" vote by GCs had led the international community, and particularly the Europeans and the United States, to strive toward ending the TCs' economic isolation, in line with the recommendation of the UN secretary-general. Greatly alarmed that this would somehow bestow recognition on the TC state, the Papadopoulos administration desperately reversed its traditional stance, exhibiting unprecedented "benevolence" toward the

TC side by proposing to the EU various "confidence-building measures" entailing economic assistance and trade with the TC north.

But GC assistance to the TCs was offered on condition that it take place exclusively under the legal umbrella of the Republic of Cyprus. In other words, Papadopoulos was offering to foster economic aid to the TCs in exchange for their integration into Republic of Cyprus—an attempt to normalize the situation without negotiating a federal settlement. Papadopoulos sought to defer negotiations for a final settlement indefinitely, hoping that confidence-building measures under the aegis of the Republic of Cyprus would eventually render them unnecessary. The prioritization of confidence-building measures over a negotiated settlement marked a fundamental deviation from the traditional GC approach to the Cyprus problem—the very approach to which the Turkish side had been resistant for three decades but had finally accepted.

Not surprisingly, Papadopoulos's apparently magnanimous gesture of economic assistance appeared less than politically credible to the Europeans. The TCs resisted the Papadopoulos offer, perceiving it as a means of evading a final solution and rendering the TCs economically dependent on the GC government. Even the newspapers of the GC community, such as *Politis,* and the *Cyprus Mail,* took note that the GC government's new approach sharply contrasted with the past position of the parties making up Papadopoulos's coalition government, as the following excerpts from contemporary and past news reports indicate.

> when, 10 years ago, the UN Security Council proposed the adoption of confidence-building measures in order to bring the two communities closer, Papadopoulos and his current allies were outraged. Papadopoulos described the measures as the "Fourth Attila." Christofias [of the communist AKEL party] went as far as to suggest a showdown with the UN. (*Cyprus Mail* 2004)

> He said at the time: "It is time we said 'no' to the Security Council. If the need arises, we will adopt a confrontational stance towards the Security Council. When it meets a brick wall it will understand that we are not making any more concessions. We must tell them that we refuse to water down our wine any more . . . we call on you to adopt alternative forms of

action so that there can be discussion on the substance of the Cyprus problem" (*Apogevmatini* 1994)

Meanwhile, the hard-line leader of EDEK, Dr Vassos Lyssarides [the former leader of the socialist party now in government], had threatened to withdraw from the National Council if the measures were accepted by the government. He was particularly eloquent. "If we say that the measures constitute national suicide, will we participate (in the National Council) in order to choose the way in which the suicide will be conducted and to say whether our steps on the way to the gallows would be small or big?" (*Phileleftheros* 1994; quoted in Charalambous 2004)

Since the invasion of 1974, in their attempt to normalize the status of the breakaway TRNC, it was always Denktash and Turkey that preferred confidence-building measures to substantive talks on the Cyprus problem. And it was always the GCs that ranked substantive negotiations for a comprehensive final settlement as the highest priority, eclipsing by far the importance of any confidence-building measures. However, following the referenda and the GC-controlled republic's entry into the EU, the respective Cypriot sides in effect switched positions in their approach to the Cyprus problem.

Clearly, in his "confidence-building" offer to the TCs, Papadopoulos had assumed that because the likelihood of the TRNC gaining recognition was rapidly diminishing, the TCs would naturally fall back into the Republic of Cyprus. This assumption was fundamentally erroneous. Even though the EU definitively refused any formal recognition of the TC state, it simultaneously endorsed the political standing of the TCs. Conversely, even though the EU fully recognized the formal status of the Republic of Cyprus as a matter of EU law, it simultaneously questioned the GC government's nationalism and criticized its attempt to usurp the new European status of the republic for partisan ethnocentric political ends as an effort to circumvent the UN process.

Sadly, at the very time the Turkish side gave up its long-standing demand for secession and recognition, Papadopoulos, rather than seizing the historical opportunity to bring closure to the Cyprus problem, adopted his own agenda of "recognition": the demand that Turkey recognize the

Republic of Cyprus in view of the fact that it was now an EU member-state. From the republic's acceptance into the EU, this demand became the vanguard of Papadopoulos's approach to the Cyprus problem, as evidenced in the ongoing debates from the run-up to the European Commission's October 2004 report on Turkey to the EU summit decision of October 2005 on commencing Turkey's accession negotiations. The approach demarcated what the Papadopoulos administration referred to as a "European solution" to the Cyprus problem, which, it was assumed, would replace and render superfluous any negotiated UN-based solution. It was a matter of time before the GC government started to realize that the European solution it sought had no foundation within the EU, especially in its conceptualization as an alternative to the UN process.

However, the apogee of the role reversal in the two sides' approach to the Cyprus problem struck as lightning three years after the failed referenda, when the eccentric GC nationalist Marios Matsakis declared that ethnic partition would be preferable to any form of bicommunal, bizonal federation. An EU parliamentarian and former member of the Papadopoulos's DIKO party, Matsakis made his position public on the occasion of announcing his candidacy for the presidential elections of February 2008. He explained that short of a unitary state he preferred "the option of a clean, two-state solution than the bi-zonal, bi-communal federation that was the Annan plan" (*Cyprus Mail* 2007a). In direct contradiction to all UN resolutions that the GCs had traditionally invoked, he openly denounced the UN blueprint for a biethnic, bizonal federation.

What followed among the GC political leadership and mass media was a torrent of debates, accusations, and confusion as to what the GCs really want. The opposition parties accused Papadopoulos and his DIKO party of fostering a disguised but determined antifederalist approach to the Cyprus problem, which the Papadopoulos government rushed to deny. The truth of the matter was that while the Papadopoulos camp never articulated support for the option of partition, its long-standing resistance to and final rejection of any biethnic federation coincided exactly with that of Matsakis. While a marginal figure in the GC presidential race, Matsakis explicated perfectly the likely practical consequences of rejecting federation. Having been placed repeatedly on the defensive by his European colleagues in the EU parliament over the GC rejection of the Annan Plan, he naturally arrived at the "logical" conclusion of his ethnocentric nationalism: If the UN and EU's long-standing backing for Annan-like plans could not be superseded, then partition would be the best option for GCs.

The most astonishing aspect of the uproar Matsakis triggered through his open support for ethnic partition was that it pushed the GC leadership into endless public debates about what a federal system is. The outcome of this brief but intense episode of GC politics was that it not only left the matter inconclusive but further entrenched public confusion, especially as the DIKO representatives, facing fierce criticism, vainly attempted to put forward an unheard of concept of federation that somehow did not include constituent federated states, while tacitly resisting altogether the principle of ethnic bizonality in regard to a Cyprus settlement. The fact that such a debate took place among the GC leadership thirty years after signing the top-level agreements for a bizonal, bicommunal, federal solution, and after full engagement, on the same premise, in top-level negotiations for four and half years leading to the 2004 referendum, indicates the degree of dissociation and disarray that befell the GC leadership in the aftermath of the failed referenda.

Even though Matsakis's position was absolutely contrary to the *formal political position* the GCs articulated for more than three decades, his declaration in favor of complete ethnic segregation in effect reflected the traditional *psychological predisposition* among GC nationalists to resist any form of ethnic mixing—an exact replica of the traditional psychological predisposition among TCs nationalists. For Matsakis, as for all nationalists, the second-best option to an ethnocentric unitary state, in which the ethnic majority essentially wields power, is not interethnic federation but rather radical ethnic separation. For the nationalist mind, full ethnic separation via two separate states is more acceptable than any form of interethnic power-sharing. Moreover, in a choice between optimal territory under an interethnic power-sharing arrangement or less territory under a purely monoethnic power arrangement, the latter would be preferable. This is because clear ethnic separation is closer to the uncompromising nationalist postulation that the "authentic" society and its national state rest on being exclusively monoethnic. One of the supreme principles of ethnocentric nationalism is to be ethnically clean. This was precisely what lay behind Matsakis appeal for "a clean, two-state solution." In this, he explicated the common stubborn motif among ethnocentric nationalists of vehemently rejecting national interethnic institutions, especially national interethnic power-sharing arrangements—the very motif that led the Papadopoulos camp to reject the Annan Plan. In his rather naïve but consistent ethnocentric nationalism, Matsakis unmasked the quintessential position of Papadopoulos and his nationalist supporters.

The postreferendum stalemate resulting from Papadopoulos's erroneous pursuit of a Hellenic-based unitary state precipitated, through Matsakis's words, in the first open acknowledgment of what would be the next step in preserving the nationalists' original ethnocentric agenda. The logic underpinning Matsakis's declaration is that given that a Hellenic-based unitary state is the nonnegotiable objective of GC nationalism, if such a state proves impossible to establish over the whole of Cyprus, it should be firmly secured over half of Cyprus, and in an ethnically purer form, for that matter. While Papadopoulos's pursuit of a unitary state under the camouflage of federation led by default to a future partition, Matsakis's uncamouflaged nationalism acknowledged and embraced partition. The historical irony in all this is that, like Denktash's ethnocentric nationalism, Matsakis's ethnocentric nationalism led to the same final end: total ethic segregation through ethnic partition. Sadly, the GC voice for partition was first heard in the immediate aftermath of the referendum in which the TCs had voted to abandon partition.

THE CHANGING INTERNATIONAL POLITICS ON CYPRUS

Inevitably, following the historical apogee of the referendum and the entry of Cyprus in the EU, the international community's political position on the Cyprus problem underwent a fundamental shift. Its efforts focused less on the quest for a settlement and more on containing the damage resulting from the outcome of the GC referendum (Loizides 2004). With 75.8 percent of the GC vote cast against the UN peace plan and 64.9 percent of the TC vote cast in favor, the international political dynamics regarding Cyprus changed considerably. The day after the referendum, *The Economist* stated that "by rejecting the [UN] proposal the Greek-Cypriots will have gained nothing other than the resentment of their fellow EU members; and they have lost the moral high ground they enjoyed in 30 years in which the Turkish-Cypriot side continually resisted a deal" (*The Economist* 2004a).

On the purely abstract and formal legal level, the international community retained its original stance on the illegitimate status of the TRNC. However, on the political and economic level, it started to modify its approach. The change was ushered into the international political arena with Annan's Cyprus report to the Security Council following the referendum. From the outset, summarizing the essence of his report, the secretary-general asserted that

> the decision of the Greek Cypriots [to vote against the UN peace plan] must be respected. However, it is a major setback. They may wish to reflect on the implications of the vote in the coming period. If they remain willing to resolve the Cyprus problem through a bicommunal, bizonal federation, this needs to be demonstrated. Lingering Greek Cypriot concerns about security and implementation of the plan need to be articulated with clarity and finality. The Security Council would be well advised to stand ready to address such concerns.
>
> The decision of the Turkish Cypriots [to vote in favor of the UN peace plan] is to be welcomed. The Turkish Cypriot leadership and Turkey have made clear their respect for the wish of the Turkish Cypriots to reunify in a bicommunal, bizonal federation. The Turkish Cypriot vote has undone any rationale for pressuring and isolating them. I would hope that the members of the Council can give a strong lead to all States to cooperate both bilaterally and in international bodies, to eliminate unnecessary restrictions and barriers that have the effect of isolating the Turkish Cypriots and impeding their development—not for the purpose of affording recognition or assisting secession, but as a positive contribution to the goal of reunification. (United Nations 2004c)

While maintaining the UN's refusal to recognize the TRNC, the secretary-general succinctly recommended opening legitimate international economic and political relations with the TCs. Even though his recommendation was not formalized by the UN, it still marked a significant shift in international politics on Cyprus.

In line with the secretary-general's suggested approach, the European Commission recommended specific policies explicitly aiming at assisting the TCs economically, especially as the enlargement process brought Cyprus under the jurisdiction of its competences. During the week between the April 24 referendum and the May 1 entry of Cyprus into the EU, Brussels set the stage for the postreferendum era. The European Commission decided that the green line dividing the TC north from the GC south would not be classed as an external border of the EU, even though conditions for the full implementation of the *acquis communautaire* in northern Cyprus were not yet in place. It subsequently approved measures to ease restrictions on trade and to allow TC goods to cross the green line and be exported to the European markets. The measures, which excluded certain items, required that all goods and products be governed by EU health and safety standards and be of TC origin, with certificates issued by the Chamber of Commerce of the TC north. By late August 2004, this policy came into effect. Because of the GCs' "no" vote in the referendum, the GC government lost considerable political leverage in objecting to the EU measures for opening trade between northern and southern Cyprus. The GC government simply had to accept the European-proposed trade package—a practice antithetical to traditional GC policy toward the TC north.

The commission recommended that EU funds to the north not be placed under the management of the TRNC, which the union continued to view as an illegitimate state entity. But in light of the new political environment that emerged in the postreferendum era, neither did the commission recommend that the funds be place under the management of the Republic of Cyprus, even though it continued to recognize the republic as the sole legitimate state entity of the Island. Instead, it suggested that aid to the TCs be administered directly by the European Commission. This is indicative of the European political perspective on postreferendum/European Cyprus. It underscored not only the commission's continuing refusal to recognize the TRNC but also its affirmation of a new fact—namely, the political diminution of the Republic of Cyprus insofar as it continued to be an exclusively GC-controlled entity within the EU.

The political implication of the stance of the European Commission was that as long as the Republic of Cyprus was controlled by GCs, its government couldn't fully represent and manage TC affairs in northern Cyprus. Through this approach, the Europeans were not making a judgment on the *legal status* of the republic but rather on the *political status* of its GC government. In other words, as long as the Republic of Cyprus functioned under monoethnic GC control, its political status with respect to the TCs would remain ambivalent, particularly as it was originally founded as a biethnic state and was to be restructured through a settlement into a bizonal, bicommunal federation. This action of the EU propelled to the political foreground the fact that the interethnic federal political settlement of the Cyprus problem remained an imperative. It clearly suggested that a negotiated settlement on the UN model was the way forward to full normalization of political life in Cyprus. Once again, the union's approach to the Cyprus problem was grounded on policy decisions directed and forged by a conflict-transcending and peace-enhancing diagnosis and vision of Cyprus.

However, in addition to facilitating the opening up of trade across the green line between the two Cypriot communities, the commission made the unprecedented recommendation to open up trade directly between the TC north and the EU. The Papadopoulos government reacted vehemently to the latter proposal, as it was reasoned that such a step would undermine the political legitimacy of the GC-controlled Republic of Cyprus in favor of the TRNC. The GC government's fear that direct trade between the TC and the union would bestow indirect state recognition on the TRNC was in principle unfounded. More accurately, the arrangement proposed by the European Commission, while having nothing to do with recognizing the TRNC, prevented the government of the Republic of Cyprus from exercising direct, administrative management over the TC north—contrary to what Papadopoulos had hoped would happen in taking Cyprus into the union without a settlement. Here again, the clear political message underlying the commission's recommendation was that, given the results of the referendum, the GC government, even though it would continue to operated as the administrator of the recognized Republic of Cyprus, stood to politically lose rather than gain jurisdiction over the affairs of the TCs and of northern Cyprus.

Direct trade between the TCs and the EU would have dissociated the management of TC-European relations from any of the organs of the TRNC. But simultaneously, it would have brought TC-EU relations further under the jurisdiction of EU institutions and less under that of the Republic of Cyprus. This proposed European policy plainly reflected the political consequences of the referenda results. As when the European Commission recommended that it manage European aid to the TC north, direct trade with northern Cyprus stood to curb the authority of the TRNC further. But it also stood to further limit the authority of the Republic of Cyprus over the TC community, practically replacing it with the EU's superseding authority.

This approach by the Europeans was deemed temporary until a resolution of the Cyprus problem. The European perspective was that until a new Cyprus emerged—and given that as of yet there was neither a recognized federated TC state nor an interethnic federal state—political authority in managing the state affairs of the north would practically rest with the EU, even though formally and abstractly the Republic of Cyprus retained its legal monopoly on recognition. This demonstrated President Papadopoulos's error in assuming that if Cyprus entered the EU without a settlement, then the status of the recognized GC-controlled Republic of Cyprus would be reinforced and its jurisdiction automatically extended over northern Cyprus, with the full backing of the EU. Papadopoulos's assumption would have been correct only if the EU had chosen to neglect the political aspects of the Cyprus problem and treat it as purely legal. However, the matter was not that simple, as the unresolved political aspects of the Cyprus problem were bound to pose challenges as complex as the unresolved legal ones.

The importance that the EU ascribed to the political dimension of the Cyprus problem was affirmed when in 2005 the European Parliament, while denouncing recognition of the TRNC, proceeded to set up a permanent contact group with the TC authorities. There was no intention of granting TCs official EU representation. But the gesture signified an attempt to curb, to the degree possible, the continued political isolation of the TCs.

As postreferendum Cyprus became a full member of the EU, the United States, in turn, began to pursue a policy aligned with that of the Europeans. As the new international status of Cyprus was hitherto defined by the UN as well as by the institutions and politics of the EU, the United States had no reason to treat Cyprus differently, but rather in a manner identical to the political and legal policy decisions of the union. Hence, like the EU, the United States expressed its intention of offering direct financial aid to the TC north as well as of opening direct relations with northern Cyprus in every way short of formal recognition of the TRNC. As stated among diplomatic circles, its treatment of northern Cyprus would be similar to its treatment of Taiwan (EU Business 2004b).

The visit to northern Cyprus by American businessmen in February 2005 and by American congressmen in June 2005, with the accompaniment of the U.S. commercial attaché from Turkey and U.S. ambassador to Cyprus, marked the beginning of the changed U.S. policy toward the TCs. It was the first time since 1974 that U.S. delegations visited TC leaders by entering northern Cyprus directly, circumventing the recognized GC-south. The outrage expressed by the Papadopoulos administration, and suggestions about issuing EU arrest warrants against the Americans for entering Cyprus illegally, led merely to public rhetoric and letters of complaint to the U.S. ambassador. The TCs, in contrast, while stressing that recognition of the TRNC was not their objective, associated the American visit with the UN secretary-general's recommendation to the international community to end the isolation of the TC community.

Of all the GC leaders, the moderate former president Vassiliou was the only one to exhibit the realism and courage to remind the GCs that, although regrettable for the Greek side, such changes in policy toward the TC north were only the beginning. This statement insinuated that they all had arisen from the GC rejection of the historic UN effort for a settlement (*Cyprus Mail* 2005c).

In response to the European Commission's recommendations of opening up direct EU trade with northern Cyprus, the Papadopoulos administration resorted to a series of diplomatic and legal moves aimed at obstructing the prospect of direct trade with the north by appealing to European law. The result was the emergence within the EU of the first in a series of political and legal entanglements around the Cyprus issue. On the formal level, Papadopoulos was correct in that European law does not provide for establishing trade relations with nonstate entities. Again, the position of the GC government was that all EU dealings with the TCs should go through the GC-controlled Republic of Cyprus. However, the overwhelming European perspective was that without addressing the political problem and its resolution, European law could not in and of itself address and fix the entire residue of ambiguities brought into the union as a result of the failure of the referendum. Within the EU, this led to a complex legal and political impasse that dragged on, resulting in the union taking successive steps to postpone any decision and action on the commission's recommendations. Simultaneously, for every legal victory Papadopoulos secured in absolutely restricting TC economic activities within the bounds of the Republic of Cyprus, he also earned political discredit in the eyes of the Europeans.

The TC perspective was that the opening of trade between northern and southern Cyprus was not sufficient to lead to the rate of economic growth necessary for the TCs to reach parity with the GCs, while the support promised by the Europeans was not forthcoming, as decisions were perpetually delayed. The TCs felt that even though they had supported the UN plan for reunification and given up secession, they were still underdogs, with no international status. Moreover, they felt that the GCs, who had rejected the peace plan, still enjoyed the upper hand within Europe, with the union taking no action.

The perception among the TCs was that while the Europeans were at a standstill in attending to the needs of the TC community, the Papadopoulos government was aiming to entrap the TCs anew, this time by attempting to disempower them through legal processes inside the EU. Using the powers granted by EU law to member-states, Papadopoulos also managed to block the aid package of € 259 million that the EU had promised to the TCs following the referendum to help the north's economy and infrastructure harmonize with its norms. Again, Papadopoulos wanted the aid money to be disbursed to the Republic of Cyprus and not directly to the TC community.

The TCs saw Papadopoulos's efforts as a strategy to impose the Republic of Cyprus onto the TC community as a substitute for negotiating a comprehensive UN-based settlement. Under these conditions, the TCs started to approach the newly established opportunities for trade between north and south with great reservations, retarding the positive potential of the EU-initiated arrangement. Furthermore, as Turkey became preoccupied with the EU's upcoming decision on its accession prospects, the TCs became concerned that Turkey's support for their community could become lukewarm and passive. At this point, the TCs felt a renewed sense of abandonment, particularly in light of their historic effort in overcoming the Denktash legacy in favor of a reunified Cyprus.

The Europeans felt very frustrated with the fact that the Papadopoulos government had been complacent in proposing how to move forward to a final Cyprus settlement, while fully mobilizing to use any legal means at its disposal to deter the union from establishing direct ties with the TC community. Consequently, the Europeans began to view the Papadopoulos administration as attempting to insert a wedge into the European process to dissociate the union's political deliberations on Cyprus from its legal deliberations, bringing the two into conflict.

More precisely, Papadopoulos was seen as using European law to undermine European policy on Cyprus—a policy that had long focused on facilitating and fully supporting a negotiated, comprehensive political settlement for the Island on the basis of the UN peace plan. Viewed as distorting the union process, these entanglements led the Europeans to postpone any decision on the commission's recommendations for direct trade with the TCs until after the union made its decision on Turkey's European progress. Among other things, this was a strategic decision. The Europeans kept Turkey in a state of attentiveness while indirectly communicating to Papadopoulos that the GC stance on Turkey would be an issue to be reckoned with before any decisions are made on the commission's recommendations for Cyprus.

Under the overarching EU process, changes in Cyprus politics also occurred at the regional level in the Eastern Mediterranean. Prior to the referendum, the European integration process was viewed as facilitating the GC and Greek quest for a UN-based settlement, while challenging Turkey and the TCs to abandon their intransigent nationalist policy of secession in favor of a federal, interethnic settlement. By contrast, after the referenda and the republic's accession to the EU, the union, while accepting the GC "no" vote, began to facilitate the TCs' and Turkey's European aspirations within the bounds of EU law despite strongly expressed discontentment by Papadopoulos and his administration.

Former Greek prime minister Costas Simitis, who had sent an unheeded message encouraging the GC leadership to vote in support of the Annan Plan, anticipated this changing EU role in relation to Cyprus. Already prior to the referendum, EU officials, noting the relapsing nationalist strategies and tactics of the Papadopoulos government, conveyed that the solution of the Cyprus problem need not be a necessary precondition for Turkey's progress toward Europe. This idea evolved from originally a diplomatic suggestion to finally the formal European position following the referendum.

Two highlights of this process stand out. The first came in June 2004 when the EU Council concluded that Turkey had made a substantial contribution toward solving the Cyprus problem and that therefore Turkey's accession process should not be associated with the Cyprus solution (as was the case prior to the referendum). Interestingly, the commendation of Turkey for its efforts was unanimous among the council's heads of state, which included President Papadopoulos. The second highlight was the statements of Enlargement Commissioner Verheugen, who reiterated this European position during a visit to Turkey in preparation for the commission's recommendation on Turkey's readiness for accession—the final decision by the European Council being due in December 2004. These developments were formalized in the recommendations of the commission released on October 6, 2004. Overall, the report concluded that Turkey was ready for commencing its accession process. While noting numerous areas still awaiting reform, the report unequivocally dissociated the Cyprus problem from Turkey's progress. In fact, it asserted that "Turkey has and continues actively to support efforts to resolve the Cyprus problem; in particular, Turkey agreed to the solution put forward in the peace plan of the UN Secretary General" (Europa 2004).

While praising Turkey for its persistent reforms, Verheugen simultaneously repeated his concern over its implementation of them. But he anticipated that the critical mass of legislative and institutional changes was attainable to warrant a favorable recommendation by the commission. However, while absolved from the previously costly political burden of the Cyprus problem, Turkey was reminded of its further legal obligations, which now included extending its customs union to the enlarged EU that also encompassed Cyprus as a new member-state. The clear message of the European Commission's recommendation to the EU Council was that no matter what the outcome would be in the upcoming December 2004 decision on Turkey, it should not be associated with the solution of the Cyprus problem.

Most interesting was that in the postreferendum era, Greek prime minister Karamalis shared the EU's position on Turkey, while his government attempted to maintain diplomatic balances vis-à-vis the Papadopoulos government by asserting support for Turkey under certain conditions. In September 2004, the *EU Observer* noted that the prime minister of Greece publicly said that "he did not believe that the situation in the divided island of Cyprus could be an obstacle for opening negotiations with Ankara" (*EU Observer* 2004a). This indicated a shift in the political dynamics in the Eastern Mediterranean, where Greece and Turkey, despite Cyprus, started to move toward increasing bilateral cooperation, while the GC leadership was facing rising political challenges within the EU because its nationalism stood in contradiction to the union's political culture. In the postreferendum era, the solution to the Cyprus problem was not only dissociated from Turkish-European relations, but was also substantially demoted in its bearing on Greek-Turkish relations.

The content of the European Commission's report on Turkey was no surprise to those GCs who understood the magnitude of the missed opportunity for solving the Cyprus problem through the April referendum. However, to those GCs still operating within the adversarial nationalist framework, the report was insufficient. The absence of any substantive link between Turkey's European progress and the solution to the Cyprus problem was outrageously disturbing. It was the first time an official EU report had dissociated Turkey from Cyprus in this manner.

The GC political leadership was dismayed that the commission made no reference to Turkish troops in Cyprus, to occupation, or to the need for Turkey "to withdraw its troops from EU soil" (EU Business 2004c). But the commission's shifting perspective appears stunningly unacceptable only when one fails to grasp the implications of the referendum results and the changes that subsequently ensued in the international politics on Cyprus. Former GC president Vassiliou, who fully anticipated what had transpired, asserted that only under one precondition could the GC side persuade the Europeans to reengage Turkey: The GC side had to "state clearly what it is that we really want." Vassiliou's statement underscored that the Cyprus issue remained a political problem waiting to be clearly and directly addressed, rather than evaded, as the Papadopoulos administration had done.

As far as the Europeans were concerned, the dissociation of Turkey's European aspirations from the solution of the Cyprus problem was henceforth taken for granted. Among political leaders and in public opinion in member-states, the political solution of the Cyprus problem no longer factored into the stance on Turkey. At this stage, no one knew what decision the Europeans would make in December 2004 regarding Turkey's future. But the dialogue within Europe between those who favored and those who were reserved about Turkey's eventual accession centered on the country's size, culture, religion, economy, relation to European security and the fight against terrorism, and on its capacity to adopt and implement EU law—but no longer on Turkey's relation to the solution of the Cyprus problem (*BBC News*, 2004; *Turkish Daily News* 2004c, 2004d, 2004e, 2004f).

Under these conditions, the Papadopoulos administration felt anew the European political constraints limiting the political legitimacy and viability of nationalist agendas. Not surprisingly, when Papadopoulos's DIKO party and its coalition partner EDEK expressed outrage at Commissioner Verheugen's statements supporting the dissociation of Turkey's European progress from the solution of the Cyprus problem, Papadopoulos assumed a mild and reserved stance. By the summer of 2004, rumors were circulating that the Karamalis government of Greece had privately convinced Papadopoulos that the GC side should not veto Turkey in

December when the EU member-states would decide on its readiness to commence accession negotiations. This agreement, the rumor implied, was to be kept a secret in order not to jeopardize the GCs' diplomatic effectiveness in negotiating Turkey's future with EU member-states.

Meanwhile, in anticipation of the decision of the EU on Turkey, the Papadopoulos administration had launched a vehement but desperate diplomatic campaign to persuade its European partners to relink the solution of the Cyprus problem to Turkey's European progress. The GC effort became increasingly ambivalent and strenuous following the European Commission's report on Turkey, which made only a scant reference to Cyprus. Throughout the fall of 2004, the Papadopoulos administration occasionally flashed its right to cast its veto against Turkey unless that country complied with international law.

To the keen observer, however, Papadopoulos's nationalist approach to the UN-led negotiations and his influence on the GC vote on the Annan Plan had offered Turkey considerable political protection, if not political immunity, from international law. As attested to by the EU decisions and reports, it was clear to European leaders that to a great measure Turkey had been absolved from political responsibilities regarding Cyprus. Although the Europeans acknowledged that complex legal issues regarding Turkey and Cyprus remained, they assumed that these no longer carried the same weight against Turkey as they did prior to the Cyprus referendum. This fact contradicted the prereferendum expectations of the Papadopoulos government and gradually caught up with the GC leadership. It finally became clear that if the rest of Europe favored the commencement of Turkey's accession process, a veto by Papadopoulos would amount to the political and diplomatic isolation of the GCs within the union, in turn undermining any empowerment that the European accession of Cyprus had bestowed on the GCs.

It was therefore not surprising that Papadopoulos began making increasingly unclear and ambiguous statements during this time. Speaking in Athens in October 2004, he stated, "Turkey has obligations toward the EU and the Republic of Cyprus which it must fulfill," only subsequently to elaborate that "this does not mean we will exercise a veto; it does not mean we won't exercise a veto." And Papadopoulos ended his remarks by acknowledging that "when a small country exercises a veto it causes many difficulties, so it is very difficult to make such a decision" (*Eleftheros Typos* 2004).

Merely pursuing nationalistically designed legal tactics while failing to articulate its specific position and recommendations on a Cyprus solution, the GC administration sounded unconvincing. Papadopoulos's effort to persuade the EU to revert to its prereferendum position on Turkey appeared less than credible and unrealistic to the Europeans. Prior to the Cyprus referendum, the Europeans repeatedly asserted that if the TCs voted "yes" and the GCs voted "no" to the UN peace plan, things would not remain the same. The Papadopoulos administration failed to heed this vital word of caution. Instead, it erroneously proceeded with the expressed assumption that entry into the union would strengthen the GC side over against Turkey.

The repeated calls on Papadopoulos to state clearly what he wanted, to reopen the negotiations anew, fell on deaf ears. Having become entrapped in his nationalist approach, Papadopoulos faced two insurmountable diplomatic and political dilemmas. On the one hand, articulating his true position, as derived from his monoethnic concept of statehood, would reveal that he was operating outside the UN framework and resolutions, which clearly he could not afford. On the other hand, refraining from stating what he would support so as to avoid exposing his anti-UN approach, would leave him vulnerable to charges of intransigence and of lacking the political will to resolve the Cyprus problem. Of the two options, Papadopoulos chose the latter, as it better served both his intent to circumvent the need for negotiations and, perhaps, his more personal interest of continuing his presidency unimpeded by any restructuring of governance that a settlement would inevitably bring.

Ironically, AKEL's leader, Christofias, divulged in 2007 that Papadopoulos had been reluctant to articulate his position from the very beginning, including his approach at the crucial high-level talks at Bürgenstock, Switzerland. "To this day," he explained, "we are paying the price for that, in that our side is accused of being unwilling to negotiate" (Hazou 2007b). This revelation was belated, coming after AKEL withdrew from the Papadopoulos government, when Christofias announced his nomination for the presidential elections of 2008.

In the prereferendum/pre-European integration era, the UN and the EU had always regarded the GC side as more forthcoming in its readiness to strive for a comprehensive settlement, and the Turkish side as more reluctant and resistant. Since the referendum and Cyprus's EU membership, however, it was the Turkish side that was viewed as the willing party and the GC side as the rejectionist one.

8

The Changing Parameters of the Cyprus Problem (I)

EU SUMMITS: TURKEY'S EUROPEAN FUTURE AND CYPRUS

On December 16 and 17, 2004, the European Council met for the highly anticipated Brussels Summit, with Turkey's European future the most important issue on its agenda. The European Union's heads of state and of the commission unanimously decided that the EU would commence accession negotiations with Turkey on October 3, 2005. To the great dismay of GC nationalists, the decision included the consent of President Papadopoulos despite his presummit rhetoric over the right of the Republic of Cyprus to veto Turkey if certain requirements were not met. Also to the disappointment of Turkish nationalists, particularly from the opposition People's Republican Party, Turkish prime minister Recep Tayyip Erdogan accepted the EU offer despite the fact that the conditions attached to it did not meet Turkey's declared objectives but went beyond what it had originally identified as nonnegotiable. Elaborated on the basis of the European Commission's earlier report, the issue of Turkey's future was a contentious one. The fact that intensive dialogue at the EU summit resulted in a unanimous decision is indicative of the high premium the EU places on forging interstate and unionwide political consensus aimed at outcomes that all parties can support as viable and legitimate.

The arduous two-day marathon dialogue among EU leaders brought together an array of conflicting positions on the handling of Turkey's accessions prospects. General opinion was undoubtedly in favor of supporting and enhancing Turkey's European orientation based on its continuing appropriate reforms—a policy that European leaders viewed as serving peace, democratization, and stability in the Eastern Mediterranean. However, countries such as France, Austria, and Denmark were reticent about absorbing Turkey—such a large, poor, and Muslim country—without numerous safeguards in place (*EU Observer* 2004b). Originally, the French had recommended that rather than aiming for full membership, negotiations with Turkey ought to be restricted to a lesser associate membership. Clearly, the central concerns of the Europeans had little to do with Cyprus.

While issues arising from Turkey's relation to Cyprus remained contentious, they no longer carried the same political weight among Europeans with respect to Turkey's future as they had before the Cyprus referendum of April 24, 2004. Now, the EU's prime interest was not to put forward the solution of the Cyprus problem as a political condition for Turkey's European advancement but rather to regularize the EU legal framework and process in which Cyprus had become an anomaly. For the EU, this anomaly had two components that needed to be addressed: first, the requirement to regularize the relationship between Turkey and all EU member-states, including Cyprus, on the basis of European law; and second, the continuing imperative that the concerned parties willfully negotiate a political solution of the Cyprus problem on the basis of the UN directives. In the minds of European leaders, the first requirement weighed heavier on Turkey. But the second requirement weighed heavier on Papadopoulos, now the president of an EU member- state.

In light of this background, the Dutch presidency of the EU, along with the commission, put forward the requirement that Turkey first fulfill its legal obligation of extending its 1963 customs union agreement to the ten new EU member-states, which would entail Turkey's recognition of the Republic of Cyprus. Papadopoulos demanded that Turkey recognize the republic as a condition for receiving a date for starting accession negotiations. Moreover, he declared that not even the signing by Turkey of the adaptation agreement extending its customs union to the new union members would suffice. All along, Papadopoulos had asserted that nothing less than the explicit and direct recognition of the Republic of Cyprus would open the way for Turkey. In talks with Turkish prime minister Erdogan, Greek prime minister Karamalis suggested that initially Turkey could sign a customs union protocol covering all new EU members; later it could formally recognize Cyprus (*Cyprus Mail* 2004h).

While having no official say in the deliberations of the European Council summit, Erdogan and his foreign minister, Gul, propagated the position that Turkey's early direct or indirect recognition of the Republic of Cyprus was out of the question, as it constituted a "red line" for Turkish policy. The Turkish leaders also expressed concern that recognizing the republic as a prerequisite would be very difficult to sell to Turkish public opinion, especially since the GC side had been the one that rejected the UN peace plan. Furthermore, Turkey expressed the firm expectation that the EU would employ the same criteria in its treatment of Turkey as it does for other countries, and that it would not resort to double standards and additional requirements in the case of Turkey. The hope was that Turkey would be given an early start date for accession negotiations in April 2005.

Impressive about the EU dialogue on Turkey's future was that while no stakeholder achieved all of its aims, the EU summit ended with a unanimous decision, as well as with Turkey formally agreeing to and supporting the EU terms. An essential feature of the summit dialogue process was that it identified, isolated, and extricated or tempered the most polarizing positions while reframing, integrating, and reconciling the views and approaches that could be most widely embraced as legitimate and constructive for all concerned. In their collective deliberations, the representatives of the twenty-five EU member-states and of the commission sidestepped the French position that Turkey ought to be considered for a lesser "privileged membership" instead of full membership; the GC demand that Turkey first recognize the Republic of Cyprus directly and explicitly before being given a starting date; and the Turkish assertion that recognition of Cyprus was out of the question before a commencement date was given.

Reflecting the values of consensus-building and conciliatory politics as a central feature of European democracy, the final unanimous agreement of the EU summit, to which Turkey consented, entailed an optimal consideration of everyone's concerns by conjoining and casting them in a framework of mutual relativization. In the formulations of the EU's decision, Turkey was given the date of October 3, 2005, to commence accession negotiations, but it could not join the EU until at least 2014. Further, prior to starting its accession negotiations, Turkey should sign the protocol adoption of the Ankara agreement, extending its customs union to all new EU members, including Cyprus—a condition required by EU law, as well as being the basis on which the GCs had articulated their more unqualified original demand.

Taking into account the reservations expressed by countries such as France, Austria, and Denmark, it was agreed that, although the goal of Turkey's negotiations is full accession, there is no guarantee as to the outcome. Echoing an essential aspect of the summit conclusions, the presiding head of the European Council, Dutch prime minister Jan-Peter Balkenende, explained that if at the end of the lengthy process of harmonization Turkey's membership is not possible, Turkey should be "anchored to the European structure" to sustain its European linkages and orientation (*EU Observer* 2004b). Appeasing one European fear that the entry of Turkey could flood Europe with cheap labor and drain EU subsidies, the EU leaders agreed that "long transition periods, specific arrangements, or permanent safeguard clauses . . . may be considered" along the way of Turkey's long road of accession. These would apply to the free movement of Turkish workers within the EU and to the EU's structural and agricultural policies.

Simultaneously, recognizing sensitivities in Turkish opinion of perceived double standards, the EU specified that, although the possibility to use the safeguards is permanent, the employment of the safeguards would not be. That is to say, the safeguards would be activated only if and when needed. Emphasizing that Turkey is obliged to continue its Europeanizing reforms, the EU summit conclusions also stipulated that as negotiations with Turkey will be open-ended, they may be broken off in "case of a persistent breach . . . of the principles of liberty, democracy, respect for human rights, and fundamental freedoms and the rule of law" (*EU Observer* 2004b).

It must be stressed that, while the specific agreed-upon terms pertinent to Turkey's relation to Cyprus were politically soft, the conditions surrounding its accession talks and obligation to the EU as a whole were deemed "the strongest ever attached to an EU hopeful" (*EU Observer*

2004b). The outcome of the EU summit was celebrated as positive, both by the EU leaders and by Turkey. However, it was clear to all that Ankara's road to the EU would be tough, demanding, and filled with challenging harmonization milestones and ratifying referenda to be held by countries including France and Austria in the years ahead. By contrast, the EU demands regarding Cyprus, while addressing Turkey's responsibility for normalizing the legal aspect of its relationship to the Island, left its responsibility regarding the political dimension of the Cyprus problem loose and indeterminate.

Turkey accepted the EU requirement that Ankara would formally extend its customs union agreement to include all new EU members prior to starting accession negotiations. Yet, it is noteworthy that Turkey consented to the EU terms under the condition that the content of the extended customs union agreement be adapted first. Exactly how the content would be adapted was essentially a political issue, not a legal one. What was certain was that the formulation of the summit conclusions reflected the general acknowledgment that Turkey would not be held primarily and indefinitely responsible for the Cyprus problem, following the GCs' determined rejection of the UN peace plan in the April 2004 referendum.

EU president Balkenende referred to this significant fact in a public statement. He noted that the EU requirement that Turkey consented to is in itself "not a formal and legal recognition of Cyprus, but . . . a step that can lead to progress" (*EU Observer* 2004b). This statement reflected the crucial fact that the EU summit conclusions, and Turkey's acceptance of them, left the specific allocation of political responsibilities for solving the Cyprus problem wide open. It did so in a manner that tacitly acknowledged both the positive stance pursued by Turkey in support of the Annan Plan and the need for the GC leadership to assume responsibility in constructively pursuing a political settlement. Papadopoulos's widely publicized, firm position that Turkey ought to recognize the GC-controlled Republic of Cyprus before being given a date for accession talks was not heeded by the EU leaders.

Under these conditions, one question naturally arises. Why, then, did Papadopoulos refrain from using his rightful veto power to obstruct Turkey's course? For the first time, the GC president was directly confronted with the fact that democratic dialogue at the level of the European Council is all about consensus building (McCormick 2002). From a strategic point of view, Papadopoulos's presummit warnings about the possibility of vetoing Turkey are understandable. However, beyond the realm of diplomatic strategy, it became clear that Papadopoulos could not act as the odd leader out. European leaders already viewed him as the person who frustrated the time and energy-consuming efforts of the UN and the EU to conclude the Cyprus problem in April 2004. In persuading his GC electorate to vote against the UN plan, Papadopoulos was seen by the EU as responsible for derailing the most comprehensive diplomatic effort ever undertaken for resolving the problem. This, as well as the reprimands and criticisms by both the UN and the EU that followed the referendum, meant that vetoing Turkey's progress would have been politically reckless on the part of Papadopoulos. He would risk being seen again as the leader who disrupts and dismantles the consensus-building dialogue of the EU at the highest level of its democratic process.

The role Papadopoulos played in the referendum prior to the republic's entry into the EU politically disempowered him in the role he wished to play after membership was achieved. His experience was typical of what happens to politicians of nationalist backgrounds who come in direct contact with the EU. In the union's democratic processes, ethnocentric and adversarial politics carry little legitimacy compared with dialogic, proactive, conciliatory, and creative consensus-enhancing approaches to conflict. In the EU, simply saying "no" does not suffice. The political culture of the EU expects its leaders to resolve their differences by constructively pursuing collective-security and peace-building agreements and to display the determination to do so. In this EU postnationalist culture, Papadopoulos could not merely repeat the *OXI* of the Cyprus referendum, the "resounding 'no,'" without further undermining his political credibility and effectiveness in the EU. Abandoning adversarial nationalism in relation to one's neighbor was a central condition that the 1999 EU Helsinki Summit had set for Turkey upon the latter's acceptance as an EU candidate—the very condition that finally compelled Turkey to shift its Cyprus policy from forced, ethnocentric secession to a negotiated, interethnic, federal settlement. In the eyes of the EU, if this condition is deemed the standard to be attained by the politics of candidate-states, it is the unquestionable norm for the politics of the member-states.

The EU Brussels Summit was Papadopoulos's first full-fledged experience with the EU's political process at the highest level of collective decision making. Here, Papadopoulos was forcibly confronted with the fact that, within the EU, his government's approach of confining its effort only to the legal aspects of the Cyprus problem, while ignoring the political dimension, was bankrupt. Despite the pre- and postsummit rationalizations, without pursuing a determined, creative, and proactive approach to resolving the political aspects of the Cyprus problem, the legal dimensions would remain forever ambivalent and even irresolvable. It is noteworthy that the presence of Turkish troops in northern Cyprus had not been at all part of the EU agenda and deliberations regarding Turkey's future. As far as the EU was concerned, there was no European solution for Cyprus to replace the UN solution, as Papadopoulos had strategized.

The anticlimax of Papadopoulos's first high-level attempt to capitalize on Cyprus's EU membership was widely reflected in the GC media immediately following the summit. The press noted that Papadopoulos, upon his return, "slipped back into the country in the early hours, making no statements to add to those made in Brussels, while state broadcaster CyBC led its main lunchtime bulleting on contaminated apricots." Papadopoulos's DIKO party was also "strangely silent" (*Cyprus Mail* 2004c). Interestingly, upon his return from Brussels, Papadopoulos came under severe fire by the most nationalist GC parties that backed his presidency as well as by hard-line factions within his own party. The disappointment with, and accusations against, Papadopoulos ranged from his being too soft, to lacking in firmness in his stance against Turkey, to not delivering what he had promised.

It was interesting, but not surprising, that the opposition parties such as DISY and the United Democrats rallied to his support, indicating that despite the limitations, not vetoing Turkey at the EU summit was the responsible European thing to do—a position shared by Greece. Papadopoulos's decision not to veto was viewed as a first step by his administration toward aligning its politics with the values and modus operandi of the EU.

However, it was pointed out that this alignment would not serve the interests of Cyprus unless complemented by a convincing and active initiative by the GC government to reactivate negotiations for a political settlement. Former GC president Vassiliou was particularly articulate about this fact. As the most European-minded, GC politician, he emphasized the imperative of reactivating the UN-based negotiation process by reminding his colleagues that "there is no room for polarities in the EU" and that "the EU sees understanding between everybody" (*Cyprus Mail* 2004c). In this anticipated development, history took a most interesting twist. The strongest critics of Papadopoulos's role at the December 2004 EU summit were those who opposed the Annan Plan most feverishly, while the strongest backing and encouragement for Papadopoulos came from those who supported it.

In summary, the European Council unanimously decided at the EU summit to offer Turkey October 3, 2005, as the date for commencing accession negotiations. But Turkey was also formally obligated to extend its customs union protocol in recognition of all the new EU members. Yet Turkey was to do so not in advance of its date for starting accession negotiations, as Papadopoulos wanted, but along the way. As for Cyprus, the conclusions of the EU summit amounted to one essential outcome: the creation of another opportunity to resolve the Cyprus problem. This was the optimal outcome of the EU consensus-building process.

Not surprisingly, Erdogan, recognizing that the EU had opened a new time frame for solving the problem, informed the UN secretary-general, immediately following the summit's decision that Turkey was ready to resume the Cyprus talks, a statement demonstrating Erdogan's understanding that Turkey's road to Europe is a tough one, going far beyond the Cyprus problem. By maintaining its support of a UN-based, negotiated solution to the problem, Turkey stood to accumulate valuable political capital, which it could invest in its long road to Europe. Erdogan's quick postsummit move posed a further challenge to Papadopoulos.

The critical historical question for the GC president was whether he would reciprocate and rise to the challenge of addressing the Cyprus problem through political negotiations. The pressure on Papadopoulos to engage genuinely in negotiations reached its apogee on April 17,

2005, when TC propeace candidate Mehmet Ali Talat won the presidential elections in northern Cyprus. Talat's victory marked the decisive end of the lifelong leadership of nationalist Denktash. It also affirmed the TCs' renewed readiness for a final settlement.

In the run-up to the EU Luxemburg Summit of October 2005, set to decide whether Turkey would formally start accession negotiations, one could observe an almost exact repetition of the scenarios leading to the Brussels Summit of the previous year. The polarization between Ankara and Nicosia stubbornly continued. Papadopoulos used Cyprus's membership in the EU to persistently block any direct, formal links between the TCs and the EU. In retaliation, Turkey unremittingly used its membership in NATO to block GC-controlled Cyprus from participating in EU-NATO strategic meetings, which in turn impeded transatlantic security talks.

Again, Papadopoulos threatened to veto Turkey unless his demands were met, particularly his demand that Turkey must formally recognize the Republic of Cyprus before starting accession negotiations with the EU. Again, Turkey warned that in view of the referendum results, recognizing the Republic of Cyprus constituted a nonnegotiable issue. Further, it attempted to exclude means of transport from the customs union with the Republic of Cyprus. While signing the protocol extending its customs union agreement to include the new EU members in July 2005, Turkey thus included an addendum declaring that it did not recognize the Republic of Cyprus. In response, the EU dismissed the addendum as void since it did not constitute part of the EU legal process.

After the GC government fiercely resisted the inclusion of any reference to the Cyprus referendum, the EU's declaration succinctly stated that the EU regretted Turkey's refusal to recognize Cyprus and that Turkey was obliged to implement the customs union agreement fully. But it also made reference to the need for a Cyprus settlement within the UN framework, thus emphasizing the need for a return to the UN process.

Interestingly, neither the absolute condition set by Turkey nor the one set by Papadopoulos was adhered to in the conclusions of the Luxemburg Summit. After marathon negotiations, in which the main objector to Turkey's full membership was Austria, a unanimous agreement was ultimately reached. The summit concluded that Turkey was to start accession negotiations toward full membership, and that recognition of all member-states was a necessary component of the process. While recognition of Cyprus was expected to take place *sometime after* the negotiations started, the time frame remained open and unspecified.

Originally, Papadopoulos had demanded that Turkey recognize the Republic of Cyprus *before* the start of accession talks. At the last moment, he modified his position to a demand that Turkey be given a specific date for recognizing Cyprus *soon after* accession talks begun. Neither condition was included in the summit conclusions. Turkey did not walk away, despite its original objections to the EU requirements on Cyprus, and Papadopoulos did not exercise his veto power against Turkey, despite his initial insinuations that he would. Turkey was required to align its policies and positions to the EU progressively, including ending its obstruction of any EU member-state from participating in international organizations. However, to the disappointment of Papadopoulos, Turkey was given *two years* to do so.

Again, the EU process attempted to forge convergence around EU law and process while underscoring the continuing need for a negotiated, UN-based Cyprus settlement. Within the broader EU process, the two-year grace period granted to Turkey was accompanied by the political expectation that the Cyprus problem would be addressed and resolved by the two sides. Throughout these weighty deliberations, Turkey expressed frustration over the fact that the EU had not ended the isolation of TCs, while the GC leadership acknowledged that its political influence in the EU was marginal, compelling it to settle with lower expectations.

A EUROPEAN SOLUTION AND INTERETHNIC TRUST?

The hard lesson learned by Turkey was that it could not ignore the EU law in its relation to the union and that its accession process was going to be long and arduous. The hard lesson learned by the Papadopoulos administration was that it is far more difficult to pursue nationalistic, belligerent, and legalistic approaches inside the EU than outside. Given the EU decisions on Turkey's European path, this realization stood to become more profound as time went on. The Papadopoulos government's original strategy to disengage from the UN-based solution and pursue a so-called "European solution," assuming that European law could replace the requirement for negotiating a political settlement, was proving untenable. Repeatedly, high-ranking leaders within Europe made it abundantly clear that Turkey's accession was no longer associated with a solution to the Cyprus problem. Simultaneously, it was further clarified that Turkey's harmonization and alignment to EU law could not constitute a substitute for a UN-based negotiated settlement.

More than a month prior to the EU Brussels Summit, the long-standing British envoy for Cyprus, David Hannay, echoed this crucial fact. In an interview on the occasion of the publication of his book *Cyprus: The Search for a Solution,* Hannay indicated that the GC rejection of the Annan Plan and abandonment of the UN process in favor of a "European solution" had no foundation in reality and contradicted the UN and the EU. He further noted that opposing the UN plan in an effort to secure a European solution was a strategic error that had poisoned every previous negotiation on Cyprus. "I am afraid," he asserted, "that from the beginning, many Greek Cypriots have regarded the European Union not as a balance of rights and responsibilities that people assume when they join, but as a one-way ticket to getting everything they want and haven't been able to get out of the international community over the previous period" (*Cyprus Mail* 2004e).

Being critical of "zero-sum" approaches, he also strongly criticized Denktash for walking away from the talks in the Hague in March 2003, at a time when GCs might have had an incentive to support a UN settlement. Hannay argued that the view among the GC political leadership that a European solution was a viable and realistic possibility was unwise and demonstrated their ignorance of the EU. The title of the article by which the GC *Cyprus Mail* reported Hannay's interview was "European solution? Dream on" (*Cyprus Mail* 2004e). Inevitability, reality was gradually sinking into GC public opinion.

On the same issue, the president of the EU parliament, Joseph Borrell, made even stronger statements during his visit to Cyprus immediately following the October Luxemburg Summit. He stressed that, sadly, the Cyprus problem "has become a European problem." However, he reminded Cypriots, it required a quick solution that could come only with the resumption of high-level talks between the two sides. Borrell reiterated that, to be admitted into the EU, Turkey would have to implement the protocol of the customs union fully. But he also emphasized that a solution to the Cyprus problem would only be found within the auspices of the UN, based on a bizonal, bicommunal federation. Borrell explained that while the EU would help in a facilitative capacity, Cypriots should "not expect a magical solution, as if the EU had a magic wand with which it can pull a white rabbit out of the hat." Sending a strong message to Papadopoulos, he noted that "we are not thinking of exchanging the UN framework with a European framework" (*Cyprus Mail* 2005a).

Borrell also commented on the renewed mistrust between the two Cypriot communities, adding that this could only be overcome through dialogue and a show of goodwill. Bringing the European experience and vision to bear on the current Cyprus situation, he tactfully challenged the polarizing ethnocentrism of the nationalist mind that continued to underpin the Cyprus problem. Appealing to both GCs and TCs, he asserted that "the most difficult walls are not those made of stones. They are made of biases and prejudices in the mind. This is a very dangerous wall. We have to avoid at all cost the creation of this psychological wall between the two communities and we have to do that by breaking down this wall, by contacts between the communities and leaders of both sides" (*Cyprus Mail* 2005a).

The troubling observations by the president of the European Parliament, as well as by other EU officials, that there were signs of renewed alienation between the GC and TC communities were further confirmed in the fall of 2005. The return to belligerent, nationalist approaches by the Papadopoulos administration reached its zenith when in October 2005, the GC government unilaterally decided to revive Nikiforos, the large-scale, highly profiled, annual military exercises of the past. For several years before 2001, the Nikiforos war drills were conducted jointly with forces from Greece, code-named Toxotis under the Joint Defense Dogma. The scenario was to counter the Turkish occupation of northern Cyprus and the threat posed by the presence of Turkish troops on the Island. The annual Nikiforos Toxotis military exercises took place in parallel with the equally high-profile "Taurus" military drill on the Turkish side, involving Turkish troops and Turkish Cypriot Security Forces (TCSF). The show of force by both sides, which consistently reflected Turkish superiority in air power, always precipitated into an annual escalation of tension, often reaching dangerous limits.

However, in the run-up to the entry of the Cyprus republic into the EU, in parallel to the ongoing top-level negotiations for a Cyprus settlement, Greece and Turkey, together with their Cypriot counterparts, consented to abstain from the huge military exercises in and around Cyprus in order to facilitate the rapprochement process. As a result, since 2001 there had been no Nikiforos or Taurus military drills. In reactivating the Nikiforos exercise in the fall of 2005, the GC government upset and reversed the trend of deescalating tension and building confidence, which was evident throughout the years preceding Cyprus's accession to the EU. The Papadopoulos administration officially announced that the military exercise would in fact be on "a vast scale," and that the scenario would simulate a gradual escalation of hostilities leading to all-out warfare (*Cyprus Mail* 2005b).

Predictably, the Turkish side announced that unless Papadopoulos reversed the decision to revive Nikiforos, Turkey would follow suit by relaunching its traditional Taurus military exercises in northern Cyprus. At this time, the GC National Guard amounted to around 10,000 soldiers on active duty with 88,000 reserves, traditionally supplemented by about 1,000 Greek mainland troops and 1,300 Greek mainland officers. In the north, the numbers amounted to 4,000 Turkish Cypriot Security Forces, with 26,000 reserves, plus the additional 40,000 Turkish mainland soldiers. These were the resources from which the two sides drew as they returned to actions that were thought to have been relegated to the past. With Papadopoulos hiding behind the legality of his government's action, and Turkey unwilling to resist Papadopoulos's provocation of reengaging through the adversarial mode, the massive remobilization of troops in and around Cyprus marked a regressive development. Inevitably, it brought to the forefront of high-level politics the old belligerent, ethnocentric nationalism; it transgressed fundamental EU values; and it struck a severe blow to interethnic rapprochement between the GC and TC communities.

Attending one of the Nikiforos exercises, Papadopoulos assured the GCs that the purpose of the drill was peace. He elaborated that "in order to maintain peace, you must prepare for war." Inadvertently, Papadopoulos had articulated the very nationalist principle on the basis of which Turkish and TC nationalists vehemently opposed the Annan Plan, as its provision for the progressive demilitarization of Cyprus undercut what they termed the Turkish army's "peace operation" in Cyprus. It was ironic that after arguing for the rejection of the Annan Plan on security grounds, Papadopoulos resorted to confrontational strategies that could potentially reescalate tension to a renewed phase of Greek-Turkish cold war in and around Cyprus.

However, despite all this—but also because of it—an unprecedented policy decision simultaneously occurred that moved developments counter to the negative trend initiated by the military exercises. Stunningly, and contrary to what Papadopoulos had originally assumed, Greece refused to join the GCs in the military drill. This was the first time that Greece exempted itself from joining GC Nikiforos. Greece had in fact distanced itself from Papadopoulos's war game to such an extent that it did not even send observers. Ideologically, the GC government had always taken Greece's support for granted, particularly since the advent of the Joint Defense Dogma. Yet, despite Greece's stance, Papadopoulos decided to go it alone, eventually triggering a heated public debate among GCs as to whether the Joint Defense Dogma of the 1990s had been practically annulled.

What transpired from this extraordinary change in Greek-GC relations was Greece's decision to sustain the six-year-long process of building peace-enhancing bilateral relations with Turkey, while refusing to be part of Papadopoulos's nationalism. Following the postnationalist politics initiated by the socialist PASOK government, the wisdom of this national policy shift by the center Right New Democracy government, brought to the forefront the Greek government's continuing identification of Greece's national interest with regional peace and stability. Greece chose to persevere in the promotion and institutionalization of bi- and multilateral relations with neighboring countries, in line with the EU vision and policy approaches. It was clear that had Greece followed the old nationalist line by participating in Papadopoulos's war game, the situation in the Eastern Mediterranean could have reverted to those dangerous days of absolute and clear-cut ethnonational polarization between Greeks and Turks. Deviating from the dangers of unqualified ethnocentrism, the distancing of Greece from the GC government at the time of the Nikiforos military exercises revealed yet another new dimension of postreferendum Cyprus.

THE EUROPEAN COURT OF HUMAN RIGHTS AND THE PROPERTY ISSUE

In the purely legal realm, developments during the postreferendum/EU-integration era introduced new ambiguities and challenges. Key legal aspects of the Cyprus problem proved not to be as black and white as nationalists on the Greek side had assumed, nor as easy to circumvent as nationalists on the Turkish side had assumed. Within the broader system of the Council of Europe and European Law, a most interesting development was the ruling of the European Court of Human Rights (ECHR) on the case of *Xenides-Arestis v. Turkey* of December 22, 2005, as it had an unprecedented bearing on the thorny property issues of GC refugees.

As in the famous 1998 Loizidou case, the ECHR ruled that GC plaintiff Myra Xenides-Arestis had been deprived of the right to use her property. But in specifying the required remedy, the court went beyond the Loizidou case, as it had adjourned the case, and ordered Turkey to set up an "effective reparation mechanism" not only for the plaintiff but also for another fourteen hundred similar cases submitted by GCs. "Such a remedy," the court said, "should be available within three months and redress should occur three months after that" (*Xenides-Arestis v. Turkey* 2005).

Moreover, the execution of the court's ruling was to be supervised by the Committee of Ministers of the Council of Europe. The decision was a reaffirmation that Turkey was guilty of human rights violations for denying GCs access to their property in Turkish-controlled northern Cyprus. The court's judgment posed the most powerful challenge ever to both Turkey and the TRNC's manner of handling of GC property. Following the Turkish invasion of Cyprus, the TC authorities nationalized all the property in the occupied areas that belonged to GCs, distributing most of it to TCs displaced from the south and to settlers from Turkey. The ECHR was now requiring Turkey effectively to dismantle the particular regime by which the TRNC had hitherto managed GC property.

Equally noteworthy was that in anticipating the court's decision, with so many similar cases in the queue, Ankara pressured the TC administration to adopt legislation that allowed GCs to seek either compensation or the return of their properties. The new property law, adopted by the TRNC parliament three days before the ECHR issued its judgment, was historically unprecedented as well as of enormous consequence for thousands of TCs. The new legislation took the more nationalistically inclined TC as well as the more nationalistically oriented GCs by surprise. TC and Turkish nationalists saw the move as placating the Europeans and as a national sellout to the Greeks. GC nationalists saw the change as ambivalent and perplexing. It certainly vindicated them, as it gave credence to GC property rights, but at the same time, it eroded their enemy image of a "barbarian Turkey" around which they had built their entire political agenda, approach, and strategy to the Cyprus problem.

At the official level, both sides claimed victory. The Turks noted that while the ECHR found Turkey guilty, it did not order it to pay compensation as it did with the Loizidou case. Most importantly, Turkish diplomatic sources argued that the most significant part of the decision was that it required an "internal remedy" to be initiated and executed within the TRNC. On its part, however, the GC government publicly hailed the court's decision as further proof of human rights violations by Turkey and as an opportunity to put things right.

Upon closer examination, however, the implications of the ECHR's ruling were not as straightforward as either side had officially claimed. Like other European-related political and legal developments since 2003, the particular ruling of 2005 drove a wedge to the heart of the Cyprus problem, further deconstructing its familiar traditional structure. The Turkish side was now challenged with a new historical dilemma. It could continue its unilateral support of the TRNC and its administrative control of GC property in northern Cyprus in the name of Turkish national interest and the self-determination of the TCs, and be in defiance of the ECHR. Or it could comply with the court's decision, proceed with the restitution of GC property, and thus bestow a significant measure of international, legal legitimacy on the regime of northern Cyprus.

In essence, the dilemma before the Turkish side was either to continue operating on the basis of a nationalistic concept of Turkish interests and TC sovereignty and defy the ECHR, or to obey the court and redefine its national interest and sovereignty in alignment with the rule of law. In choosing the latter, Turkey would also face the prospect of returning to its GC owners the ghost city of Famagusta. But if it did so, it would lose a major negotiating card that it held in hand since taking the city in 1974.

The GC side was confronted with an equally challenging dilemma, but one far more nuanced than that facing Turkey. If the Turkish side proceeded with the restitution of GC property, the GC government would have to decide whether the Turkish-managed mechanism for remedy in northern Cyprus implied any legitimacy to the TC administration and hence to the TRNC. The Papadopoulos government had already declared that the GCs would reject the authority of any institution in the TRNC. But clearly, the institutional entity under consideration had been ordered, authorized, and mandated by the ECHR to implement the court's ruling.

Ironically, the institutional deliberations over the mechanism for remedy that GCs had to now reckon with by the order of the European court was in certain respect similar, although not identical, to the Claims Settlement Council that Denktash wanted to launch unilaterally prior to the referendum for resolving the GC property issue in northern Cyprus. The TRNC-authorized commission offered GC refugees the option of barter or compensation, but not the return of GC property. The international community outright rejected Denktash's effort, as his move was universally viewed as both illegitimate and a political scheme to undermine and evade the mounting Annan-based negotiations for a comprehensive settlement.

In the postreferendum era, the GCs confronted a most peculiar reality: What Denktash had tried to do prior to the referendum and which had been discredited and dismissed, the ECHR was now not only requiring but also extending under international law. One of the reactionary opinions formed in GC nationalist circles was that the court's decision was an attempt to punish the GCs for rejecting the Annan Plan. Such an argument indicates a fundamental lack of understanding of the ECHR and how it operates. Turkey had used the GCs' rejection of the Annan Plan as a point in its defense. But the court explicitly stated "that the fact that the Greek-Cypriots had rejected the Annan Plan did not have the legal consequence of bringing to an end the continuing violation of the displaced persons' rights" (*Xenides-Arestis v. Turkey* 2005). Although the court's ruling made mention of the Cyprus referendum as one of the facts contextualizing the case, its decision was clearly made in reference to Article 8 of the Convention and Article 1 of Protocol No. 1, and not on political considerations. In essence, GC nationalists refused to understand that, short of a final political settlement, the remedy required by the court's ruling was the sole legal way open for the practical restitution of GC property.

While formally neither the EU nor the Council of Europe recognized the TRNC, the GC government was compelled to come to terms with the legal and political consequences of the judgment of ECHR. The court's call on Turkey for the restitution of GC property in northern Cyprus struck at the heart of not only the traditional Turkish approach but also the traditional GC approach to the Cyprus problem. If GC property rights were to be restored, the GC government would be compelled to acknowledge the legal authority of at least the institution in northern Cyprus implementing the remedy. However, if the GC government deemed that the institution in question was illegitimate, it would inevitably come in conflict with the very process designated by the ECHR for restoring GC property rights. Further, a most critical issue for the GC government concerned how to react if any of the thousands of GC refugees decided to submit their property claims to the remedying institution in northern Cyprus.

This issue had the potential of posing a huge challenge to the Papadopoulos government, particularly in view of the fact that, had the GC side accepted the Annan Plan, two-thirds of GC refugees would have had their properties not only immediately reinstated but also placed under GC administration. Would the GC government charge these GCs with formally dealing with an illegal entity and thereby appear to be undermining the opportunity granted to the GCs by the ECHR to have their property rights restored? Would it label these GCs as traitors operating contrary to national interest? Some GC nationalists even suggested that the government should prosecute any GC who deals with the TC administration. In such a case, wouldn't the GC government be obstructing the implementation of the ECHR's ruling? Moreover, what would the implications be if the revived nationalism in GC public opinion were strong enough to deter individual GCs from appealing directly to the Turkish side for restitution? What would happen if no GC stepped forward to claim his or her property? Would the GCs themselves nullify the very ruling that intended to restore their human rights? And how would this impact the international credibility of the GC government, particularly within the EU?

If Turkey refused to execute the court's decision fully, it would face isolation and a further stalling of an already difficult EU accession process. This was clear to all concerned. But if it proceeded, it would be taking a significant step toward aligning Turkish policy on Cyprus with international law. Thus, international law not only would cease to be the monopolized instrument of the GC side, but also would reinforce Turkey's political standing in both the EU and the UN. Even in the face of fierce criticism by Turkish nationalists, the Erdogan government clearly understood this eventuality, which also explains Ankara's determination to depart from traditional Turkish policy on Cyprus.

However, what would this mean for the Papadopoulos government in the postreferendum era? If under the directives of the ECHR the Turkish side institutionalized a mechanism that started to effectively address GC property claims, then one of the major aspects of the Cyprus problem would be dissolved, but still without a final political settlement in place. Such a prospect stood to weaken the GC government's legalistic approach to the Cyprus problem considerably, further exposing as bankrupt the ethnocentric nationalism that it had reactivated since Papadopoulos came to power. Following his rejection of the Annan Plan and subsequent refusal to engage in negotiations, Papadopoulos's pursuit of a purely legal approach to the Cyprus problem instead was contingent on maintaining and propagating the image of an intransigent, defiant, and law-transgressing Turkey. Surely, Turkey had a long way to go before harmonizing with European norms. However, for Turkey, restoring GC property would constitute a huge step in that direction. And if Turkey convincingly appeared to be complying with international law, especially against the backdrop of its acknowledged active support of a UN-based Cyprus settlement, then the dark enemy image of Turkey projected by GC nationalists would become politically untenable and strategically ineffective.

Not surprisingly, in the face of the ECHR's decision, the greatest fear among GC nationalists was not that Turkey would refuse to comply with the court's ruling, but rather that it would comply! Ironically, this same fear was shared by staunch Turkish nationalists of both the Right and the Left. In particular, hard-liners of the old Turkish establishment, in collusion also with the former TC leader Denktash, were known to have been actively mobilizing within Turkey to curb what they perceived as Erdogan's treacherous policy on Cyprus, all in preparation for making a bid for power during the next election. Under these conditions, the longer the Cyprus problem remained unresolved, the greater its prospects of being nationalistically exploited through the power dynamics of Turkey's domestic party politics. Clearly, if the nationalists in Turkey made a comeback, the Cyprus issue would again regress to a new stalemate with unpredictable consequences. At this moment in the development of the Cyprus problem, the new GC nationalism brought to the forefront of the political process since the referendum, and the potential reempowerment of nationalism within Turkey, constituted the two interrelated factors most likely to drive the Cyprus problem into a new historical impasse.

By 2007, the property issue had become severely complicated for both TC and GC nationalists. To the great disappointment of the TC nationalists, the Property Commission in northern Cyprus started to settle the first case brought forward by GC plaintiffs. To the great disappointment of the GC nationalists, the first 180 GC refugees had applied to the Property Commission in the Turkish north with claims ranging from $200,000 to $4.2 million. Of these cases, twelve had already been successfully resolved. The situation for the GCs became even thornier when nationalist television station Sigma handed to the attorney general a list of the GC refugees who had applied for restitution, insinuating that the government should prosecute them (Christou 2007b). While referring to the Property Commission as an illegal entity, the GC government refrained from taking a position on whether to prosecute. What was clear, but unspoken, was that action against the refugees would have clashed with European law. The irrationality of the situation reached its climax when nationalist voices in parliament suggested that the refugees in question be stripped of their refugee status and hence of government benefits. In response, GC refugees, who now saw the solution of the Cyprus problem as remote, prepared to launch a class-action suit against the Republic of Cyprus, demanding the equal division of the economic burden that had resulted from the Turkish invasion (*Cyprus Mail* 2007b).

The decision of the ECHR was a landmark case of restorative justice that simultaneously exposed both sides to the antinomies and paradoxes inherent to the nationalism perpetuating Cyprus conflict. Still more significantly, it indirectly brought into sharper focus the imperative for a final settlement as the only way to decisively supersede innumerable similar dilemmas that would inevitably continue to plague Cyprus. Again, all postreferendum developments in both GC and TC politics, including those associated with Turkey's progress toward EU accession, clearly pointed to the urgent need for the disputants to address multilaterally both the legal and political aspects of the Cyprus problem. And the sole avenue for doing so was the resumption of negotiations within the framework of the UN, which invariably meant reengagement within the framework of the Annan Plan.

9

The Changing Parameters of the Cyprus Problem (II)

EU BRUSSELS SUMMIT, DECEMBER 2006

By the Brussels summit of 14–15th of December 2006, the EU was compelled to face two interrelated issues: The first was that Turkey continued to keep its sea and air ports closed to the Republic of Cyprus. The second was that Papadopoulos continued to exhibit no willingness to reengage in the search for a comprehensive Cyprus settlement. The former, being legal in nature, was tackled through a strong reproof of Turkey in the formal deliberations and conclusions of the summit. The latter, being political in nature, was addressed through diplomatic reprimand and challenge of the Papadopoulos government. But this dual approach was initiated only after the EU had exhausted all efforts for a constructive conciliatory outcome.

In the run-up to the summit, the Finnish EU presidency attempted to mediate an agreement between the GC-controlled Republic of Cyprus and Turkey by exploring an interim plan that would have provided Cyprus access to Turkish sea and air ports in exchange for direct trade between the TCs and the EU. The Finnish initiative also explored the possibility of placing the port of Famagusta, through which the TCs would presumably conduct their foreign trade, under the administration of either the UN or the EU.

The Papadopoulos government continued to resist allowing any TC trade directly with the EU. In the process of Finland's diplomatic exploration, the GC government demanded the return of the ghost city of Famagusta to its rightful owners as a condition for any progress on the matter at hand, declaring simultaneously that the issue concerned the human rights of GCs and, as such, could not be part of a negotiated process of give-and-take. Conversely, hitting at Papadopoulos's general evasion of substantive talks for a comprehensive settlement, Turkey's response was that the return of Famagusta was a major and integral part of a final comprehensive settlement and not a bargaining chip for presolution negotiations on confidence-building measures. The GC side, adamant about TC trade with the EU, wanted all TC trade to go through the southern city of Limassol, the republic's major port—an approach that the TCs always perceived as an attempt by Papadopoulos to subjugate the TCs under the authority of the GC-controlled republic while evading a comprehensive settlement. Turkey's position was that the termination of TC isolation was an EU promise and that Turkey would not open its sea and air ports to the republic unless this promise was fulfilled. This interaction between the GC government and the Turkish side reflected, yet again, the regressive trends that the failed Cyprus referendum of 2004 had revived in GC-Turkish/TC relations as well as in Turkish-EU relations.

The Finnish presidency's initiative toward an interim agreement aimed at partially reintegrating the legal and the political aspects of EU policy toward the Eastern Mediterranean that fell into disarray after the failed 2004 referendum. The vast majority of the EU leadership shared a common historical perspective on Cyprus, Turkey, and their evolving relationship with the EU. In an article published in the *International Herald Tribune* a month before the EU summit, Swedish foreign minister Carl Bildt, stressing the significance of EU enlargement for peace and stability in the Eastern Mediterranean, articulated the European perspective on Cyprus quite succinctly.

> One of the most painful failures of the international community in recent years was the 2004 failure to achieve a solution to the division of Cyprus, and it was obvious from that day that it would complicate the accession process of Turkey.
>
> We should not forget that these efforts did not fail because of Turkey, but because key parts of the Greek Cypriot leadership refused to accept a plan by the UN secretary general that had the clear support of the European Union.

> As the Finnish presidency of the EU tries to overcome the present difficulties, we must neither ignore our long-term strategic interests nor forget where the key responsibility for the 2004 failure lies. (Bildt 2006)

The Finnish presidency, however, was unable to mediate an agreement between the GC government and Turkey. At the Brussels summit, following intense negotiations by the EU foreign ministers two days earlier, with the Cyprus government at the center of controversy, the EU leaders came to a unanimous conclusion regarding Turkey: suspend accession negotiations on eight of the thirty-five chapters required for harmonization with the EU. The suspended chapters were on trade, transport, financial services, and agriculture, covering the very issues bearing on Cyprus-Turkish trade relations. However, the decision also underscored the fact that accession negotiations on all remaining chapters would continue unimpeded.

Despite insinuations about employing his veto power to halt Turkey's accession, Papadopoulos was compelled to endorse the summit conclusions, as the gravity of collective compromise, an integral part of EU conciliatory politics, contained and curbed the degree to which he could play unilateralist nationalist politics within the EU. Banking on its veto power and EU accession regulations, the Papadopoulos administration was hoping to block Turkey's accession path altogether unless Turkey unconditionally recognized the Republic of Cyprus and opened to it its sea and air ports. Instead of freezing Turkey's accession process, the EU essentially deferred the eight problematic chapters to the end of it. But in so doing, the EU also indirectly deferred to the end of Turkey's long accession process Papadopoulos's veto power regarding these chapters. Simultaneously, the EU Commission encouraged a speedy opening of negotiations on the remaining chapters.

While the EU leaders reprimanded Turkey, they did not include any ultimatums or deadlines for it to open its sea and air ports to Cypriot traffic, as the GC government wished. Moreover, they reiterated the promise to end the economic isolation of the TC community while leaving the details to be worked out the following year. The commission was subsequently mandated to find legitimate ways to open up direct trade between the TCs and the EU and to generally upgrade the TC community in every way, short of any recognition of the TRNC. Thus after more than two-and-a-half years of effort by the Papadopoulos government to use EU law to curb any prospect of TC-EU trade, the EU leaders returned to the commission's 2004 postreferendum recommendation for direct trade between northern Cyprus and the EU. This decision may be characterized as a *political* deliberation of finding legal ways to economically upgrade the TC community in light of the fact that the GC side, more than the TC side, has been fundamentally reluctant to reengage in negotiations under the UN for a comprehensive Cyprus settlement.

It was therefore not surprising that the EU's summit deliberations ended with a simultaneous short but succinct presidency statement which made two key points: First, it welcomed the positive responses of the GC and TC leaders to the call by UN undersecretary-general Gambari to start confidence-building talks through technical committees, as was expected by their July 8 agreement. But second, and more importantly, the EU presidency stated that after discussions in the council it expressed "its full support for the ongoing efforts of the United Nations Secretary General to resume the negotiations for a comprehensive settlement of the Cyprus problem in line with relevant UN Security Council Resolutions and the principles on which the EU is founded" (*EU Press* 2006). The presidency further emphasized "the need to quickly start this preparatory work in order for the United Nations Secretary General's Good Offices mission to resume without unnecessary delay."

Unfortunately, while the technical committees produced very little, this call to action on a final settlement was not heeded. But the EU presidency's statement underscored the need for the resumption of top-level negotiations, which were systematically evaded, mainly by Papadopoulos. While Turkey faced endless entanglements and tough challenges for not complying with the EU requirement to extend the Ankara protocol to include Cyprus, the GC government was becoming politically isolated from an increasing number of EU leaders who viewed the GC side as responsible for precipitating this stagnating situation. EU leaders were increasingly upset with the GCs, especially in view of Turkey's repeated proposals for reviving the top-level UN talks for the reunification of Cyprus (*BBC News* 2006b).

At the General Affairs Council that preceded the Brussels summit, the foreign ministers strongly castigated the GC government for its behavior. Only this time around, the strongest words came from countries that the GCs normally considered friendly. Diplomats and analysts in Brussels pointed out that GCs had lost all their friends in the EU, including Greece, despite their political rhetoric to the contrary (Charalambous 2007). One observer noted that key actors in the EU "are in a state of complete despair with regard to the Cyprus problem," while another indicated that there was increasing frustration in Brussels with GCs. As one diplomat put it, the GC government "has a one-dimensional foreign policy while the rest of us have multi-dimensional foreign policies" (Christou 2007b).

EU UPGRADING OF TURKISH CYPRIOTS AND THE RELAPSE OF NATIONALISM WITHIN TURKEY

In February 2006, the EU member-states adopted the long-delayed Aid Regulation of €259 million. Its purpose was to facilitate the economic development and integration of the TCs, to improve contacts between the two communities and with the EU, and to prepare the TCs for the gradual adoption of the EU's legal order. In the same year, under the direct control of the commission (not of the GC government), €177.1 million had already been granted to the TCs. By this time, however, the EU also began to address the political isolation of the TCs—a significant step that went beyond mere economic assistance.

Procrastination in the pursuit of a comprehensive settlement in the post-2004 era, for which the Europeans held mainly Papadopoulos responsible, inevitably raised persistent questions concerning the fact that while the TCs supported the UN peace plan, they had been completely left out of all the EU institutions. While TCs were accepted as legitimate EU citizens vis-à-vis the Republic of Cyprus, all Cypriot representation in the EU was held by GCs. By default, the failure of the 2004 referendum pushed the TCs back into the unrecognized TRNC. Mindful of these ambiguities, the Europeans launched an ongoing quest for ways to upgrade the status of the TCs in every possible legal and political way short of state recognition.

While disappointing the GC government, which went to great lengths to obstruct any upgrading of the TCs that was not placed exclusively under the GC-run Republic of Cyprus, the EU, particularly through the commission and parliament, remained persistent in this general objective despite disagreement on specifics.

In 2007, following the December 2006 summit, the German presidency of the EU initiated an examination on how to assist TCs in coming out of both their economic and political isolation. A confidential report was prepared by the European Parliament's High-Level Contact Group for relations with the TCs in northern Cyprus, a cross-political group of EU parliamentarians established by the EU assembly in September 2005. The contact group examined the matter and made proposals on issues ranging from the Direct Trade Regulation—proposed by the commission soon after the 2004 referendum to allow TC trade with the EU—to upgrading TC educational institutions with the prospect of integrating them into EU programs, to the introduction of a number of institutions that would end the political isolation of the TC north. Initially there were disagreements over "whether or not to grant Turkish Cypriots a form of representation in the European Parliament, with all six MEPs from Cyprus currently being Greek Cypriots." The contact group's consensus was to propose that TCs be granted the status of observers so that their voices will be heard in the EU parliament (*EU Observer* 2007). The group also proposed that Turkish be recognized as an official EU language.

While the Papadopoulos administration fiercely resisted these initiatives, the succeeding German presidency of the EU made it clear that its aim was to find a solution acceptable to both sides but also oriented toward ending TC isolation. All along, the Papadopoulos administration strongly objected to any upgrade of the TCs, even to having one or two TC universities participate in the EU-led, twenty-nine-country Bologna Process for integrating higher education. As time went on, the GC government became increasingly confronted with political challenges that emanated directly from Papadopoulos's strategy of indefinitely postponing negotiations for a final settlement, erroneously thinking that Cyprus's EU membership would give the GC side a huge advantage over the Turkish side. Even though many issues pertaining to the upgrading of the TCs entailed intergovernmental agreements that inevitably excluded the illegitimate TRNC, the EU became persistent in finding interim solutions so as to keep the TCs close to the EU, rather than isolating and alienating them. This was a strategy that the EU deemed prudent for maintaining the TC incentive for a final settlement. European officials explained their concern over the condition of the TCs in July 2007, when the European Parliament's High-Level Contact Group strongly criticized the EU for failing in its promises by not having managed to lift sufficiently the political and economic isolation of the TC community (Bahceli 2007b).

In addition, the European leadership gradually started to focus on how the cumulative politico-legal complications in GC-TC relations, Cyprus-Turkish relations, and EU-Turkish relations—all direct consequences of the failed 2004 referendum—could potentially impact domestic developments within Turkey, especially in view of the upcoming 2007 presidential and general elections. The combination of Papadopoulos's obstructionist strategy toward Turkey and the TCs, fears of Islam among portions of European opinion, and the resultant EU demands and criticism, often harsher than usual, of the Turkish government carried a high risk of a dual negative impact within Turkey. The first entailed the prospect of empowering the hard-line nationalist groups within Turkey, who relentlessly attacked the Turkish government, accusing it of treason over its support for a reunified Cyprus and of selling out to the EU. The second concerned the possibility that a harsh stand toward Turkey could undermine rather than aid the Erdogan government in its strenuous push for reforms against the historically entrenched conservative political establishment and judiciary of Turkey (International Crisis Group 2007).

The EU's reprimand of Turkey for slowing accession reforms in 2005–6 was inevitably tempered by a sobering realization of these dynamics. While in September 2006 the EU parliament adopted a critical report on the slow pace of Turkey's reforms, it also voted to delete a clause that would have required as a precondition for EU membership that Ankara officially recognize as genocide the mass killing of Armenians by Ottoman Turks (Ennis 2006). Earlier attempts by the EU parliament to add the Armenian issue as a condition for Turkey's eventual membership had vexed, mobilized, and emboldened anti-European nationalists within Turkey. Even pro-EU reformers in Turkey argued that admitting to genocide as a condition for accession entailed a double standard that went way beyond the Copenhagen criteria, especially since the event in question had occurred under Ottoman rule and not under that of the Republic of Turkey. Erdogan's proposal to convene a joint group of Turkish and Armenian historians to research and bring to closure the complex and controversial issue of Armenian killings during World War I—which unfortunately was rejected by Armenians—gave the Europeans further reason to suspend the issue.

The slowness of reforms within Turkey was directly linked to the relapse of nationalism and its emerging strength on the eve of the national elections. The assassination of Turkish-Armenian newspaper editor Hrant Dink in January 2007, the fact that Orhan Pamuk, the Nobel laureate for literature, had to leave the country for his safety, and the fact that the Turkish government had to provide bodyguards for prominent writers, academics, and journalists was indicative of the seriousness of the situation. But the Turkish government's strong condemnation of Dink's murder and the more than one hundred thousand pro–freedom-of-speech Turks who gathered at his funeral, many chanting "We are all Armenians," was also reflective of the mounting tensions within public opinion between prodemocracy, European-minded Turks, and ethnocentric nationalists. Following these events, the EU, mindful of both the delicate situation within Turkey and the need to sustain the momentum of reforms, stressed the expectation that the Turkish government ought to steadily proceed in 2007 with its harmonization process, especially on freedom of speech and rights of religious minorities. In response, the Turkish government expressed its determination to continue its reform efforts, including the abolition of Article 301 of the Turkish Penal Code, which makes the denigration of Turkishness and of state institutions a punishable offense (Güvenc 2007). The pro–EU Justice and Development Party's victory in the elections of July 2007 renewed hopes that the Turkish government would reinvigorate the reform process (International Crisis Group 2007).

DEALING WITH SYMPTOMS RATHER THAN SUBSTANCE: THE LEDRA STREET CROSSING

All of these complications in GC-TC relations, Cyprus-Turkish relations, and EU-Turkish relations point directly or indirectly to one basic historical fact: Failure to achieve a comprehensive Cyprus settlement in 2004 inevitably diverted thereafter all of the political energy of the stakeholders away from addressing the substance of the Cyprus problem to merely fighting over its symptoms. This post-2004 shift subsequently created an obdurate political stalemate that tended to complicate even relatively simple issues and to render explosive the more weighty and far-reaching issues. The drawn-out efforts to demolish the respective forty-three-year-old barricade walls across Ledra Street in the center of the divided capital was one of the most vivid and highlighted examples of the first type of issue. The unilaterally declared intention by each side to tap oil and gas reserves off the coast of Cyprus was one of the most spectacular and highlighted examples of the second.

While talks were on the way about removing the barricades for reopening Ledra Street, a thoroughfare running along the divided capital, the Turkish army decided to build a footbridge across the street to facilitate its patrols along the green line. Naturally, the move angered GCs, and even though the TCs had removed their barricade in 2005, the GCs argued that the bridge encroached into the UN buffer zone, separating the two sides (*BBC News* 2006a). After much debate and UN mediation, TC leader Talat, despite initial objections by the Turkish army, ordered the demolition of the bridge just before Christmas of 2006, demanding the removal of the barricade wall on the GC side in return. The GC government insisted further that Turkish troops disengage from the area, neglected buildings be strengthened, and mines (believed to exist) be removed. The GCs also demanded the removal of all TRNC and Turkish flags, which in turn angered the Turkish side. The two sides spent more than a year at loggerheads over the opening of the Ledra Street crossing. They became embroiled in endless debates, engaging much of the UN's labor time.

Discussions on opening Ledra Street started in 2005. But it was not until March 2007 that the GC side decided to demolish its own barricade.

President Papadopoulos ordered the wall to come down in the midst of the European Commission's initiatives for finding a mutually acceptable formula for ending the political and economic isolation of TCs, including direct trade with the EU. Since the last EU summit of 2006, Papadopoulos had been under severe criticism by European leaders for his unconstructive approach to the Cyprus problem, which consequently complicated Cyprus-Turkish and EU-Turkish relations. Under EU pressure, he was eventually compelled to knock down the wall despite the fact that not all of the conditions he originally set for doing so were met. Interestingly, the wall came down a little after midnight on the day he was due to leave Cyprus to meet with EU leaders. Though on a smaller scale, Papadopoulos's move was reminiscent of Denktash's opening of the checkpoints in 2003: a unilateral attempt to exhibit goodwill for the purpose of salvaging political credibility while avoiding a comprehensive settlement. The GC government rushed to warn that demolishing the Ledra Street wall did not mean opening the crossing, as all other conditions were still pending (Christou and Leonidou 2007). But, Papadopoulos explained, this was a gesture of goodwill, and he called on Turkey to withdraw its troops from Cyprus.

He even went a step further and unilaterally ordered the commencement of works that would facilitate the opening of the crossing in the Kato Pyrgos–Limnitis area. His government expressed the desire to open this crossing irrespective of progress on Ledra Street. The GCs resorted to this move knowing that the Turkish army had a base nearby that would either have to withdraw for the crossing to open; otherwise the Turkish side would be accused of intransigence and obstruction to the building of confidence. Not surprising, the Turkish side responded in kind. Talat accused the Papadopoulos government of unilateralism and suggested that the GC side first open the Ledra crossing before they entertained the opening of another. But, copying Papadopoulos, the Turkish side now demanded that for the security of the TCs, the GC government must also remove its military from the Ledra Street crossing. Combating the GC side's demands for the withdrawal of Turkish troops from the crossing, the TCs argued that it is not the Turkish army but TCs that man the green line there. In this context, the GC sweeping proposal to open eight more crossing points was viewed by TC "foreign minister" Turgay Avci as ridiculous in view of the fact that the GC government prevented the opening of Ledra Street to begin with by its increasing list of preconditions (Evripidou 2007).

But what was the deeper issue that determined this counterproductive interaction between the two sides? Papadopoulos's strategy was to pursue the opening of multiple crossings for the purpose of pushing the Turkish army to disengage along the green line without the GC side making any substantive concessions. The assumption here was that since the presence of the Turkish army was illegal, its removal from portions of the republic's territory should not require reciprocation. While refraining from negotiating a comprehensive settlement, the idea was to use the route of piecemeal confidence-building tactics as a way of changing a huge factor on the ground, namely getting the Turkish army to partially withdraw. For TCs, however, changing the status and function of the Turkish army was considered a substantive issue to be addressed as part of a comprehensive settlement and not as a peripheral issue of confidence-building measures. In the mind of the TCs and Turkey, the Turkish side had consented to the progressive demilitarization of the whole of Cyprus when it accepted the Annan Plan. Thus, to pull back the Turkish army without securing any substantive benefits in return appeared completely unacceptable, especially after Papadopoulos's 2005 reintroduction of Nikiforos. (The respective approaches to the possible opening of the green-line crossing paralleled exactly those concerning the return of the city of Famagusta. The TCs saw these issues as part of a comprehensive settlement while the GCs viewed them as piecemeal issues to be tackled outside of a comprehensive settlement.)

Despite this confusion, the downing of the Ledra Street barricade, even without the opening of the crossing, was met with jubilation on both sides of the ethnic divide, briefly rekindling a positive climate that reminded Cypriots of the goodwill of 2003 (Bahceli 2007c; Morgan 2007). However, at this stage in the evolution of the Cyprus problem, piecemeal confidence-building measures, though important, could not replace a negotiated settlement. Exhibiting goodwill in removing a barricade could never substitute for the badly needed political will to negotiate a comprehensive settlement. Suggesting that Turkey withdraws its troop without such a settlement was a notion that only existed in the unfounded dreams of GC nationalists. It was in fact contrary to both the provisions of the UN resolutions and EU thinking on Cyprus.

DEALING WITH SYMPTOMS RATHER THAN SUBSTANCE:
TAPPING OIL AND GAS RESERVES

In 2003, in anticipation of a possible settlement, the demolition of barricades for opening crossings along the green line occurred swiftly and in a relatively straightforward manner. By contrast, the attempts to open the Ledra Street crossing resulted in endless entanglements from 2005 to 2007. With no prospect of a settlement in view, intercommunal interactions became oriented to the symptoms of the Cyprus problem, rendering even simple matters exaggeratedly weighty and unmanageable. It was not surprisin, therefore, that more complex issues, such tapping oil and gas reserves off the shores of Cyprus, would raise tensions and inflate ethnocentrism on both sides, even dangerously so.

The issue of oil and gas reserves surged to the forefront of events when the GC press divulged in January 2007 that the Papadopoulos government had recently signed an agreement with Lebanon and Egypt for joint oil and gas exploration in an area 125 miles wide between Cyprus and the Mediterranean's southern coast. The wealth of the energy reserves was initially estimated at more than $400 billion. As these developments came to light, TC leader Talat declared that TCs and Turkey also had rights to the reserves and that any deal should include them and required their consent. He further revealed that he had protested in writing to both Lebanon and Egypt, warning that if the project went ahead, it would likely raise tensions. Talat even insinuated that the reason GCs had rejected the 2004 reunification plan had much to do with their reluctance to share the wealth from the energy reserves. Even though he presented no evidence of this, Talat's reaction exemplified TC feelings of rejection resulting from the 2004 GC vote.

The GC government responded by asserting that as the legitimate state of the Island, the Republic of Cyprus had every right to exploit any and all resources, that the reserves rightfully belong to it, and that it was not obliged to share them with anyone (Hazou 2007a). While the EU held that it was certainly within the legal rights of the republic to engage in energy exploration, it simultaneously questioned the political prudence of the move in view of Papadopoulos's persistent disinterest in pursuing a comprehensive settlement. A suggestion originating from Greece that future energy revenues be kept in a fund until the Cyprus problem was solved was rejected outright by the GC government.

By early February 2007 the GC press was reporting the unexpected movement of Turkish warships along the southern coast of Cyprus and blamed Turkey for power posturing over the GC government's oil and gas exploration plans. General Yasar Buyukanit, chief of Turkey's general staff, attempted to calm things down by stating that the movement was a routine patrol in the Mediterranean. But his statement came after the Turkish television channel NTV reported that the warships had been sent as a warning that Ankara "would safeguard its rights in the area" (Borowiec 2007). The GC government subsequently characterized Turkey's action as an unacceptable provocation and a threat to peace in the area, while the Greek government was compelled to add its voice to that of the GCs. By February 15, the *Turkish Daily News* announced that Turkey was launching its own plans for oil and gas exploration. By March, in response to GC complaints, the German EU presidency called on Turkey to refrain from threats, as this approach violated the Helsinki (1999) and Brussels (2004 and 2006) decisions that stressed the commitment of member-states as well as candidate- states to maintain good neighborly relations.

While the two sides attempted thereafter to exhibit restraint and Greece completely distanced itself from the issue, the incident was indicative of the fact that outside a comprehensive Cyprus settlement, the matter of energy reserves could easily trigger dangerous conflict escalation in the Eastern Mediterranean (Christou 2007d). After all, this was the very reason why similar efforts in the past had been aborted. It was in fact former GC minister of commerce Rolandis who warned that any attempts at energy exploration that did not include the TCs could lead to war. The entire issue was the direct result of failing to address the substance of the Cyprus problem and thus diverting all political energy toward its symptoms, which as such can only generate further antinomies and irreconcilable interests.

In hindsight, a question naturally arises: What would the impact of the energy reserves have been on developments in and around Cyprus had the Cyprus problem been resolved in 2004? For those who dare pose this question, the answer is that the function of the energy reserves, in both the political and economic domain, would have been the exact opposite of what it became in 2007. In the context of a settlement, the oil and gas exploration would have been a significant factor in consolidating the final agreement, in forging interethnic peace, and in heightening motivation for interethnic cooperation. As one of the most formidable interethnic ventures, it would have united the economic interests of the GC and TC communities in a historically unprecedented manner., creating a shared anticipation for an ever-rising standard of living for all Cypriots and furnishing a high-profile success story of economic prosperity through interethnic peace. Moreover, it would have easily offered Greece and Turkey the opportunity to partner in the joint energy venture, thus creating a peace-enhancing energy consortium in the Eastern Mediterranean.

Within the framework of a Cyprus settlement, the energy issue would have become a significant catalyst for peace; outside a settlement, the same energy issue transformed into a catalyst for conflict, and dangerously so. Against the backdrop of the failed 2004 referendum, the 2007 incident over oil and gas reserves is likely to complicate any new attempts at a settlement, as the energy issue will inevitably require of any future peace plan an additional chapter on how the two ethnic communities will share the revenue, thus rendering negotiations more intricate and difficult.

THE NEW POLITICAL IMPASSE

It has already been noted that after the referenda, the GCs and TCs reversed roles in their approach to the Cyprus problem. This pattern persisted, conditioning interethnic interaction in many different ways and permeating all subsequent disputes between the two sides. Prior to 2004, GCs incessantly accused the Turkish side of intransigence, as Denktash was always reluctant to engage in negotiations that aimed at a comprehensive settlement. Meanwhile, TCs constantly accused the GC side of intransigence since GCs were not even willing to engage in small confidence-building measures through incremental, step-by-step agreements. The GC side objected to piecemeal approaches unless a comprehensive settlement was first on the agenda, while the TCs insisted that unless confidence was first built through piecemeal agreements, they would not address a comprehensive settlement.

After the referenda, however, the two sides essentially switched approaches. On the surface it appeared that the GCs simply continued to charge the Turkish side of intransigence, as they had always done. But the GC charge no longer focused on the Turkish side's refusal to negotiate a comprehensive settlement, as there were no grounds for it. Instead it focused on the Turkish side's reluctance to engage in piecemeal confidence-building agreements. In contrast, the Turkish side appeared to continue to accuse the GC side of intransigence, as it, too, had always done. Only now the accusation no longer concerned the GCs' unwillingness to engage in confidence-building measures but rather on their refusal to seek a comprehensive settlement.

This role reversal was the major obstacle behind the impasse and paralysis that followed the July 8, 2006, UN-initiated agreement between GCs and TCs to commence talks through the technical committees. Papadopoulos wanted an approach that would first show progress on partial issues before considering any reference to a comprehensive settlement. In essence, the strategy of Papadopoulos was to gradually pass through the confidence-building process not just technical matters that aimed at removing obstacles to the daily interactions between GCs and TCs (as was first intended by the UN) but also major substantive issues of the Cyprus problem. This approach underpinned all of Papadopoulos's efforts, such as his failed pursuits of the return of the city of Famagusta; his attempt at the opening of multiple crossings with the aim of getting the Turkish army to disengage and withdraw; his strategy of trying to absorb the TCs into the GC-controlled economy; his attempts at placing TC trade with the EU exclusively under the authority of the GC-controlled government of the republic, etc. (Even his unilateral effort to tap oil and gas resources reflected the same approach, as it intended to pressure the TCs to accept absorption into the republic as the absolute condition for securing a piece of the economic benefits.)

In the context of this overall approach, Papadopoulos's specific strategy of adding substantive issues to the task of the technical committees was met with TC indignation and objection, as it was perceived as yet another attempt to substitute a UN-based, high-level negotiation process for an overall settlement with a low-level intercommunal process that endeavoured to take on the substantive issues, one by one, without ever addressing the overall parameters of a final settlement. Not surprising, for almost a year following the agreement to commence talks through technical committees, nothing was accomplished, while the question as to what exactly the mandate of the committees was remained blurred and controversial.

The key idea in Papadopoulos's mind was that as long as technical as well as substantive issues were approached on a piecemeal basis, the GC government would somehow be able to deal with all the major aspects of the Cyprus problem without having to negotiate a federal, bizonal, bicommunal final settlement, as the UN resolutions required. In other words, his attempt was to address all the major issues of the Cyprus problem, piece by piece, and solve it without a fundamental restructuring of the constitutional polity of Cyprus. Reacting to this strategy, the Turkish side became increasingly reluctant and greatly cautious as to how far they would engage on any of these issues without having in place a serious, internationally backed negotiation process formally aimed at a comprehensive final settlement. This dynamic inflicted a great blow to the process of intercommunal rapprochement.

In contrast to Papadopoulos, Talat wanted the pursuit of a comprehensive settlement back on the table as the primary agenda for negotiations before major issues would be addressed. Papadopoulos's attempt to deal with substantive issues under the guise of confidence- building measures without having in place a UN-backed framework for negotiating a final settlement was thus strongly resisted by the TCs. Talat went as far as to suggest to the Papadopoulos government to forget the Annan Plan altogether and start negotiations for a comprehensive settlement from scratch (Christou 2006a). Even to such a proposal, Papadopoulos remained mute.

In the absence of any internationally based momentum for a final settlement, the Turkish side, while repeatedly asserting that secession was no longer on its agenda, maintained a definitive distance from the GC-controlled Republic of Cyprus, pursuing instead political upgrade and direct trade with the EU.

The pattern of the GC side had been to constantly try to offset the severe criticisms of the EU by exhibiting economic "benevolence" toward the TCs through endless proposals for the economic integration of northern and southern Cyprus, arguing that this was the European approach (Christou 2007a). However, in light of his incessant resistance to negotiating a comprehensive settlement, Papadopoulos's persistent push for the economic integration of north and south was far from European. While the EU strongly recommended and pursued the economic upgrade of the TC community, it never considered the economic integration of north and south under the exclusive umbrella of the Republic of Cyprus as a substitute for a negotiated final settlement, as the Papadopoulos's administration strategized. The European perspective was that the full economic integration of north and south could be achieved only through a negotiated, comprehensive political integration of both regions.

With no recourse to a final political settlement, the more Papadopoulos attempted to integrate the TCs into the republic, the more alienated and resistant the Turkish side became. And the more resistant the Turkish side became, the more paranoid the GC government became, as it equated the TC administration's quest for political upgrade and trade vis-à-vis the EU as a bid for recognition and thus a reversion to the politics of secession.

Moreover, the reservation of the Turkish side was also parallelled by the reservation of the UN since 2004 to engage the Cyprus problem at the high level. Despite statements by the GC government that it continued to be interested in a settlement, the UN repeatedly refrained from taking on the problem, explaining that under current conditions there was no ground for doing so. Even though the UN maintained equal distances from the disputants as a matter of protocol, in the minds of officials and diplomats it was clear that the major responsibility for the impasse rested on Papadopoulos's shoulders.

Behind Talat's resistance to piecemeal approaches lay Papadopoulos's refusal to engage with him in pursuing a comprehensive and final settlement. But as time went by, Talat was also confronted with rising criticism from TC and Turkish nationalists who started to attack him and the Turkish government because of a failed Cyprus policy due to their abandonment of ethnic secession. Conversely, in its attempt to manage GC opinion, the Papadopoulos government evaded and systematically downplayed the fact that since 2004, the Turkish side had made the pursuit of a comprehensive settlement for Cyprus its priority, above and beyond partial approaches. By so doing and simultaneously drawing attention to the Turkish side's resistance to engage in piecemeal approaches, the GC government persistently projected onto Talat images of intransigence, suggesting that he was just like Denktash. Stunningly, at this point in the evolution of the Cyprus problem, Papadopoulos's approach was in fact more similar to Denktash's than Talat's. Talat's preference for a comprehensive settlement was in fact closer to the pre-Papadopoulos GC approach than Denktash's. Denktash's perennial preference for confidence-building measures over negotiating a final settlement always aimed at achieving piecemeal agreements with the GC side that would leave the TRNC intact and legitimize it in perpetuity, thus evading the need to negotiate the reunification of Cyprus. Similarly, Papadopoulos resorted to piecemeal approaches to the Cyprus problem so as to leave the republic intact and sustain its legitimacy, but also render it *the permanent state entity over all of Cyprus,* thus bypassing the need for negotiating a comprehensive settlement.

NEGATIVE REVERSIBLES: THE MISSED OPPORTUNITY OF 2004

The convergence of factors favoring a comprehensive settlement, as they occurred in anticipation of the 2004 April referendum and of the subsequent integration of Cyprus into the EU, is extremely rare, historically speaking. If and when the noise of nationalist rationalizations subsides, April 2004 may appear, in hindsight, as the most tragic of missed opportunities for a final Cyprus settlement. As anticipated early on, the failed referendum had the capacity to push the two communities apart, thus rendering partition a renewed prospect (Loizides 2004).

The diplomatic inaction characterizing the years following the 2004 referendum fundamentally pacified the GC and TC communities, as both became psychologically overwhelmed with the emotional anticlimax of the referenda and the endless politicolegal entanglements arising thereafter. The mess resulting from the tensions between the GC government and other EU states over the handling of the Cyprus problem, the irreconcilable stresses in Cyprus-Turkish relations, and the difficulties that subsequently emerged in EU-Turkish relations, as well as the complications that ensued vis-à-vis the issues of TC trade, energy reserves, and property issues of refugees, established a new kind of alienation between the two Cypriot communities. Conditioned by all these postreferendum trends, the psychopolitical state of mind of the two communities calcified into a new and peculiar form of interethnic estrangement that prevented them from fully capitalizing on the unprecedented opportunities for rapprochement and peace building that free movement and EU membership offered them. The International Crisis Group's 2006 recommendation to maintain the spirit and momentum of interethnic rapprochement for the purpose of sustaining the enormous goodwill that was exhibited prior to the referendum debacle was unfortunately not heeded (International Crisis Group 2006).

By 2006–7 it became clear that the GCs had lost their motivation and become fundamentally passive about seeking a settlement. As time went by, fewer GCs remained genuinely focused on pursuing a comprehensive settlement, particularly as the energy of the GC community was increasingly absorbed by the new economic opportunities and challenges that EU membership introduced. The GCs refused to invest any hope and energy into a prospective Cyprus solution. With a dispirited and placated GC public, domestic GC politics reverted to the anachronistic but familiar political rhetoric and squabbles around the old nationalist polarization of "us" versus "them," sustaining the traditional images of the presumed moral rightness of one's own side in juxtaposition to the presumed immoral "enemy other"—a position that in the postreferendum era came to exist solely in the minds of GC nationalists and domestic opportunists but was nowhere to be found in the EU or the UN. During the years following the referendum, the GC leadership fundamentally shifted attention from the search for a solution to the politics of domestic consumption by reactivating the politics of psychosis and self-victimization and the exclusively legalistic approach to the Cyprus problem of the 1970s.

It is important to note that during the 2004 referendum, the hyped emotionalism and nationalist frenzy that the government-led rejectionist camp generated, and the high anxiety as well as confusion it brought about among GCs, resulted in mass psychological exhaustion that subjugated the GC community under a prolonged state of what may be called "solution fatigue." The GC government's incessant inaction to pursuing a comprehensive solution came to fit perfectly the solution-fatigued state of mind of the GC community—the very state that the Papadopoulos administration instated by its fear-mongering approach to the UN peace plan during the 2004 referendum.

Under a leadership presenting the 2004 UN peace plan as the utter "catastrophe of Cypriot Hellenism," the referendum experience left the GCs deeply, albeit unconsciously, traumatized, instilling within them a profound fear of proposed solutions as well as great uncertainty about their capacity to individually assess and judge the rightness of any solution (especially since the nationalists convinced the majority of GCs that the Annan Plan was a conspiratorial, bogus initiative by foreigners intending to cheat them). In the postreferendum era, the greatest fear of the GCs ceased to be the Turks or the Turkish army. Rather, their greatest fear became the prospect of having to make yet another historic decision on a final settlement of the Cyprus problem. The GCs' anxiety of having to encounter and decide on another settlement plan had in effect superseded their traditional anxiety about the Turks, the loss of northern Cyprus, and even partition. While peripheral domestic politics among the GC community thrived in intensity and interparty antagonisms, the solution of the Cyprus problem became captive to a general political lethargy. The antisolution coalition government of the Papadopoulos administration had essentially damaged the political will of the GC community. At least in the years that followed the referendum, it had psychologically and politically incapacitated the GCs from courageously seeking and facing anew the likelihood of a final settlement.

Given the prevalence of this state of mind among the GC community, the natural outcome, by default, was to avoid and refrain from reengaging the other side in pursuit of any settlement, Annan-like or not. Escaping and seeking comfort in the familiar status quo thus emerged as the sole alternative, since in the eyes of GCs, leaving things as they were now appeared less painful and dreadful than facing another proposed plan for a solution. However, opting for the status quo psychologically could only mean one thing politically: an increased tolerance, if not preference, for ethnic segregation. Interestingly, according to a December 2006 political circular by former GC foreign minister Rolandis, most GCs have psychologically arrived at the point of preferring independence and separation from the TCs to reunification and power sharing.

Unfortunately, this is where the Papadopoulos administration had led GC opinion with its rejectionist approach to the 2004 Annan Plan and its politics of evasion and inaction during the years that followed. By opting for legalistic and drawn-out piecemeal approaches to the Cyprus problem while refusing to genuinely pursue a comprehensive final settlement, the Papadopoulos administration reactivated an old paradox in the GC soul. It brought forward, yet again, that peculiar state of mind where what GCs assert they want politically, namely the reunification of the Island, comes to stand in direct contradiction to what they feel they want psychologically— namely, an ethnically homogeneous national life free of admixtures with the other ethnic community. This conflicted state of mind has historically emerged every time the GCs came under the influence of concentrated dosages of nationalism. The very same ethnocentrism that induces their potent claim for reunifying Cyprus under the presumption of being a Hellenic state simultaneously induces within them an aversion and a fear of ethnic remixing. Paradoxically, the latter triggers a tacit emotional preference for ethnic separation.

Following the failed referendum of 2004, the historical challenge for GCs had crystallized into facing the fundamental fact that they cannot have it both ways. If indeed they have reached a historic milestone of not wanting to reunite, cohabit, and hence share power with TCs in an interethnic federal Cyprus, GCs will do well to face it and admit it. In which case, the solution to the Cyprus problem would not be reunification, as they have been politically declaring since 1974, but rather partition, as they have been psychologically demonstrating, especially since 2004. The historical irony of these trends is that, as never before, they appear to both vindicate and elate Denktash, the father of ethnic secession, at the very time in the history of Cyprus when Denktash has been removed from power altogether. However, if GCs truly want reunification, they must reexamine their feelings and their politics toward the TCs while prioritizing the pursuit of a comprehensive settlement. Indeed, the GC long-declared desire to reunify the Island will remain void unless it is accompanied by the will for interethnic cohabitation, reconciliation, normalization, and especially power sharing.

The greatest shock in regressive trends, however, came in January 2007, when a survey in northern Cyprus revealed that, in contrast to 65 percent in 2004, only 20 percent of TCs now support a federal solution akin to that proposed in the Annan Plan. Stunningly, this is even lower than the percentage among GCs who supported the 2004 plan. Muharrem Faiz, the head of the KADEM research group that conducted the survey, attributed the trend to the disappointment of the TCs over the GCs' rejection of the Annan Plan, but also to the fact that in the aftermath, the left-wing TC parties (formerly been avid supporters of reunification as well as Denktash's severest critics) have shifted to increasingly nationalist rhetoric. Simultaneously, the TC media had been portraying the GCs in the worst light. Faiz explained that "In the past, parties on the left clearly differentiated between the Greek Cypriot administration and the people. Now, that distinction is not being made" (Bahceli 2007a). He further noted that TCs perceived GC obstruction of Turkey's EU accession process as a slur on Turkish people in general. The KADEM survey finally revealed that overall TC willingness to live next door to, work with, or marry GCs has been significantly on the decline.

The alienation between the GC and TC communities was also reflected in the retardation of even the simplest forms of interethnic economic activities. By the end of 2007, the resistance to TC-GC economic transactions reached new levels of expression, when both TC and GC media were reporting incidents of TC police harassing and intimidating TCs at the checkpoints when returning from shopping excursions to the GC south. Critical voices among TCs were arguing that any obstructive tactics by

Talat's government were a violation of the EU's Green Line Regulation. The Turkish Cypriot Chamber of Commerce responded by declaring that "within the framework of the Green Line Regulation, TRNC-originated goods/products (not including live animal and animal products) can be exported to the South Cyprus with Certificate of Origin given by the Chamber" (Turkish Cypriot Chamber of Commerce 2007). What became evident was that while the TC side remained within the formal framework of the Green Line Regulation, the motivation to trade with the south had all but disappeared (Pope 2008).

All these regressive trends have been evolving while the TCs became increasingly uncertain as to whether they should support any future solution like they did in 2004, and while GCs became increasingly uncertain as to whether they did the right thing in voting against the 2004 peace plan. To the degree that these negative tendencies are not decisively halted, the two sides run the risk of historically missing each other yet again.

Since the referendum, TCs have been both angry and confused with GCs. But most of all they have been fiercely frustrated with them, as they cannot understand what it is that the GCs really want by way of an acceptable settlement. TC frustration cannot be defused until the GCs confront realistically and practically what it is they want. But to do this GCs must go beyond the false and evasive comfort of thirty-three-year-old blanket slogans such as "the withdrawal of all Turkish troops from Cyprus" and "the return of all refugees to their ancestral home" and start attending the practical parameters of a likely settlement. After all, according to all UN resolutions, these perennial and rightful GC demands on refugees and troop withdrawal are to be fulfilled as *a result* of a negotiated settlement and not as a *condition* for it. Simultaneously, the new historical challenge for the TC and Turkey is to recapture and sustain their 2003–4 conciliatory and rapprochement spirit, as this is the greatest catalyst for empowering the GCs to face up to the fact that it is now their turn to make the decisive break from past fears and from ethnocentric nationalism. But TCs will be able to pose this constructive challenge only to the degree that they resist the temptation to recoil into their own familiar, defensive, secessionist nationalism.

POSITIVE IRREVERSIBLES: NEW OPPORTUNITIES AND CHALLENGES

Despite the regressive political trends that precipitated in Cyprus as a result of the April 2004 referendum, it is vital not to lose sight of the fact that numerous peace-enhancing factors, however incomplete and ambiguous, have become an integral part of Cypriot reality in the postreferendum/European-integration era. In the context of the EU, the relevance and significance of the many multilevel rapprochement initiatives that have emerged in the recent history of Cyprus, Greece, and Turkey were neither cancelled nor diminished in value and legitimacy. While in perpetual competition with the continuing presence of adversarial nationalist politics, the possibility for conciliatory, peace-enhancing initiatives in Cyprus, though heavily burdened, weakened, and at times stalled, remained tangibly within reach, reflecting its affinity with EU political culture. Postreferendum/European Cyprus, despite the unresolved political problem, manifested the EU-empowered potential for transformational peace-promoting change, which stood to help continue the effort to transcend ethnocentric nationalist politics as an imperative for resolving the Cyprus problem. In view of such a prospect, some of the positive elements that became irreversible and permanent because of the integration of the Cyprus republic into the EU ought to be explicitly noted.

Following the referendum, by deciding not to view the ethnically dividing "green line" in Cyprus as its outer border, the EU had in fact consolidated the mixing of the Cypriot ethnic communities, even in the absence of a final political settlement, as an integral part of freedom of movement and contact among all EU citizens. The prospect for future interethnic citizen rapprochement had thus become empowered and legitimized. Since the entry of Cyprus into the union, citizen contact and joint bicommunal projects became formally and politically expected, generously funded, and strongly encouraged by the EU. This marked a strengthening of civil society as a vital factor in society-wide peace building, which stood to grow as European integration deepened.

Henceforth, the challenge was whether GCs and TCs would act on these new opportunities. While numerous bicommunal events continued to take place, including regular meetings between GC and TC political parties, GCs and TCs have failed to fully seize the new opportunities for rapprochement in the years following the referenda (Hadjipavlou-Trigeorgis 2007). However, the path for bicommunal contact and cooperation had been opened widely and irreversibly. The objective obstacles of complete physical separation that formerly prevented GCs and TCs from meeting together had evaporated. The problem that remained was one of subjective psychological and political attitudes. Nevertheless, bicommunal rapprochement will remain imperative for the future of Cyprus, no matter what the end settlement looks like. Yet contrary to this fact, the respective administrations have not been forthcoming in supporting and promoting broad-based intercommunal rapprochement, especially the GC side.

Nevertheless, to their credit, the GC and TC administrations were able to generate the political will to make unprecedented progress in one specific area: jointly addressing the most vexing humanitarian issue of the Cyprus problem, that of missing persons. Within the EU context, and in the face of persistent calls by the Committee of Ministers of the Council of Europe, the long-overdue issue of missing persons on both sides of the ethnic divide underwent significant and irreversible changes. The process was also greatly assisted by the joint efforts of two investigative journalists, TC Sevgül Uludağ and GC Andreas Paraschos, who arduously and sensitively managed to gather information leading to the unmarked graves of many missing persons, both GCs and TCs (Uludağ 2006). The belligerent nationalist practices of the past—of withholding information and of politically exploiting human losses by keeping the wounds of the conflict perpetually open—could no longer withstand the increased weight of human rights' requirements regarding this exceedingly sensitive issue. Unavoidably, the leadership of the TC and GC communities, through the Committee of Missing Persons, proceeded with the sharing of information, the designation of unmarked graves (including mass graves), and the exhumation, identification, and return of human remains. Under sobering conditions, the year 2007 saw the two Cypriot communities engaged in an endless array of painful and highly emotional funerals during which many remains of missing TCs and GCs were finally put to rest (*Cyprus Mail* 2007c).

While the issue of the missing persons was a grim reminder of the evils of the past, the identification and burials of their remains marked the commencement of a process of closure of one of the most devastating aspects of the Cyprus problem. More importantly, as the management of this humanitarian issue occurred in full transparency in the public domain, with the respective mass media openly reporting on the matter, the two communities became consciously aware of a crucial historical fact that the nationalism of each side had denied for decades: namely, that both sides had their victims and culprits and that both sides had suffered the pain and agony of the conflict. Paradoxically, the pain that surfaced with the exhumation of the bodies of the missing—which simultaneously amounted to the exhumation of history—also initiated a solemn healing process, as the two communities encountered the harsh acknowledgment that the past had been clearly tainted with mutual tragedies that need not be part of the future of Cyprus. Though highly nuanced and silent, this realization signified, at a very basic level of GC and TC humanity, a positive irreversible reality in post-EU-integration Cyprus.

Positive and hitherto irreversible phenomena also emerged in the form of unprecedented challenges that henceforth faced both the GC and TC sides at the highest level of politics. Though not enacted into policy, the recommendation to the international community by the UN secretary-general to end the political and economic isolation of northern Cyprus implied a political demotion of the GC government insofar as it resisted an interethnic federal settlement in preference to preserving the GC-controlled Republic of Cyprus. This demoted political status of the Papadopoulos government ought to be distinguished from the legal status of the Republic of Cyprus. While continuing to recognize the Republic of Cyprus as the legitimate state of Cyprus, the international community did not view it as the polity of the solution. This perspective brought to focus, yet again, that the Cyprus problem was not exclusively a legal one, as GC nationalists had assumed for decades, but rather a complex mixture of legal and political issues. To the extent that the Papadopoulos government continued to employ the recognized status of the Republic of Cyprus as a belligerent, legal instrument, it was bound to come in increasing political and diplomatic conflict with the EU and the UN. It did not follow, as Papadopoulos had assumed, that the legal status of the Republic of Cyprus would automatically confer international political credibility to the GC government, especially when the latter pursued unilateral ethnocentric approaches.

Within the EU framework, the TRNC had been radically delegitimized, with the prospect of recognition more remote than ever before. The decisive rejection of any formal role for the TRNC in European institutions and politics reflected the UN position that, while it called upon the international community to end the political and economic isolation of the TCs, it objected to any action that would imply state recognition of northern Cyprus. Thus, the TCs and Turkey were compelled to face an unprecedented and crucial historical fact: Recognition of the TRNC was rejected outright, even after the Turkish side was internationally hailed for its decision to support the resolution of the Cyprus problem in alignment with the UN plan. In light of this, the old nationalist politics of secession had been decisively disclosed as untenable and historically bankrupt.

Immediately following the Cyprus referendum, Turkish prime minister Erdogan acknowledged this by publicly noting that it is politically futile to reject the international recognition of the Republic of Cyprus as a way of endorsing the TRNC (*Turkish Daily News* 2004g). In the absence of a final political settlement, although lip service to the TRNC continued due to historical habit, it fundamentally lacked any grounding in reality. This historical dead end, which faced the TC nationalists, was the correlate of what the GC nationalists faced as they attempted to usurp the EU legal status of the Republic of Cyprus in order to pursue a reclaiming of Cyprus as a presumed monoethnic, Hellenic state. Within the EU this too was proving an irreversibly unrealistic agenda, lacking any substantive reality or future.

Although Cyprus entered the EU with the political problem unresolved, and although the TCs secured no formal statehood status, the union's decision not to view the ethnic divide along the green line as its outer border resulted in incorporating the TC community into an internationally credible and recognized legal framework extending beyond the confines of the Republic of Cyprus. The TC community thus acquired a peculiar, yet irreversible, form of European status at the level of civil society.

This was unprecedented, as the TCs had operated for decades outside any internationally recognized legal structure with legitimacy and mechanisms of enforcement that encompassed equally the TC and the GC civil society. Unlike during the era preceding European integration, the TCs acknowledged that the more they complied and operated within the EU framework and aligned themselves with the UN, the more they would be empowered to offset any attempt by the GC nationalists to impose on the TCs the legal status of the Republic of Cyprus as the presumed solution to the Cyprus problem.

This fact disclosed two irreversible realities: first, EU responsibilities and benefits were no longer the exclusive privilege of the GCs; and second, the nature of the Cyprus problem could not be confined to its political dimensions, as the TCs were traditionally inclined to treat it; it also entailed an array of serious legal dimensions intertwined with the political.

It must also be noted that since the referendum, a number of TCs, having acknowledged the premium the EU places on the rule of law, have resorted to the courts in order to have their property in southern Cyprus reinstated. With the TC community's new access to European law, the victory of TC Arif Mustafa at the Supreme Court of the Republic of Cyprus constituted a landmark of the new legal possibilities for the TCs. In the midst of a war of words within the GC community, the filing of an appeal by the GC attorney general against the Supreme Court's decision prompted Mustafa to express his willingness to take the issue to the European Court of Human Rights if the decision to have his property reinstated was reversed. For some GCs, such a prospect marked the beginning of what could become the TC counterpart of Titina Loizidou, the GC who won a case against Turkey at the ECHR for obstructing access to her property (*Cyprus Mail* 2004a).

The concern of these GCs was absolutely correct. By January 2007, four TC siblings—Hasan Huseyin Cakartas, Nejla Cagis, Mumin Cakartas, and Gokcen Bayer—who owned much property in Limassol, located in the GC south, applied to the ECHR demanding from the GC government compensation and restitution of their properties. The lawsuit demanded at least € 7 million if the court qualified the case as "acceptable." In the petition to the ECHR, the lawyer of the TC plaintiffs referred to the precedent of the case of GC Titina Loizidou (*Turkish Press* 2007). Interestingly, as was the case with GC refugees, TC refugees started to line up in the hundreds, ready to follow suit.

TC access to new legal instruments also led to action in other domains. In July 2006, seventy-eight TCs living in the north appealed to the Supreme Court of the republic demanding the right to vote for their own Turkish Cypriot deputies in parliament as provided by the 1960 constitution, which the GC government claims to be upholding and defending. Presumably, if the TC plaintiffs are not satisfied with the final ruling of the Cypriot Supreme Court (which was delayed because of the GC government's failure to translate court documents into Turkish), such a case could easily end up in European courts as well.

However, as long as the Cyprus problem remained unresolved, recourse to the law by either side ran the risk of placing a wedge in interethnic relations.

As the cornerstone of the EU system, strict adherence to the rule of law became an irreversible reality that also extended to Turkey. Particularly since the EU summit of December 2004, and more so following the October 2005 EU decision to open accession talks, Turkey could not treat the Cyprus problem as simply political. The Turkish government also had to address an array of legal dimensions pertaining to both European and international law. The requirement for Turkey to extend its customs union agreement with the EU to include Cyprus was a case in point, even while the EU did not view these types of legal alignments as a substitute for a negotiated Cyprus settlement.

In this context, Turkey continued to be burdened with the legal implications of its continued military presence in northern Cyprus. However, this burden was lightened by Turkey's forthcoming stance on the UN peace plan and by the prevalent EU conviction that Papadopoulos failed to demonstrate the political will to solve the Cyprus problem. To a great measure, while still confronted with the *legal* responsibilities concerning Cyprus, Turkey had been absolved from the weighty *political* responsibilities in the search for a Cyprus settlement, which had formerly tarnished its political credibility.

With the Republic of Cyprus a full member of the EU, the prospect that Turkey would pose a threat to GC community became irreversibly remote and diminished. The decision of the UN to reduce UNFICYP personnel by one-third was indicative of the changed security situation. This postreferendum fact stands in contradiction to the exaggerated security-risk arguments put forward by the Papadopoulos administration for rejecting the Annan Plan. Similarly, questions can be raised as to whether the troop levels maintained by Turkey in northern Cyprus are necessary following the integration of the republic into the EU, since the pre-1974 GC and Greek threat to the security of the TC community had also become irreversibly nullified.

As noted above, the traditional Turkish approach that the Cyprus problem is mainly political in nature had become increasingly untenable. But the traditional GC approach to the Cyprus problem being primarily legal had also become untenable, if not counterproductive. Without taking cognizance of the fact that the problem also entailed a substantive complex of political dimensions, the GC government stood to stall any progress toward a settlement. After Cyprus joined the EU, the GC government became increasingly challenged with the stark reality that its struggle to resolve the Cyprus problem on merely legal grounds could not eradicate the historical imperative for a negotiated, comprehensive political settlement establishing a new Cyprus polity. This was yet another irreversible trend confronting the GC side in the postreferendum/European-integration era.

Against the backdrop of multilevel rapprochement initiatives since 1999, the relationship between Greece and Turkey within the EU framework has also assumed a new and irreversible dimension. Up until the referendum, and the integration of Cyprus into the EU, the full potential of Greek-Turkish relations was strongly dependent on the progress toward a resolution of the Cyprus problem. Thereafter, however, Greece and Turkey started to tacitly view their bilateral relations as considerably dissociated from their formerly belligerent relationship vis-à-vis Cyprus, which limited and blocked the full development of Greek-Turkish relations. The gradual but steady build-up of conciliatory relationships and the establishment of mutual economic interests in the region brought the neighboring countries to the point where neither would risk falling out with the other over Cyprus. This orientation was reinforced following the October 2005 EU summit, which anchored Turkey's future even more firmly to the EU. It has become historically clear that it was in the mutual benefit of Greece and Turkey to continue emulating the EU model by building, expanding, and institutionalizing conciliatory relationships.

Already, there were many signs that Greece and Turkey were willing to move forward with rapprochement despite the Cyprus problem. Some of the highlights were Greece's refusal to follow Papadopoulos in reviving the joint Nikiforos-Toxotis military exercises in October 2005; the ongoing tensions between Greece and Cyprus over Papadopoulos's approach to Turkey's accession that frequently surfaced despite attempts to conceal them from the public eye; and the decision of Greece to stay out of the oil and gas controversy that erupted between Cyprus and Turkey, which Greece clearly communicated to Papadopoulos. In the midst of denials, the reports in the Greek and GC media that Greece was tacitly exploring the possibility of convincing AKEL not to support Papadopoulos in the next presidential elections were not completely unfounded (Christou 2006b). Behind its public face, Greece not only felt disempowered and entrapped by the unresolved Cyprus problem but saw Papadopoulos's nationalism as potentially damaging to its now-European-based foreign policy, which was increasingly redefining its national interest in terms of peace and stability in the Eastern Mediterranean.

Indicative of how Greece and Turkey were moving to a new phase of bilateral relations was the effective manner in which they cooperatively contained the political impact of a midair collision of Greek and Turkish F-16 fighter jets in the context of the unresolved issue of air corridors in the southern Aegean (Grohmann 2006). An incident that in earlier years could have escalated into a dangerous crisis was successfully defused by quick practical actions and direct bilateral communication. Mutually recognizing the dangers of belligerent past approaches, the two sides ended the episode by jointly declaring that, while regrettable, the incident will not deter the two countries from continuing to improve their relations.

Since 2004, Greek-Turkish trade and investment has continued to increase. In May 2006, the National Bank of Greece, the biggest financial institution in the region, purchased 46 percent of Istanbul-based Finansbank's common shares as well as 100 percent of its preferred shares from the Fiba Holding Group for $2.774 billion. Halkbank, the largest branch network in Turkey, signed a contract worth € 2.5 million for the purchase of office chairs from The Chair Company, a subsidiary of Greek-listed Sato Group in Turkey. In the first two months of 2006, Greek exports to the EU rose 10.4 percent, while exports to Turkey increased by 4 percent compared to the same period a year earlier, ranking Turkey as Greece's fourth trade partner (Greek Embassy 2006). All of these bilateral economic activities, including the opening of Turkish businesses in new shopping centers in Athens, are a testimony to the continuing efforts by the neighboring countries to foster a transformation of their past conflict-habituated relations (Fisher 2007). Moreover, in continuation of this trend, Greece and Turkey announced the founding of a Greek-Turkish business council in 2007 (*Hellenic Journal* 2007).

Greek-Turkish rapprochement reached new heights in November 2007, when the Greek prime minister Costas Karamalis and his Turkish counterpart Recep Tayyip Erdogan inaugurated the opening of the natural gas pipeline, a cooperative project that was agreed in 2004. The pipeline was designed to carry Azerbaijani natural gas from the Shah Sea to European markets, constituting an integral part of the EU's policy of diversifying and decentralizing its energy sources. Appearing in front of a giant banner depicting a handshake sleeved with the Greek and Turkish flags, the prime ministers of Turkey and Greece underscored the significance of the project for all concerned. The event, which was celebrated on the northern Greek-Turkish border, was seen as yet another major step in transforming Greek-Turkish relations in the interest of peace, cooperation, and shared national interests (Carassava 2007; *Hellenic Journal* 2007; *The New Anatolian* 2007).

Strengthened by the successful completion of the pipeline project, Greece and Turkey proceeded further in their rapprochement initiatives by announcing a new agreement on a package of confidence-building measures on military cooperation. The agreement entailed expanding high-level exchange visits at the Greek-Turkish border, conducting joint missions in NATO and overseas peacekeeping, as well as establishing a joint all-branch military unit to manage natural disaster relief and humanitarian assistance.

The rapprochement process reached a symbolic zenith in January 2007, when Greek prime minister Karamalis travelled to Turkey for an official high-level visit. The historic significance of the event is underscored by the fact that the last Greek premier to visit Turkey was in 1959.

Following talks with Turkish prime minister Erdogan, Karamanlis called for the "full normalization of Greek-Turkish relations," stressing that this was "the only road toward essential progress that will allow us to exploit future opportunities within a European framework" (Altan 2008). In their joint public appearances and press conferences, the two leaders, while exuding an air of hope and optimism, did not shy away from acknowledging the existence of problems that await resolution. Karamanlis pressed Turkish authorities to improve the rights for Greeks living in Turkey, primarily by reopening the Halki Orthodox Seminary off the coast of Istanbul. Erdogan, with whom Karamanlis developed a close personal relationship, noted that Turkey was working on a solution for reopening the seminary but also stressed that Athens must do more to protect the Turkish minority living in northern Greece, noting that improving the situation of minorities in both countries "would boost the bridge of friendship between our countries." The Greek premier urged Turkey to normalize its relationship to Cyprus as required of an EU candidate-member, while the Turkish premier focused on the need for fresh negotiations on Cyprus, as expected by the UN and EU, while calling for "a period of cooperation and solidarity in the Aegean" (Altan 2008).

The visit of the Greek premier to Turkey was more symbolic than substantive. Its significance, however, lay in the fact that it focused public opinion on the ongoing process of Greek-Turkish rapprochement, on the now public and official commitment of the neighboring countries to jointly work toward peaceful and mutually beneficial solutions to their remaining bilateral problems.

The event also reminded Greeks and Turks of past periods of Greek-Turkish peace and rapprochement—periods that Greek and Turkish nationalists have tended to suppress for decades. This came to the forefront when Karamalis, after laying a wreath at Atatürk's tomb, wrote the following in the visitors' book: "Kemal Atatürk and (then Greek leader) Eleftherios Venizelos had the political courage, will and vision not to allow the conflicts and tragedies of the past to become an obstacle to . . . building a better future of peace and co-operation to the benefit of the two peoples" (*Cyprus Mail* 2008). This was a reminder of the hitherto evaded fact that after the wars between Greeks and Turks that coincided with the collapse of the Ottoman Empire and the founding of the Republic of Turkey in the early 1920s, Atatürk and Venizelos successfully restored cordial bilateral relations.

The timing of the visit was particularly significant for Cyprus, since it took place less than a month before the GC presidential elections of February 17, 2008. Erdogan noted this significance when he stated that "the process after the [GC] elections is very important" and appealed for "an effort from Mr. Karamanlis to restart the [Cyprus] negotiations" (*Cyprus Mail* 2008). It was perhaps the first time that the leaders of Greece and Turkey, rather than unqualifiedly aligning themselves in polarizing mode with their ethnic counterpart in Cyprus, jointly declared the need for a final settlement of the Cyprus problem, along with all other remaining bilateral issues.

In the context of this rapprochement process, the path forward for postreferendum Cyprus may come to hinge on whether Greek-Turkish relations will become strong enough to enable the two countries, as guarantors of Cyprus's integrity and independence, to jointly mediate and assist GCs and TCs in negotiating a solution to the Cyprus problem—akin to how Ireland and the UK cooperated in addressing the conflict in Northern Ireland (Byrne 2007).

Prior to the referendum and European membership of Cyprus, the Cyprus problem led the way in its conditioning of Greek-Turkish relations. However, with the European integration of the Island, it seemed likely that the Cyprus problem would be dragged along, behind the improving Greek-Turkish relations. Attesting to this was the Greek government's full alignment with the EU in maintaining and supporting Turkey's European orientation, even in the face of specific objections by the Papadopoulos government. Greece's support of Turkey thus began to surpass the Cyprus problem, despite the political rhetoric to the contrary.

A ray of hope may have loomed over the horizon when in April 2007 a UN opinion survey indicated that while only a third of the TCs and GCs rejected a federal settlement, the majority on both sides of the ethnic divide considered it a tolerable compromise (United Nations Forces in Cyprus 2007). Clearly, under such conditions, the prospect for a settlement rested decisively on courageous and creative leadership on the part of the stakeholders in the Cyprus problem.

Conclusion

By failing to arrive at a final settlement in 2004, Cyprus became the first EU member-state to usher into the union an ethnically divided society. This has presented the EU with an unprecedented anomaly within its own political and legal edifice that stands in sharp contrast to its very principles and foundation. By 2007, many EU countries—even skeptics such as France, which had concerns about Turkey's full membership—have concluded that it was a mistake to accept a divided Cyprus into the union (International Crisis Group 2007). With the complete absence of any substantive diplomatic initiatives since the failure of the Cyprus referendum, and with more urgent challenges within the EU as well as in the broader international arena overshadowing Cyprus, it was possible for the Cyprus problem to enter into a long-drawn period of inertia and stagnation with regressive effects on interethnic relations.

Any scrutiny of the developments on Cyprus between the 2004 referenda and 2007 reveals that the effort to negotiate a final and comprehensive settlement had been forfeited by ongoing political squabbling and legalistic battles over issues that are peripheral or symptomatic of the unresolved Cyprus problem. This was evident in the stresses and strains that emerged between the Papadopoulos government and other EU members over his reluctance to engage the political dimension of the issue based on the UN directives. It was also evident in the complications and entanglements between Turkey and the EU over the unresolved legal dimensions still pertaining to its relationship to Cyprus and the Cyprus problem. While the legal aspects of the Cyprus problem continued to haunt Turkey's EU accession process, its political aspects weighed heavier on the Papadopoulos administration. The complexities, antinomies, and contradictions that emerged in practically every commission report and EU summit from April 2004 till the end of 2007 brought into focus two key facts: First, that there can be no alignment of the legal and political aspects of the Cyprus problem without a comprehensive settlement; second, that in the absence of a comprehensive settlement, the politicolegal contradictions and ambiguities in the relationships between the EU and Turkey, GCs and TCs, and Cyprus and Turkey are likely to persist indefinitely.

As difficult as it may be for the Greek side to face, even as Turkey continues the illegal occupation of northern Cyprus, the Papadopoulos administration has burdened the GC government with an ongoing credibility problem—one that may persist beyond his presidency. This was evident in the fact that since the referenda, the international community and the UN have assumed a position of both disinterest in Cyprus and of strong reluctance to take Papadopoulos seriously when claiming after his rejection of the UN plan that he was still interested in resolving the Cyprus problem. GC opinion did not quite fathom that the wholesale rejection of the Annan Plan, led by Papadopoulos, amounted to the most spectacular rejection of the UN resolutions and directives in the problem's history.

Under the circumstances, bringing the Cyprus problem back on the path of a possible resolution hinged on whether the two sides, but especially the GC government, could genuinely convince the international community of their readiness to reengage in negotiations on the basis of the UN framework for an interethnic democracy. Only then would the UN, the EU, and the international community be moved to put Cyprus back on their agenda and proceed to reassemble the diplomatic infrastructure necessary to tackle the problem effectively.

On February 17, 2008, the GCs held their presidential elections with incumbent president Tassos Papadopoulos, AKEL's leader Dimitris Christofias, and DISY-backed EU parliamentarian Ioannis Kasoulides as the main contenders. As always, the Cyprus problem and the appropriate leader for achieving its resolution was central to the public debates. Not surprisingly, questions as to what exactly happened in the run-up to the 2004 referendum abounded: who did what and why; whether the GC side had handled the negotiations prudently; whether the GC leadership had acted responsibly in agreeing to hold the 2004 referendum since it planned to reject the Annan Plan; whether the GC government had acted with transparency. Even Christofias openly accused Papadopoulos of clandestine decisions during the 2004 negotiations, of alienating the TC side, and of deviating from the long-held UN-based agreements for a bizonal, bicommunal federation. It was as though Christofias had been struck by amnesia, forgetting that Papadopoulos became president through his party's support and that it was with his party's full participation in Papadopoulos's government that Papadopoulos was empowered to act as he did. On the other hand, running as an independent, former foreign minister Kasoulides, who over the years had adopted a more European outlook, and whose party, contrary to its far-right nationalist past, supported the Annan Plan, questioned the credibility of both Christofias and Papadopoulos.

In the first round of the presidential elections, Kasoulides emerged as the front runner with 33.51 percent of the votes, followed by Christofias with 33.29 percent. Contrary to the polls, Papadopoulos was knocked out of the race as he ranked third with 31.79 percent of the vote. In the runoff of February 24, Dimitris Christofias was declared the new president of the GC-run Republic of Cyprus with 53.37 percent of the vote, prevailing over Kasoulides, who received 46.63 percent.

It was perhaps a striking coincidence that on February 17, 2008, the very day the GC elections commenced, Kosovo, with the backing of numerous EU countries, was declaring independence from Serbia. Given the historical dynamism of the postmodern era, Kosovo's independence came as a stark reminder that unresolved interethnic conflicts cannot be left open indefinitely without eventually affecting the legal status of the states and the communities involved. This fact, together with Turkey's intent since 2004 to remove the Cyprus problem from its European path, may create a new convergence of interests and a mutual incentive toward peace.

However, the reality confronting the new GC president was all that precipitated with the failed 2004 referendum: domestic and international diplomatic stalemate; interethnic alienation; and mounting politicolegal entanglements vis-à-vis EU-Cyprus-Turkish relations. President Christofias was now confronted with a historical paradox, namely of fundamentally undoing the outcomes of the Papadopoulos presidency that he and his party had helped bring about and sustain since 2003. At this point in time, the great challenge for the new president is to free GC policy and public opinion from the legacy of the Papadopoulos administration and supersede the erroneous notion that the Cyprus problem can be resolved merely as a legal issue in the EU framework and outside the UN process. His task is to immediately demonstrate a return to the premise that the Cyprus problem also entails a fundamental political dimension that can be addressed only through UN-based negotiations for a final settlement. From this perspective, he must convincingly declare readiness to constructively engage in top-level negotiations on the basis of a bizonal, bicommunal federation, as agreed by GCs and TCs since the 1970s and as established for more than three decades by the UN Cyprus resolutions.

To empower such a process, the TCs and Turkey must revive at least part of the momentum of 2002–4 to meet the new GC president halfway, sustaining their abandonment of secession and exhibiting their readiness to reengage the GC side in a last but decisive effort to reunite Cyprus as a biethnic federation. Simultaneously, the UN, and especially the EU, ought to assume a more proactive role, reinvigorating their leadership and mediation efforts in pursuit of a Cyprus settlement. This is imperative, as it is doubtful whether the Cyprus disputants will be able of themselves to initiate a substantive peace process.

With the new GC president in office, the two sides would need to move beyond the July 8th process and jointly invite the UN to restart high-level negotiations. If, with the backing of the UN and the EU, the parties concerned generate the political will to resume negotiations, a new process of hope-inducing rapprochement may commence. It would be the last chance of the parties concerned to act on the historic realization that only through the prospect of a negotiated comprehensive settlement of the Cyprus problem can the array of complex politicolegal issues that burden interethnic Cypriot relations, Greek-Turkish relations, and EU-Cyprus-Turkish relations become convergent in a sustainable manner (Pope 2008). If the parties concerned fail again, it is very likely that Cyprus will go the way of Kosovo.

In 2004, nationalists on both the GC and TC sides had hoped that the entry of a divided Cyprus into the union would undermine the UN by permanently placing the Cyprus problem outside the UN's framework and proposals. Following the GC elections of February 2008, the EU and the UN were presented with a new opportunity to vigorously assist the parties achieve a final settlement. Under the new circumstance, the European integration of Cyprus, once again, stood to reinforce the UN proposals on Cyprus. As always, the EU remained oriented to and firmly aligned with the UN's directives. More than it did prior to Cyprus's European membership, the EU must now undertake the challenge to fully engage as a proactive intermediary, linking the Cyprus problem to the UN's directives for a final settlement. The union's own conciliatory legal and political instruments and institutions constitute an unprecedented, regional, intermediary system of democracy with the potential to both assist and reinforce the credibility and effectiveness of the UN—the sole international institution assigned to serving the interest of global peace and stability in an era of new and changing global challenges.

WORKS CITED
INDEX

Works Cited

ABC. 2002. "EU Hails Turkey's Democracy Reforms but Monitoring Impact." August 4.
Aletheia. 2004. Untitled. Nicosia, May 16.
Altan, Adem. 2008. "MP Upbeat in Landmark Turkey Visit." *Kathimerini,* January 24. http://www.ekathimerini.com/4dcgi/_w_articles_politics_100007_24/01/2008_92512 (accessed January 26, 2008).
Alter, Peter. 1994. *Nationalism.* London: Edward Arnold, Hodder Headline Group.
Anastasiou, Harry. 1996a. "Conflict 0." *The Cyprus Review* 8, no. 2:79–96.
———. 1996b. "Peace Builders at the Crossroads." In *The Multi-Cultural Carpet: Reflections on Bi-communal Work in Cyprus,* 1–4. Nicosia: American Center.
Anastasiou, Harry, and Birol Yesilada. 2003. "The Annan Plan: A Historic Challenge for the Cypriots." TUSIAD–US Web site. www.tusiad-us.org, March 11.
Anastasiou, Nicos. 2003a. "Two Mothers." Bicommunal internet circular, April 28.
———. 2003b. "Why Am I Not Going." Bicommunal internet circular, May 14.
Apogevmatini. 1994. Article. June 21. http://www.apogevmatini.gr/.
Bahceli, Simon. 2007a. "Most Turkish Cypriots Want Two States." *Cyprus Mail,* January 30. http://www.cyprus-mail.com/news/ (accessed February 3, 2007).
———. 2007b. "Things Are Not Improving." *Cyprus Mail,* July 5. http://www.cyprus-mail.com/news/ (accessed July 10, 2007).
———. 2007c. "Turkish Cypriots Hail Symbolic Gesture." *Cyprus Mail,* March 9. http://www.cyprus-mail.com/news/ (accessed March 12, 2007).
Barash, David P., and Charles P. Webel. 2002. *Peace and Conflict Studies.* London: Sage Publications.
BBC News. 2004. October 14. http://news.bbc.co.uk (accessed October 20, 2004).

———. 2006a. "Turkey Urges Fresh Cyprus Talks." January 24. http://news.bbc.co.uk (accessed January 26, 2006).

———. 2006b. "Turkish Cypriots Move to End Row." December 29. http://news.bbc.co.uk/2/hi/europe/6216355.stm (accessed January 4, 2007).

Bildt, Carl. 2006. "Open Wide Europe's Doors." *International Herald Tribune*, November 7. http://www.iht.com/articles/2006/11/07/opinion/edbildt.php (accessed November 28, 2006).

Birand, Mehmet Ali. 2003. "Denktash Wins Again." *Turkish Daily News*, March 12. http://www.turkishdailynews.com.tr (accessed March 14, 2003).

Bohm, David. 2000. *On Dialogue*. New York: Routledge.

Borowiec, Andrew. 2007. "Turkey Defiant over Oil Deposits." *The Washington Times*, February 3. http://www.washtimes.com/ (accessed February 19, 2007).

Broome, Benjamin J. 1998a. "Designing Citizen-Based Peace-Building Efforts in Cyprus: Interactive Management Workshops with Greek Cypriots and Turkish Cypriots." In *Analysis for Peace Operations*, ed. Alexander Woodcock and David Davis, 33–58. Lester B. Pearson Canadian International Peacekeeping Training Centre, Cornwallis Park, Nova Scotia: Canadian Peacekeeping Press.

———. 1998b. "Overview of Conflict Resolution Activities in Cyprus: Their Contribution to the Peace Process." *The Cyprus Review* 10, no. 1:47–66.

———. 1998c. "Views from the Other Side: Perspectives on the Cyprus Conflict." In *Readings in Cultural Context*, ed. Judith Martin, Thomas Nakayama, and Lisa Flores, 422–33. Mountain View, Calif.: Mayfield Publishing Company.

———. 2005. *Building Bridges Across the Green Line: A Guide to Intercultural Communication in Cyprus*. Nicosia: United Nations Development Program.

Byrne, Sean. 2007. "Mired in Intractability: The Roles of External Ethno-Guarantors and Primary Mediators in Cyprus and Northern Ireland." *Conflict Resolution Quarterly* 24, no. 2:149–72.

Carassava, Anthee. 2007. "Greece and Turkey Open Gas Pipeline." *The New York Times*, November 19. http://www.nytimes.com/2007/11/19/world/europe/19greece.html?_r=1&scp=1&sq=Carassava+Gas+pipeline&oref=slogin (accessed November 25, 2007).

Charalambous, Loucas. 2004. "Their Audacity Knows No Bounds." *Cyprus Mail*, July 25. http://www.cyprus-mail.com/news/ (accessed July 30, 2004).

———. 2007. "How to Lose All Your Friends." *Cyprus Mail*, January 21. http://www.cyprus-mail.com/news/ (accessed January 26, 2007).

Christophorou, C., and C. Webster. 2004. "Greek Cypriots, Turkish Cypriots, and the Future." *College of Tourism and Hotel Management/CYMAR* (Nicosia). http://www.cothm.ac.cy (accessed June 20, 2004).

Christou, Jean. 2006a. "Forget the Annan Plan and Start from Scratch." *Cyprus Mail*, June 20. http://www.cyprus-mail.com/news/ (accessed June 27, 2006).

———. 2006b. "The Issue Ends Here." *Cyprus Mail*, June 28. http://www.cyprus-mail.com/news/ (accessed July 1, 2006).

———. 2007a. "New Economic Plans for the Turkish Cypriots." *Cyprus Mail*, April 3. http://www.cyprus-mail.com/news/ (accessed April 5, 2007).

———. 2007b. "Sigma Hands Property Commission List to AG." *Cyprus Mail*, June 7. http://www.cyprus-mail.com/news/ (accessed June 20, 2007).

———. 2007c. "Upsetting Another Commissioner." *Cyprus Mail*, March 11. http://www.cyprus-mail.com/news/ (accessed March 13, 2007).

———. 2007d. "We Will Fight the EU on Direct Trade Proposal." *Cyprus Mail*, February 23. http://www.cyprus-mail.com/news/ (accessed February 27, 2007).

Christou, Jean, and John Leonidou. 2007. "Ledra Wall Comes Down." *Cyprus Mail*, March 9. http://www.cyprus-mail.com/news/ (accessed March 13, 2007).

CNN. 2003. "Reunification Rally in N. Cyprus." January 14. http://www.cnn.com/WORLD/ (accessed January 14, 2003).

Curle, A. 1971. *Making Peace*. London: Tavistock.

Cyprus Action Network. 2004."Human Rights Violations in Cyprus Before the Referenda." April 23. http://www.cyprusaction.org (accessed April 23, 2004).

Cyprus Mail. 2002a. Article. December 28. http://www.cyprus-mail.com/news/ (accessed December 30, 2002).

———. 2002b. "Thousands Gather in the North in Favor of a Solution." November 28. http://www.cyprus-mail.com/news/ (accessed November 30, 2002).

———. 2004a. "AG Seeks to Overturn Turkish Cypriot Property Ruling: Tramountas Calls for Caution over Bringing Refugee Cases to Court." September 30. http://www.cyprus-mail.com/news/ (accessed October 7, 2004).

———. 2004b. "Bishop Warns 'Yes' Voters Will Go to Hell." April 20. http://www.cyprus-mail.com/news/ (accessed April 28, 2004).

———. 2004c. "Coming to Terms with EU Debacle." December 19. http://www.cyprus-mail.com/news/(accessed December 24, 2004).

———. 2004d. "DISY Leader Goes Back on the Rampage." April 22. http://www.cyprus-mail.com/news/ (accessed April 26, 2004).

———. 2004e. "European Solution? Dream on." November 4. http://www.cyprus-mail.com/news/ (accessed November 10, 2004).

———. 2004f. "Leaders Told to Sleep on It: New York Talks to Continue Today after Papadopoulos and Denktash Given the Morning to Reflect." February 11. http://www.cyprus-mail.com/news/ (accessed February 18, 2004).

———. 2004g. "New Study Shows 'No' Camp Clearly Dominated the Airwaves." May 1. http://www.cyprus-mail.com/news/ (accessed May 7, 2004).

———. 2004h. "Turkish EU Date Hangs on Cyprus." December 17. http://www.cyprus-mail.com/news/ (accessed December 22, 2004).

———. 2005a. "Borrell Calls on Turkey to Recognize." October 5. http://www.cyprus-mail.com/news/ (accessed October 10, 2005).

———. 2005b. "Nikiforos 2005 Will Be 'on a Vast Scale.'" October 15. http://www.cyprus-mail.com/news/ (accessed October 23, 2005).

———. 2005c. "Visit to the North Roundly Condemned." February 18. http://www.cyprus-mail.com/news/ (accessed February 22, 2005).

———. 2007a. "Matsakis: I Want Unified State or Two-state Solution." December 29. http://www.cyprus-mail.com/news/.

———. 2007b. "Refugees Prepare to Sue the Government." June 12. http://www.cyprus-mail.com/news/ (accessed August 1, 2007).

———. 2007c. "Remains of Missing Persons Laid to Rest." July 24. http://www.cyprus-mail.com/news/ (accessed July 28, 2007).

———. 2008. "Karamanlis Lauds Atatürk on Historic Trip to Turkey." January 25. http://www.cyprus-mail.com/news/ (accessed January 26, 2008).

Cyprus News Agency. 2004. "AKEL Maintains 'No' Position on UN Plan." April 22. http://www.cna.cy (accessed April 23, 2004).

Cyprus Weekly. 2004. Article. January 9–19. http://www.cyprusweekly.com (accessed January 22).

Demiris, B. 2004. "EU Endorses First Cross-border Pact for Greece and Turkey." Circular, February 10. Washington, D.C.: Embassy of Greece.

Diamond, Louise. 1997. "Training in Conflict-Habituated Systems: Lessons from Cyprus." *International Negotiation* 2:353–80.

Djavit An v. Turkey. 2003. European Court of Human Rights. Application no. 20652/92. Strasburg, February 20.

The Economist. 2003. "Is it a Warning Influence?" June 14. http://www.economist.com/index.html (accessed June 21, 2003).

———. 2004a. "A Chance for Peace and Unity Wasted." April 25. http://www.economist.com/index.html (accessed April 30, 2004).

———. 2004b. "Costas Karamanlis Wins." March 10. http://www.economist.com/index.html (accessed March 14, 2004).

———. 2004c. "An Ominous European Debut." April 29. http://www.economist.com/index.html (accessed April 30, 2004).

Eleftheros Typos. 2004. Article. October 25.

Ellul, Jacques. 1973. *Propaganda: The Formation of Men's Attitudes.* New York: Vintage Books.

Ennis, Darren. 2006. "Eu Assembly Adopts Critical Report on Turkey." *Cyprus Mail,* September 28. http://www.cyprus-mail.com/news/ (accessed October 3, 2006).

EU Business. 2004a. "Cyprus Gives Lukewarm Response to Turkey's EU Progress." October 7. http://www.eubusiness.com (accessed October 19, 2004).

———. 2004b. "EU Commission Praises New Cyprus Talks as 'Historic Breakthrough.'" February 13. http://www.eubusiness.com (accessed February 13, 2004).

———. 2004c. Article. April 28. http://www.eubusiness.com (accessed April 28, 2004).

EU Observer. 2004a. Article. September 8. http://euobserver.com (accessed September 8, 2004).

———. 2004b. "Turkey and the Long Road to Prosperity." December 17. http://euobserver.com (accessed December 17, 2004).

———. 2007. "MEPs Consider Turkish Cypriot Observers in EU Parliament." March 14. http://euobserver.com/9/23696/?rk=1 (accessed March 20, 2007).

EU Press. 2006. *EU Presidency Statement on Efforts Towards a Comprehensive Settlement of the Cyprus Issue under Un Auspices.* Press Release # 16644/06 (Presse 363), December 12. http://www.consilium.europa.eu/Newsroom (accessed December 24, 2006).

Europa. 2004. "Communication from the Commission to the Council and the European Parliament: Recommendation of the European Commission on Turkey's Progress Toward Accession," October 6, Brussels. [Annex, CELEX Nr. 52004DC0656.] http://europa.eu.int/comm/enlargement/report_2004/pdf/tr_recommandation_en.pdf (accessed November 1, 2004).

Europarl. 2004. "The Outlook for Cyprus after the Failure of the Referendum." News Report, April 27. http://www.europarl.europa.eu/sides/getDoc.do?pubRef=-//EP//TEXT+PRESS+NR-20040427-1+0+DOC+XML+V0//EN&language=EN#SECTION4 (accessed April 27, 2004).

Evripidou, Stefanos. 2007. "Work Starts on Pyrgos Crossing as Little Action Seen on Ledra Street." *Cyprus Mail*, March 15. http://www.cyprus-mail.com/news/ (accessed March 20, 2007).

Financial Mirror. 2003. Article. June 4. http://www.financialmirror.com (accessed June 8, 2003).

Fisher, Ian. 2007. "Cultural Thaw Nudges Greeks and Turks Closer." *International Herald Tribune*, January 18. http://www.iht.com/articles/2007/01/18/news/journal.php (accessed January 20, 2007).

Fisher, Roger, and William Ury. 1991. *Getting to Yes: Negotiating Agreement without Giving In*. New York: Penguin Books.

Fitzgibbons, R. P. 1986. "The Cognitive and Emotive Uses of Forgiveness in the Treatment of Anger." *Psychotherapy* 23:629–33.

Greek Embassy. 2006. News Bulletin, April 4. (Accessed from e-mail circular.)

Greek-Turkish Forum. 2002. "Cem Meeting Papandreou in Athens." http://www.greekturkishforum.org (accessed January 30, 2003).

Grohmann, Karolos. 2006. "Greek, Turkish Jets Collide in Interception Moves." Reuters, May 23. http://news.yahoo.com (accessed May 23, 2006).

Gundogdu, Ayten. 2001. "Identities in Question: Greek-Turkish Relations in a Period of Transformation." *MERIA Journal*, March. http://meria.idc.ac.il/journal/2001/issue1/jv5n1a8.html (accessed June 3, 2001).

Güvenc, Duygu. 2007. "EU Is Doubtful about the Election Period in Turkey." *Turkish Daily News*, March 16. http://www.turkishdailynews.com.tr/ (accessed March 20, 2007).

Hadjipavlou-Trigeorgis, Maria. 2007. "Multiple Stories: the 'Crossings' as Part of Citizens' Reconciliation Efforts in Cyprus?" *Innovation* 20, no. 1:53–73.

Hazou, Elias. 2007a. "All Sides Need to Tone Down the Rhetoric." *Cyprus Mail*, January 27. http://www.cyprus-mail.com/news/ (accessed January 31, 2007).

———. 2007b. "Christofias to Tassos: 'I'll Meet You in the Runoff.'" *Cyprus Mail*, July 10. http://www.cyprus-mail.com/news/ (accessed July 21, 2007).

Hellenic Journal. 2007. "Greece to Expand Military Cooperation with Turkey." *Hellenic Journal* 7, no. 49 (December 12).

International Crisis Group. 2006. "The Cyprus Stalemate: What Next?" March 8. http://www.crisisgroup.org/home/index.cfm?id=4003&l=1 (accessed March 20, 2006).

———. 2007. "Turkey and Europe: The Way Ahead." August 17. http://www.crisisgroup.org/home/index.cfm?id=5021&l=1 (accessed June 23, 2007).

International Herald Tribune. 2003. "Turkey and Greece: Aegean Peoples Begin to Share Stories Again." December 10. http://www.iht.com (accessed December 14, 2003).

Jenkins, Gareth. 2001. "Turkey's Changing Domestic Politics." In *Greek-Turkish Relations in the Era of Globalization*, ed. Dimitris Keridis and Dimitios Triantaphyllou, 19–41. Dulles, Va.: Brassey's.

Kasaba, Reşat, and Sibel Bozdoğan. 2000. "Turkey at the Crossroad." *Journal of International Affairs* 54, no. 1:1–20.

Keridis, Dimitris. 2001. "Domestic Developments and Foreign Policy: Greek Policy Toward Turkey." In *Greek-Turkish Relations in the Era of Globalization*, ed. 2–18. Dulles, Va.: Brassey's.

Keridis, Dimitris, and Dimitrios Triantaphyllou. 2001. "Greek-Turkish Relations the Era of European Integration and Globalization." In Keridis and Triantaphyllou, *Greek-Turkish Relations in the Era of Globalization*, xvi–xxii. Dulles, Va.: Brassey's.

Khaleej Times. 2004. "We Said No Because We Feel Insecure." September 4. http://www.khaleejtimes.com/DisplayArticleNew.asp?section=exclusiveinterview&xfile=data/exclusiveinterview/2004/september/exclusiveinterview_september2.xml.

Lacher, Hannes, and Erol Kaymak. 2005. "Transforming Identities: Beyond the Politics of Non-Settlement in North Cyprus." *Mediterranean Politics* 10, no. 2.

LaFranchi, Howard. 2004. "Why the White House Is Pushing Cyprus Solution." *The Christian Science Monitor* 96, no. 45 (January 1).

Lederach, John Paul. 2002. *Building Peace: Sustainable Reconciliation in Divided Societies*. Washington, D.C.: United States Institute of Peace Press.

Loizides, Neophytos. 2004. "In the Aftermath of the Cyprus Referendums." *European Balkan Observer*, May 2004. http://www.wiiw.ac.at/balkan/files/EBO%203.pdf (accessed July 3, 2007).

Loizidou v. Turkey. 1998. European Court of Human Rights. Article 50, Case No. 40/1993/435/514. (Strasburg, July 28, 1998).

Lordos, Alexandros. 2005. *Civil Society Diplomacy: A New Approach for Cyprus? An Evidence-based Report in Cooperation with CYMAR Market Research and KADEM Cyprus Social Research*. www.help-net.gr/CivilSocietyDiplomacy.pdf (accessed March 10, 2005).

Mavratsas, Caesar V. 1998. "Greek Cypriot Political Culture and the Prospect of European Union Membership: A Worst Case Scenario." *The Cyprus Review* 10, no. 1:67–76.

McCormick, John. 2002. *Understanding the European Union: A Concise Introduction.* New York: Palgrave.

Montville, J. V. 1993. "The Healing Function in Political Conflict Resolution." In *In Conflict Resolution Theory and Practice: Integration and Application,* ed. Dennis J. D. Sandole and Hugo Van Der Merwe, 112–27. Manchester: Manchester Univ. Press.

Morgan, Tabitha. 2007. "Symbolic Nicosia Wall Comes Down." *BBC News,* March 9, 2007. http://news.bbc.co.uk/ (accessed March 16, 2007).

Moustakis, Fotios, and Rudra Chaudhuri. 2005. "Turkish-Kurdish Relations and the European Union: An Unprecedented Shift in the Kemalist Paradigm?" *Mediterranean Quarterly* 16, no. 4:77–89.

The New Anatolian. 2007. "Turkish, Greek Premiers Open Taps on Europe's First Supply of Caspian Gas." November 19. http://www.thenewanatolian.com/tna-29608.html (accessed November 28, 2007).

Papadakis, Yiannis. 2005. *Echoes from the Dead Zone: Across the Cyprus Divide.* London: I. B. Tauris.

Papadopoulos, Tassos. 2004. *National Address of the President of the Republic Tassos Papadopoulos for the Referendum of April 24, 2004,* April 7, 2004.

Papandreou, George. 2000. "Revision of Greek Foreign Policy." Western Policy Center, January 2000. http://www.papandreou.gr/february2000/wpc_jan2000.html (accessed December 2000).

Pfaff, William. 1989. *Barbarian Sentiments.* New York: Hill and Wang.

Phileleftheros. 1994. Article. February 13. http://www.phileleftheros.com.cy.

———. 2002. Article. November 27. http://www.phileleftheros.com.cy (accessed November 28, 2002).

———. 2003. Article. March 11. http://www.phileleftheros.com.cy (accessed March 12, 2003).

Pope, Hugh. 2008. "Settling Cyprus." *The Wall Street Journal, Europe,* February 14.

Quetteville, Harry de. 2004. "EU accuses Greek Cypriots of betrayal." *The Age,* April 23. http://www.theage.com.au/articles/2004/04/22/1082616262769.html?from=storyrhs.

Reuters. 2002. "Turkey's EU Reform Laws Passed by Parliament." Reuters, August 3. http://today.reuters.com (accessed August 3, 2002).

———. 2003. "UN Abandons Cyprus Peace Effort After Talks Fail." Reuters, March 11. http://today.reuters.com (accessed March 2003).

Rifkin, Jeremy. 2004. *The European Dream: How Europe's Vision of the Future is Quietly Eclipsing the American Dream.* Cambridge, UK: Polity Press.

Silver, Eric. 2004. "Cypriots Who Back UN Plan Face Damnation, Says Bishop." *The Independent,* April 20. http://www.independent.co.uk/news/europe/cypriots-who-back-un-plan-face-damnation-says-bishop-560568.html.

Turkish Cypriot Chamber of Commerce. 2007. *Foreign Trade,* October 4. http://www.ktto.net/english/foreigntrade.html (accessed October 20, 2007).

Turkish Daily News. 2003. "Cyprus solution will have to wait until 2004." *Turkish Daily News,* March 11. http://www.turkishdailynews.com.tr (accessed March 15, 2003).

———. 2004a. "Germany puts full weight behind Turkey." *Turkish Daily News,* October 19, 2004. http://www.turkishdailynews.com.tr (accessed October 22, 2004).

———. 2004b. "Lamy says Turkey has European vocation, but calls for debate." *Turkish Daily News,* October 19, 2004. http://www.turkishdailynews.com.tr (accessed October 22, 2004).

———. 2004c. Article. February 11. http://www.turkishdailynews.com.tr (accessed February 14, 2004).

———. 2004d. "Opposition gets tough on government's Cyprus issue." *Turkish Daily News,* February 19. http://www.turkishdailynews.com.tr (accessed February 23, 2004).

———. 2004e. "PM: Recognition of Greek Cypriots is a reality." *Turkish Daily News,* May 3, 2004. http://www.turkishdailynews.com.tr (accessed May 5, 2004).

———. 2004f. "Solana: Turkey must be in EU for Europe's security." *Turkish Daily News,* October 19. http://www.turkishdailynews.com.tr (accessed October 22, 2004).

———. 2004g. "Zapatdro: Europe's open door to Turkey." *Turkish Daily News,* October 19. http://www.turkishdailynews.com.tr (accessed October 22, 2004).

Turkish Press,. 2007. "Turkish Cypriots Apply To E.C.H.R. for Their Properties." January 2. www.Turkishpress.com (accessed January 14, 2007).

Uludağ, Sevgül. 1996. "We are the New Culture." In *The Multi-Cultural Carpet: Reflections on Bi-communal Work in Cyprus,* 5–9. Nicosia: American Center.

———. 2006. *Oysters with Missing Pearls: Untold Stories about Missing Persons, Mass Graves, and Memories from the Past of Cyprus.* Nicosia: IKME Sociopolitical Studies Institute.

United Nations. 2003a. *Report of the Secretary-General on His Mission of Good Offices in Cyprus,* April 1. [S/2003/398.] http://daccessdds.un.org/doc/UNDOC/GEN/N03/305/59/PDF/N0330559.pdf?OpenElement.

United Nations. 2003b. *Report of the Secretary-General on the United Nations Operation in Cyprus*, May 27. [S/2003/572.] http://daccessdds.un.org/doc/UNDOC/GEN/N03/372/58/IMG/N0337258.pdf?OpenElement.

———. 2003c. *Report of the Secretary-General on the United Nations Operation in Cyprus*, November 12. [S/2003/1078.] http://daccessdds.un.org/doc/UNDOC/GEN/N03/609/59/IMG/N0360959.pdf?OpenElement.

———. 2004a. *The Annan Plan for Cyprus: The Comprehensive Settlement of the Cyprus Problem*, March 31. http://www.hri.org/docs/annan/.

———. 2004b. *In Briefing to Security Council on Cyprus, Under-secretary-general Cites Need for Accurate Assessment of Situation, Appropriate Recommendations*, April 28. [Press Release# SC/8074]. http://www.un.org/News/Press/docs/2004/sc8074.doc.htm (accessed May 20, 2004).

———. 2004c. *Report of the Secretary-General on His Mission of Good Offices in Cyprus*, May 28. [S/2004/4370.] http://daccessdds.un.org./doc/UNDOC/GEN/NO4/361/53/PDF/NO436153.pdf?OpenElement (accessed May 30, 2004).

———. 2004d. *Report of the Secretary-General on the United Nations Operation in Cyprus*, May 26. [S/2004/427.] http://daccessdds.un.org/doc/UNDOC/GEN/N04/366/24/IMG/N0436624.pdf?OpenElement.

United Nations Forces in Cyprus. 2007. "The UN in Cyprus: An Intercommunal Survey of Public Opinion by UNFICYP." United Nations Forces in Cyprus, April 24.

Wolleh, Oliver. 2001. *Local Peace Constituencies in Cyprus: Citizen Rapprochement by the Bi-communal Conflict Resolution Trainer Group*. Berlin: Berghof Research Center For Conflict Management.

Wood, David M., and Birol A. Yesilada. 2004. *The Emerging European Union*. New York: Pearson Longman.

Xenides-Arestis v. Turkey. 2005. European Court of Human Rights. App. No. 46347/99. Strasburg, December 22.

Yesilada, B., J. Kugler, H. Anastasiou, A. Sozen, and B. Efird. 2004. *A Bounded Rationality Analysis of the Cyprus Problem*. Paper presented at the International Studies Association 45th Annual Convention, Montreal, Canada, March 17–20.

Index

absolutism, 4, 6, 24, 168–69
academics, 46, 97, 124
acceding states: privileges/obligation of, 104–7; requirements of, 6–8, 14, 118, 155, 183–84, 210–11, 238. *See also* Cyprus; Turkey
accession process: Copenhagen criteria for, 14, 118, 119, 155, 183; demilitarization of Cyprus under Annan Plan and, 58; effects of rejection of Annan Plan on Cyprus's process, 59; for Turkey, 136, 145, 189, 198–203, 205–9, 212, 213–14, 227–28, 232–33, 254, 260–61
accession to EU: of Cyprus, 3, 6, 59, 60, 61–62, 74, 102, 108–9, 114, 132, 157, 167, 217; effects of rejection of Annan Plan on Turkey's application, 59, 71; Papadopoulos's view of, 114; privileges/obligation of acceding states, 104–7; requirements for, 6–8, 14, 118, 155, 183–84, 210–11, 238; role in peacebuilding/conflict transformation, 50, 254
Accession Treaty. *See* Treaty of Accession to EU
acquis communautaire (EU law): GC integration with, 185; harmonization of national institutions with, 6–8; TC harmonization with, 137, 185, 193. *See also* European Union law

Act of Adoption, 136
adversarial stance/politics: of Cypriot communities, xv; dissolution of in Greece, 10; of ethnocentric nationalism, xii, xiii, 41, 45, 49, 87, 89, 93, 98, 109, 114; EU membership and, 3–4, 105–7, 182, 184, 200, 210; of Greece/Turkey, xv, 47; of Greek nationalism, 11–12; of Greek Orthodox Church of Cyprus, 155; intergroup communication through mediation of, 88; of nationalism, 121, 148–49; nationalist definition of identity and, 41; Papandreou-Çem initiatives' movement beyond, 32–35; peace negotiations and, 130, 249; remobilization of troops in Cyprus and, 217; rendered obsolete in Greece, 131; resurgence of in postreferendum Cyprus, 112, 114; revival of by "no" campaign, 144; solution to Cyprus problem vs., 49; of TC Right, 45; understanding of EU culture and, 114
Aegean Sea, 30, 123, 125, 256, 258
AGB research, 154–55
Aid Regulation, 230
AKEL: acceptance of rapprochement, 95–96; election for presidency (2008) and, 261–62; request for postponement of referenda, 167; role in failure

AKEL (cont.)
of Annan Plan, 158, 163–68, 169–70; support of DIKO, 159, 163; support of Papadopoulos, 256; withdrawal from Papadopoulos government, 203

Aletheia, 160

alienation: acts of humanity in presence of, 83; between AKEL/DISY, 165; effects of, 88, 247; precipitated by failure of Hague talks, 73; "no" campaign reestablishment of, 170, 176, 184, 262; precipitated by politicolegal entanglements, 244; resources for peace in spite of, 84

All Cyprus Union Forum, 38

Alter, Peter, 70

Amer/Nielsen poll, 65–66

An, Djavit, 77–79

Anastasiades, Nicos (leader of DISY), 153, 159

Anastasiou, Harry: article on Annan Plan, 59–60; as member of citizens peace movement, 37, 38, 64; speech delivered in mid-1990s in Nicosia, 39–40

Ankara agreement, 208

Annan, Kofi: AKEL's request for postponement of referenda, 167; on bicommunal events in Cyprus, 97; call for referendum in Cyprus, 67; EU's recommendation for renewed talks, 229; on failure of Hague talks, 126; on final version of Annan Plan, 133; Hague talks and, 67–68; negotiations in Switzerland, 133; New York talks, 127–29; Papadopoulos's response to postreferendum report, 176–81; postreferendum report, 172, 174, 192; proposal for ending TC isolation, 186, 251; proposal for solution of Cyprus problem, 52–66; revision of Annan Plan, 133–38, 171–72; timing of proposal, 66–67; view of free movement in Cyprus, 80–81

Annan Plan: aims of, 179; basic principles of, 52–55, 180–81; benefits of acceptance of, 60–61; call for referendum on, 67, 73; campaign against in TC community, 152; consequences of both sides' rejection of, 59; criticism of Denktash's refusal to negotiate on, 101; Denktash's rejection of, 111, 114; election for presidency (2008) and, 261–62; EU response to campaign against, 171, 181–84; failure of, xi, 68–71, 139–40, 157–58; failure of Hague talks and, 157–58; final version of, 133–38; GC media campaign against, 154–55; Greek Orthodox Church's campaign against, 155–57; Hague talks concerning referendum on, 67–70; indirect referendum on in TRNC, 117–18; international support of, 117; nationalist response to, 58, 67–68, 112–15; negotiations in Cyprus on, 129–30, 131–32; negotiations in Switzerland on, 132–33; New York talks, 127–29, 171–72; Papadopoulos's campaign against, 142–48, 150, 151–59, 244–45; Papadopoulos's delays of negotiations on, 113–14; Papadopoulos's objections to, 110; Papadopoulos's position on, 67–68, 71, 116, 255; peace rallies calling for acceptance of, 62–66, 93; postreferendum need for negotiations on, 225, 229; public understanding of, 65–66; referenda of April 24, 2004 on, 139; resumption of talks based on, 125–33; role of political parties in failure of, 158, 163–70; security measures in, 147; situation of proposal of, 52; sustainability of, 55–58; TRNC legitimacy and, 107; Turkey's readiness to resume talks on, 212; Turkish acceptance of, 119–22; UN response to campaign against, 171–75; violence against supporters of, 160–62. *See also* referendum/referenda

Annan Plan: A Historic Challenge for the Cypriots, The (Anastasiou/Yesilada), 59–60

ANT1, 155
anticolonialism, 145–46, 156
Archbishop, 143, 146, 156
Armenian issue, 232–33
Article 301 of Turkish Penal Code, 233
artists, 46, 97
assassinations, 22
Association Agreement, 106
Atatürk, Kemal, 15, 258–59
Austria, 206, 208, 213
Avci, Turgay, 236

Balkans, 11
Balkenende, Jan-Peter, 208, 209
Barash, David P., 122
Barcelona Declaration, 60
Basis for the Comprehensive Settlement of the Cyprus Problem. *See* Annan Plan
Bayer, Gokcen, 253
Belgium, 181
betrayal: EU outrage over "no" campaign, 181–84; "no" campaign as, 142–51; UN outrage over Papadopoulos's "no" campaign, 174–81; yes vote on Annan Plan portrayed as, 146
bicommunal, bizonal federation: Annan Plan for, 52–66, 133–38, 180–81; bicommunal groups vision of, 40; Denktash's rejection of, 117; Matsakis's denunciation of, 189–91; as only solution acceptable to EU, 216, 263–64; Papadopoulos's objections to, 110, 116, 117; Papadopoulos's rejection of, 176–81; referenda on, 139, 192

bicommunal communications, 39
bicommunal events, 89, 97–99, 249–50
bicommunal groups, 38–39. *See also* citizen peace movement (Cyprus)
bicommunal meetings. *See* citizen peace movement (Cyprus)
bicommunal movement. *See* citizen peace movement (Cyprus)
bicommunal republic. *See* bizonal, bicommunal federation
bilateral agreements, 33–34
Bildt, Carl, 227
Birand, Mehment Ali, 69
Bishop of Morphou, 156
blood donation event, 97–99
Bohm, David, 89, 90
Bologna Process, 231
border crossings, 72–93, 100
Borrell, Joseph, 215–16
Broken Olive Branch, vol. 2, The Impasse of Ethnonationalism, The (Anastasiou), xii–xiv, xvi–xv, 1
Brussels: endorsement of cross-border pact between Greece/Turkey, 124; frustration with GC government, 230; opening of trade with TC community, 193; Papadopoulos's comments to Annan, 173; pledging conference, 175; position on admission of Cyprus to EU, 61
Brussels Business Group, 38
Brussels Summit (2004), 205–11, 238, 254

Brussels Summit (2006), 226–30
buffer zone: bicommunal meetings in, 38, 42; bridge across Ledra Street and, 234–35; opening of border crossings in, 100; speech delivered in mid-1990s in, 39–40, 42
Building Peace: Sustainable Reconciliation in Divided Societies (Lederach), 1
Bürgenstock, Switzerland, 132–33, 142
Bush administration, 126–27
business, 28, 257
Buyukanit, Yasar, 238

Cagis, Nejla, 253
Cakartas, Hasan Huseyin, 253
Cakartas, Mumin, 253
Canada, 181
candidate states, 6–8, 14, 119, 130. *See also* Turkey
capital punishment. *See* death penalty
Çem, Ismail, 32–34
Central Bank, 134
Central Bank law, 137
Certificate of Origin, 106, 109, 193, 248
Chair Company, The, 256
Chamber of Commerce (TC), 106, 109, 193, 248
Chamber of Deputies, 54, 56–57, 180–81
children, 98. *See also* youth
Christodoulakis, Nikos, 125
Christofias, Dimitris, 169, 187, 203, 261–63
Christophorou, C., 168
Chrysostomos (Bishop of Paphos), 156
Chubais, Denis, 95
church, 152, 155–57
Ciller, Tansu, 17, 21
citizen-initiated activities, 46, 62–65
citizen organizations, 101

citizen peace movement (Cyprus): Annan Plan and, 62; challenges of, 38, 46; change in mental framework, 47–50, 89; conflict transformation through, 3, 91; interethnic conceptualization of democracy, 41–42; justification of, 94–95, 99; leadership of, 37–38; majority of population following, 99; members response to peace rallies, 64; mobilization of civil society, 35–46; as peace-enhancing process, 3; requirements for effective role in peacebuilding process, 36–37; training of members, 37; transcendence of political lines, 45; TRNC refusal to allow members access to, 77–78; utilization of middle-range leadership flexibility, 43; widening of possibilities for, 94–95; work of, 39–46
citizenship, 53–54, 55, 102, 109
Citizens' Movement for Reunification and Coexistence, 38
civil politics (Turkey), 16–18, 21–22
civil society: ; emergence of voices of peace, 35–47, 92 (*see also* citizen peace movement [Cyprus]); EU-based reforms in Turkey and, 28; nationalist retardation of development of, 41; peace rallies in northern Cyprus, 62–66, 74–75; popularization of in Cyprus, 40; relaxation of state controls over in Turkey, 120; role in peacebuilding/conflict transformation, 65, 93–94, 112–13, 249–50. *See also* free movement across green line; peace rallies; as threat to nationalism, 112–13; of Turkey, 16–18, 22, 24
civil society initiatives, 2–3, 46, 123
civil war (Greece), 8
Claims Settlement Council, 111

Clerides, Glafkos, 66, 113, 133, 159, 165
CNN, 63
cold war, xiii, 8, 15
colonialism, 4
Commission of Compensation, 221
Committee of Missing Persons, 250
common state, 53, 54, 56, 57. *See also* Annan Plan
common state law, 53
communication, xii, xiv
communism/communists: civil war in Greece and, 8; contact between GC/TC left, 95–96; role in failure of Annan Plan, 158, 163–68, 169–70; support of DIKO, 159, 163. *See also* AKEL; DIKO; left-wing groups/ideologies
Communist Party, 9
Communist Progressive Workers Party (AKEL). *See* AKEL
community (nationalist concept), xi
component states, 53, 54, 55, 57. *See also* Annan Plan
conciliatory politics of EU: at Brussels Summit, 207; culture/framework of, 3–8; in Cyprus, 106, 226; effect on Cypriot politics, 228–29; effects on Greek politics/society, 9–14; in Greek-Turkish relations, 255–56; Kurdish problem in Turkey and, 19–20; nationalism vs., 210; positive impact of, 49; rapprochement efforts and, 51
confidence-building measures: Denktash's preference for, 243; between Greece/Turkey, 257; low-level political cooperation as, 32–35; Papadopoulos's strategy behind, 236; Republic of Cyprus's recommendation of for TCs, 186–88; talks with Gambari, 229; talks with technical committees, 240–42
conflict, 1–2

conflict-conditioned societies, xi, xii, xiv, 3, 88–89, 148
conflict entrenchment, 1–2, 79, 92–93, 116–17, 147–48
conflict resolution: Annan Plan for, 52–66; EU strategy for Cyprus/Greek-Turkish relations, 62; role of low-level politics, 33–35; role of peace constituency in, 42; training of members of citizen peace movement in, 37
conflict transformation: citizen peace movement and, 35–46; EU's role in, xvi, 6–8; progression of, 1–3; requirements for effective role of citizens in peace-building process, 36; response to free movement across green line as, 81–104; role of civil society in, 93–94; role of middle-range leadership in, 43; role of peace constituency in, 42
confrontation, 2
consensus building in EU, 3, 7, 207, 210, 212
Constantinides, Alecos, 160
constitution (1960), 253
Copenhagen criteria: creation of, 14; Cyprus's lack of compliance with, 155, 183; GC violation of, 155; reforms in Turkey in compliance with, 118, 119
Copenhagen Summit (1993), 14
Copenhagen Summit (2002), 6
copresidents, 54
corruption, 16, 17–18, 24, 74
Council of European Union (Council of Ministers): amplification of democracy, 6; consideration of Act of Adaptation, 136; Cypriot voting power in, 181; dissociation of Turkey's accession from Cyprus problem, 199–203; functions of, 4–5, 6; missing person of Cyprus issue and, 250; property rights issues and, 219; responsibilities of, 5, 6

coups: in Cyprus, xiv, 166; in Greece, xiv; in Turkey, 15, 16, 21
Court of Primary Federal Jurisdiction, 134
cross-border economic pact, 124–25
culture: cooperation between Greece/Turkey on, 124–25; created by citizen peace movement, 35–46; effects of low-level political cooperation on, 33–34; EU development of, 3–4; peace rallies and, 65; shared values between Greece/Turkey, 13, 123–24; shared values between rival ethnic groups, 84
Curle, Adam, 1, 42
currency, 6
customs union agreement (Turkey): acceptance of EU requirement, 209; addendum to, 213; full compliance with as EU requirement, 216, 254; inclusion of Cyprus as EU requirement, 200, 206–7, 208, 212
CyBC, 152, 153, 155, 211
cyberspace, 39
Cypriot government. *See* Annan Plan; Denktash, Rauf R.; Denktash administration; Papadopoulos, Tassos; Papadopoulos administration; Republic of Cyprus; Turkish Republic of Cyprus (TRNC)
Cyprus: accession to EU, 3, 6, 55, 60, 61, 108–9, 114, 119, 127, 132, 155, 167, 183–84; Annan Plan for, 52–66; call for referendum in, 67; cancellation on Greek/Turkish military operations in, 124; citizen peace movement in, 35–46; conflict-conditioned societies of, xi, xiv; conflict transformation in, 2–3 (*see also* citizen peace movement [Cyprus]; free movement across green line); consequences of both sides' rejection of Annan Plan, 59; coup d'état in, xiv; demilitarization of under Annan Plan, 54, 58; deviations from nationalism in, xiii, xv, 47–50, 80–101 (*see also* citizen peace movement [Cyprus]); economic impact of "no" vote on Annan Plan, 237–39; effect of EU membership on, 244, 249–59; EU membership, 186; EU process in Eastern Mediterranean and, 31; EU requirement for UN-based settlement of, 214; free movement across green line, 72–93; Greek-Turkish relations and, 259; incompatibility of democracy with nationalism in, xiii; integration into EU, xvi, 67, 186, 193, 252, 255, 260; interethnic impact of "no" vote on referendum, 216–19, 237–39, 240, 243, 244–48; memories of pain in, xiii, xiii–xiv, 73, 85–86, 85–93, 101, 250–51; nationalist rejection of Annan Plan, 58–59; negotiation for peace in, xi, 129–32; obstacles to solutions to, 73–74; opening of crossings in, 234–37; outcome of Brussels Summit, 212; peace-enhancing processes in postreferendum era, 249–51; persistence of nationalist thinking in, 108–17, 142–51, 162, 172–74, 176–81, 184–91, 200, 203, 216–19; political changes in Eastern Mediterranean, 198–99; postnationalist approach to problem of, 30; postreferenda change in politics of, 191–204, 206, 209, 228–29, 230, 234–37, 239–45, 251, 261; postreferendum reversal of roles, 184–91; privileges/obligation of under EU framework, 104–7; remobilization of troops in, 216–18; significance of EU culture in, 6; tapping gas/oil reserves off coast of Cyprus and, 234, 237–39;

Treaty of Accession to EU, 53; Turkey's customs union agreement including, 200, 206–7, 208, 209, 212, 213, 216, 254; Turkish invasion of, xi, xiv, 103, 166, 219; UN opinion on (2007), 259; U.S. facilitation of renewed talks, 125–27. *See also* Greek Cypriot (GC) community; Republic of Cyprus; Turkish Cypriot (TC) community; Turkish Republic of Northern Cyprus (TRNC)
Cyprus Action Network (CAN), 151–52
Cyprus Justice Party (KAP), 118
Cyprus Mail, 154–55, 186–87, 215
Cyprus Peace Center, 39
Cyprus problem: anomalies to Turkish accession concerning, 206; central question concerning, xii–xiii; challenge of interethnic democracy and, 20; citizen peace movement and, 36–46; crossing openings and, 234–37; developments between 2004/2007, 260; EU-based reforms in Turkey and, 120–22; EU dissociation of Turkey's accession from, 199–203, 206, 209, 215, 228, 254; EU political/legal entanglements concerning, 196–97; EU process and, 6–8, 104–7; EU's recommendation for renewed talks, 229; failure of peace initiatives, xi–xii, xiv, 139–51; GCs' approach to, 255; Greek Europeanization and, 12–14; Greek-Turkish rapprochement and, 123–25, 255–59; jokes about, xi; Justice and Development Party in Turkey and, 24; low-level political cooperation between Greece and Turkey and, 35; movement across green line and, 72–104; nationalist underpinning of, xii–xiii; necessity of comprehensive settlement, 261; negotiation based on Annan Plan in, 129–33; new understanding of through rapprochement efforts, 47; New York talks on, 127–29; opportunities for solutions to, 249–51; outcome of Brussels Summit, 212; Papadopoulos's postreferenda approach to, 186–89; Papadopoulos's strategy for negotiation and, 240–41; referenda of April 24, 2004 on Annan Plan and, 139–51; response to free movement across green line and, 80–104; reversal of approaches to in Cyprus, 184–91; Talat's willingness to negotiate settlement, 241–42; tapping gas/oil reserves off coast of Cyprus and, 234, 237–39; TCs' approach to, 254, 255; tension between prosolution/antisolution secessionist factions in TRNC, 92–93; Turkey's customs union agreement and, 200, 206–7, 208, 209, 212, 213, 216, 254; Turkey's EU accession and, 118–19; Turkish internal problems and, 18–19; Turkish military as obstacle to solution of, 70; unilateral good will policies, 100–104; UN proposal for solution of. *See also* Annan Plan; U.S. facilitation of renewed talks, 125–27
Cyprus: The Search for a Solution (Hannay), 215
Cyprus-Turkey relations: Brussels Summit (2004) and, 205–11; complication of postreferendum period, 234, 244; customs union agreement and, 254; demand for Turkish recognition of Republic of Cyprus, 188–89, 206–7, 213, 214, 228; Famagusta and, 221, 226–27, 236, 240; necessity of comprehensive settlement, 261; Nikiforos war drills and, 216–18; opening of crossings in Cyprus and, 234–37;

Cyprus-Turkey relations (*cont.*)
run-up to Brussels Summit (2006), 226–27; tapping gas/oil reserves and, 234, 237–39, 244, 256; Turkey's customs union agreement and, 200, 206–7, 208, 209, 212, 213, 216, 254

death penalty, 19–20, 28
Demetriades, Lellos, 64
demilitarization of Cyprus, 54, 58, 136–37, 147–48, 182
democracy: acceding states responsibility toward, 7, 30, 183; correlation to foreign policy, 122; development in Turkey, 120–21, 122; EU concept of, 4–6; EU goals and, 6, 30, 31; Europeanization process and, 8; incompatibility with ethnocentric nationalism, xii–xiii, 4, 112; interethnic conceptualization of, 41–42; intertwining of domestic/international, 32; *metapoliteysi* and, 8–9; nationalist understanding of, 57, 177–81; relationship to peace process, 40, 42, 65; response to free movement across green line as, 81–93; stability of Turkish civil society and, 17–18, 22; in Turkey, 15–17, 18; Turkish Islamic fundamentalists' appeal to EU for, 23
Democratic Left Party. *See* DIKO
Democratic Left Party (Turkey), 17
Democratic Party (DP), 118
Democratic Rally Party (DISY). *See* DISY
democratization, 40, 45, 70, 71
Denktash, Rauf R.: agreement/disagreement with peace-builders' assumptions, 117; Annan's call for referendum, 67; Annan's postreferenda report on, 175; appeal against Annan Plan, 132, 142; approach to Cyprus problem, 111–12, 114–15, 130, 132, 254, 255; compliance with ECHR ruling on GC property and, 224; concept of security, 150; criticism of, 101, 215; demythologizing of image of in Turkey, 121–22; difference in views over joint governance by, 66; election of 2005 and, 213; EU concept of security and, 150; EU view of, 160; Hague talks and, 67–70, 73; international criticism of, 73, 116, 117; lifting of restrictions on movement across green line, 72–80; loss of support from Turkey, 121–22; loss of TC support, 169, 173, 175; message of peace rallies for, 63–64; negotiation based on Annan Plan, 129–30, 131–33, 174; New York talks, 128–29; objection to European integration, 157; as obstacle to TC interests, 73–74, 116; persistence of nationalist thinking, 108–13, 116, 117, 150, 174, 178, 179; political exposure due to failure of Hague talks, 73; position on Annan Plan, 67, 186; postnationalist reforms in Turkey/Greece and, 125; preference for confidence-building measures, 188, 243; proposal of Commission of Compensation, 221; referendum and, 152; refusal of further negotiations, 68–69, 132, 239–40; rejection of Annan Plan, 101, 102, 114–15, 117; rejection of interethnic citizen contact, 96; resumption of talks on Annan plan, 131; satisfaction with outcome of referenda, 139; security concerns of, 148; TC criticism of position on negotiations, 63, 73, 117–18; tension between prosolution/antisolution secessionist factions and, 92; use of Papadopoulos's rejection of Annan Plan, 116; vindication of, 247

Denktash, Serdar, 133
Denktash administration: establishment of Claims Settlement Council, 111–12; EU process and, 107; interethnic rapprochement and, 99–100; persistence of nationalist thinking in, 108–9, 110–11, 112–13, 162; TCs' requests for identity cards/passports from Republic of Cyprus and, 102
Denmark, 206, 208
dialogue: bicommunal events facilitating, 97; breakdown of under ethnocentric nationalism, 88–89; concerning interethnic relations, 216; on Cyprus issue in Turkish media, 121; established by citizen groups in Cyprus, 35–36, 38; between Greece/Turkey, 12–14; low-level political cooperation establishing, 33; positive impact of, 49. *See also* negotiations
dictatorship (Greece), 8
DIKO: AKEL support of, 159, 166; concept of federation, 190; criticism of, 189–90; election for presidency (2008) and, 261–62; EU political culture and, 107; nationalistic approach of, 110, 165; opposition to federal solution, 176; reestablishment of nationalist agenda, 152; response to EU's dissociation of Turkey from Cyprus problem, 201; rise to power, 159; silence following Brussels Summit, 211
Dink, Hrant, 233
Direct Trade Regulation, 231
DISY: addition of citizen peace building to agendas for Cyprus, 44–45; election for presidency (2008) and, 261–62; influence of EU policy on, 159; on outcome of Brussels Summit, 211; rapprochement policies of, 165; rebuke of Papadopoulos, 153; support of Annan Plan, 165, 166; violence against leader of, 160
Djavit An v. Turkey, 77–79
domestication of foreign policy, 29
domestic policy, 12
drug trafficking, 33–34

earthquake diplomacy, 3, 46
earthquakes, 17–18, 46
Eastern Mediterranean: benefits of acceptance Annan Plan to, 60–61; conflict transformation in, 2–3; EU process in, xv, 31, 50, 205–6, 227, 255–56; Greek Europeanization and, 12–14; oil drilling issue in, 237–39; peace-enhancing processes in, 3; remobilization of troops in Cyprus and, 218–19; shift in politics in postreferendum era, 198–200, 226–27
economic assistance, 197–98, 230, 242
economic development: EU assistance to TC community for, 105–7, 197–98, 230, 242; EU proposal to open direct trade with TC community for, 185, 186, 193–97, 213, 226–27, 228; in Greece, 131, 256–57; Greek-Turkish cross-border economic pact, 33–34, 124–25, 255, 256–57
Economist, The, 131, 170, 174, 192
economy: acceding states responsibility toward, 7; benefits of acceptance Annan Plan to, 60; benefits of accession to EU for TCs, 61, 62; cross-border economic pact between Greece/Turkey, 124–25, 255, 256–57; EU acceleration of globalization of, 30; EU aid to TC community, 105–7, 230, 242; EU framework and, 4; free movement across green

economy (*cont.*)
  line and, 75, 103; of Greece, 11, 131, 256–57; interethnic activities, 247; of TRNC, 74, 103; of Turkey, 13, 17, 24, 74
EDEK, 158, 159, 165, 201
education, 28, 101, 151–52
Egypt, 237
elections: for GC presidency (2008), 259; in Greece (2004), 130–31; of parliament in TC community (2003), 117–18; for President of Republic of Cyprus (2003), 66; for TRNC president in 2005, 213; for Turkish presidency (2007), 232, 233; for Turkish president (1995), 21; for Turkish president (1999), 22; for Turkish president (2002), 24; for U.S. president (2004), 126
embargo on TRNC, 103, 105–6, 186
enclaves, 73, 74, 81
energy reserves: opening of natural gas pipeline between Greece/Turkey, 257; tapping gas/oil reserves off coast of Cyprus, 234, 237–39, 244, 256
enosis (unification with Greece), 53, 91–92, 157
environmental issues, 7, 33–34, 124
Erbakan, Necmettin, 21, 22
Erdogan, Recep Tayyip: acceptance of accession plan, 205; acceptance of Annan Plan, 122; on Cyprus referenda, 170; on Kurdish problem, 120; nationalist opposition to Cyprus policies of, 224, 232; negotiation based on Annan Plan and, 130; negotiations at Brussels, 206–7; at New York talks, 129; opening of natural gas pipeline, 257; readiness to resume Cyprus talks, 212; on recognition of Republic of Cyprus, 252; at talks in Switzerland, 133; top-level talks with Karamalis, 258–59

ESDI, 59
Ethnarch, 143
ethnically mixed societies, xiii
ethnic segregation, 243–44, 246–47
ethnocentric nationalism: Annan Plan and, 55, 56; competition with European, postnational reformers, 127; concept of security, 218; deconstruction of in Turkey, 20, 119–22; effect on conflict between Greeks/Turks, 49; elimination of shared culture, 84; erosion of in TC community, 65; EU framework of conciliatory politics and, 3–4, 6–7; globalization trends and, 50; historiography of, xiii–xiv, 86–87; incompatibility with democracy, xii–xiii, 112; interethnic relations and, xiii; monoethnic state polity of, xii, 57, 116–17, 132, 158, 177–79, 189–91; negotiation based on Annan Plan and, 130, 131–33; rejection of Annan Plan, 58–59, 140–58; relapse to in GC community, 160–61, 244; remobilization of troops in Cyprus, 216–18; in Turkey, 14–31; as underpinning of Cyprus problem, xii; understanding of democracy, 177–81. *See also* Greek Cypriot nationalism/nationalists; nationalism; Turkish Cypriot nationalism/nationalists; Turkish nationalism/nationalists
EU Council. *See* Council of European Union (Council of Ministers)
EU-Cyprus Association Council, 106
EU-Cyprus Joint Parliamentary Committee member, 182
EU Federation Study Group, 38
EU-NATO strategic meetings, 213
EU Observer, 200
euro, 6, 131

European Commission: amplification of democracy, 6; Brussels pledging conference, 175; criticism of "no" campaign, 153–54; on decision made at New York talks, 129; proposal for opening of trade with TC community, 185, 186, 193–95; recommendation report on Turkey, 120, 121, 200–201, 202, 205; responsibilities of, 4–5, 6

European Commission for Enlargement, 136

European Community, 6, 8–9, 14

European Convention of Human Rights, 77

European Council. *See* Council of European Union (Council of Ministers)

European Court of Human Rights (ECHR): Annan Plan and, 136; *Djavit An v. Turkey*, 77–79; establishment of Claims Settlement Council and, 112; *Loizidou v. Turkey*, 76–77, 112, 253; Mustafa case and, 253; property rights issues, 76–77, 219–22, 253; ruling on execution of Ocalan, 20; *Xenides-Arestis v. Turkey*, 219–20, 221–22

European Court of Justice, 5, 6, 106, 185

European integration: of Cyprus/Turkey, 119; Denktash's objection to, 157; dissociation of nationalism from political culture of members, 4; evolution of EC to EU, 6; requirements of, 183–84; security provided by, 148. *See also* accession process to EU membership; accession to EU

Europeanization: effect on Cyprus problem, xv–xvi; effects in Turkey, 25–27, 31, 119–22; failure of Hague talks and, 71; of Greece, 8, 9–14, 31; liberalization of media and, 121; Turkish military as obstacle to, 70

European law, 76–79, 219

European Parliament: Cypriot representation in, 181; discussion of failed referendum, 182–84; establishment of permanent contact group with TC authorities, 195; functions of, 5, 6; Verheugen's reprimand of Papadopoulos, 182

European Parliament's High-Level Contact Group, 231, 232

European Security and Defense Identity (ESDI), 59

European solution, 188–89, 195, 211, 214–19

European Union: acceptance of Turkish candidacy, xiv–xv, 3, 12, 27, 46, 59; accession of Cyprus to, 6, 59, 60, 61–62, 74, 102, 108, 114, 127, 132, 157, 167, 183–84; accession of Turkey to, 145, 189, 198, 199–203, 205–9, 212, 260–61; address to political isolation of TC community, 230–32; Anastasiades's revelation of human rights violations to, 153; Annan Plan's role for, 53, 55–56; Armenian issue and, 232–33; assistance to candidate states, 14; Brussels Summit (2004), 205–11; Brussels Summit (2006), 226–30; challenge to Papadopoulos government, 226; Christofias administration and, 263–64; concept of democracy, 4, 181; concept of security, 4, 149–50; concerns over Turkish presidential election (2007), 232–33; conciliatory politics of, 3–8, 19–20, 106, 207, 210, 226, 228, 255–56; conflict resolution strategy for Cyprus problem, 62; conflict with Papadopoulos government, 251; Copenhagen Summit (1993), 14; Copenhagen Summit (2002), 6;

European Union (*cont.*)
criticism of Papadolpoulos's European solution, 188, 189; cross-border economic pact between Greece/Turkey, 124–25; Cypriot representation in, 230; decision on Turkey's accession, 228; demilitarization of Cyprus under Annan Plan and, 58; denial of TRNC role in, 252; deviations from nationalist world view in Cyprus/Greece/Turkey and, 47–50; dismissal of Turkish addendum to customs union requirement, 213; dissociation of Turkey's accession from Cyprus problem, 199–203, 206, 209, 215, 254; economic aid to TC community, 105–7, 230, 242; economic opportunities of membership, 244; effect of accession process on Cyprus, 91, 100, 104–7; effect of globalization on membership in, 25; endorsement of citizen peace movement, 95, 99; endorsement of TCs' political standing, 188; enlargement process, 6–8, 50, 105; *EU Federation Study Group*, 38; Europeanization process of, 8; evolution from European Community, 6, 14; as factor of political/social change in Cyprus, 62–65, 74–75, 76–77, 101, 102–7, 108, 244, 249–59; as factor of political/social change in GC community, 159; as factor of political/social change in Greece, 6, 9–14, 218, 238, 255–59; as factor of political/social change in Turkey, 6, 14–15, 19–20, 23–31, 70–71, 75–77, 118, 119–23, 130, 254, 255–59; failure of Hague talks and relations with Turkey, 71; Finnish initiative, 226–28; focus on politico-legal complications in Eastern Mediterranean, 232; founding of, 3; GC administration's consideration of court case against, 185; goals of, 3–4; governance of, 4–7; Greek-Turkish low-level politics and, 32–35; Green Line Regulation, 247–48; institution of euro, 6; institutions of, 4–6; integration of Cyprus into, xvi, 3, 67; Islamic fundamentalism in Turkey and, 24–27; Kurdish problem and, 19–20; low-level political cooperation between Greece and Turkey and, 32–35; Luxemburg Summit, 213–14; Maastricht Treaty (1992), 6, 14; measures for promotion of trade between northern Cyprus/EU, 105–7, 109; mediators prevented from explaining Annan Plan in GC community, 152; nationalism vs., 3–4, 6; nationalist rejection of Annan Plan and, 58–59; Ocalan trial and, 19–20; Papadopoulos's goals for accession to, 172–73; Papadopoulos's lack of understanding of culture of, 114; Papadopoulos's "no" campaign and, 153–54, 155, 160, 181–84; peace-enhancing process in Cyprus, 249–51; peace rallies calling for entrance into, 62–66; political culture of, 3–8, 20, 25, 40–41, 60, 79, 105, 114, 115, 123, 125, 183–84, 200, 209–10; political/legal entanglements around Cyprus problem, 196–97; postreferenda view of TC administration, 185; postreferendum approach to Cyprus problem, 193–96; pressure over Ledra Street crossing, 235; pressures for resumption of Cyprus talks, 127; privileges/obligation of Cyprus under framework of, 104–7; proposal to open trade with TC community, 185, 186, 193–95, 196–97, 228; psychological isolation of Papadopoulos, 117;

questioning of Denktash's nationalism, 160; recognition of citizen peace movement, 36; reforms induced in Turkey by, 19–20, 28–30, 70–71, 118, 119–22; refusal to recognize TRNC, 192, 195, 222; reprimand of Turkey, 226, 228, 232; requirements for accession to, 6–8, 76–77, 79, 210–11; response to Papadopoulos's "no" campaign, 171, 185; review of Central Bank in Turkish Cypriot State, 137; rule of law as cornerstone of, 5, 76, 221, 253, 254; signing of Treaty of Accession by Republic of Cyprus, 67, 74–75, 80, 116; status of TC community in, 252–53; support of Annan Plan, 117; tapping gas/oil reserves off coast of Cyprus and, 238; TC Left's politics of peace and, 45; TCs' desire for unification with, 73–74, 102, 118; tension between GC government/other states, 244; TRNC attempted backdoor entry into, 79–80; Turkey's accession talks, 118–19; Turkish Islamic fundamentalists' appeal to, 23–24; U.S. entrenchment in Iraq crisis and, 126; view of Cyprus's membership, 260, 261; view of failure of Hague talks, 73; view of freed movement in Cyprus, 80; view of GC government, 229–30. *See also* acceding states; accession process to EU membership; accession to EU; *acquis communautaire* (EU law); Council of European Union (Council of Ministers); European Parliament; European Union law

European Union institutions, 3–8

European Union law: enforcement of, 5; Europeanization and, 8; GC administration's appeal to, 196–97; harmonization of national institutions with, 6–8; Papadopoulos's attempt to use to advantage, 188–89, 195, 206–7, 209–11, 213–14, 215, 226, 228–29, 252; ratified Annan Plan as part of, 136; as solution to Cyprus problem, 186; TC harmonization with, 137; Turkey's obligation to, 254

European Union treaties, 7. *See also* Treaty of Accession to EU

Euro-reformers. *See* postnationalist reformers

EU-Turkish relations: acceptance of Turkish candidacy, xiv–xv, 3, 12, 27, 46, 59; accession negotiations, 71, 145, 189, 198, 205–9, 212, 213–14; accession process, 214, 227–28, 232–33, 260–61; application for membership, 14, 19; aspirations for accession to EU, 53, 71, 74–75, 76–77, 115, 118–19, 145; benefits of acceptance Annan Plan to, 60–61; Brussels Summit (2004), 205–11; Brussels Summit (2006), 226–30; candidacy accepted, xiv–xv, 3, 12, 27, 46, 59; complications from failed referendum, 71, 75, 199–203, 232–33, 234, 235, 244; concerns over Turkish presidential election (2007), 232–33; dissociation of Turkey's accession from Cyprus problem, 199–203, 206, 209, 215, 254, 262; *Djavit An v. Turkey* and, 77–79; EU reprimand of, 226, 228, 232; EU requirement of negotiation for solution in Cyprus, 119; failure of Hague talks and, 71; Finnish initiative and, 226–28; *Loizidou v. Turkey*, 76–77; Luxemburg Summit, 213–14; need for revival of 2003–4 momentum and, 263; Ocalan sentence and, 19–20; *Xenides-Arestis v. Turkey* and, 219

Evert, Miltiades, 10
Expected Utility Analysis methodology, 140–41

Faiz, Muharrem, 247
Famagusta, 221, 226–27, 236, 240
Far Right nationalist colonels, 8
fascism, 165
federation (GC understanding of), 177, 190
Fiba Holding Group, 256
Financial Mirror, 95
Finansbank, 256
Finnish initiative, 226–28
Finnish Presidency, 226–27, 228
Fisher, Roger, 34
Flight Information Regions (FIR) regulations, 123
force, xiii, 4
foreign policy: correlation between internal democracy and, 122; Europeanization and, 12–13; of GC government vs. EU, 230; of Greece, 125, 131, 146; modification of Greece policy toward Turkey, 12–13, 30; of PASOK government in Greece, 11; of Turkey, 15, 121–22, 125
foreign powers argument, 145–46, 153, 156, 159, 171
Former Yugoslav Republic of Macedonia, 11
France, 206, 207, 208
freedom, 99, 120
freedom of assembly, 78–79
freedom of movement of citizens, 77–78
freedom of speech, 78–79, 233
free movement across green line: consequences of, 80–104; EU peace-enhancing initiatives and, 249; Greek Orthodox Church and, 156; nationalist objections to, 96; opportunity offered by, 244; Papadopoulos's interpretation of results, 109–10; rationale for lifting restrictions, 72–80

Gambari, Ibrahim A., 229
gas pipeline, 124
GC refugees. *See* refugees (GCs)
GCs. *See* Greek Cypriot (GC) community; Greek Cypriots (GCs)
General Affairs Council, 230
genocide, 232
German Presidency, 231
globalization: Cyprus problem and, 68; effect on Cyprus problem, xv; effect on Greek society/economy, 11–12; ethnocentric nationalism and, 50; EU acceleration of, 30; EU institutions and, 6; need for EU membership and, 25; TCs' view of TRNC and, 73–74
governance: of bicommunal federation, 53–54, 55, 56–57; in Greece, 8–11; in Turkey, 14–18
grassroots movement: against Annan Plan, 156; interethnic encounters across green line as, 80–104; peace rallies as, 62–66. *See also* citizen peace movement (Cyprus)
Great Britain: Annan Plan and, 53, 55; envoy to Hague talks, 68; GC nationalist view of Annan Plan and, 145; New York talks and, 128; representation at Hague talks, 67
Greece: acceptance of Turkish candidacy to EU, 12; alignment with GC position on Annan Plan, 183; Annan Plan negotiations and, 171; Balkan crisis, 11; benefits of acceptance Annan Plan

to, 60–61; change in policy toward Turkey, xv, 12–13, 29, 30, 91, 259; citizen-initiated activities for reconciliation in, 46, 123; civil war in, 8; coup d'état in Cyprus by, xiv; coup in, xiv; deconstruction of nationalism in, 10, 11–14, 30, 32–35, 33; deviations from nationalist world view in, xiii, 47–50; dictatorship in, 8; earthquake diplomacy, 3; economy of, 11, 131, 256–57; ethnocentric nationalism in, xii, 8–14, 30, 33; EU as factor in political/social change in, 9–14; EU peace-enhancing initiatives in, 249; Europeanization of, 8–14, 31; exports to EU, 256–57; foreign policy of, 12–13; as guarantor power in Cyprus, 54, 134, 136–37, 147, 259; incompatibility of democracy with nationalism in, xiii; intervention in Cyprus, xii; junta in, 8; low-level political cooperation between Turkey and, 46; membership in EU, 8; membership in European Community, 8–9, 14; membership in NATO, 8, 15, 257; *metapoliteysi*/democracy in, 8–9; negotiations on Annan Plan and, 129, 132; New York talks, 127–29; Nikiforos war drills and, 216–18, 256; oil drilling issue and, 238, 256; Olympic Games in, 131; opening of natural gas pipeline, 257; on outcome of Brussels Summit, 211; participation in Cypriot blood donation event, 98; PASOK government, 10–12, 130–31, 218; political parties process of reconciliation, 165; political support of Papadopoulos, 256; rapprochement with Turkey, 3; refusal of final Annan Plan, 138; relapse to nationalism in, 10–11; relations with Turkey (*see* Greek-Turkish relations); representation at Hague talks, 67; resumption of talks based on Annan plan and, 131; role in Annan Plan, 53, 54, 55, 135–36; shared culture with Turkey, 123–24; significance of EU culture in, 6–7; support of Annan Plan, 127, 173, 175; support of Turkish accession to EU, 200, 201–2; tension between right and left wings in, 8; as threat to northern Cyprus, 255. *See also* Greek-Turkish relations

Greek Civil War, 8

Greek coup, xiv

Greek Cypriot (GC) community: approach to Cyprus problem, 255; bridge across Ledra Street and, 234–35; challenge of interethnic democracy in, 20; citizen groups in, 35–46; communication with TC community, xiv; conflict between right and left wing, 44–45, 166; criticism of Papadopoulos's reservations on renewed negotiations, 101–2; desire for reunification, 246–47; dilemma of TC property law, 224–25; economic impact of "no" vote on Annan Plan, 237–39; effect of nationalistic thinking on, 88–89; election for presidency (2008), 259, 261–62; ethnocentric nationalism in, xii, xiii–xiv; human rights violations in prior to referendum, 151–52; impact of EU acceptance of Turkey's candidacy, xv; interethnic impact of "no" vote on referendum, 216–19, 237–39, 240, 243, 244–48; international community's acceptance of referendum results, 185; jokes about Cypriot problem, xi; Leder Street barricade and, 234–35; left wing in, 44–45; loss of motivation for settlement, 244;

Greek Cypriot (GC) community (*cont.*) media coverage of peace rallies, 64; memories of pain in, xiii–xiv, 73, 85–93, 101, 250–51; modernization of, 41; monocommunal groups in, 39; nationalist view of democracy, 57; "no" campaign in, 140–51; opening of Kato Pyrgos-Limnitis crossing, 235; opposition to items in Annan Plan, 66; persistence of nationalist thinking in, 112–13, 181, 216–19; political effects of "no" vote on referendum, 191–204, 206, 209, 228–29, 230, 234–37, 239–43, 244, 245, 251, 261; position on reunification, 141, 143; postreferendum report, 226–27; preference for negotiation of solution, 188; proposals for Annan Plan revisions, 133–35; referendum of April 24, 2004 in, 139, 181; relapse into extreme nationalism, 151–59; relationship with TC community, xii, xv–xvi, 216–19, 227, 239–40, 243–48, 261 (*see also* free movement across green line); representation in EU, 230, 231; response to EU's dissociation of Turkey from Cyprus problem, 200–201; response to free movement across green line, 81–104; response to Papadopoulos's campaign against Annan Plan, 143–47, 150, 157–59; response to peace rallies, 64; revelation of missing persons information, 250–51; revival of nationalism in, 160–62, 244–45; revival of Nikiforos war drills, 216–18; security of, 254–55; significance of EU culture in, 6–7; support of Annan Plan, 64, 65–66; UN outrage over "no" campaign of, 171–75; uproar triggered by Matsakis, 189–91; view of Annan Plan in, 58–59; violence against GCs, xi, 160–62; violence against TCs, xiii–xiv. *See also* Greek Cypriots (GCs); refugees (GCs); Republic of Cyprus

Greek Cypriot National Guard, 84, 216–18

Greek Cypriot nationalism/nationalists: Annan Plan and, 55, 56–57; campaign against Annan Plan, 142–51; challenges to, 116–27; as challenge to citizen peace movement, 38; conflicts of 1960s and, 179; EU process and, 104–7; GC defiance of, 81–93; negotiation based on Annan Plan and, 130, 131–33; Papadopoulos's response to postreferendum report, 176–81; persistence of, 108–10, 112–13; rejection of Annan Plan, 58–59; revival of, 160–62, 244–45; view of Cyprus problem, 251; view of ECHR ruling on property rights, 220–24; view of final Annan Plan, 138. *See also* Papadopoulos, Tassos; Papadopoulos administration

Greek Cypriots (GCs): Annan Plan for property rights of, 134–35; application for compensation for property, 224; arrests for crossing into TRNC, 85; bicommunal events involving, 89, 97–98; class action suit against Republic of Cyprus, 225; conflicted state of mind, 246; effects of free movement across green line, 72; establishment of Claims Settlement Council and, 111–12; *Loizidou v. Turkey* case of, 76–77, 112, 253; noncommunication with TCs, xiv; positions of citizen peace movement members, 45; rapprochement activities of, 96; response to free movement across green line, 81–88; TC property law and, 220, 222–23, 224; view of Annan Plan, 58–59; *Xenides-Arestis v. Turkey* and, 219

Greek government: change of date for referenda in Cyprus, 139; coup, xiv; dictatorship as, 8; Kurdish problem in Turkey and, 19; low-level politics between Turkey and, 32–35; PASOK government, 10–12, 130–31, 218; Simitis government, 159; support of Annan Plan, 146; support of Turkish accession to EU, 201–2; Tzanetakis government, 9. *See also* Greece; Greek-Turkish relations

Greek identity, 11–12

Greek military (troops): Annan Plan for presence in Cyprus, 54, 134, 136–37; confidence-building measures with Turkey, 257; junta/dictatorship by, 8; redeployment of under Annan Plan, 54; Toxotis exercises, 216–18, 256

Greek Ministry of Foreign Affairs, 124

Greek nationalism, 10, 11–14, 30, 33

Greek Orthodox bishop, 152

Greek Orthodox Church of Cyprus, 152, 155–57

Greeks, xiv, 46

Greek society, 11–12

Greek-Turkish business council, 257

Greek-Turkish Forum, 46

Greek-Turkish relations: acceptance of Turkish candidacy to EU and, xv; Aegean Sea and, 30, 123, 125, 256; Annan Plan and, 62; benefits to of acceptance of Annan Plan, 60–61; central question of, xii–xiii; citizen-initiated activities for reconciliation, xiv, 46, 123–24; cross-border economic pact, 124–25, 255, 256–57; Cypriot nationalists and, 108–9; effect of Europeanization on, xv–xvi, 12–14, 200; emergence of voices of peace in civil society, 35; EU-based reforms in Turkey and, 29–30; Justice and Development Party in Turkey and, 24–25; Karamalis's visit to Turkey, 257–59; Kurdish problem and, 18–19; low-level politics of rapprochement, 32–35, 123; military cooperation agreement, 257; nationalist conditioning and, xiii–xiv; natural gas pipeline agreement, 124, 257; Olympic Truce, 124; peace-enhancing postnationalist politics and, xv–xvi, 255–56; political cooperation, 124; rapprochement, xv, 3, 30, 91, 108, 123–24, 255–56; rejection of Annan Plan and, 58, 59; rise of New Democracy Party in Greece and, 131

green line: consequences of movement across, 81–104, 94–95, 96–99, 101–4; EU peace-enhancing initiatives and, 249; free movement across, 72–80; nationalist objections to movement across, 96; regulation of, 247

Green Line Regulation, 247

Green Party, 158

Grey Wolves, 152, 161

Gül, Abdullah, 69, 133, 207

Gül government, 69–70

Hade, 39

Hague talks, 67–70, 73, 92, 116, 215

Halkbank, 256

Halki Orthodox Seminary, 258

Hannay, David, 215

Harvard Study Group, 39, 45

Hellenic state: attempt to use EU to reestablish Cyprus as, 252; fear of ethnic remixing in, 246; Papadopoulos's view of Cyprus as, 110, 178; view of Annan Plan in light of, 58

Hellenism, 145–46, 155–57, 171, 245

Helsinki Summit (EU), xiv–xv, 12, 27, 210, 238
heroism/heroes, xiii–xiv, 151
history: of Cypriot communities, xiii–xiv, 97; of Greeks/Turks, 258; nationalist treatment of, xi, xiv, 86–87, 150–51, 258
hospitality, 82–84
Hulsman, John, 126
humanity, 86–88, 93, 97–99
human rights: acceding states' responsibility toward, 7; association with interethnic peace/reconciliation, 65; *Djavit An v. Turkey* concerning, 77–79; as goal of reform Islamists, 23; Kurdish problem in Turkey and, 18–20; *Loizidou v. Turkey* concerning, 76–77, 112, 253; missing persons information and, 85–86, 101, 250–51; new realizations concerning violations of, 48–49; obstruction of free movement of citizens and, 77–78; in Turkey, 233; violation in GC community prior to referendum, 151–52; *Xenides-Arestis v. Turkey* and, 219
Hussein, Saddam, 126

Iacovou, George, 168, 176
identity: citizens' responsibilities dissociated from nationalist concept of, 41–42; Greek nationalist concept of, 11–12; Islamist views of in Turkey, 23; nationalist concept of, xi, 98–99; of Turkish society, 119–20; Turkish state's aim for establishing, 14–15
immigration, 28, 33–34
Imnia/Kardak islet, 125
infrastructure, 125
institutions. *See* European Union institutions

intercommunal relations. *See* interethnic relations
interethnic communications, xii, xiv, 39, 88–89
interethnic democracy: as challenge for Cyprus solution, 20; of EU, 183; nationalist exclusion of, 63, 175; rejection of, 177–81; TC/GC readiness to reengage in negotiations on, 261; in Turkey, 20; under Annan Plan, 180. *See also* Annan Plan
interethnic economic activities, 247–48
interethnic rapprochement: citizen-initiated activities between Turkey/Greece, 46–47; established by citizen groups in Cyprus, 35–46; revelations concerning missing persons and, 85–86, 101, 250–51. *See also* free movement across green line
interethnic relations: citizen peace movement and, 35–46; effect of ethnocentric nationalism on, xii, xiii; EU peace-enhancing initiatives and, 249; EU requirements concerning, 7; exhumations/funerals of missing persons and, 251; following failure of Annan Plan, 216–19, 237–39, 243, 244–48, 260; free movement across green line and, 80–99, 101–4; nationalist conditioning of, xiii–xiv; necessity of comprehensive settlement, 261; opening of crossings in Cyprus and, 237; Papadopoulos's interpretation of, 109; renewal of mistrust following failure of Annan Plan, 216–19, 239–40; during run-up to referenda, 162
interethnic violence: in Cyprus, xii, xiii–xiv; healing for, 85–88, 101, 250–51; in Turkey, 18–20

international community: criticism of Papadopoulos by, 154, 171, 185; disinterest of in Cyprus problem, 261; failure of Hague talks and, 126; Iraq disarmament and, 68; modification of approach to TRNC by, 192; nationalist rejection of Annan Plan and, 58; postreferenda view of TC administration, 185, 192–95; proposal for ending TC isolation, 251; recognition of citizens in peace-building process, 36; recognition of citizens' role in peace building process by, 45; refusal of to recognize TRNC, 192; response of to free movement across green line, 72, 80; support of Annan Plan by, 117; U.S. entrenchment in Iraq crisis and, 126; view of Denktash's/Papadopoulos's resistance to Annan Plan by, 115. *See also* European Union; United Nations
International Crisis Group, 244
International Herald Tribune, 123, 227
international law, 4, 169, 254
International Monetary Fund, 137
Internet, 39
intraethnic conflict, 160–62
invasion of Cyprus, xi, xiv, 103, 166, 219
Iraq, 18, 68–70, 126
Islamic fundamentalism, 18, 20–27
Islamic nationalism, 23
Islamic Raiders of Greater Eastern Front, 22, 26

Jenkins, Gareth, 16, 17
Joint Defense Dogma, 216–17, 218
journalists, 46, 97
junta in Greece, 8
justice, 1, 2, 42. *See also* European Court of Human Rights (ECHR); European Court of Justice; human rights; property rights
Justice and Development Party (Turkey): EU process and, 24–26; rapprochement policy toward Greece, 24–25; reforms of, 70; rise of reformist voices within, 25–27; rise to power in Turkey, 24, 69; September 11, 2001 terrorist attacks on U.S. and, 26; victory in 2007 election, 233

KADEM, 65–66, 247
Karamalis, Costas: official visit to Turkey, 257–59; opening of natural gas pipeline, 257; suggestions by for Turkey's accession plan, 206–7; support of Turkey's accession to EU, 200, 201; at talks in Switzerland, 133
Karamanlis, Constantine, 9
Karpas, 135
Kasoulides, Ioannis, 261–62
Kemalism, 14–16, 21–22, 24
Kemalist nationalism, 21–22
Keridis, Dimitris, 9, 13, 29, 30
Ketencoglou, Muammer, 123–24
Khaleej Times, 177
Kibris, 161
Kormakit, 135
Kosovo, 262, 263
Kurdish nationalism, 18
Kurdish problem, 18–20, 28, 120
Kurdish Workers Party (PKK), 18–20, 120

Lausanne Treaty Foundation, 124
law. *See acquis communautaire* (EU law); European Union law; international law
Lebanon, 237

Lederach, John Paul: on conflict transformation, 1–3; on connections across conflict lines, 85; on middle-range leaders, 43–45; on requirements for effective role of citizens in peacebuilding process, 36; on role of peace constituency, 42; on shared cultural values, 84
Ledra Street Crossing, 234–37
left-wing groups/ideologies: citizen peace movement and, 44–45; civil war in Greece and, 8; compliance with ECHR ruling on GC property and, 224; conflict between right wing and, 166; in Cyprus, 44–45; nationalistic shift in TC community, 247; reconciliation with right wing in Greece, 9–10; role in failure of Annan Plan, 163–68, 169–70; of TC community, 44–45; and TC parliamentary elections (2003), 118; tension between right wing and in Greece, 8; in Turkey, 17. *See also* AKEL; communism/communists; PASOK government
Limassol, 227
Loizidou, Titina, 76–77, 253
Loizidou v. Turkey, 76–77, 112, 253
lop-level leadership, 43. *See also specific leader by name*
loss (revisitation of), 82–88, 101, 250–51
low-level politics, 32–35, 46, 123
Luxemburg Summit, 213–14, 255
Lyssarides, Vassos, 188

Maastricht Treaty (1992), 6, 14
Macedonia, Former Yugoslav Republic of, 11
majoritarian nationalism/nationalists, 55–56, 58–59, 106, 168–69, 177–81.

See also Greek Cypriot nationalism/nationalists
majority (Annan Plan), 53
Makarios, Archbishop, 143, 146
Marshall Plan, 8
Matsakis, Marios, 189–91
media: attacks on citizen peace movement, 38; bicommunal participation in, 97; campaign against Annan Plan, 151–55; coverage of exhumations/funerals of missing persons, 251; coverage of peace rallies in Nicosia, 62, 64; criticism of Turkish politics, 18; on Greek support of Papadopoulos, 256; on Greek-Turkish relations, 123; liberalization of in Turkey, 13, 28, 121; on Matsakis's denunciation of biethnic federation, 189; middle-range leadership and, 43; on Papadopoulos's return from Brussels, 211; reports of humanity/kindness, 97; reports of Turkish military movements, 238; on tapping gas/oil reserves, 237; TC representation of GCs, 247
mediation, 2
Mega, 155
memories of pain, xiii–xiv, 73, 85–93, 101, 250–51. *See also* free movement across green line
metapoliteysi, 8–9
middle-range leadership, 43, 50
militant interventionism, 160–62
missing persons, 85–86, 101, 250–51
Mitsotakis, Constantine, 9, 11
modernization, 41
Monitoring Committee, 134
monocommunal groups, 39. *See also* citizen peace movement (Cyprus)
monoethnic state polity: Annan Plan and, 57; of ethnocentric nationalism,

xii, 177–79, 189–91; peace negotiations and, 132; of rival nationalist leaders, 116–17
Motherland Party, 17
Movement for the Independent and Federal Cyprus, 77
multiethnic societies (nationalism in), 15, 173
Mustafa, Arif, 253

narcissistic psychology, xiii–xiv, 6, 7, 111
nation, 41, 169
National Bank of Greece, 256
National Council (GC), 172
National Guard, 84, 217–18
national identity. *See* identity
national interests, 49, 50
nationalism: absolute value of nation/sovereignty to, 4, 6, 41, 169; absolutist approach of, 168–69; adversarial stance of, xii, xiii, 41, 45, 47, 49, 87, 88, 89, 93, 98, 109, 130, 182, 184, 200, 210, 249; aims of in Turkey, 14–16; of AKEL, 163–67; Annan Plan and, 55, 142–51; challenges to, 86–88, 99–100, 101, 102–4; concept of democracy, 4, 57; concept of security, 218; conditions conducive to during crisis, 70; conflict-transforming capacity of EU and, xvi, 3–8, 101; defiance of national/international law, 4; deviations from in Cyprus, xiii, xv, 47–50, 80–101 (*see also* citizen peace movement [Cyprus]); deviations from in Greece, xiii, xv, 10, 11–14, 30, 32–35, 47–50 (*see also* low-level politics); deviations from in Turkey, xiii, xv, 32–35, 47–50, 119–22, 130 (*see also* low-level politics); of DIKO, 159; elimination of shared culture, 84; erosion of in TC community, 65; ethnocentric, majoritarian understanding of democracy, 177–81; EU framework of conciliatory politics and, 3–4, 6–7; EU process and, 104–7; Europeanization of Greece and, 11–12; EU strategy for resolution of Cyprus problem and, 62; of GC media, 154–55; Greek Orthodox Church and, 155–57; historiography of, xiii–xiv, 86–87, 251, 258; hopes for EU membership and, 263–64; incompatibility with democracy, xii–xiii, 4, 112; interethnic relations and, xii, xiii–xiv; introduction of religion into in Turkey, 21; justification of use of force/violence, xiii, 4, 216–18; of Kurdish Workers Party, 20–21; low-level political cooperation vs., 33; monoethnic concept of, xii, 158; narcissistic mind of, xiii–xiv, 6; peace process and, 70; persistence of in TC/GC administrations, 108–15, 142–51, 162, 173, 184–91; reality vs., 146–48, 150; rejection of Annan Plan, 58–59; relapse to in GC community, 151–59, 160–62, 160–63, 244–45; relapse to in Greece, 10–11; relapse to in Turkey, 232–33; retardation of the development of civil society, 41; shattering of concept of identity, 98–99; shift back to in TC community, 247; and treatment of pain/suffering, xiii–xiv, 86, 250–51; in Turkey, 14–18; as underpinning of Cyprus problem, xii–xiii, 163; violence arising from, 86–88, 99, 160–62; and withholding of information concerning missing persons, 250. *See also* ethnocentric nationalism; Greek Cypriot nationalism/nationalists; Greek nationalism;

nationalism (*cont.*)
  majoritarian nationalism/nationalists; secessionist nationalism/nationalists; Turkish Cypriot nationalism/nationalists; Turkish nationalism/nationalists
nationalist mind: association of security with military in, 148–49; concept of democracy in, 177–81; entrapment in tautologies of, 108–15; EU's dissociation of from political culture of nation-state/international relations, 4; interpretations of rapprochement efforts within, 108–15; reactivation of in GC community, 140–58, 160–62; reality vs., 146–48, 150; shift away from, 46; view of interethnic power sharing in, 190
Nationalist Movement Party, 22
Nationalist Peace Party (MBP), 118
nationalist psychology, 30
nationalist rhetoric, 10
nationalists: Annan Plan and, 56, 137–38; citizen peace movement and, 38; competition with European, postnational reformers by, 11, 12–13, 70, 127; conflicted state of mind generated by, 246; dialogue with Turkey and, 12; failure of Hague talks and, 71; impact of on negotiations for peace in Cyprus, xiv; negotiation based on Annan Plan and, 130, 131–33; New York talks and, 128; objections to citizen-initiated activities between Greeks/Turks, 46; opposition to Talat's Cyprus policy, 243; rejection of Annan Plan, 58; remobilization of troops in Cyprus, 216–18; response to peace rallies, 62, 63; response to UN postreferendum report, 176–81; understanding of "federation," 177–81; view of Cyprus problem, 251; view of property law, 220–24; view of UN, 122. *See also* Denktash, Rauf R.; Papadopoulos, Tassos
nationalist stereotypes, 13, 47–50, 81, 82–90
nationalist symbols, 150
nationalist world- and life view, xii–xiv, 3–4, 145–48
National Movement Party, 17
National Order Party, 21
National Salvation Party, 21
National Security Council (Turkey), 15, 120
national sovereignty, 4, 6, 30
National Unity Party (UBP), 118
nation-states: ethnocentric nationalist view of, xii, 6; EU demand for reconceptualization of, 30; EU framework of conciliatory politics and, 3–4, 6; justification of use of violence in maintenance of, xiii, 4
NATO: Greece's membership in, 8, 15; Greek-Turkish military cooperation agreement, 257; rejection of Annan Plan and, 59; Turkey's membership in, 15; Turkey's use of against Cyprus, 213
negotiations: based on Annan Plan, 130–33, 142, 175; in Bürgenstock, Switzerland, 132–33, 142; in conflict transformation, 2; in Cyprus, 131–32; Denktash's approach to, 132; Denktash's refusal to attend, 68–69, 132, 239–40; effect of ethnocentric nationalism on, xii; failure of, xiv; Hague talks, 67–70, 73, 92, 116, 215; led by UN, xi, xiv; New York talks, 127–29, 171–72; Papadopoulos's refusal to resume, 204, 230, 231, 243; Papadopoulos's strategy, 110, 113–14, 115, 132–33, 142,

172, 240–41, 242, 243; solution fatigue and, 244–46
New Democracy Party (Greece), 9, 12, 130–31
New York talks, 127–29, 171–72
Nicosia, 39–40, 62–66
Nikiforos war drills, 216–18, 236, 256
noncommunication, xiv, 88–89
nongovernmental organizations (NGOs), 28, 40, 62, 89, 94
North Atlantic Treaty Organization. *See* NATO
northern Cyprus. *See also* Turkish Cypriot (TC) community; Turkish Republic of Northern Cyprus (TRNC)
"no to a solution" front, 69–70
NTV, 238

Ocalan, Abdullah, 18, 19–20
Ocalan, Osman, 19, 28
occupation of Cyprus, 166, 216–17, 219, 261
oil/gas reserves: crisis between Cyprus/Turkey over, 234, 237–39, 244, 256; opening of natural gas pipeline between Greece/Turkey, 257
Olympic Games (2004), 124, 131
Olympic Truce, 124
open-market systems, 7
organized crime, 33–34
Ortam (TC newspaper), 65–66
OXI, 150, 210
Ozal government, xi

pain/suffering, xiii–xiv, 48, 85–86, 251
Pamuk, Orhan, 233
Pan-Hellenic Socialist Movement (PASOK). *See* PASOK
Papadakis, Yiannis, 90

Papadopoulos, Tassos: agreement/disagreement with peace-builders' assumptions, 117; agreement to tap oil/gas reserves, 237–39, 240, 244, 256; AKEL's support of, 163–70; Anastasiades's rebuke of, 153; and Annan's call for referendum, 67; approach to Cyprus problem, 109–10, 111–15, 255; attempt to use EU law to GC advantage, 114, 185–86, 188–89, 195, 206–7, 209–11, 213–14, 215, 226, 228–29, 252; blocking of TC trade with EU, 213; campaign against Annan Plan, 142–48, 150, 151–52, 153–54, 155–59, 172–73, 175, 202, 210, 245; commendation of Turkey's efforts in negotiations, 199; concept of federation, 177, 190; concept of security, 148, 150, 218; consent to Turkey's accession to EU, 205, 209–11; criticism of, 101–2, 154, 189; demand for Turkish recognition of Republic of Cyprus, 188–89, 206–7, 213, 214, 228; demands at Brussels Summit, 206–7, 208, 209; and dilemma of TC property law, 220–25; diplomatic reprimand of, 226; dispatch of Iacocou to Russia, 168, 169; election for presidency (2008), 261–62; election of (2003), 66, 159; EU and nationalistic goals of, 181–82, 214; EU castigation of, 229–30; EU concept of security and, 150; EU outrage over "no" campaign of, 171, 181–84; and European solution to Cyprus problem, 186, 188–89, 195, 215; Finnish initiative and, 226–28; Greece's support of, 256; Hague talks and, 67–68; integration into EU and, 184; international community's view of, 251; legacy of, 262–63; negotiation based on Annan Plan, 129–30, 131–33, 142, 175;

Papadopoulos, Tassos (*cont.*)
  New York talks, 127–29, 171–72; objection to EU upgrades of TCs, 231, 240; opening of crossings, 235–37, 240; opposition to Annan Plan, 67–68, 71, 116, 117, 255; outcome of Brussels Summit for, 210–11, 212; persistence of nationalist thinking by, 108–10, 112–14, 116–17, 142–48, 150, 172–73, 176–81, 184, 185–86, 203, 216–19; postnationalist reforms in Turkey/Greece and, 125; postreferendum approach to Cyprus problem, 186–89, 195, 215; pressures for solution in Cyprus and, 127; proposal of confidence-building measures for TC community, 186–88, 240; proposals for Annan Plan revisions, 133–34; refusal of final Annan Plan, 138; refusal to resume negotiations on comprehensive settlement, 230, 231, 240–41, 243, 244–46, 260; response to EU's dissociation of Turkey from Cyprus problem, 201–3; response to UN postreferendum report, 176–81; return from Brussels Summit, 211; revival of Nikiforos war drills, 216–18, 236; satisfaction with outcome of referenda, 139; signing of Treaty of Accession, 175; strategy for negotiations, 110, 113–14, 115, 130, 132–33, 142, 172, 240–41, 242, 243; strategy for opening crossings, 236; at talks in Switzerland, 132–33, 142; UN outrage over "no" campaign of, 171–75; UN resistance to resuming negotiations and, 242; UN's view of, 242, 261; view of Republic of Cyprus, 113
Papadopoulos administration: agreement with Lebanon/Egypt on oil reserves, 237–39, 244, 256; attempt to use EU law to GC advantage, 185–86, 188–89, 195, 206–7, 209–11, 213–14, 215, 226, 228–29, 252; bridge across Ledra Street and, 234–35; campaign against Annan Plan, 151–52, 153–54, 162, 230, 231, 240–41, 244–46, 254; concerns over free movement across green line, 102–3; consideration of case against EU in European Court of Justice, 185; criticism of "no" campaign of, 154; denial of antifederalist approach, 189; dilemma of TC property law, 220–25; EU castigation of, 229–30; EU challenge to, 226; EU outrage over "no" campaign of, 171, 181–84; European solution to Cyprus problem, 215–19; Finnish initiative and, 226–28; human rights violations by, 151–52, 153–54; immobility following referenda, 170; interethnic rapprochement and, 99–100; international community's view of, 251; legacy of, 262–63; nationalist mind of, 95–96; objection to EU upgrades of TCs, 231; opening of Kato Pyrgos-Limnitis crossing, 235; persistence of nationalist thinking, 108–10, 112–13, 162, 176–81, 216–19; privileges/obligation of under EU framework, 104–7; proposal of confidence-building measures for TC community, 186–88; reaction to opening of trade between EU/TC community, 194, 196–98, 226–27; refusal to return to negotiating table, 226–27, 244–46, 254, 260; rejection of Annan Plan, 191, 255; rejection of interethnic citizen contact, 96; reservation about Annan Plan concerning territory, 140–41; response to EU's dissociation of Turkey from Cyprus problem, 200–203; response

to UN postreferendum report, 176–81; response to U.S. policy toward TC north, 196; revival of Nikiforos war drills, 216–18; strategy within EU, 214–15; UN outrage over "no" campaign of, 171–75; uproar triggered by Matsakis, 189–91

Papandreou, Andreas, 10, 32–33, 34–35

Papandreou, George, 12, 131

Papandreouem initiatives, 32–33

Papapetrou, Michalis, 64, 161

parliament, 54, 56–57

partition: Annan Plan's prohibition of, 53; Denktash's attempt at entrenchment of, 132; effect of failure of referenda on, 243–44, 246–47; interethnic relations and, 88; Matsakis's view of, 189–91

PASOK, 10–12, 130–31, 146, 218

PASOK government, 10–12, 130–31, 218

Pavlos (Bishop of Kyrenia), 157

peace, 65

Peace and Conflict Studies (Barash/Webel), 122

Peace and Democracy Movement (BDH), 118

peace building: Annan Plan for. *See* Annan Plan; civil society initiatives, 35–47, 52. *See also* citizen peace movement (Cyprus); Cyprus's movement through stages of, 2–3; definition of, 1; institutions of EU for, 60; of low-level politics between Greeks/Turks, 32–35; movement across green line as, 80–104; protection of human rights through, 48–49; stages of, 1–2

peace constituency, 42–45, 101

peace-enhancing postnationalist politics, xv

peace-enhancing processes. *See* accession process; citizen peace movement (Cyprus); Europeanization; Greek-Turkish relations; rapprochement

peace-grounded democracy, xv

peace movement. *See* citizen peace movement (Cyprus)

peace process: assumptions of architects of, 117; bicommunal events facilitating, 89, 97–98; Bürgenstock talks, 132–33, 142; citizen-initiated activities between Turkey/Greece, 46–47; consequences of free movement across green line, 81–93; Cyprus negotiations, 129–30, 131–32; deviations from nationalist worldview in Cyprus/Greece/Turkey and, 47–50, 62–66, 81–104; earthquake diplomacy, 46; established by citizen groups in Cyprus, 35–46; EU process and, xv–xvi, 4, 104–7, 108; Hague talks and, 67–70; lifting of restrictions on movement across green line and, 80–104; low-level politics between Turkey/Greece, 32–35, 46; movement toward in Cyprus, 2–3; nationalism and, 108–15; need for bilateral engagement, 101; negotiations in Cyprus, 129–30; New York talks, 127–29, 171–72; relationship to democratization, 40, 42; renewed talks on Annan Plan, 125–27; requirement of full engagement of political leaders/civil society, 49; revelations concerning missing persons and, 85–86, 101, 250–51; role of civil society in, 93–94, 112–13; role of middle-range leadership in, 43; role of shared cultural values in, 84; shift away from nationalist thinking in Cyprus/Greece/Turkey, 47–50; stages of conflict transformation, 1–3; tension between pro- and antisolution

peace process (*cont.*)
  secessionist factions in TRNC, 92–93; unilateral gestures, 72–80, 93, 100–101; unilateral good will policies, 100–104. *See also* Annan Plan; Greek-Turkish relations
peace rallies, 62–66, 74–75, 93
People's Republican Party, 24, 205
PKK. *See* Kurdish Workers Party (PKK)
political accountability, 7, 49
political culture: changes in Cyprus/Greece/Turkey, xiii, xv, 33, 35–36; of Cyprus, xv; of ethnocentric nationalism, 41, 84, 88–89, 114; of EU, 3–8, 20, 25, 40–41, 60, 79, 105, 114, 115, 123, 125, 183–84, 200, 209–10; EU curbing of nationalist culture, 107; of GC community, xii, xiii, 91, 114, 143–44, 183, 200, 249–50; of Greece, xii, xiii, xv, 8–14, 47; of Greek nationalism, 11–12; initiated by citizen peace movement, 95; nationalist conditioning in Cyprus/Greece/Turkey, xiii; in nationalist states, 41; of TC community, xii, 79–80, 91; of Turkey, xii, xiii, xv, 14–31, 33, 35–36, 47, 79–80, 123; of Tzanetakis government, 9
political Islam, 20–27
political parties: addition of citizen peace building to agendas for Cyprus, 44–45; criticism of Denktash's refusal to negotiate, 101; dialogue with Turkey and, 12–13; EU influence on, 159; Europeanization of in Greece, 11–12; interaction between Greeks/Turks, 97; nationalist effect on functioning of, 41; "no" campaign and, 159–63; results of 2003 parliamentary election in TRNC, 118; role in failure of Annan Plan, 158, 163–70; in Turkey, 16–18. *See also specific party*

Politis (GC newspaper), 65–66, 187
polyethnic democracy, 57
postnationalist Europeanization. *See* Europeanization
postnationalist politics, 32–35
postnationalist reformers: competition with nationalists, 11, 12–13, 70; Europeanization and, 31; in Greece, 11–14; impact on Greek-Turkish relations, 12–13, 24–25, 32–35, 125; pressure for solution to Cyprus problem, 127; Simitis as, 11; in Turkey, 24–31
postreferendum Cyprus: change in political status of, 191–98, 206, 228–29, 230, 234–37, 239–43, 244, 251, 261; democracy and, 249; economic status, 247–48; EU proposal to open trade with TC community, 186, 193–95, 196–97, 228; interethnic relations, 216–19, 237–39, 243, 244–48, 262; international view of TC community, 185; loss of motivation for settlement, 244–47; opportunities/challenges for, 249–59; politicolegal entanglements of, 234–37, 237–39, 244, 251, 256, 262; positive changes in, 249–59; reversal of roles between TC/GC communities, 184–91
postreferendum report, 192
Powell, Colin, 128
power rebalancing, 2
Prendergast, Kieran, 173, 174
president (Annan Plan), 54, 56, 133
Presidential Council, 54, 56, 57, 133
press. *See* media
Principles of the Charter of the United Nations, 134
process of conscientization, 1–2
Prodi, Romano, 129
propaganda, 88–89
Property Board, 135

Property Commission, 224
property rights: under Annan Plan, 55, 66, 134–35; contestation of Annan Plan for, 141; establishment of Claims Settlement Council and, 111–12; EU-based reforms in Turkey, 28; European Court of Human Rights and, 219–25; *Loizidou v. Turkey*, 76–77, 112, 253; of TCs, 253; *Xenides-Arestis v. Turkey* and, 219
public opinion: on Armenian problem in Turkey, 233; basis for GCs', 143–44; change in as challenge for Christofias, 263; concerning recognition of Republic of Cyprus, 207; debates on Cyprus talks, 130; foreign powers argument and, 145–46; led by Denktash/Papadopoulos administrations, 95–96; media's impact on, 154–55; "no" campaign shaping of, 142–59; property rights applications and, 223; reality sinking in for GCs, 215; of TCs concerning federation, 92; TCs' questioning of secessionist nationalism, 65; Turkish view of Denktash, 121–22; on use of force/violence, xiii

al Qaeda, 26

rapprochement: AKEL policy of, 163–64; bicommunal events facilitating, 89, 97–98; citizen-initiated activities for reconciliation in Turkey/Greece, 46; citizen peace movement in Cyprus and, 35–46, 94–95; confidence-building measures between Greece/Turkey, 257; cross-border economic pact between Greece/Turkey and, 124–25, 255, 256–57; Denktash's view of, 110–11, 112–13; effects of, 51; EU initiatives for, 249–51; EU process and, 104–7, 108; free movement across green line and, 81–104; Greek-Turkish military cooperation, 257; in Greek-Turkish relations, xv, 3, 12–14, 24–25, 32–35, 62, 91, 123–24, 255–58; lack of support of by Cypriot administrations, 250; low-level politics and, 32–35, 46, 123; nationalist response to, 108–15; Papadopoulos's interpretation of, 109; Papadopoulos's strategy for negotiation and, 240–41, 242; Papadopoulos's view of, 109–10, 112–13; remobilization of troops in Cyprus and, 216–18; revelations concerning missing persons and, 85–86, 101, 250–51; shift away from nationalist thinking in Cyprus/Greece/Turkey, 47–50; top-level talks between Greece/Turkey, 257–59; unilateral gestures, 72–80, 93, 100–104
reconciliation: association of human rights/civil society/democracy with, 65; citizen peace movement promotion of, 35–46; between Greece/Turkey, xv; Greek Orthodox Church's plea for, 156; requirements for in Cyprus, 247; between right/left in Greece, 9
referendum/referenda: Annan's call for, 67; of April 2004, xvi, 139; critical events deterring, 68–72; economic impact of failure of, 237–39; effect of failure on TC community, 185, 186, 192–97, 213, 226–27, 228, 230; effect of on UN engagement, 242; election for presidency (2008) and, 261–62; EU response to "no" campaign prior to, 171, 181–84; failure of, 227–28; failure of Hague talks and, 73; on final

referendum/referenda (*cont.*)
   version of Annan Plan, 133, 136, 171; government voting manipulation, 152; Hague talks concerning, 66–70; interethnic impact of failure of, 216–19, 237–39, 243, 244–48, 262; New York talks on, 127–29; Papadopoulos's "no" campaign, 142–48, 150, 151–54, 245; political effects of failure of, 191–204, 206, 228–29, 230, 234–37, 239–43, 244, 251, 261; politicolegal entanglements precipitated by failure of, 262; secured at New York talks, 129; UN response to "no" campaign on, 144, 171–75, 185

reformists. *See* postnatonalist reformers

reforms: in Greece, 10–14; in Turkey, 19–20, 25–30, 70–71, 118, 119–22

refugees (GCs): Annan Plan for property rights of, 55, 134–35; application for compensation for property, 224; class action suit against Republic of Cyprus, 225; establishment of Claims Settlement Council and, 111–12; free movement across green line and, 72; objections to citizen-initiated activities between Greeks/Turks, 46; property rights cases, 76–77, 219–25, 253; return visits to northern Cyprus, 81–93; TC property law and, 222–23, 224

refugees' (TCs) property rights, 220

religion, 21–27. *See also* Greek Orthodox Church of Cyprus

Relocation Board, 137

Republican Party, 152

Republican People's Party (Turkey), 69, 130

Republican Turkish Party (CTP), 118

Republic of Cyprus: accession to EU, 3, 6, 55, 61, 114, 119, 127; agreement with Lebanon/Egypt on oil reserves, 237–39, 256; bridge across Ledra Street and, 234–35; court cases for property rights of TCs, 253; court cases for voting rights of TCs, 254; demand for restoration of territorial integrity/sovereignty, 96; demand for Turkish recognition of, 188–89, 206–7, 213, 214, 228; diffusion of incidents concerning border crossing, 85; dilemma of TC property law, 220–23, 224–25; economic impact of "no" vote on Annan Plan, 237–39; election for presidency (2008), 259, 261–62; election of Papadopoulos, 66; embargo on TRNC, 103, 105–6, 186; EU-based reforms in Turkey and, 29; EU castigation of, 229–30; EU outrage at failure of Annan Plan, 181–84; EU's recommendation for renewed talks, 229; EU upgrading of TCs and, 231; failure of negotiations, xi; final version of Annan Plan and, 133–38; Finnish initiative and, 226–28; GC nationalist view of establishment of, 145; incompatibility with resolution of conflict, 117; integration into EU, 61, 186, 193, 254–55; interethnic rapprochement and, 99–100; international community's view of, 251; lack of support of intercommunal rapprochement, 250; nationalist administration of, 95; negotiation based on Annan Plan, 129–30, 131–33; New York talks, 127–29; Papadopoulos's attempts at preservation of, 172–73; Papadopoulos's view of, 113–14; persistence of nationalist thinking in, 108–10, 112–13, 162, 181, 200, 216–19; political effects of "no" vote on referendum, 191–204, 206, 228–29, 230, 234–37, 239–43, 244, 245, 251, 261; privileges/obligation of under

EU framework, 104–7; property rights of TCs and, 253; proposal of confidence-building measures for TC community, 186–88; proposals for Annan Plan revisions, 133–35; recognition of TRNC and, 107; refusal of final Annan Plan, 138; rejection of interethnic citizen contact, 96; representation in EU, 230; revival of Nikiforos war drills, 216–18; signing of Treaty of Accession, 74–75, 80, 116, 175; tension between EU states and, 244; TRNC position on, 102, 104; Turkey's obligation to recognize, 206; Turkish threat to, 254–55; UN outrage over "no" campaign of, 171–75; uproar triggered by Matsakis, 189–91; Vassiliou's/Clerides's views of, 113–14. *See also* Greek Cypriot (GC) community; Papadopoulos, Tassos; Papadopoulos administration

Republic of Greece, xii

Republic of Turkey, xii, 258–59. *See also* Turkey

residency ceilings, 135

restoration of historical sites, 101

Reuters, 63

Right New Democracy, 218

right to assembly, 28

right-wing groups/traditions: changes in Greece under, 9; citizen peace movement and, 45; civil war in Greece and, 8; communist Left's criticism of, 9; compliance with ECHR ruling on GC property and, 224; conflict between left wing and, 166; reconciliation with left wing in Greece, 9–10; support of Annan Plan, 165; in TC community, 45; TC parliamentary elections (2003), 118; tension with left wing in Greece, 8; in Turkey, 17

Rolandis, Nicos, 238

Royalists, 8, 9, 10

rule of law: as cornerstone of EU system, 5, 76, 254; sphere of competency of, 5; TC acknowledgement of EU stress on, 221, 253; Turkey's obligation to, 208

Russia, 168

Sato Group, 256

secession, 18–19, 252

secessionist nationalism/nationalists: Annan Plan and, 55–56; deconstruction of, 185; disclosed as untenable, 252; establishment of Claims Settlement Council and, 112; hope for legitimization through open border policy, 79–80; as obstacle to TC interests, 63, 65–66; rejection of Annan Plan, 58–59; tension between prosolution factions and, 92–93; view of interethnic relations, 110–12. *See also* Turkish Cypriot nationalism/nationalists

security: Annan Plan's provision of, 53, 54, 55, 58, 61, 134, 136, 147, 182; within EU framework, 4, 107, 149, 182; of GC/TC communities following integration into EU, 254–55; nationalist concept of, 148–49; Papadopoulos's "no" campaign on, 147–49, 159

Security Council: briefing on referenda failure, 173, 174; Papadopoulos's response to postreferendum report, 176–81; postreferendum report, 172, 174, 192; proposal of confidence-building measures for TC community, 187; vote on Annan Plan, 168

Senate, 54, 56–57, 136, 180

September 11, 2001, terrorist attacks, 26

Serbia, 262

Sezer, Ahmet Necdet, 69
Sigma, 155, 224
Simitis, Costas, 11, 19, 131, 159, 199
Simitis government, 159
singers, 46, 97, 123–24
smuggling of people, 28
social transformation, 40
society: citizen-initiated activities for reconciliation in Turkey/Greece in, 46; citizen peace movement's inroads into, 44–45; effects of low-level political cooperation on, 34; Europeanization of in Greece, 11–12, 13; gestures of good will toward rivals, 81–85; Islamic influence in Turkey, 22; Kurdish problem and, 18–20; legitimization of ethnic pluralism in Turkey, 20; recognition of citizens' role in peace building process, 45; of Turkey, 13, 17, 27, 120
Solution and EU Party (CAP), 118
solution fatigue, 244–45
Soto, Alvaro de, 129, 153
southern Cyprus. *See* Greek Cypriot (GC) community; Republic of Cyprus
squatter towns, 17
state, 7
statehood, xi
stereotypes, 13, 47–50, 82–93, 88–89
Straw, Jack, 128
suffering. *See* pain/suffering
Supreme Court (Annan Plan), 54
Supreme Court of Republic of Cyprus, 253, 254
Switzerland, 53, 132–33, 181
Syria, 18

taksim (partition of Cyprus), 53, 91–92
Talat, Mehmet Ali: bombing of house of, 161; as countervailing force to Denktash, 152, 173; election to presidency, 213; nationalist opposition to Cyprus policies of, 243; at New York talks, 128; order for demolition of bridge across Ledra Street, 234; presence at European Parliament, 183; proposals for Annan Plan revisions, 135–38; resistance to piecemeal approaches, 241–42, 243; at talks in Switzerland, 132; on tapping gas/oil reserves, 237; as unofficial prime minister, 184; willingness to negotiate on comprehensive settlement, 240–41
Taurus military drill, 217–18
TC administration. *See* Denktash, Rauf R.; Denktash administration
TC Left, 164
TC refugees. *See* refugees' (TCs) property rights
TCs. *See* Turkish Cypriot (TC) community; Turkish Cypriots (TCs)
technical committees, 240–42
Technology for Peace, 39
territorial adjustments: under Annan Plan, 55, 140–41; opposition to, 66; relocation of TCs, 137; UN responsibility for, 134
terrorism/terrorist organizations (Turkey), 22, 33–34
think tanks, 39, 44, 46
This Country Is Ours, 39
top-level negotiations: abstention from military drills during, 217–18; Bürgenstock talks on Annan Plan, 132–33; Christofias administration and, 263–64; culmination in Annan Plan, 52; in Cyprus on Annan Plan, 129–33; failure of, xi, 68–72, 73, 190; between Greece/Turkey, 124; Hague talks, 67–70, 73; New York talks, 127–29, 171–72

tourism, 33–34, 125
Toxotis, 216–18, 256
trade: cross-border economic pact between Greece/Turkey, 124–25, 255, 256–57; EU economic assistance for TC community, 105–7; EU proposal to open trade with TC community, 185, 186, 193–95, 196–97, 228; free movement across green line and, 103; GC administration's interpretation of EU plan, 109; Greek exports to EU, 256–57
Trainers Group, 39
transitional government (Annan Plan), 54, 67, 133–34
Treaty of Accession to EU, 53, 67, 74–75, 80, 116, 175
Treaty of Alliance, 53, 54, 134, 136
Treaty of Establishment, 53
Treaty of Guarantee, 53
Treaty of Paris (1951), 6
Triantaphyllou, Dimitrios, 30
TRNC. *See* Turkish Republic of Northern Cyprus (TRNC)
True Path Party, 17, 21
Turkey: acceptance of Annan Plan, 119, 127, 131; accession negotiations, 71, 189, 198, 205–9, 212, 213–14; accession process of, 214, 227–28, 232–33, 260–61; adherence to rule of law in, 254; aims of nationalism in, 14–16; Annan Plan negotiations and, 171, 229; Annan Plan provisions concerning, 53, 54, 55, 135–36, 146; application for EU membership, 14, 19; aspirations for accession to EU, 53, 71, 74–75, 76–77, 115, 118–19, 145; benefits of acceptance Annan Plan to, 60–61; candidacy to EU accepted, xiv–xv, 3, 12, 27, 46, 59; challenge to recapture conciliatory spirit, 248; change in Greek policy toward, 12–13, 30, 91, 259; citizen-initiated activities for reconciliation in, 46, 123; competition between nationalist/postnationalist reformers in, 69–70; conflict with Cyprus prior to Luxembourg Summit, 213; coups in, 16; customs union agreement, 200, 206–7, 208, 209, 212, 213, 216, 254; deconstruction of nationalism in, xiii, xv, 20, 32–35, 47–50, 119–22, 130 (*see also* low-level politics); democracy in, 18; depoliticization of military, 120–21; dissociation of accession from Cyprus problem, 199–203, 254, 262; divisions within military, 123; *Djavit An v. Turkey*, 77–79; domestic difficulties, 74; earthquake diplomacy, 3; economic impact on TC community, 74; economy of, 13, 17, 24, 74; effect of failure of Annan Plan on, 71, 115, 198–204, 226–27; effects of Europeanization in, 25–27; elections of 2007, 232, 233; ethnocentric nationalism in, xii, 14; EU as factor in political/social change in, 14–18, 28–30, 70–71; EU-based reforms in, 19–20, 25–30, 70–71, 118, 119–22; EU peace-enhancing initiatives in, 249; EU reprimand of, 226, 228, 232; EU requirement of negotiation for solution in Cyprus, 119; Europeanization of, 31; failure of Hague talks and relations with EU, 71; Finnish initiative and, 226–28; foreign policy of, 18; as guarantor power in Cyprus, 54, 134, 136–37, 147, 259; incompatibility of democracy with nationalism in, xiii; international legal challenges to, 76–79; invasion of Cyprus, xii, xiv, 103, 166, 219; Iraq situation and, 68–69; Kurdish problem

Turkey (*cont.*)
in, 18–20, 28, 120; lifting of restrictions on movement across green line, 72–80; *Loizidou v. Turkey*, 76–77; low-level political cooperation between Greece and, 46; Luxemburg Summit, 213–14; membership in NATO, 15; military as obstacle to Europeanization in, 70; need for revival of 2003-4 momentum, 263; negotiations on Annan Plan and, 129, 130, 132; New York talks, 127–29; occupation of Cyprus, 261; oil/gas issue and, 238, 244, 256; opening of natural gas pipeline, 257; participation in Cypriot blood donation event, 98; persistence of statist nationalism within, 79–80; pluralization in, 13; political fragmentation in, 16–17; preference for confidence-building measures, 188; readiness to resume Cyprus talks, 212; refusal to recognize Republic of Cyprus, 213; relations with Greece (*see* Greek-Turkish relations); representation at Hague talks, 67; reprimand of Denktash, 122; restoration of property rights and, 220–24; rise of Islamic fundamentalism in, 18, 20–27; shared culture with Greece, 123–24; significance of EU culture in, 6–7; support of Annan Plan, 173, 175, 254; tapping gas/oil reserves off coast of Cyprus and, 237; Taurus military drill and, 217–18; as threat to Cyprus, 254–55; troops in northern Cyprus, 106; *Xenides-Arestis v. Turkey* and, 219. *See also* Erdogan, Recep Tayyip; Greek-Turkish relations; Turkish government
Turkish appeals court, 120

Turkish Constitutional Court, 22
Turkish Cypriot (TC) community: acceptance of Annan Plan, 139, 181, 185; Annan's postreferenda report on, 175; approach to Cyprus problem, 254, 255; benefits of Annan Plan to, 61–62; challenge of interethnic democracy in, 20; challenge to recapture conciliatory spirit, 248; citizen groups in, 35–46; communication with GC community, xiv; criticism of Denktash's refusal to negotiate, 101; Cyprus's accession to EU and, 105–7; economy of, 74, 75; effect of nationalistic thinking on, 88–89; effects of failure of Hague talks on, 71; embargo on, 103, 105–6, 186; erosion of demand for recognition of TRNC, 186, 188, 191; establishment of permanent EU contact group with, 195; ethnocentric nationalism in, xii, xiii–xiv; EU address to political isolation of, 230–32; EU economic assistance to, 105–7, 197–98, 230, 242; EU proposal to open direct trade with, 185, 186, 193–97, 213, 226–27, 228; EU status of, 252–53; Finnish initiative and, 226–27; free movement across green line as remedy for economic isolation, 75; human rights violations in, 153; impact of EU acceptance of Turkey's candidacy, xv; indirect referendum on Annan Plan, 117–18, 122; international credibility of, 185; jokes about Cypriot problem, xi; Kurdish problem, 18–20; left wing in, 44–45; memories of pain in, xiii–xiv, 73, 85–93, 101, 250–51; modernization and, 41; monocommunal groups in, 39; nationalist view of democracy, 57; nationalist violence against supporters

of Annan Plan, 161; nationalization of GC property, 219–20; need for revival of 2003–4 momentum, 263; opening of Kato Pyrgos-Limnitis crossing, 235; opening of trade with southern Cyprus, 185, 186, 193–94, 198; opinion on EU membership within reunited Cyprus, 117–18, 175; opposition to items in Annan Plan, 66; Papadopoulos's plan for absorption of, 110; peace rallies, 62–66, 74–75; perception of EU political/legal entanglements, 197–98; persistence of nationalist thinking in, 110–11; position on reunification, 141; postreferendum international approach to, 192–95; proposals for Annan Plan revisions, 135–38; referendum of April 24, 2004, 139; relationship with GC community, xii, xv–xvi, 216–19, 227, 239–48, 261 (*see also* free movement across green line); representation in EU and, 230, 231; requirement for state legitimacy, 117; response to free movement across green line and, 81–104; revelation of missing persons information, 250–51; security of, 255; significance of EU culture in, 6–7; support of Annan Plan, 62–65, 108; support of federal solution, 247; tapping gas/oil reserves off Cyprus coast and, 237; Taurus military drill in, 217–18; tension between prosolution/antisolution secessionist factions, 92, 118; U.S. policy toward, 186; view of Annan Plan in, 58–59; violence against GCs, xi, xiii–xiv; willingness to negotiate settlement, 241–42. *See also* Denktash, Rauf R.; Turkish Cypriots (TCs); Turkish Republic of Northern Cyprus (TRNC)

Turkish Cypriot nationalism/nationalists: Annan Plan and, 55, 56–57; challenges to, 116–27; as challenge to citizen peace movement, 38; disclosed as untenable, 252; establishment of TRNC and, 178, 179; EU process and, 104–7; European legal challenges to, 76–79; internal challenges to, 73–76, 117–18; international exposure of, 73; international pressures against, 122; negotiation based on Annan Plan and, 130, 131–33; opposition to Talat's Cyprus policy, 243; persistence of, 79–80, 108–9, 110–13; rejection of Annan Plan, 58–59; TC defiance of, 81–93; view of Cyprus problem, 253; view of final Annan Plan, 138; view of property law, 220, 224

Turkish Cypriots (TCs): bicommunal events involving, 89, 97–98; demand for right to vote for representatives in parliament, 253; *Djavit An v. Turkey*, 77–79; enclaves of, 73, 74, 81; free movement across green line and, 72, 81–88, 100; lists of missing made public, 101, 250–51; new property law and, 220–21; noncommunication with GC, xiv; peace rallies of, 62–66, 74–75, 93; positions of citizen peace movement members, 45; property rights cases against GC government, 253; rapprochement activities of, 96; relocation under Annan Plan, 137; request for identity cards/passports for Republic of Cyprus, 102, 109; view of Annan Plan, 59, 61–66; view of failure of Hague talks, 73–75

Turkish Cypriot Security Forces (TCSF), 217–18

Turkish Cypriot State, 137

Turkish Daily News, 70, 128–29, 238
Turkish government: acceptance of Annan Plan, 119, 121–23; depoliticization of military, 120–21; EU-based reforms, 119–22; failure of negotiations, xi; instability of, 16–18; invasion of Cyprus, xiv; Justice and Development Party agenda, 24–27; low-level politics between Greece and, 32–35; military's role in, 14–31; mismanagement of economy, 24; nationalist history of, 14–18; need for consensus on Annan Plan concerning territory, 140–41; negotiations on Annan Plan and, 130; Ozal government, xi; political system of, 15–18; rapprochement with Greece, 3; response to Kurdish problem, 18–20; security of academics/journalists and, 233; state politics of, 14–18; U.S. attempt to communicate directly with military and, 69; under Welfare Party, 21–22. *See also* Talat, Mehmet Ali
Turkish Hezbollah, 22, 26
Turkish identity, 14–15, 23
Turkish invasion, xiv
Turkish military: abolition of National Order Party/ National Salvation Party, 21; bridge across Ledra Street, 234; confidence-building measures with Greece, 257; conflict with PKK, 18; coups of, 15, 16, 21; crossing openings and, 234–36; depoliticization of, 120–21; EU process and, 25, 27; guaranteeing of structural integration of Turkish state, 14–31; Islamic fundamentalism and, 20, 70; movement of warships along coast of Cyprus, 238; part in rejection of Annan Plan, 69; position on Annan Plan, 123; U.S. attempt to communicate directly with, 69. *See also* Turkish troops

Turkish nationalism/nationalists: Armenian issue and, 233; compliance with ECHR ruling on GC property and, 224; deconstruction of, xiii, xv, 20, 32–35, 47–50, 119–22, 130 (*see also* low-level politics); EU challenge to, 24; European legal challenges to, 76–79; international pressures against. 73–76; introduction of religion into, 21; low-level political cooperation vs., 33; opposition to Erdogan, 224, 232; opposition to Talat's Cyprus policy, 243; persistence of, 79–80; view of property law, 220
Turkish parliament, 28, 130
Turkish Republic of Northern Cyprus (TRNC): acceptance of Annan Plan, 185; Annan's postreferenda report on, 175; arrest of GCs for crossing at unauthorized points, 85; attempt to gain recognition, 111–12; demand for recognition of, 96, 102, 103, 104, 107, 111, 185; *Djavit An v. Turkey*, 77–79; economy of, 74, 75; embargo on, 103, 105–6, 186; erosion of demand for recognition of, 186; establishment of, 178, 179; establishment of Claims Settlement Council, 111; European Court of Justice's ruling on, 106; failure of Hague talks and, 73; final version of Annan Plan and, 133–38; GC embargo on, 103, 105–6; hope for legitimization through open border policy, 76, 79–80; indirect referendum on Annan Plan in, 117–18, 122; interethnic rapprochement and, 99–100; international legal challenges to, 76–79; lack of support of intercommunal rapprochement,

250; lifting of restrictions on movement across green line, 72–80, 93; message of peace rallies concerning, 63–64; nationalization of GC property, 219–20; and negotiation based on Annan Plan, 129–30, 131–33; and New York talks, 127–29; as obstacle to TC interests, 73–74; opening of border crossings, 100; parliamentary elections (2003), 117–18; peace rallies in, 62–66, 74–75; persistence of nationalist thinking in, 79–80, 108–9, 162 (*see also* Denktash, Rauf R.; Denktash administration); postreferendum international approach to, 192–95; property law, 220–23; proposals for Annan Plan revisions, 135–38; recognition denied to, 192, 195, 222, 230, 252; referendum of April 24, 2004, in, 139, 152; rejection of interethnic citizen contact, 96; Republic of Cyprus's signing of Treaty of Accession and, 74–75; role in EU denied to, 252; Talat as president of, 213; Taurus military drill in, 217–18; tension between pro- and antisolution secessionist factions in, 92; U.S. policy toward, 196. *See also* Denktash, Rauf R.; Talat, Mehmet Ali; Turkish Cypriot (TC) community

Turkish society, 13, 17, 22, 26, 27, 120

Turkish troops: Annan Plan for presence in Cyprus, 54, 134, 136–37, 147–48; control of northern Cyprus, 77–78; in Cyprus, 254–55, 261; EU as factor in political/social change in, 15–18; gestures of good will in spite of, 84; invasion of Cyprus, xiv; Nikiforos war drills as counter to, 216–17; redeployment of under Annan Plan, 54; security of TCs and, 148; Taurus military drill and, 84. *See also* Turkish military

Turks, xiv, 46

Tzanetakis government, 9

UNFICYP. *See* United Nations Force in Cyprus (UNFICYP)

unilateral gestures, 72–80, 93, 100–101

unitary state, 55, 66, 112, 130, 168, 189–91

United Cyprus Republic, 67. *See also* Annan Plan

United Democrats, 211

United Nations: Christofias administration and, 263–64; concept of federation, 180; conflict with Papadopoulos government, 251; cooperation with EU on economic assistance to Cyprus, 105; Denktash's view of, 122; discussions on opening Ledra Street crossing, 234–35; efforts to restart Cyprus negotiations, 126; expectations for Cyprus solution, 100; failure of 2003–4 initiative, xi; focus on Iraq disarmament, 68; GC denunciation biethnic federation, 189–91; GC nationalist view of Annan Plan and, 145; initiative for solution to Cyprus problem, xi, xiv (*see also* Annan Plan); mediators prevented explaining Annan Plan, 152, 153–54; nationalist rejection of Annan Plan and, 58; New York talks over Cyprus problem, 127–29; opinion on Cyprus problem (2007), 259; Papadopoulos's response to postreferendum report, 176–81; postreferenda view of TC administration, 185, 192; postreferendum report, 172, 174, 192; Prendergast's briefing on referenda, 173, 174; proposal of

United Nations (*cont.*)
confidence-building measures for TC community, 187–88; recognition of citizen peace movement's role in peace building, 36; refusal to recognize TRNC, 192; reservation to engage Cyprus problem, 242, 261; resolutions for settlement of Cyprus problem, 117, 263; response to Papadopoulos's "no" campaign, 144, 171–75, 185; responsibilities under Annan Plan, 134; Security Council vote on Annan Plan, 168; view of failure of Hague talks, 73; view of freed movement in Cyprus, 80. *See also* Annan, Kofi; Security Council

United Nations Force in Cyprus (UNFICYP), 97–99, 254–55

United Nations resolutions, 117, 263

United States: ending of TCs' economic isolation, 186; envoy to Hague talks, 68; facilitation of renewed Cyprus talks, 125–27; GC nationalist view of Annan Plan and, 145; involvement in Iraq, 68–69, 126–27; policy toward TC north, 186; pressure on AKEL for "yes" vote on referendum, 164–65; recognition of citizen peace movement's role in peace building, 36; representation at Hague talks, 67; support of Annan Plan, 117; Turkish ties with, 15; view of freed movement in Cyprus, 80

UN peacekeeping operation, 54

UN secretary general. *See* Annan, Kofi

Ury, William, 34

Vassiliou, George Vasos: on changes in policy toward TC north, 196; concern about Papadopoulos's approach to negotiations, 128; on EU dissociation of Turkey's accession from Cypress problem, 201; intraethnic violence and, 161; political objectives of, 113; on reactivation of UN negotiation process, 212; view of "no" campaign, 154

Vassiliou government, xi

Venizelists, 10

Venizelos, Eleftherios, 9, 258–59

Verheugen, Günter: on Cyprus's EU membership, 183; dissociation of Turkey's accession from Cypress problem, 201; Papadopoulos's "no" campaign and, 153; on reforms in Turkey, 28–29, 71, 199, 200; reprimand of Papadopoulos, 182

vice president (Annan Plan), 54, 56, 133

violence: against Annan Plan's advocates, 160–62; EU view of, 4; within GC community over referendum, 151–59; of Islamic terrorist organizations in Turkey, 22–23; as means of securing human rights, 19–20; between military and PKK in Turkey, 18–20; nationalist justification of, xiii, 4; between 1958 and 1974, xi; PKK cessation of, 120; between TCs and GCs, xi, xiii–xiv

Virtue Party, 22

Vision of the Turkish Cypriots for a Solution and Joining of the EU, 62

Volkan (nationalist newspaper), 62

voting rights, 253

warfare, 4

Webel, Charles P., 122

Webster, C., 168

Welfare Party (WP), 21–22

"Why the White House is Pushing the Cyprus Solution" (*Christian Science Monitor*), 126
women, 39
Women's Group, 39
World War I, 149
World War II, 3, 8, 149

Xenides-Arestis, Myra, 219
Xenides-Arestis v. Turkey, 219, 222

Yesilada, Birol, 59–60
Yilmaz, Mesut, 17
youth: beatings of supporters of Annan Plan, 161; as catalyst for peace, 39; impact of "no" campaign on, 162; position on reunification, 141, 142
Youth Encounters for Peace, 39

Zana, Leyla, 120